# ZEPPELIN INFERNO

Dedicated to the memory of
Richard Ansell
1964-2021

A talented craftsman and a good friend

# ZEPPELIN INFERNO

## The Forgotten Blitz 1916

### IAN CASTLE

FRONTLINE
BOOKS

First published in Great Britain in 2022 by
Frontline Books
An imprint of
Pen & Sword Books Ltd
Yorkshire - Philadelphia

ISBN 978 1 39909 392 7

Printed and bound in England
By CPI (UK) Ltd.

Pen & Sword Books Ltd. incorporates the Imprints of Pen & Sword Archaeology,
Atlas, Aviation, Battleground, Discovery, Family History, History, Maritime,
Military, Naval, Politics, Railways, Select, Transport, True Crime, Fiction,
Frontline Books, Leo Cooper, Praetorian Press, Seaforth Publishing,
Wharncliffe and White Owl.

For a complete list of Pen & Sword titles please contact

PEN & SWORD BOOKS LIMITED
47 Church Street, Barnsley, South Yorkshire, S70 2AS, England
E-mail: enquiries@pen-and-sword.co.uk
Website: www.pen-and-sword.co.uk

or

PEN AND SWORD BOOKS
1950 Lawrence Rd, Havertown, PA 19083, USA
E-mail: uspen-and-sword@casematepublishers.com
Website: www.penandswordbooks.com

# Contents

# Introduction

At the beginning of the 20th century, the Wright Brothers' experiments in aeronautics resulted in the completion of the first recognised manned, controlled and powered aeroplane flight in history. Soon the buzzing of aeroplane engines could be heard not only in America but across Europe too. Rapid progress in aeroplane development ensured they had a role to play when Europe descended into war in 1914. In Germany in particular, another area of flight had also made great strides – airships, especially the large rigid type developed by Count Ferdinand von Zeppelin and first flown in 1900. Such was the progress that aeroplane and airship met in combat over Britain in 1915, just twelve years after the Wright Brothers' first flight. Flight was in its infancy in 1914, but by the end of the conflict in 1918 it had changed the face of war forever.

The impact on Britain when these giant airships – Zeppelins – first appeared over the country has been explored in my previous book, *Zeppelin Onslaught – The Forgotten Blitz 1914-1915* and now I have continued that history through 1916 in *Zeppelin Inferno*. The stories of 1915 and 1916 are very different and can be read in isolation or as a continuing narrative. It took rapid development to progress from those first tentative flights to German bombs dropping on Britain in 1915, yet the continuing advances in 1916, both offensive and defensive, pushed aviation to ever greater heights.

It has always been my intention to tell the story of this campaign, the first sustained aerial bombing campaign in history, by intertwining the personal experience of the individual with grand strategy. That has required diligent research and much detective work – press censorship meant newspapers reported on the raids but could not say where they had occurred. But by marrying these two types of report – military and personal – we can discover the full impact of the raids and how they were experienced by ordinary people on the ground and those intrepid young men in the air.

During the course of this research I have made extensive use of the historical Ordnance Survey maps made available by the National Library of Scotland on the 'Old Maps Online' website. These have enabled me to track individual bombs falling on obscure farms and in streets that no longer exist, adding to our understanding of how each raid developed, and with a level of accuracy completely unknown to those who took part.

This period of Britain's history is an important one, yet it is one too often overlooked, consumed by the enormity of the Blitz of the Second World War. Yet the lessons learnt painfully during this time helped lay the foundations for the air defence system that proved effective in the later air conflict. As such the thrilling, emotional, heroic and sometimes even amusing stories of this 'Forgotten Blitz' deserve to be more widely acknowledged.

# Acknowledgements

I have encountered many people while writing this book and all have been enthusiastic with their support and have generously made contributions that have added to the story I set out to tell. It would have been a lesser book without their help.

Local historian Ron Borsberry was of great help regarding the raid on Scartho, while in Loughborough, Lynne Dyer is always happy to help with questions concerning the history of the town. I have exchanged interesting emails with Colin Turner regarding the raid on Eldon and the Dene Valley and discussed elements of the raids on the Midlands with Mick Powis.

In a similar vein, Michael Bardell was happy to share his research on the Braintree raid as well as his mother's account. I exchanged numerous emails during my research with Dr Hamish McLaren regarding the bombing of his family's house in Edinburgh; sadly Dr McLaren passed away before this book could be published. Nigel Wood contacted me and passed on details of his interview with Thomas Charity, who had a painful reason to remember the first Zeppelin raid of 1916, and Phil Redman got in touch regarding his grandfather, a casualty of an air raid, who appears to have slipped through the net. Ian Holmes kindly shared his grandmother's letters about the Zeppelin raid of 31 January 1916, as did Haydn Gate regarding family letters concerning Norah Chapman, a raid victim in York. I was also delighted to hear from Jan Soley whose grandfather, Richard Turner, was killed in a raid on south-east London in August 1916.

Kathy Perkins made me aware of the diaries of Alex Morley in the Northampton Archives and provided me with transcripts, while Alf Small alerted me to an old article on the Scottish raids in *The Scots Magazine*. Rachel Field kindly undertook some research for me at the Suffolk Record Office and Alexander Corde, the archivist at the Aeronauticum Museum at Nordholz, helpfully answered a question about Peter Strasser that had bugged me for a long time.

I value my friendship with Ray Rimell, an expert on the Zeppelins of the First World War era, who is always happy respond to any questions I may throw at him, and I know if I ever have any Norfolk related questions regarding the raids, Steve Smith will be happy to help. Email exchanges with Eileen Bostle have helped clarify some aspects of the final raid by SL 11, while Mark Barnes alerted me to an interesting anecdote that has found its way into the book. I owe thanks to Steve Hunnisett, a historian of the later Blitz, who kindly gave me permission to use a photo from his collection. I am also extremely grateful to Frederik Gerhardt, a German historian living in Sweden. Through him I have gained access to many reports filed by Zeppelin commanders that now reside in the German military archives in Freiburg. Incredibly, we both happened to be in the same small Cornish fishing village at the same time in the summer of 2019.

Much of the work that has gone into this book relies on material held by the National Archives and I would like to express my gratitude to the nameless members of staff who at some point in the past brought all the individual reports and documents relating to each individual air raid together into a series of single folders. I am also greatly indebted to those creating the rapidly growing digitised content of the British Newspaper Archive.

I cannot end without expressing my thanks to two stalwarts of my Forgotten Blitz project – David Marks and Ian Campbell. David Marks holds a unique collection of postcards from this period and his generosity in making them available has made a significant impact on the look of the finished book – and he's always good company for a beer and a chat about Zeppelins. Ian Campbell, however, I have never met for a beer as he lives in Australia. Perhaps, one day! He found me through my website a few years ago and we too have become good friends, albeit at a great distance. He reads my chapters and lets me know if any aspect needs greater clarification or suggests ways to improve readability. If you think anything in the book isn't quite up to the mark then it's probably because I foolishly overruled him!

Finally, I must thank my partner Nicola. She tolerates, without comment, my strange existence whereby I disappear into my study for up to ten hours each day to fly with the Zeppelins as though it were the most normal thing in the world... it is isn't it?

Ian Castle
April 2021
www.IanCastleZeppelin.co.uk

## Map 1: German Airship Bases – 1916

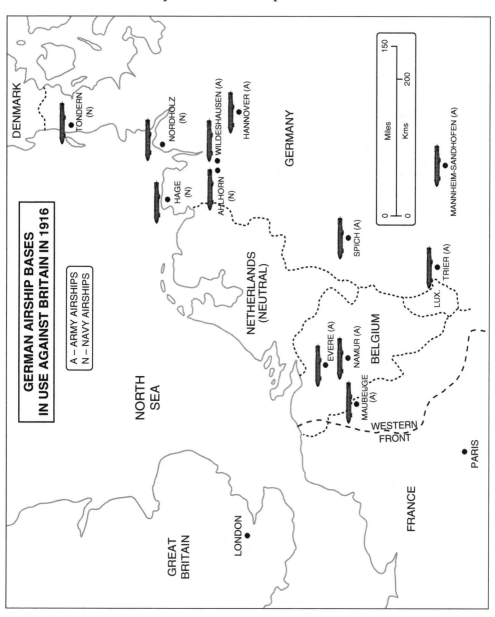

GERMAN AIRSHIP BASES
IN USE AGAINST BRITAIN IN 1916

A – ARMY AIRSHIPS
N – NAVY AIRSHIPS

DENMARK

TONDERN (N)

NORDHOLZ (N)

WILDESHAUSEN (A)

HANNOVER (A)

HAGE (N)

AHLHORN (N)

GERMANY

SPICH (A)

MANNHEIM-SANDHOFEN (A)

NETHERLANDS (NEUTRAL)

TRIER (A)

LUX.

BELGIUM

EVERE (A)

NAMUR (A)

MAUBEUGE (A)

WESTERN FRONT

NORTH SEA

PARIS

GREAT BRITAIN

LONDON

FRANCE

Miles

150

Kms

200

xi

## Map 2: Air Raid Warning Districts

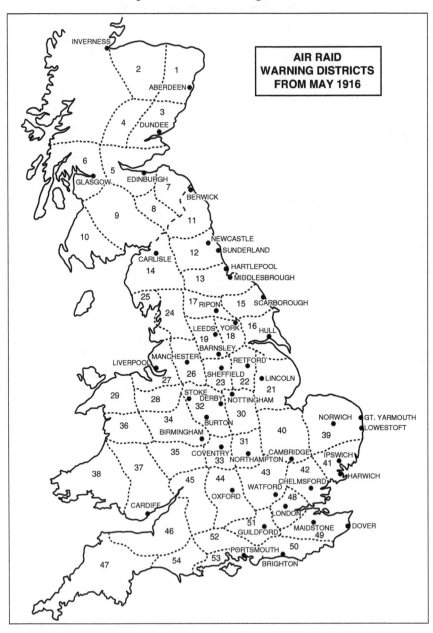

# Map 3: Zeppelin Raid Penetration – 1916

## Map 4: Zeppelin Types Over Britain – 1916

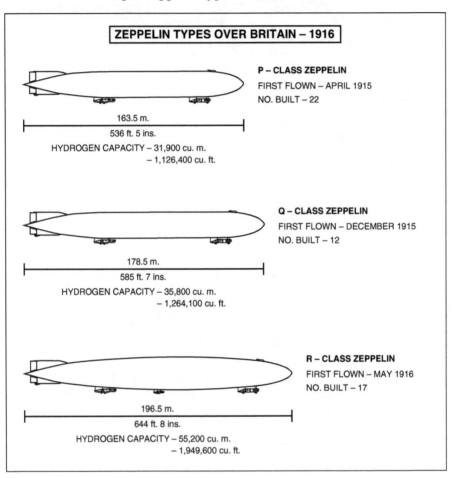

ZEPPELIN TYPES OVER BRITAIN – 1916

**P – CLASS ZEPPELIN**
FIRST FLOWN – APRIL 1915
NO. BUILT – 22

163.5 m.
536 ft. 5 ins.
HYDROGEN CAPACITY – 31,900 cu. m.
– 1,126,400 cu. ft.

**Q – CLASS ZEPPELIN**
FIRST FLOWN – DECEMBER 1915
NO. BUILT – 12

178.5 m.
585 ft. 7 ins.
HYDROGEN CAPACITY – 35,800 cu. m.
– 1,264,100 cu. ft.

**R – CLASS ZEPPELIN**
FIRST FLOWN – MAY 1916
NO. BUILT – 17

196.5 m.
644 ft. 8 ins.
HYDROGEN CAPACITY – 55,200 cu. m.
– 1,949,600 cu. ft.

# Map 5: RFC Home Defence Wing

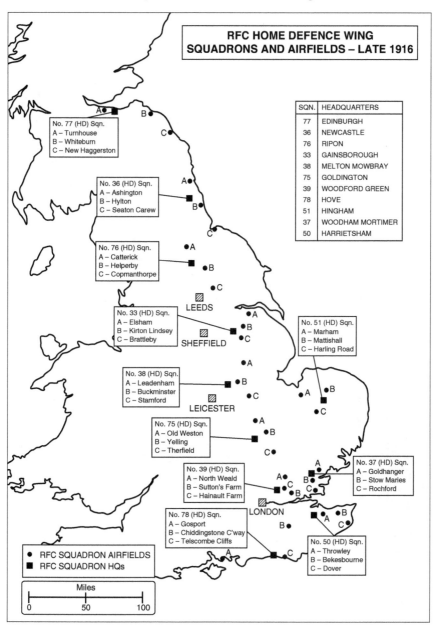

**RFC HOME DEFENCE WING
SQUADRONS AND AIRFIELDS – LATE 1916**

No. 77 (HD) Sqn.
A – Turnhouse
B – Whiteburn
C – New Haggerston

No. 36 (HD) Sqn.
A – Ashington
B – Hylton
C – Seaton Carew

No. 76 (HD) Sqn.
A – Catterick
B – Helperby
C – Copmanthorpe

LEEDS

No. 33 (HD) Sqn.
A – Elsham
B – Kirton Lindsey
C – Brattleby

SHEFFIELD

No. 51 (HD) Sqn.
A – Marham
B – Mattishall
C – Harling Road

No. 38 (HD) Sqn.
A – Leadenham
B – Buckminster
C – Stamford

LEICESTER

No. 75 (HD) Sqn.
A – Old Weston
B – Yelling
C – Therfield

No. 37 (HD) Sqn.
A – Goldhanger
B – Stow Maries
C – Rochford

No. 39 (HD) Sqn.
A – North Weald
B – Sutton's Farm
C – Hainault Farm

LONDON

No. 78 (HD) Sqn.
A – Gosport
B – Chiddingstone C'way
C – Telscombe Cliffs

No. 50 (HD) Sqn.
A – Throwley
B – Bekesbourne
C – Dover

| SQN. | HEADQUARTERS |
|------|--------------|
| 77 | EDINBURGH |
| 36 | NEWCASTLE |
| 76 | RIPON |
| 33 | GAINSBOROUGH |
| 38 | MELTON MOWBRAY |
| 75 | GOLDINGTON |
| 39 | WOODFORD GREEN |
| 78 | HOVE |
| 51 | HINGHAM |
| 37 | WOODHAM MORTIMER |
| 50 | HARRIETSHAM |

● RFC SQUADRON AIRFIELDS
■ RFC SQUADRON HQs

Miles
0    50    100

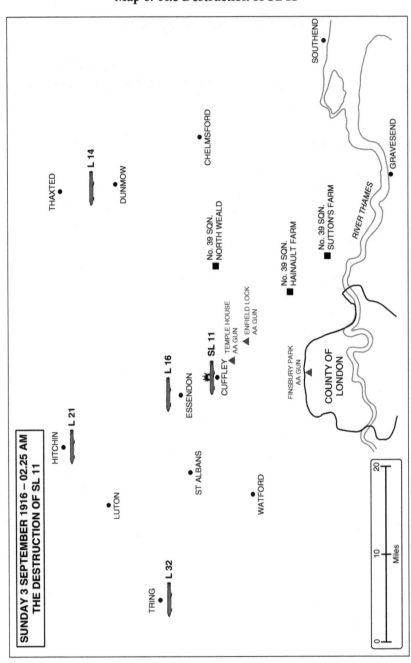

SUNDAY 3 SEPTEMBER 1916 – 02.25 AM
THE DESTRUCTION OF SL 11

L 32
TRING

L 21
HITCHIN

LUTON

L 16
ST ALBANS

ESSENDON

WATFORD

SL 11
CUFFLEY
TEMPLE HOUSE
AA GUN
ENFIELD LOCK
AA GUN

THAXTED

L 14

DUNMOW

CHELMSFORD

No. 39 SQN.
NORTH WEALD

No. 39 SQN.
HAINAULT FARM

No. 39 SQN.
SUTTON'S FARM

FINSBURY PARK
AA GUN

COUNTY OF
LONDON

RIVER THAMES

GRAVESEND

SOUTHEND

Miles
0    10    20

# Map 7: The Last Flight of L 21

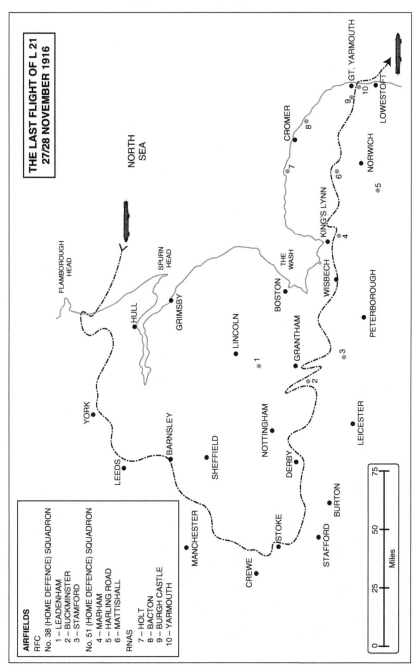

# Map 8: Airships Destroyed Over Britain – 1916

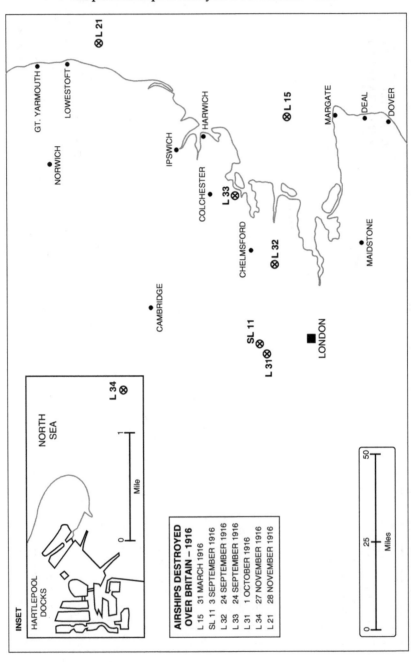

INSET

NORTH SEA

HARTLEPOOL DOCKS

L 34 ⊗

0 ___ Mile ___ 1

**AIRSHIPS DESTROYED OVER BRITAIN – 1916**

L 15    31 MARCH 1916
SL 11   3 SEPTEMBER 1916
L 32    24 SEPTEMBER 1916
L 33    24 SEPTEMBER 1916
L 31    1 OCTOBER 1916
L 34    27 NOVEMBER 1916
L 21    28 NOVEMBER 1916

0    25    50
Miles

⊗ L 21

GT. YARMOUTH ●
LOWESTOFT ●
NORWICH ●
HARWICH ●
IPSWICH ●
⊗ L 15
MARGATE
DEAL ●
DOVER
COLCHESTER ●
L 33 ⊗
CHELMSFORD ●
L 32 ⊗
MAIDSTONE ●
CAMBRIDGE ●
SL 11 ⊗
L 31 ⊗
LONDON ■

# Chapter 1

# Frightfulness

In 1915 the previously unthinkable had happened. British civilians had been subject to aerial bombing by German aircraft, in particular by airships – the dreaded Zeppelins. Always approaching under the cover of darkness, these aerial monsters had roamed over British towns and countryside largely unopposed, while Home Defence forces struggled to come to grips with this new form of warfare. In that first full calendar year of the war over 200 men, women and children, had died in air raids, with over 500 injured.

The Admiralty had assumed the mantle of mounting Britain's aerial defence at the beginning of the war while the Army's Royal Flying Corps (RFC) supported the British Expeditionary Force in Europe. It was planned as a temporary arrangement, but at the end of 1915 it remained in place, although an end was in sight with the Army preparing to take back responsibility in February 1916. It had been an uneasy role for the Admiralty, a make-do arrangement in which they lacked the weapons and organisation to make a significant impact, but they had made the best of a bad job. In October 1915, under pressure from the top, the Army added some weight to the aerial defence of London in what proved to be the last raid of the year. Even so, one Zeppelin reached central London and dropped a string of bombs across the city.

The effect of these raids on the people very much depended on how close they were to the bombs when they exploded. Given that Zeppelins tended to follow a direct course over a target, it became possible for those on the ground to get a reasonable idea if they were in the line of fire.

For those finding themselves outside the Zeppelin's path the experience could become a fascinating must-see spectacle, provided you had taken the necessary precautions. Hallie Miles, who lived with

1

her husband Eustace and their staff in a large London flat, was very organised, as she wrote in summer 1915.

> I am putting up beds in our downstairs flat which we use as offices, so that if a bomb crashed through the roof of this flat, which is near the top of the building, we should sleep downstairs. The Zeppelin pile of emergency clothes and bags, etc., ready at our bedroom door for the fatal raid (if it comes) has grown bigger! Eustace now has a little pile all of his own by his bedside, including a pair of trousers and overcoat, and I have added a soft little hat to my clothes, to pull down over my hair... I am going to have a 'dress rehearsal' to see how quickly we can 'escape' and get into our garments.[1]

Hallie and Eustace Miles followed their routine nightly, as she wrote again two months later.

> I still go on making my solemn preparations every night before we go to bed. Eustace now always has a pair of trousers by his bedside ready to jump into if necessary. We call them the 'Zeppelin trousers'![2]

The couple were at home when that last Zeppelin raid of October 1915 struck London.

> We, at our flat, were given a timely warning by our porter. It was only a little past 9 p.m., so we were dressed this time. We collected our bags, etc., and the same procession again walked solemnly down the stairs to the basement, to the music of the guns and bombs... It was rather amusing that, as the bombs were further away this time, most of the people collected at the open front door and watched the Zeppelin, and the shrapnel from our guns exploding all round it, but alas, not hitting it. Even *I*, after depositing our possessions in the basement... crept cautiously upstairs, and peeped, with frightened eyes, out of the open front door and up at the sky. I did not see the Zeppelin, but I saw the shrapnel bursting into flame in the sky, as if a star had suddenly exploded. It was very beautiful, but awful too. The sounds were so ghastly and the knowledge

that each thud of a bomb falling to earth carried death and destruction with it added to the horror of it all.[3]

It was, however, those living in the houses and streets where the bombs fell that faced the full horror of an air raid. Their traumatic experience was one of terror, shock, bewilderment and devastation, as their homes fell around them and loved ones' helpless bodies were mutilated, burned or torn apart before their eyes.

A study comparing the effects of injuries from high-explosive (HE) bombs with those caused by bullets summarized the findings as follows.

> Shell fragments, shrapnel, etc., have no fixed weight or shape. They have lower initial velocity, which is lost more rapidly. They are haphazard in action, often cause multiple injuries, and depend less upon velocity than on the size and shape of the fragments. They have a lower power of penetration and often lodge in the body. They frequently carry clothing and gross dirt into the tissues. Explosive exit wounds are rare. The effect of the explosive is as destructive as the fragmentation.[4]

When a HE bomb detonates, first there is enormous expansion of gas, variously referred to as an explosive wave or, more commonly, blast. After the initial blast there follows a second wave, a sudden inrush of air. This could manifest itself by window glass blown out into the street and walls falling inwards, while lethal fragments of jagged hot metal flew in all directions, cutting and ripping into soft flesh.

> By far the greatest number of casualties resulting from detonation of heavy HE shells and bombs is caused by flying fragments of shell, brick, stones and debris, which are impelled at great velocity and may cause death hundreds of feet from the exploded bomb or shell. A considerable percentage of the casualties are caused by crushing, by burying, and by asphyxiation from the collapse of buildings, entrances to cellars, etc.[5]

As well as HE bombs, German airships also dropped incendiaries. They came in two designs, a cylindrical-shape used by Navy Zeppelins and a conical version favoured by the Army vessels, but both worked in the same way, utilizing a process developed by a German chemist, Hans Goldschmidt. Incendiary bombs did not explode, they ignited and burned fiercely.

The central core of the bomb consisted of thermite, which burned at extreme heat in the region of 2000° centigrade. Around this core the bomb contained a quantity of benzol (motor fuel) while tarred rope covered the exterior. When an incendiary bomb smashed through the roof of a building an inertia fuse ignited the thermite causing an intense fire, setting alight any combustible material in its proximity. In addition, the benzol would flow from the bomb and ignite other surfaces, with the burning liquid also dripping between floorboards spreading the conflagration throughout the property. The tarred rope helped to keep the bomb burning after the initial chemical reaction had died down. In Britain these were considered further evidence of German *schrecklichkeit* – frightfulness – as indeed was the whole concept of bombing the civilian population.[6] British records estimated that in 1915, German airships dropped bombs on England with a combined weight of 35 tons, although the total was in all probability higher.

Those who experienced the bombing first-hand often made demands for retaliation while others chose to debate the matter in newspapers. In January 1916, *The Times* published a series of letters, the first by Sir Arthur Conan Doyle, under the heading 'A preventative of air raids'. Sir Arthur argued that as the current defences appeared unable to deal effectively with Zeppelin raiders then perhaps retaliation would make Germany reconsider its approach, and to do that he proposed a great British centre of aviation at Nancy in France.

> Without any delay we should establish such an aviation centre, defend it with numbers of the best aircraft guns against the persistent attempts which will be made to destroy it, and announce to the German Government through the American Embassy at Berlin that we can tolerate no more outrages upon our civilian population, and that any further raids will be followed by immediate reprisals.
>
> If such a policy were at once put in force it might act as a preventative – which is better than vengeance. But if it must be vengeance, then the blood is on the head of those who with

their eyes open have provoked it... For the sake of our own women and children the time has come when these murders must be stopped.[7]

Sir Arthur's views received complete support from another letter writer, M.W. Mitchell, who advocated that Britain take steps immediately.

We can no longer plead ignorance of his intentions or of the approval with which the whole German nation regards such monstrous barbarities. What right have we to expose our own non-combatants to such dangers without making any and every effort to counteract them?[8]

An officer serving in France with the Royal Field Artillery, however, took exception to this, but not on moral grounds.

Surely it is not asking too much of the inhabitants of London to take their chance of a few dozen bombs at very long intervals without squealing for reprisals which can have no military result. By what right do you in London demand that we in France should drop bombs on anything except the German Army and its communications? Merely to make you a little safer than you are – and God knows the risk to each one of you is not very great.[9]

Alfred E. Turner joined in the debate, supporting Sir Arthur's stance, with a jingoistic response.

These raids serve no military purpose; they are the outcome of pure blood lust and venomous hatred of us. The Germans say they are for the purpose of hurting us and frightening us; and so shortening the war; they do hurt us, because through them women and children are murdered; but far from frightening us, they only increase our intense hatred of Germany and steel our hearts to exact punishment to the last jot and tittle.

Another letter writer, Charles Bright, tried to refocus the discussion on matters of defence and suggested a very British response.

But surely what we really have to consider in this matter is the best steps to take to safeguard our arsenals, munition and other factories, docks, &c., against the ravages of Zeppelins.

In view of the wide diversity of opinions, and perhaps lack of adequate action, is it not time that a committee was appointed – independent of any special and possibly conflicting departmental interests – to investigate exhaustively and report on the best means of guarding against seriously destructive air raids?

The question of retaliation resurfaced regularly after major raids in the coming year and although raids into Germany did commence in summer 1916, they were on a strategic, not retaliatory, basis.

In 1915, while German airship crews were gaining experience operating over Britain, other than for attacks on London they rarely ventured far inland, preferring to keep close to the coast. With London being successfully targeted in September and October 1915, there was a confidence, particularly at the top of the Naval Airship Division, that the time had come to penetrate deeper into Britain, to the areas of heavy industry in the Midlands and North of England and up to the Naval dockyards on the Firth of Forth in Scotland. New 'p-class' Zeppelins were being delivered, as were an upgrade, the 'q-class', while designs for a new type, the 'r-class' were coming off the drawing board. These would be able to fly higher, faster and carry a greater bombload than those that had gone before and Peter Strasser, commander of Germany's Naval Airship Division, firmly believed they would give him a decisive edge in the coming campaign.

But there was frustration too for Strasser. Zeppelins restricted their raiding to a limited period around the new moon, the eight days either side offering the darkest skies each month, which provided valuable protection for the Zeppelins. But within this limited window of opportunity the weather had to be right too – the increased likelihood of encountering snow, ice and heavy rain during the winter months further restricted options for attack. Despite Strasser's desire to keep the pressure on Britain, after that raid in October 1915, the weather prevented any further attacks that year, or in the opening weeks of the next. Throughout the war new, improved Zeppelin designs appeared but all needed the weather and the phase of the moon to be in their favour for a successful mission. In January 1915, at the time of the first Zeppelin raid on Britain, the Navy operated six Zeppelins but a year later, in mid-January 1916, they had 12 Zeppelins and one Schütte-Lanz in service, although one, Zeppelin L 6, was reserved for training purposes. The Army's strength had grown too in the same period, from six Zeppelins and a Schütte-Lanz to ten and one respectively, although four of their Zeppelins were serving on the Eastern Front.

As the year turned from 1915 to 1916, responsibility for aerial defence still lay with the Admiralty but, with the knowledge that it would soon pass to the War Office, special arrangements made by them to assist the Admiralty in defending London during the last Zeppelin raid in October 1915 were extended. By the end of December there were ten RFC airfields encircling London. At each airfield two night-flying trained pilots and a pair of BE2c aircraft stood by waiting to be called into action. However co-ordination remained haphazard with the ten airfields occupied by four separate squadrons. No.10 Reserve Aeroplane Squadron (RAS) flew from Joyce Green and Farningham, No.17 RAS from Chingford, Croydon, Hainault Farm, Hendon, Sutton's Farm and Wimbledon Common (Chingford and Hendon were shared with the Royal Naval Air Service (RNAS)), while No.11 RAS operated from Northolt. No.24 squadron at Hounslow took on Home Defence duties while awaiting transfer to France. Even so, there was little attempt to provide an effective aerial defence away from London and the aircraft that did defend Britain lacked effective weapons with which to seek and destroy enemy airships.

As 1916 dawned both sides waited for the next move. The new moon in January rose on the fifth but bad weather prevented the Zeppelins emerging from winter hibernation. The next moon would rise on 3 February so Strasser looked to that and hoped for a change in the weather. The phase of the moon, however, had far less impact on the German aeroplanes and seaplanes based in Belgium, who aimed their hit-and-run raids on Kent coastal towns. On the night of 22/23 January 1916, it was they who dropped the first bombs of the year on England.

## 23 January 1916, 1am, Dover, Kent

A single Friedrichshafen FF 33b floatplane of Seeflieger Abteilung 1 (SFA 1) took off from Zeebrugge with the town of Dover as its target. It was the first time an aeroplane had attacked at night and over Dover a brilliant moon shone down on the town. Unseen on his approach, shortly before 1.00am the pilot announced his presence by dropping three HE bombs close to a memorial erected by the 60th Rifles to commemorate their participation in the Indian Mutiny. It stood just a few yards from the seafront at the junction of Waterloo Crescent, Cambridge Road and Camden Crescent.[10] Windows shattered in houses in each of the roads, doors were blown in, brick coping tumbled into the streets, bomb fragments marked walls and one chipped out a fist-sized chunk from the Rifles monument. About five seconds later a bomb smashed through the roof of a 'common lodging house' upstairs at the Red Lion public house on the corner of St. James's Street where it joined St. James's Lane.

The bomb exploded in a room where four men were sleeping, killing 43-year-old barman Harry Sladden When a doctor arrived he found Sladden lying on a bed covered with debris. Both his femur and tibia in the right leg were broken but the critical injury came from a bomb fragment that sliced open his stomach from where his intestines protruded. The other three men in the room all suffered injuries but survived. Just a couple of seconds more and another bomb struck a malting at the Phoenix Brewery on Dolphin Lane. After crashing through the roof tiles, a fire started in the rafters but workers at the brewery, supported by a number of police officers who rushed to help, dealt with the flames, the only loss being a quantity of barley damaged by the water used to extinguish the fire.

The bombs continued to fall in rapid succession. The next landed in the roadway in Russell Street. It dug a hole in the road outside the gas company's offices, landing just beyond a large gasometer, smashing more windows and scarring the walls of the building. Moments later another struck a wall between Castle Street and St James's Street at the back of 10 Golden Cross Cottages. Fragments of the bomb flew into the house where they injured three children. Another fragment shot through an upper floor window at 2 Golden Cross Place, injuring 71-year-old Julia Philpott as she lay in bed. In Victoria Park a bomb exploded in soft earth behind a retaining wall close to the junction of Castle Hill and Laureston Place before the final bomb burst in the garden of 9 Victoria Park where the blast broke a number of windows.

Although the damage appeared relatively light, the raid caused consternation down by the harbour where Lieutenant Commander Stanley W. Coxon, RNVR, was on duty.

> At the time I was engaged decoding a cipher telegram. Suddenly, in the stillness of the night, there occurred what I, on the spur of the moment, concluded was a short and sharp bombardment

8

by an enemy submarine which had entered the harbour and was engaging our ships. We all rushed out, the orderly, the operator and myself, and practically before we were out it was over and there was silence again. What was it? Then in the town there arose a big sheet of flame from a burning house, and I knew at once that it must have been an enemy aircraft dropping bombs. Only one remark was made, and it was by Witt… and to the point: 'Oh, be God! it's the brewery.' And the brewery it was.[11]

Completely taken unawares by the raid, no aircraft took off in response and no guns opened fire. When daylight arrived on Sunday morning, great crowds flocked into the town to see the damage.

## 23 January 1916, 1.10pm, Dover, Kent

Those same people were still milling about when two German seaplanes, a Friedrichshafen FF 33b and a Hansa-Brandenburg NW, approached the town from the west in the middle of the day. Having crossed the coast unobserved between Folkestone and Dover, they appeared over the town at 12.52pm. The raiders attracted immediate fire from the Dover anti-aircraft guns and from ships moored in the harbour as both passed out to sea. One circled around and appeared over the town again at 1.10pm, greeted once more by the guns.

Lieutenant Commander Coxon had just arrived for duty on the pier.

No sooner was I on the spot than they dropped a bomb within about fifty yards of me, fortunately a 'dud', and in the water. A second one fell immediately after, just short of a hospital ship lying alongside… I then ascended our look-out platform and had a beautiful view of the attack and the defence. From one-pounder pom-poms up to three-inch and even seven-inch, both from the ships and the forts, they were all blazing away for all they were worth…

During the raid I noticed the Chief Officer of the [Hospital Ship] *Dieppe*, one Mahoney by name, busily engaged lowering and manning one of his lifeboats, and when the show was all over I called him up and inquired what the brain wave was, and whether if we had brought a Hun down it was his intention to take his boat to rescue the occupants? His reply was quite to my liking: 'No, divil a bit, sir,' he said. 'I was just making ready, in case I saw any of them floating around, to go out and slit their bloody gullets!'[12]

There is no doubt that the barrage fired by the Dover anti-aircraft guns was an intense one. The post-engagement report states that the 6-pdr at Drop Redoubt fired 71 rounds, the three 1-pdrs at Dover Castle 381 rounds, the 1-pdr at Langdon Battery another 118 and that battery's 3-inch, 20 cwt gun 30 rounds. It appears, however, that all fell short of the target.

While that seaplane passed over Dover for a second time, the other re-crossed the coast near Folkestone to make an attack on the RNAS base at Capel-le-Ferne, which housed small, non-rigid airships used for anti-submarine patrols. At 1.23pm the raider dropped five bombs but all missed the airship sheds. Four aircraft took off from RFC Dover, joined by an RNAS FBA flying boat, which unfortunately attracted fire from the anti-aircraft gunners after it became airborne at 1.30pm, although no damage was done and the raiders escaped.

## 31 January 1916, Evening, London

Back in London, Hallie Miles welcomed the January full moon as she would the return of a trusted friend and protector. For the previous few weeks, memories of the autumn 1915 Zeppelin raids had kept her and her husband at home in the evenings but Londoners had learnt by experience that Zeppelins favoured the darker nights of the new moon.

> It will be the first time that I have had courage to go out in the evening since the cruel raids. But as there is a moon I am venturing. I don't think any of us loved the moon as we do now. She seems like a protecting angel shining down upon us from the sky; when she disappears, the horrible dangers seem to begin again.[13]

Hallie, like many others, made the most of the full moon as she knew it would not be long before the dark nights returned, bringing with them a mood of apprehension. On 31 January, eight days after the raid on Dover and Capel-le-Ferne, Hallie Miles became aware of rumours of an imminent Zeppelin raid. When she got back to her London flat the porter added more fuel to the fire with wild tales of Zeppelins having reached Southend and heading for London.

> So we gathered up the precious bags and started off to the basement. I tried to get our old servants to come, but they said it would be time enough when the guns began to thunder forth; so we left them to their fate…
>
> Oh! the grim horror of it all, and the chilly feeling on entering the basement, not knowing what was in store for us. I lit the little lamp and got all our warm rugs and blankets, and we sat with them spread on our laps as if we were in a railway carriage… We sat shivering and expectant; every door that shut with a bang we thought was a bomb. We were down there an hour, and then the news was brought us that the Zeppelins had been turned back, and we might go upstairs again. How gladly we all left our 'dug-outs' and how beautiful our flat looked when we entered it again! The old servants were gloating with triumph that they had stayed upstairs by the warm fire, whilst we were shivering below. The wicked Zeppelins wended their way to the Midlands instead, and did frightful havoc there.[14]

While Hallie Miles could breathe a sigh of relief that London had been spared, the night of 'frightful havoc' experienced by those in the Midlands was a result of the largest raid of the war so far. After a three-month hiatus, the Zeppelin terror had returned, and with nine Zeppelins roaming at will over the country, that terror was greater and more deadly than ever before.

Chapter 2

# 'Attack England middle or south, if at all possible Liverpool.'

In October 1915 Peter Strasser, commander of the Naval Airship Division, had hoped to launch his Zeppelins against Liverpool but bad weather prevented bringing the plan to fruition. The city, however, remained a tempting target, acting as a major port for American goods transported across the Atlantic into Britain. An effective raid here on the west coast would send a clear message to Britain, that no part of the country was safe from attack by Germany's seemingly untouchable raiders.

At the beginning of 1916, Vizeadmiral Reinhard Scheer, the newly appointed commander of Germany's High Seas Fleet, gave approval for a raid targeting 'England Middle', an area including Liverpool within its boundaries. On 31 January the moon cycle was right and the weather conditions appeared good. The attack was on and orders quickly followed: 'Attack England middle or south, if at all possible Liverpool.'[1] From bases at Nordholz, Hage and Tondern, nine Zeppelins prepared for action. Hydrogen, petrol, oil, water ballast was all checked, engines tested and each loaded bombs weighing about two tons (2,120kgs), the exact combination of HE and incendiary bombs selected by their commanders. Around lunchtime all was ready and the airships took to the skies. Alert listeners at the British wireless stations on the east coast picked up the 'H.V.B' signals as the Zeppelins departed, confirming that a raid on England was under way.[2] Keen as ever to take part, Peter Strasser assigned himself to L 11. In previous raids in which he had taken part, mechanical failures or bad weather had often prevented his chosen Zeppelin from completing its mission; privately many of the men considered him a 'Jonah'. This time, for L 11, it was to be no different.

Contrary to the promising weather forecast, the conditions encountered over the North Sea were very different. On board L 11, Oberleutnant-zur-See Freiherr Treusch von Buttlar Brandenfels (von Buttlar), like all the others, struggled through thick fog, rain clouds and snow, which caused ice to form on the airship's outer covering – the envelope. L 11 accumulated about 2 tons of excess weight, preventing her from climbing above 6,700 feet.[3] With navigation difficult many commanders called for wireless bearings to determine their position over Britain, but the narrow angle of triangulation from the transmitting stations meant the returned locations were generally unreliable. When the raiders returned and filed their reports they claimed successful attacks on Liverpool, Manchester, Sheffield, Nottingham, Goole, Yarmouth and Immingham.[4] In fact not one of these places was bombed.

British observers reported L 11 over The Wash and crossing the Lincolnshire coast near Sutton Bridge at about 7.10pm. Although now clear of the snow and rain, mist and fog continued to hinder progress as von Buttlar and Strasser peered blindly into the gloom searching for a hint of a landmark. Eventually they calculated that they had reached the west coast but as they could see nothing below Strasser authorised L 11 to return, taking the full bomb load with them. British trackers surmised that the furthest west attained by L 11 was just to the east of Macclesfield, over the lonely expanses of the Peak District, some 40 miles short of Liverpool.

L 11, however, was not the only raider to have little to show for her night's work.

## 31 January 1916, 6.40pm: Holt, Norfolk

Kapitänleutnant Herbert Ehrlich had a miserable crossing in L 17, his battle against the weather compounded by engine problems. On reaching England he considered it unwise to undertake the long journey to the west coast and sought closer targets. He believed he was near the River Humber but thick cloud obscured the ground. When a searchlight tried to break through and a diffused glow softly illuminated the gloom below, Ehrlich concluded he was over the industrial area of Immingham on the Humber's south bank and prepared to drop his bombs. Ehrlich, however, was wrong.[5]

L 17 came inland at about 6.40pm, west of Sheringham on the north Norfolk coast, about 65 miles south-east of the Humber. The searchlight that lit the clouds was operating from RNAS Holt, an air station between the market town of Holt and the sea. Reacting to the light, Ehrlich dropped 20 HE bombs. Ten fell about 200 yards from the RNAS station, the others further away. A newspaper summed up the futility of the raid: 'Most of the bombs fell into a ploughed field and no one was injured. Several sheep were maimed, and a number of birds, most of them sparrows, were killed.'[6] Moments later five more HE bombs and an incendiary dropped near Bayfield Lodge Farm, where presumably lights were showing, wrecking a couple of outbuildings, but although the occupiers were deeply shocked, no one was hurt. Ehrlich then released 14 incendiary bombs over Bayfield Hall but all missed the target before a final bomb smashed a few windows at the village of Letheringsett. From there Ehrlich headed across Norfolk, back to the coast and out to sea near Great Yarmouth. Four Zeppelins had set out on the raid from Nordholz; L 17 was the first to return.

From Hage, about 55 miles west of Nordholz, three Zeppelins were participating in the raid. The first of these to return home was L 16, commanded by Oberleutnant-zur-See Werner Peterson.

## 31 January 1916, 7.15pm: The Suffolk Fens

Peterson's North Sea crossing was similar to Ehrlich's, including engine problems; he also abandoned the mission and switched to local targets. He recognised he had crossed the coastline of north Norfolk so decided make an attack on Great Yarmouth but, with cloud and fog limiting visibility, he believed he was much further east than he was. Flying south he anticipated reaching the coastal town, whereas when he dropped his first two bombs at Swaffham he was about 45 miles inland. A HE bomb landed near the police station but failed to detonate and an incendiary ignited harmlessly in a field holding horses at a camp of the 2/1st Nottinghamshire Yeomanry (Sherwood Rangers).[7] Peterson continued on his course, believing he unleashed the rest of his bombs on Great Yarmouth. According to reports in the German press, 'a factory and various industrial areas were bombed, good effects being observed'.[8] This, however, was wrong. After leaving Swaffham, Peterson continued south until he reached a point close to the border between Suffolk and Cambridgeshire, and unloaded 62 bombs (47 HE and 15 incendiaries) near Mildenhall, many falling on West Row Fen and Isleham Fen. In this rural landscape the only recorded damage was to a chicken house, where 16 birds died.[9] Having released his bombs, Peterson headed back to Germany. At the same time the remaining six Zeppelins were tentatively feeling their way westwards through the clouds, fog and mist. And now the killing began.

## 31 January 1916, 8.10pm: Tipton, Staffordshire

The commander of Zeppelin L 21, Kapitänleutnant der Reserve Max Dietrich, had only taken command of this new 'q-class' airship twelve days earlier. This class was an interim design between the existing 'p-class' models and the awaited 'r-class'. It was a lengthened 'p-class' which boosted hydrogen capacity and allowed for an increase in bombload of about 15 per cent.

It was the first time over England for both. Dietrich had previously commanded L 7 from June to September 1915, before taking over a new ship, L 18, on 6 November 1915. It was a brief command, eleven days later an accidental fire destroyed her at her Tondern base.[10] Aged 45, prior to the war Dietrich had served as a captain in the German merchant navy and had once had Count Zeppelin on board his ship. Dietrich must have been impressed with the Count because when the war started he joined the naval airship division. Back in Germany, Dietrich had a 14-year-old niece, Marie Magdalene; she later became better known as the actress Marlene Dietrich.

L 21 was one of the first to cross the British coast on 31 January, doing so at about 4.50pm near Mundesley in Norfolk. Dietrich's initial navigation was good, but when he reached a position north of Derby he believed he had found Manchester so altered course to the south-west to seek Liverpool. At about 7.50pm he believed he had found his target.

> … the lights of two cities which from dead reckoning and from their position were taken to be Liverpool and Birkenhead… Docks, harbour works, and factories of both cities were attacked with thirty five 50kg and twenty incendiary bombs. Explosion of all bombs and good results seen from on board.[11]

Dietrich, however, had miscalculated his position and was about 70 miles south-east of Liverpool at the time; it seems that his 'Birkenhead' was actually Tipton in the West Midlands and 'Liverpool' the area encompassing Wednesbury and Walsall. Tipton was a heavily industrialised town with a network of canals, supporting locks and basins. From his position in the command gondola the reflections of those canals appear to have taken on the appearance of a large body of water – the 'River Mersey' flowing between Birkenhead and Liverpool. Although the nearby major centres of Wolverhampton and Birmingham were in darkness, the lights were on in Tipton.

From Union Street, 45-year-old Thomas Morris had gone to the Tivoli Picture House. Morris was a labourer and married with six children. His wife, Sarah-Jane, had taken two of the children, Martin (11) and Nellie (eight), to her parents – William and Mary Greenshill – who lived almost next door at 1 Court, 8 Union Street. The remaining four children, Thomas (16), Rose (14), Ivy (12) and five-year-old May stayed at home. Sarah-Jane and her family were sitting around the fire when Dietrich dropped his first three bombs shortly after 8.00pm. They landed close together in Union Street and Waterloo Street. One smashed into the Greenshill's house. It 'collapsed like a pack of cards' as the bomb 'fell on the footpath of the narrow thoroughfare, smashing in the front of the house. The occupants… were terribly mangled beneath the ruins'.[12] Sarah-Jane, her parents and the two children were all dead. Her distraught and traumatised husband rushed home and helped to recover the shattered and mutilated bodies of his family from the wreckage.

The bombs in Union Street demolished two houses, damaged many others and smashed a gas main running under the road. They also cut down Benjamin Goldie, aged 43, who ran a business making iron fenders, while 26-year-old shoemaker Arthur Edwards died in his shop when a bomb fragment pierced his chest; his wife, Eliza, lost a leg. Edwards' mother was sitting in the back kitchen and ran outside when the bomb exploded. When she returned at about 8.30pm she found her son lying dead in a pool of blood in the wreckage of the shop.[13] The bombs also killed blacksmith Daniel Whitehouse, aged 34, and Thomas Henry Church, a 57-year-old estate agent. He was on his way from the Post Office to the Conservative Club when the bomb blast cut him down. Taken into a house, he died a few moments later.

The body of a soldier's wife, Elizabeth Cartwright, was found slumped in the road near a large crater[14] and two boys, George Henry Onions, aged 12, and Frederick Norman Yates, nine, were also victims. George died in the street and Frederick in a doctor's surgery. Annie Wilkinson perished inside her home at 16 Union Street, where the blast also injured her husband, Thomas. A fireman, Albert Batten of the Tipton Fire Brigade, later received the British Empire Medal in recognition of his efforts to extinguish the burning gas main in the street and rescuing the injured. The final victim was in Waterloo Street where a bomb claimed the life of a 30-year-old nurse, Louisa York.

The following morning hordes of sightseers flocked to the shattered streets of Tipton.

> So Gertie & I & Georgie went to Tipton & you cannot imagine the sight – awful. 5 killed in one house. Holes in the streets. Windows, slates, chairs, doors & glass everywhere. She took me through the Conservative Club. I can't describe it, it was a wreck. Roof slates – not a glass left whole, door posts, everything in confusion & 13 children in cellar wouldn't come up…Thousands of people & motors & crowds waiting at the Guest Hospital waiting for the news. My knees tremble under me, bodies picked up in pieces.[15]

Other bombs fell near Tipton Station followed by six incendiaries, three in gardens at Barnfield and Bloomfield roads and three at the Bloomfield Brickworks, although all but one failed to ignite. Now twisting to the north-east, Dietrich headed towards Lower Bradley, south of Bilston, where there were three canal-side ironworks. Walking along the towpath were a courting couple who shared the same surname, William Fellows, a 23-year-old furnace stoker, and Maud Fellows, aged 24, a domestic servant. The couple sought shelter by the wall of the Bradley Pumping Station but to no avail. L 21 dropped five bombs along a 500-yard stretch of the canal, from the Pumping Station to Pothouse Bridge. One exploded on the towing path just eight feet from where the terrified couple were sheltering. Arnold Wolverson went to assist them but found a shocking sight. The blast had almost severed William's head from his body, there were burns, open wounds and his right leg was shattered. Maud had suffered numerous injuries but she was still alive and, with help, Wolverson carried her to a nearby pub where a doctor attended her but she died of septicaemia in hospital twelve days later.

## 31 January 1916, 8.20pm: Wednesbury, Staffordshire

After the bombs at Lower Bradley, Dietrich took L 21 eastwards, over land that had formerly seen much coalmining activity. There were very few lights below, perhaps creating in Dietrich's mind the idea that he was now crossing the River Mersey towards Liverpool. Rather than Liverpool, however, the lights directly ahead were shining from Wednesbury where the huge Crown Tube Works industrial site was located, bordered on its western side by King Street and with the main thoroughfare of High Bullen running down the eastern side. The bombs – 12 HE and eight incendiaries – dropped in two concentrations, the first around the tube works. The impact was devastating.

At 12 King's Place, a small court off King Street, Susan Howells was alone while her husband Edward had ventured out for a walk. Adjacent to King's Place stood 13 King Street, home to Edward Shilton and his wife Betsy, and at 14 King Street, Joseph Smith and his wife Jemima were with her mother, Mary Evans, who had walked around from High Bullen; two of their children, Nellie (13) and Thomas (11) were also there. Their third child, seven-year-old Ina, was in the street playing with her friend Matilda Birt, aged 10. When Jemima Smith heard the sound of explosions (probably those from Lower Bradley) her curiosity led her outside. The rest of the family followed but she left them to go to collect her little nephew. She turned back when she heard the first booming explosion. A bomb had landed directly on the Shilton's house at No.13 killing the couple instantly. As the house collapsed the avalanche of rubble swallowed up and killed Joseph Smith, his children Nellie and Thomas, and his mother-in-law. Ina Smith's friend, Matilda Birt, was dead in the street, but of Ina there was no sign. To her distraught mother she had simply disappeared without trace. In fact the force of the blast had thrown the little girl through a window 15 feet up in the outer wall of the Crown Tube Works. There searchers found Ina some 15 hours later, her tormented body hanging grotesquely from a rafter.[16]

The same bomb that shattered 13 King Street also destroyed 12 King's Place and inflicted serious damage to other homes in the court. Edward Howells rushed back from his walk to find his wife Susan's maimed body blown out of the house into the street. There were others too. At 4 King Street widowed Mary Ann Lee was visiting her younger sister, Rachel Higgs; they both died. And at No.28 a bomb fragment killed shopkeeper Rebecca Sutton.

Harry Doige, a boatswain in the Royal Navy, was passing the end of King Street when the bombs fell and was blown off his feet. Having picked himself up, he started up the road.

> On the left side of the street on the footpath I found a human body. I struck a match to look, but it was so mutilated I could not say what sex it was. A few yards further, on the opposite

side, I found another body — nothing but a trunk. I saw that about three or four houses had been destroyed. I assisted to remove four bodies from the debris of the houses.[17]

More bombs landed on the Crown Tube Works, a major industrial site in the town employing a workforce of about 1,300. Fortunately an industrial dispute broke out earlier in the day and few workers had appeared for the night shift. The police reported on the damage.

> The roof over a larger Workshop was very considerably damaged and the walls in places shattered, much glass was broken, and Steam Pipes, Water Mains, and Gas Mains damaged. Some of the offices, brass stores, receiving shop, brass shop, and some of the warehouses were more or less damaged.[18]

After the raid the workforce abandoned their dispute but one of the workers failed to return – 16-year-old Samuel Whitehouse. Samuel was one of the few working that night. At his inquest the jury heard details of the immediate aftermath of the explosion.

> [The bomb] blew all the lights out, and threw the workmen down, some of them being injured by flying metal. A portion of the roof fell in, and for some time nothing could be seen through the cloud of dust. The youth [Whitehouse] was discovered calling for help, and was removed to hospital, where he died soon after midnight from shock following extensive burns on the back.[19]

The final group of bombs from this first salvo fell from High Bullen, across Upper High Street to Earp's Lane. In High Bullen, 'almost without exception the shop windows… were shattered and the pavement strewn with broken glass'. In Upper High Street patrons left a theatre when the sound of exploding bombs stopped the show, as did others streaming out from two cinemas close by. Incendiary bombs started a handful of small fires. Behind High Bullen bombs also damaged property belonging to the Hickman & Pullen Brewery, and in a chicken house at the back of the Crown & Cushion pub the occupants were 'roasted and completely stripped of their feathers' by the bombs.[20]

The second concentration of bombs – eight HE – fell about three-quarters of a mile away at Mesty Croft, from Brunswick Park Road, across the London & North Western Railway, to Oldbury Street. Some damage occurred on the railway embankment and at Mesty Croft Goods Yard, with two bombs exploding between the railway and Oldbury Street. Albert Madeley had finished work and was walking along Oldbury Street on his way to visit his fiancée when a jagged fragment from one of the bombs sliced across him, ripping open his stomach. The 21-year-old died in hospital three days later.[21]

## 31 January 1916, 8.25pm: Walsall, Staffordshire

Leaving the population of Wednesbury to deal with the tragedy that had befallen their town, Dietrich saw more lights two miles away to the north-east – Walsall.

PC Joseph Burrell was on duty in Wednesbury Road, which led into the centre of Walsall. He had already heard the disconcerting sound of explosions from the direction of Wednesbury when L 21 appeared high in the sky coming towards him. Seconds later a bomb struck the imposing Wednesbury Road Congregational Church – it was about 8.25pm. Debris of all kinds rained down and one piece struck Burrell a fierce blow. The church suffered badly.

> [The bomb] struck as nearly as possible in the centre.... Half the roof had disappeared…, rafters and beams were scattered about in all directions, the wood of the pews was splintered, the flooring was torn up, and most of the windows were blown out… Two gaps had been made in the gallery on either side of the church, and a great beam had fallen across the pulpit and the steps leading up to it. In the grounds around the church portions of the stonework, bricks, slates, and glass, were scattered everywhere.[22]

The church was empty at the time but the unfortunate Thomas Merrylees happened to be at the junction of Wednesbury Road and Glebe Road when the bomb exploded. A piece of debris struck him with such force that it ripped off the back of his head as his body crumpled into the gutter. But the death toll could have been much worse. In the Sunday School building attached to the church a class of 15 children were studying. Their teacher, Miss Winifred Clark, remembered a piece of the ceiling falling in 'then a blinding blue flash more vivid and fearsome than any lightning', but other than minor cuts and scratches all the children emerged unharmed from their terrifying experience.[23]

PC Burrell, having regained his wits, saw flames rising from the Walsall & District Hospital where an incendiary bomb had struck the roof of one of the wards. At the entrance Burrell found 'the nurses excited and unable to move'. He pushed his way through to the bomb. With nothing else to hand, he grabbed a length of wood and, on his hands and knees to gain a little protection from the worst of the intense heat, began to nudge the bomb away from the danger area. As a mark of their gratitude the hospital committee awarded him a gratuity of a guinea (about £100 today) and a medal. Sadly, failing eyesight, caused he believed by his exposure to the heat of the burning bomb, forced his retirement from the police force in 1923 and the following year he became blind. He eventually learnt to read and write using Braille.[24]

Dietrich dropped a brace of bombs as L 21 passed over Mountrath Street, digging craters, blowing down a wall and smashing windows, but only inflicted cuts and scratches on those nearby.[25] About 200 yards further on was Bradford Place, a triangular ornamental garden around which the traffic flowed. A grand Victorian edifice, the Institute of Science and Art, overlooked the area where inside evening classes were underway.

A student attending a chemistry class, A.L. Stephens, heard odd sounds outside and as he looked through the windows overlooking Bradford Place a bomb exploded.

> All the apparatus on the table disappeared and the lab was in confusion, everything was blown to smithereens. It was pandemonium, but no panic. We made a dash for the stairway and on the way down someone shouted 'Hey, look – he's been hurt'. So I turned round and this woman was covered in blood but a man grabbed me and said 'No, it's you.'[26]

Stephens lost a lot of blood but at hospital his injuries were stitched, 'a very painful process' he recalled, before he was helped home. Other students suffered minor injuries.

Just seconds before the bomb exploded a No.16 tram arrived in Bradford Place. The passengers had heard explosions as they approached. Amongst those on board were two friends from Wednesbury, Frank Linney and Charles Cope, on their regular Monday night out in Walsall.[27] When the tram stopped the two men alighted but as they crossed the road the bomb exploded just yards from them, smashing windows at the Institute, on the tram and in all the shops and buildings around Bradford Place. Linney sustained severe injuries to his legs and, although taken to hospital, died there later that evening. Cope was also down; he remembered the flash of the bomb and a heavy blow on his back. Helpers took him to the Hospital, where the staff were still recovering from the excitement caused by the incendiary bomb. Cope seemed to be on the road to recovery but then took a turn for the worse and died on 3 February.

Inside the tram all was chaos and confusion. The explosion smashed the lights and in darkness the passengers rushed for the two exits. Amongst them was 55-year-old Mary Julia Slater, the Lady Mayoress of Walsall, travelling with her sister and sister-in-law. Mary staggered out of the wrecked tram before collapsing on the pavement. Her horrific injuries were clear to all.

> She was bleeding freely... There was a lacerated wound on the left breast, three inches long and 1½ inches in diameter, another wound on the left side which had torn away a portion of the ribs and had opened her chest and abdomen, and there was another wound lower down which had penetrated the bone.[28]

Despite constant medical attention Mary Slater eventually succumbed to her injuries and died in hospital on 20 February.[29]

At the Walsall Workhouse another death occurred. John Powell, an inmate, was suffering from pneumonia. After the raid a nurse found him dead in his bed. When questioned at the inquest she stated that the raid had hastened his death.

Dietrich now turned for home. Taking an easterly course, after passing Kettering he observed a strong light ahead, offering him a final tempting target. It proved to be the blast furnaces of the Islip Ironworks near Thrapston in Northamptonshire. He released his last bombs – six incendiaries.

About 500 yards to the north-west of the furnaces stood two cottages, the homes of Ernest and Jane Curtis and their neighbours George Ward and his wife. Both couples were preparing for bed at about 9.15pm when they heard a strange sound. One of the women described it as 'a report, slightly louder than a gun being fired'. Through their windows the startled couples saw two distinct fires that continued to burn with light blue flames until about 10.00pm. Two other fires also started in a ploughed field in front of the cottages but, buried deeply in the soil, the flames soon died out.

The following morning the remains of five of the burnt out bombs were taken to Thrapston Police Station. Enquiries eventually revealed the location of the missing sixth bomb; a soldier had taken it away as a souvenir.[30]

With no further distractions, Dietrich took L 21 back out to sea just south of Lowestoft at about 11.35pm. When he safely reached Nordholz, L 21's mission had lasted 23 hours and 32 minutes.[31]

## 31 January 1916, 8.15pm: Great Fenton Colliery, Stoke-on-Trent, Staffordshire

Heinrich Mathy, the commander of Zeppelin L 13, came inland at about 4.50pm near Mundesley on the coast of Norfolk with Dietrich's L 21. Heading west, Mathy passed the darkened towns of Nottingham and Derby but saw lights as he approached the industrial centre of Stoke-on-Trent. The police reported that bombs dropped at 8.15pm. Six fell in a 70 yard radius of Great Fenton Colliery but there were no casualties. According to the colliery manager, 'Two fell in a field, 3 on shraff heaps [waste tips], and the sixth struck the top side of an ammonia tank and lifted the top off and a few windows were broken by concussion.' Unsure of his position and having circled the area for about 30 minutes, Mathy called for wireless bearings. As often was the case, the position he received back was inaccurate, placing him near Manchester, which stood about 50 miles to the north.

Having set a course back to the east, at 10.50pm through a break in the clouds, Mathy observed 'blast furnaces and other extensive installations' which he concluded were at Goole on the River Ouse. He had in fact already passed south of Goole and was approaching Scunthorpe with its extensive ironworks.

## 31 January 1916, 10.55pm: Scunthorpe, Lincolnshire

People in the town heard the sound of engines 'and immediately afterwards there was a heavy explosion, a bomb having fallen in close proximity to a large building without hitting it'.[32] A number of incendiary bombs also landed but had little effect.[33] In Ravendale Street a bomb practically ripped off the backs of four worker's homes but failed to injure the occupiers; an unfortunate pig, however, 'had its head completely chopped off'.[34] At Trent Cottages an incendiary bomb smashed through the roof of 86-year-old widow Sabina Markham's home. A neighbour rushed to her assistance but the doughty Mrs Markham had already doused the bomb with water.[35] The town's iron and steel works were now in Mathy's sights. His first bombs overshot the North Lincolnshire Iron Works, landing instead at the Redbourn Hill Iron Works, which was in darkness. One bomb there wrecked a water pump, damaged a locomotive shed and killed two men: Cyril J. Wright, a 24-year-old laboratory assistant, and Thomas William Danson, an engine tender, who died of his injuries later that night. Danson, aged 29, was a well-known local footballer, playing in goal for Scunthorpe and Lindsey United.[36]

L 13 now circled, lured by lights at the Frodingham Iron and Steel Works, but Mathy's bomb missed the target by 100 yards, exploding in a railway goods yard with the blast 'injuring four civilians, but an engine driver sat calmly looking on from his engine'.[37] Damage, however, was light: 'some of the bullets from one of the bombs embedded themselves deeply in a railway wagon. One struck a buffer and entered to the depth of a few inches, and another cut through a steel rail on the line as though passing through a piece of cheese.'[38]

Passing over the old Lindsey Iron Works, Mathy headed towards the Trent Iron Works, dropping more bombs as he went. One of those, exploding in Dawes Lane, claimed the life of steelworker Ernest Benson, aged 31, and injured others.

Mathy had dropped 16 HE bombs and 48 incendiaries in the eight or nine minutes he had been over Scunthorpe, killing three men and injuring seven other people. At about 11.35pm, as L 13 approached Humberston, she came under an ineffective burst of fire from the 1-pdr 'pom-pom' gun at the Waltham wireless station. It was the only gun to open fire that night. Untroubled, Mathy and L 13 headed out to sea.

## 1 February 1916, 12.10am: Derby, Derbyshire

When word about a possible Zeppelin raid spread earlier that evening, those towns that had plans in place to reduce or switch off lighting began to do so. At about 7.20pm a great cacophony burst forth in Derby.

> Every hive of industry that boasted the possession of a hooter
> of any kind let loose… The din was terrific. There were shrill

shrieking whistles, there were loud whistles. There were buzzers of varying volume and sound, and there were also a few bells, and above all rose the deep base of the great 'Bull' at the Midland [Locomotive Works]... for all the world as though it were the voice of fate.

Lights went off at the factories and works, in people's homes and in the streets. The trams came to a standstill and the railways ceased work; industrial sites began to close down their operations. The effort was effective as from 8pm onwards a number of Zeppelins passed the town without attacking. One of those was L 14 commanded by Kapitänleutnant der Reserve Alois Böcker. A captain of the *Hamburg-Amerika* shipping line before the war, Böcker had held command of L 14 since August 1915. He passed Derby once, but he found it again later.

Böcker brought L 14 inland at about 6.15pm over the coast of Norfolk north of Holkham and headed inland. At 8pm he dropped a bomb near the village of Knipton, about six miles south-west of Grantham. Although local reports dismiss its impact, Thomas Charity, a local schoolboy might disagree. Excited that a bomb had landed nearby, nine-year-old Thomas played truant from school the next morning. He found the still smouldering depression and took a jagged bomb fragment as a souvenir, one he kept for the rest of his life. There was, however, a high price to pay for this memento – when he arrived at school after lunch, 'he was soundly thrashed by the Headmaster for missing the morning session'.[39]

L 14 passed south of Nottingham and Derby and into thickening cloud that obscured any sight of land. Circling between Shrewsbury and Stafford, Böcker believed he had reached the west coast but finding no point of reference below he gave up and turned south-east. At 11.35pm Böcker reached Tamworth and, attracted by distant lights, changed course again, reaching Ashby Woulds fifteen minutes later where L 14 dropped six bombs over an industrial sanitary pipe works. One HE and an incendiary bomb landed on a large cinder heap near a furnace at the works but four other HE bombs overshot and fell at Overseal, one in a canal and three in fields. Then three more dropped at Swadlincote resulting in a few smashed windows. The time was now just before midnight and, about ten miles to the north-east, lights began to appear in a previously darkened area. The crew believed it was Nottingham, but the lights were going back on in Derby.

The sound of distant exploding bombs had reached Derby earlier in the evening but it had been quiet since 9pm. People remained cautious for some time but eventually the lights began to return.

> Sometime before midnight... the lighting at the Midland Station was restored and shortly afterwards permission was given to the trams to proceed to their depots. When the witching hour struck most people came to the conclusion that the danger was past... Then, at ten minutes past twelve, the town was shaken by a bomb that exploded in the Osmaston area.[40]

From the command gondola of L 14, Böcker observed 'big factories and blast furnaces' below. With the engines slowed he prepared to attack.

Approaching the town from the south-west the first target was a highly prestigious one – the Rolls-Royce works, which was heavily engaged in war work. Six bombs streaked down. The first two exploded on open land west of the complex, and just one exploded inside the works perimeter, gouging out a crater on the testing track and smashing around 400 windows in nearby works buildings.[41] The other three struck the Metalite Lamp Works, 200 yards away in Gresham Road, where they caused considerable damage but there were no injuries.[42] Now approaching the Midland Railway Carriage and Wagon Works on Osmaston Road, L 14 dropped five HE bombs. They damaged carriage and wagon building facilities, a blacksmith shop, railway siding tracks and a railway truck loaded with pig iron.[43] Seven incendiary bombs followed. The first three fell in the yard of W & T Fletcher's lace factory on Osmaston Road where they burnt out without causing any injury, but the other four fell in neighbouring Horton Street, where one caused a significant house fire.

L 14's course had taken her across the Osmaston Road so Böcker swung her back towards a vast target east of the London Road — the Midland Railway Locomotive Works. A bomb landed in the garden of Litchurch Villa, at the junction with Bateman Street, blasting a great hole.[44] In Rose Hill Street, 450 yards away, a well-known schoolmistress died. Sarah Constantine, aged 71, had been under the care of doctors for some time but 'the explosion of the bombs produced heart failure'.[45] The huge Midland Railway complex now lay directly ahead and Böcker ordered the release of ten bombs.

The first three ripped up sections of railway line sending chunks of track flying for great distances in all directions, while smashing an electric main and two water mains buried underground.[46] The next five bombs all exploded within the space of 80 yards, four of them digging into the asphalt and sending debris flying all around, but one exploded with deadly effect.

Although there had been no official notification that the blackout had ended, when other parts of Derby returned to normal, the Locomotive Works followed suit. Charles Coxon, the Foreman at No.3 Running Shed, noticed the lights were on again at another department and, presuming they had received 'proper authority', he switched the lights back on in the shed for those working the night shift.[47] When the first bombs were heard exploding at the Rolls-Royce Works, Coxon plunged the huge engine shed back into darkness. But by then it was too late, Böcker had already seen all he needed to.

As the sound of explosions edged closer, those men working inside the shed ran for cover just as a bomb smashed through the roof and exploded about six feet from the outer wall. A rather dispassionate report noted: 'Inside the shed were very few marks of bits of bomb and no appreciable downward effect.'[48] Those men inside, however, had a rather different experience. Five workmates scattered; the blast struck one down but he luckily escaped injury, while the other four dived into an inspection pit beneath an engine tender, which seemed to offer the best protection. The bomb exploded six or seven yards from the pit with horrific results.[49] The bodies of two engine drivers, Harry Hithersay (23) and James Gibbs Hardy (55), and assistant fitter William Bancroft (32), 'were terribly mangled and beyond all recognition'. Another man who sought shelter, Sidney Baines, a 21-year-old engine fireman, had both legs shattered by the blast, and died in hospital on 4 February, the cause of death, 'haemorrhage and shock'.[50]

The last two bombs thrown at the Midland Railway Locomotive Works exploded on No.18 Boiler Shop but, expending most of their energy on the roof, inflicted only limited damage inside. Passing over the Litchurch Gas Works, which bordered the Locomotive Works, L 14 released two final bombs.[51] They were both incendiaries; one burnt out a few feet from a gasometer and the other, which fell on a large heap of coal, failed to ignite. Both were narrow escapes. Böcker now took L 14 away from Derby and at 12.30am passed south of Nottingham then onwards to the coast, eventually passing out to sea over Lincolnshire.

The shocked populations of Tipton, Wednesbury and Walsall could be forgiven for thinking their night of terror was over, but they were mistaken. Other Zeppelins were roaming the Midlands and all three towns would hear the dull drone of Zeppelin engines again, while some would hear them for the first time.

Chapter 3

# 'Gott strafe England'[1]

While Zeppelins L 11, L 13, L 14 and L 21, had been at loose over the industrial Midlands and L 16 and L 17 had threatened the rural landscape of East Anglia, Zeppelin L 20 had also made a dramatic journey over the Midlands leaving terror and destruction in her wake. And behind her came L 15 and L 19.

### 31 January 1916, 8.05pm, Loughborough, Leicestershire

Kapitänleutnant Franz Stabbert, a 34-year-old naval officer, had command of L 20, another of the new 'q-class' Zeppelins. Stabbert came inland over The Wash at around 7pm, also battling the worst of the weather and engine problems. Undeterred, he pushed on, dropping a single HE bomb at 7.45pm in a field at Uffington in Lincolnshire, which broke a few windows. Heading west, L 20 blindly passed the darkened town of Leicester but at Loughborough, 10 miles to the north, it was a different story. Lights there were shining brightly and Stabbert attacked, claiming to have dropped four bombs to silence a battery, but there were no guns protecting the town, or any other towns in the Midlands that night. Stabbert's bombs fell amongst the population of Loughborough, the first at 8.05pm.

It exploded 100 yards from the gas works, at the rear of the Crown and Cushion Inn[2] on Ashby Square, 'bursting with a terrific report', wrecking outbuildings and smashing 'every window for a hundred yards around'.[3] Adjacent to the Inn, the glass roof of the town's Technical Institute crashed in on those attending evening classes but miraculously there were no serious injuries. Martha Shipman, however, was not so lucky. A fragment of the bomb dug deeply into her leg as she stood at the back door of her home at 5 Orchard Street. She staggered inside,

29

slumping into an armchair in shock. Her husband was away with the army; alone, and with blood streaming from her wound, she died.

Many people were walking along The Rushes, a busy thoroughfare about 150 yards from the Crown and Cushion. Among them were newly-weds Anne and Joseph Adkin; Anne had gone to meet her husband on his way home from work. Friends Ethel Higgs and Elizabeth Askew were also heading home from Caldwell's hosiery factory where they worked, happy to have had the chance of some overtime. At 13 The Rushes, the home and shop of Billy and Annie Adcock, Billy had gone out to visit a friend while Annie was at home with their two children. Many others were in the street too when the peace of the evening was shattered by the explosion of the first bomb; panic set in and as people began to scatter in all directions, the second bomb exploded in The Rushes.

> The scene just after the explosion was one of unforgettable confusion and horror... Telegraph and telephone wires lay in tangles across the pavements, and everywhere the ground was littered with broken glass. People were running in and out of their houses in terror, not daring to stay indoors, yet fearing to come out.[4]

Joseph and Anne Adkin had reached the north end of The Rushes when the first bomb exploded. Bewildered, they ran back, straight into the blast of the second and were killed. The bomb also cut down Ethel Higgs and Elizabeth Askew. Ethel died in hospital that evening while Elizabeth, who had 'a horrific wound just below the knee', managed to limp home the 700 yards to Paget Street. She remained in hospital for several months but she survived.[5]

At 13 The Rushes, Annie Adcock went outside when she heard the first explosion. As she did so the second bomb wrecked the front of the shop. When Billy got home a few minutes later he found a crowd gathered and his wife lying dead in the doorway. Upstairs his terrified children were in bed covered in glass from a smashed window.

L 20 now headed slowly towards the eastern edge of Loughborough, where the Empress Works, a large engineering establishment, was in production. Stabbert dropped two more bombs. The first exploded in a small orchard at the south end of Thomas Street but inflicted little damage of note. The sound of bombs, however, had alarmed local people. Mary Page left her house at 87 Empress Road with her children,

Joseph, aged 18 and Elsie, 16. Across the road at the Empress Works, Arthur Turnill, opened a door to see what was happening.

After Thomas Street the next bomb exploded outside 85 Empress Road. Bomb fragments and other lethal debris shot out in all directions. The Page family stood no chance. They had just reached a newsagent's shop on the corner of Judges Street when the bomb exploded right behind them. The shop's owner was a couple of streets away and had been cut by the Thomas Street bomb but, realizing his wife was alone in the shop, he ran home where…

> … a ghastly sight met his gaze, for on the pavement in front of his shop, in three pools of blood; lay a mother, her young son, and her daughter… The newsagent entered his shop after passing the dead people, remarking: 'Oh poor things!' His wife was in the shop, the front of which was blown in but she too had escaped without serious injury.[6]

On the opposite corner to the newsagent was a shop owned by Josiah Gilbert. Josiah and his 14-year-old son were talking to a travelling salesman. When the bomb exploded in Thomas Street, Josiah shouted, 'It's bombs, bombs!' and pulled his son away from the doorway. Seconds later the Empress Road bomb exploded and a jagged metal fragment slammed into his chest. Sarah, Josiah's wife, tried to pull him to safety but he stopped her saying, 'It's no use; I've been struck in the breast'. He died 15 minutes later.[7]

Directly opposite where the bomb exploded, Arthur Turnill, who had emerged from the Empress Works, also lay on the ground, badly injured by falling glass from the Works' shattered roof. Turnill, aged 51, a fitter, had eleven children from two marriages. He died from his injuries a few hours later. Inside the Works there was panic. Vicious shards of jagged glass slashed down from the roof and at least five of the workforce required treatment for their injuries. But not all lost their cool. Beatrice Smith, a crane driver, ensured the electricity was turned off, working with electrician, Ernest Stubley, who remained on the premises the whole night. Later both received the British Empire Medal.[8]

As L 20 departed Loughborough a fifth bomb landed in a field about a mile outside the town but it failed to detonate. That night the population of the town mourned the deaths of ten of their fellow citizens and felt sympathy for the 12 who bore the scars of that night of terror, but in the morning Loughborough became alive as huge numbers flocked to see the damage. At the Crown and Cushion, so many came to look that the landlord, William Oram, erected collection boxes in aid of the hospital; in two days he collected almost £19 (about £1,600 today).[9]

## 31 January 1916, 8.30pm, Ilkeston, Derbyshire

Leaving Loughborough behind, the crew of L 20 failed to notice the darkened town of Nottingham, but when Stabbert sighted a sprawl of lights to the west he believed he had found the industrial centre of Sheffield and abandoned his attempt on Liverpool. The first lights he saw, however, were shining from the Stanton Ironworks at Ilkeston, 30 miles south of Sheffield. As he neared Trowell, Stabbert dropped seven bombs. Little damage resulted although one exploded within 40 yards of the impressive Bennerley Viaduct, which carried the railway over the Erewash Valley, with another on the north side of the viaduct, bursting close to where the Midland Railway ran underneath it. All railway traffic in this area had halted but a signalman left his signal box to tell the driver of a stationary train to extinguish his lamps. While he was away a bomb exploded just five yards from the signal box.

> The front... was hammered in by the force of the explosion, many panes of glass were shattered to glittering fragments, the block instruments were knocked out of order, the telephone and telephone wires were brought down, while the rails and the permanent way were torn up.[10]

The Stanton Ironworks, at Hallam Fields, now lay directly ahead. Lights in Ilkeston were off but that was not the case at the ironworks on the south side of the town. About 8.30pm the Zeppelin loomed over the industrial complex and dropped 15 bombs as L 20 circled the area. There were great explosions close to the moulding and blacksmith's shops and a stable, but the main ironworks escaped relatively unscathed.

An unofficial warning reached the ironworks about 15 minutes before the attack and a group of four men heard sounds that one described as 'bumps' – the bombs near the viaduct. After a number of 'bumps' there was an explosion 20 or 30 yards from the group. One was hit on the arm and under the chin as he ran. He believed his workmates had all escaped too but an hour later, while receiving treatment, he heard that one of them – assistant furnace keeper James Hall – was dead. When he later saw James' body 'the head had been blown off'.[11]

The other victim, 41-year-old furnace loader Walter Wilson, and two other men had left the ironworks in a hurry. As L 20 loomed above them they ran towards the tram terminus outside St Bartholomew's Church. Bombs dropped in front and behind them. One exploded 20 yards from Walter by the boundary wall of the church, wrecking the adjacent parish room. The bomb ripped open a three-inch gash on the right side of his back through which his intestines now protruded. Although operated on, Walter did not recover and died the following day.[12]

## 31 January 1916, 8.45 - 9.45pm, Burton-upon-Trent, Derbyshire

Stabbert now headed south-west towards the next block of lights, which he felt marked southern Sheffield and the surrounding area. It was, however, Burton-upon-Trent, the famed brewery town. Following L 20's lead, over the next hour two more Zeppelins bombed the town and it is not possible to assign individual bombs to specific raiders; there were 15 HE and between 24 and 29 incendiary bombs of which about 10 failed to ignite.

Harry Hawkes, driving a shunting engine from Leicester Junction on the south side of the town, watched the bombs fall. One of the first serious fires broke out at the Ind Coope brewery's malting sheds while another fire, which lasted several hours, burnt out the hop room at Worthington's brewery. As Hawkes approached Wellington Street Junction a signalman, Tony Mycock, hailed him. He was a little unnerved by what he saw.

> He'd got a great incendiary bomb… He says, 'This here's hit the signal box and it's bounced in front of here,' and he went and picked it up and brought it into the signal box. So I says 'That's an incendiary bomb, Tony,' I says, 'you want to get shot of that bugger.'[13]

The large fires in the town now served as a beacon, drawing other roaming Zeppelins to the flames as Stabbert turned L 20 back to Germany. She crossed the country with no further incidents and exited the north coast of Norfolk at about 11.45pm.

Kapitänleutnant Joachim Breithaupt had also experienced a difficult journey over the North Sea in L 15. Two of her engines were out of action for about two hours. Those responsible for plotting the tracks of the nine incoming Zeppelins understandably struggled and their conclusion that L 15 dropped its bombs over the fens close to the Suffolk/Cambridgeshire border is impossible to reconcile with Breithaupt's belief that he had reached Liverpool.[14]

> At [8.30pm] the ship was over the west coast; a large city complex, divided in two parts by a broad sheet of water running north and south, joined by a lighted bridge, was recognized as Liverpool and Birkenhead... From [8,300] feet 1,400kg of explosive and 300kg of incendiaries were dropped in four crossings of the city mostly along the waterfront.[15]

An analysis after the war concluded that Breithaupt was describing an attack on Burton where the River Trent runs along the east side of the town and links to Winshill by a bridge that crosses the river and flood plain. Railways, canals and the extensive industrial buildings of the numerous breweries may have further convinced Breithaupt that he had found Liverpool.

It appears likely that Breithaupt made his runs over the town shortly after Stabbert had departed. Again the breweries suffered. Bombs blasted the roof off Worthington's four-storey malthouse, wrecked Allsop's sawmill and partly demolished an engine house at Bass. Others exploded at Charrington's and Robinson's breweries but in both cases they failed to damage buildings. There were no casualties at any of the breweries; however, that was not the case elsewhere in the town.

At a point where a railway track crossed High Street, about 50 people filled the Black Cat billiard hall. An eyewitness described the hall 'ablaze with light' when the bomb struck.[16] It exploded on the tracks just nine feet from the wall of the Black Cat, smashing a section of it and blasting away part of the roof.[17] While panic and confusion reigned inside the billiard hall, one person lay motionless alongside a rubble covered table; a large piece of metal had struck 16-year-old George Stephens' head and killed him.[18]

Another lethal bomb landed in Bond Street, close to the junction with Lichfield Street. At a school there the alert headmaster had just led his family down to the cellar and switched off the gas supply when 'a bomb glanced off the roof of his house, blew out a gable end, exposing to view the bedroom and smashing the drawing room and blowing the piano to fragments.' The headmaster was untouched but outside in the street it was different.[19]

When he heard the sound of the Zeppelin's engines, with commendable awareness, 13-year-old Bertie Geary climbed a lamppost to put out a streetlight. At the same time 15-year-old Lucy Simnett was walking by with her mother. Lethal metal fragments from the bomb cut down and killed Lucy; about 20 yards behind another mother and child were lucky to escape unhurt when a piece of the bomb cut through the woman's hat. Blown from the lamppost, young Bertie now lay on the ground 'with a wound in the back and perforation of the abdomen'. Another young boy tripped over him in the dark. Bertie was still alive but he told the boy he was going to die; his prediction came true the following day.[20]

The most casualties that night occurred at the Christ Church mission room on the corner of Uxbridge and Moor streets, where about 200 people had gathered. With Bible in hand, Mary Rose Morris was addressing the meeting when 'there was a blinding flash, and then all was darkness'. The bomb detonated on soft ground between the church and the mission room, opening up a crater 12 feet across. The wooden building was shattered and inside all was carnage.

Mary Rose Morris died instantly, as did Ada Brittain (aged 15), schoolmistress Margaret Anderson (60) and Rachel Wait (78). Elizabeth Smith and her husband lost each other in the panic and it was half an hour before he found her lying badly injured in an adjoining house. Mr Smith took his wife home and laid her on the settee. Their daughter Gladys looked on: 'She'd got a white blouse on, and you couldn't tell. It was bright red. Soaked in blood.'[21] Elizabeth died in hospital a few days later.

The bomb also fatally wounded 16-year-old Flora Warden. She had gone to the meeting with her friend Sybil, who escaped unscathed. They had just swapped seats because a woman was blocking Sybil's view of the speaker.[22] Inevitably in such a big crowd many were injured.

At the Midland Railway goods shed on Derby Road, just north of the main station, six men had just finished work when they heard the sound of bombs. They dived for cover under a loading dock just as one exploded in the shed. Three were injured but one, John Finney, a 53-year-old railway labourer, caught the full force of the blast and died.

At 34 Wellington Street, just to the west of the main railway station, Charles Gilson heard an explosion and went into the garden followed by his 15-year-old son, George. As he did so a bomb streaked down and exploded with tremendous force just a few yards away. Charles Gilson slumped to the ground, blood pouring from his head. The blast forced his watch into his body, stopping it at 8.45pm. His son was down too and covered in blood. George picked himself up: 'I felt something was wrong when I touched my arm. Dad was lying there and I tried to pick him up and I couldn't.' He ran into the house to find his mother and blurted out: 'They have killed my daddy, and look what they have done to me.' His left arm 'was severed as though cut through with a knife'.[23] At hospital they amputated what remained. George was lucky in that he survived the horrendous injury but he was unsuccessful in seeking compensation.

> A solicitor came from Manchester, and I had to lose half a day from work. He wasn't in the house two seconds. Just asked me to stand up. Showed him my wound. 'Oh, a big fine strapping chap you are. You might get eighteen pence a week and you might get nothing'. And he's gone through the door. Never heard from that day to this.[24]

The bomb that killed Charles Gilson also damaged other houses in Wellington Street, and next door at No.32, 10-year-old Edith Measham died the following day. Her nine brothers and sisters were all injured.

Elsewhere in Burton a bomb exploded in Shobnall Street. At No.108, 23-year-old Florence Jane Wilson was visiting her friend, Mrs Warrington, who had three children, one just a baby. Florence was just about to leave when the bomb smashed the house, reducing it to rubble and shattering others nearby. Mr Warrington returned home shortly after 9pm and joined those desperately searching through the wreckage for any survivors. As he called for his wife, rescuers heard her reply and then a baby's cry. Clawing away at the debris the rescuers pulled them both out alive. But as they continued to dig they discovered the crushed body of Florence, and then, near the fireplace, the couple's other two children, Mary, aged 11, and six-year-old George. Both were dead.

As Breithaupt turned for home he seemed pleased with the result of his raid on 'Liverpool'.

> All explosive bombs burst but fires were not seen to result. On the other hand, the incendiaries worked very well in my opinion… A huge glow of fire was seen over the city from a great distance.[25]

As L 15 left Burton many of the town's terrified population were hiding in their cellars waiting and wondering if they would be next. From her cellar in Grange Street, parallel with Shobnall Street, one woman listened fearfully to the boom of the bombs and the drone of the Zeppelin's engines.

> All we are thankful for is that God listened and took care of us. We were huddled up in the cellar, us and several of our neighbours, waiting as it were for death. Oh it was terrible, and I hope please God it may never come our way again.[26]

Burton, however, still had one more visit to come, for drawn by the glowing fires, Zeppelin L 19 was now heading towards the town.

Kapitänleutnant Odo Loewe was an experienced Zeppelin commander. Aged 32, he made his first raid on Britain commanding L 9 in August 1915 when he bombed Goole and on another occasion had attacked the Skinningrove Ironworks on the North Yorkshire coast. He took command of the Navy's last 'p-class' Zeppelin, L 19, in November 1915.

After crossing the North Sea from Tondern in Schleswig-Holstein, L 19 made landfall near Sheringham on the Norfolk coast at 6.20pm, but the Maybach HSLu engines were causing problems. This slowed progress and there are reports of L 19 circling while the crew made repairs. At 9.45pm Loewe radioed that he had reached the west coast but weather conditions were such that he could see nothing: 'Orientation and attack there impossible due to thick fog; dropped incendiaries.' Far from the west coast, those two incendiaries dropped on Burton. There is no report that they caused any damage. For Burton the night of terror was finally over. In the shattered houses and damaged streets 15 people lay dead and another 70 were receiving treatment for their injuries.

From Burton, Loewe took L 19 to the south-west, hoping to confirm his supposed position on the west coast. But at about 10.30pm, when south-west of Birmingham, engine problems struck again forcing L 19 to circle for about an hour.

With engines throbbing back to life once more, Loewe headed north, towards Wednesbury where fires still burned from the earlier attack. About midnight he dropped a single bomb less than half a mile west of the Crown Tube Works where bombs had caused such terror almost four hours earlier. It smashed the roof and damaged machinery at the works of the Patent Shaft and Axeltree Company. Between Wednesbury and Tipton, Loewe released five more bombs as he passed over Ocker Hill

Colliery, but their impact was minimal. Then, at 12.10am, Police Chief Superintendent Speke reported that L 19 attacked Dudley.

> Fourteen incendiary and four explosive bombs were dropped in fields at Netherton [just south of Dudley], in close proximity to M & W Grazebrook's blast furnaces. Incendiary bombs were also dropped in the Dudley Castle Grounds, the fields adjoining the same and at the Grain Shed at the Great Western Railway Station. The only damage done was at the shed in question, which amounts to about £5.[27]

For those living nearby it came as quite a shock.

> Everybody was running around the house, getting the kiddies up & we saw flashes and heard the bombs our house shook & poor little George trembled from head to foot. People running home from Dudley to their homes couldn't tell us anything further – than the Zeps had come!... a Zep came over our house, across the public [house] at the back (Jolly Collier) and across those fields and dropped a bomb not very far from our house but that one fortunately for us did not explode.[28]

## 1 February 1916, 12.20am, Tipton, Staffordshire

From Dudley, L 19 turned towards Tipton, where four hours earlier L 21's bombs had killed 14 people. Two bombs hurtled down towards Park Lane West. One landed in the open but the other exploded just five feet from the front of the Bush Inn. It smashed every window, tore the doors from their hinges and caused the collapse of the roof. Pinned in their bedroom, the landlord and his wife only escaped when their frantic son managed to break down the door. The pub clock stopped at 12.20am.[29] More bombs fell along the railway from Tipton Station to Blomfield before L 19 headed towards Walsall where the town was also still reeling from the earlier attack. This time bombs fell over the western districts of Pleck and Birchills.

Frederick Bromley, a dairyman living with his family at 18 Dora Street, heard the sound of distant explosions and woke his 10-year-old son, sending him out to climb and extinguish a streetlight. Outside in the cold night air the boy saw the Zeppelin and ran back into the house just as 'there was a crash, bang and then two more'. The first 'crash' was a bomb making a breach in the wall that divided the gardens on that side of the street from the field behind. The 'bang' was the second bomb destroying Frederick Bromley's stable at the back of his house killing some of his pigs, many chickens and his carthorse.[30] Seconds later a third bomb exploded on open ground east of Scarborough Road, smashing numerous windows. Now following Pleck Road, L 19 failed to bomb any of the iron or tube works it passed over, instead Loewe's final bomb smashed onto a bowling green between St Andrew's Church and a partly-built vicarage. The roofs of both buildings suffered and many of the stained glass windows on the south side of the church were smashed. The explosion also demolished part of the premises of carriage builder, John Barton, while shattered window glass frosted the streets, crunching under the feet of the curious and inquisitive as they gradually began to emerge from shelter to view the damage.

L 19's bombs claimed no lives directly although there had been some narrow escapes. One person however, did die. William Henry Haycock, a 50-year-old former policeman, now bedridden with chronic rheumatic fever, had been unsettled during the earlier raid when a bomb exploded 600 yards away. Despite his nervousness he insisted his wife went out to check on a patient she was nursing. She had not returned when the second raid commenced. When he heard the bombs, Haycock, 'impulsively' jumped out of bed. His wife returned home to find him lying dead on the floor. A doctor pronounced death due to 'shock caused by the explosion of bombs'.

Loewe now turned for home, but the engine problems that had plagued him earlier returned. The flight back to the coast – a distance of 155 miles – took five hours to complete. When she passed out to sea over Norfolk at 5.25am on 1 February L 19 had been overland and vulnerable for almost 11 hours.

The statistics of the raid compiled by GHQ, Home Forces showed that 379 bombs with a combined weight of just over 12 tons (12,500kgs), caused material damage estimated at £53,832, while killing 70 people and injuring another 113. For those in authority these were sobering figures.

Hailed in the German press, the idealistic reports filed by the returning Zeppelin commanders fuelled a wild delight, as illustrated in an article in the *Hamburger Nachrichten*.

> In England the people were living happily and free from care
> in the midst of war... Then the Zeppelin came out of the night

and taught haughty people that the war can overtake them everywhere, and that it is bloody, terrible, and serious.

England's industry to a considerable extent lies in ruins. England's own soil has been ploughed by the mighty explosive shells of the German air squadrons.[31]

It was a wildly optimistic view of the effect of the bombs and a version of events seized on with glee by the British satirical magazine *Punch*.

The Germans claim that as the result of the Zeppelin raid 'England's industry to a considerable extent lies in ruins,' is probably based on the fact that three breweries were bombed. To the Teuton mind such a catastrophe might well seem overwhelming.[32]

There was, however, no denying that it had been a traumatic night for many of those on the ground caught up in the raids. But what of those who ventured up into the air to oppose them?

\* \* \*

While the nine raiding Zeppelins had prowled over East Anglia and criss-crossed the Midlands, they had at no point encountered any British aircraft. Although the poor weather played its part in limiting the response, the night's efforts have been labelled one of the biggest fiascos in British air defence history.[33]

First in the path of the Zeppelins' approach were the RNAS stations on the Norfolk coast. When the first two raiders came inland at about 4.50pm, word immediately reached Great Yarmouth and within 20 minutes two pilots were in the air, but the atrocious weather conditions forced them down within the hour. At 5.15pm a third pilot, Flight Lieutenant C.E. Wood, went up but after losing his bearings he made an eventful forced landing in the dark.

He glided down till his altimeter said 0 – and waited developments. Suddenly there was a rending crash – both wings of his machine crumpled up – and he sat down with a bang on the lawn of an old house [in Spixworth, north of Norwich] occupied by two old maiden ladies. He had apparently glided down an avenue of trees, shorn off both wings and sat down just beyond them, absolutely unscratched.[34]

A fourth pilot ascended from Great Yarmouth at 7pm but he saw nothing.

When Zeppelins first appeared their target was unknown so warnings were widely issued, including to London. The RNAS maintained two air stations for the defence of the capital, at Chingford and Hendon. Between 7.55 and 8.30pm a pilot from each station went up searching for an enemy that was not there. Both damaged their aircraft on landing. A misfiring engine forced another RNAS pilot from Rochford to make a sticky landing in the mud of the Thames estuary.

It had clearly not been a great night for the RNAS, but for the RFC it proved a disastrous one.

## 31 January 1916, 7.35pm: Outskirts of London

At the ten RFC airfields around London, 19 BE2c aircraft were standing by when the patrol order came through, advising that Zeppelins could reach London by 8.10pm. At 7.35pm the squadron commander of No.10 Reserve Aeroplane Squadron (RAS), Major Ernest Unwin, took off from Joyce Green through fog and mist to assess flying conditions. Fifteen minutes later he smashed into trees on Erith Marshes. He died of his injuries seven weeks later. A second pilot, Second Lieutenant Claude Ridley, went up but, disorientated in the clouds, he crashed and wrecked his aircraft near Reigate. A third pilot of the squadron, flying from Farningham at 7.45pm, also crashed but, like Ridley, Second Lieutenant W. Guilfoyle walked away from the wreckage of his BE2c.

At Northolt the commander of No.11 RAS, Major Leslie da Costa Penn-Gaskell, also went up first to check flying conditions. Moments later his aircraft hit a tree at the far end of the airfield and caught fire. Penn-Gaskell died four days later.

While there were no more deaths to report, the pilots of No.17 RAS also had a night to forget. Both pilots from Hainault Farm crashed on the airfield, while the pilot from Sutton's Farm hit a fence when landing. Second Lieutenant Hugh Tomlinson took off from Wimbledon Common but seconds later hit a tree and then a house; he just managed to scramble clear before two of his bombs exploded. The two pilots who ascended from Croydon both cut short their patrols due to poor visibility and the single pilot from Hendon lost his way before spotting flares and gratefully landing at Hainault Farm. Of the 13 patrols flown by the RFC around London, two pilots were fatally injured, two had minor injuries, with five aircraft wrecked and two damaged. Yet not one Zeppelin threatened London at any time during the raid.

The situation over the Midlands was no better. Despite this being the largest raid of the war to date, no aircraft in the region opposed the attack. The inadequacies of Britain's aerial defence were fully exposed: an ineffective warning system, a lack of anti-aircraft guns and searchlights, and aircraft without effective weapons with which to threaten the Zeppelins. There had been little progress since the raids of 1915, but the green shoots of change would begin to appear in the spring of 1916.

Although it had proved a disastrous night for Britain's airborne defenders, their problems were over for now. For the crew of Zeppelin L 19, however, their problems had only just begun.

## 1/2 February 1916: The North Sea

Zeppelin L 19 had left the British coast at 5.25am on 1 February, the last of the nine raiders to depart. By 1pm all the others were back in Germany and concerns for the whereabouts of L 19 grew. At 4.05pm the navy despatched three destroyer flotillas to commence a search but as they did so, Nordholz received a radio message from the missing Zeppelin. Although experiencing difficulties, she was nearing Germany: 'Radio equipment at times out of order, three engines out of order. Approximate position Borkum Island. Wind is favourable.'[35]

Borkum, one of Germany's East Frisian Islands, would have been good news for Loewe but unfortunately his navigation was out. He was at the time about 45 miles to the west of his supposed position and 22 miles north of the Dutch island of Ameland. The radio centre at Nordholz tried to advise Loewe of his real position but received no reply. However, as L 19 was less than 70 miles from the nearest Zeppelin base at Hage, the navy recalled the destroyers. Eight hours later, however, there was still no sign of L 19 and at midnight the ships set out again. On the morning of 2 February, 12 miles north of Borkum, they recovered one of L 19's discarded fuel tanks but of the airship there was no sign. Fog and strong winds prevented any Zeppelins joining the search.

After transmitting the message to Nordholz on the afternoon of 1 February, Loewe flew towards Ameland, believing it was the German island of Borkum, but as she came in low over the sand dunes the Dutch coastguard at the village of Hollum opened rifle fire. Although the Netherlands was neutral in the war, she vigorously defended her territory against any encroachments. The bullets found an easy target in the looming body of L 19 and pierced her gasbags. Realising his error, Loewe turned away, heading back out over the North Sea where engine problems struck again, compounding the crew's difficulties as gradual hydrogen loss from the tiny bullet holes meant the airship became heavier as the wind carried L 19 westwards and away from Germany.

At some point during the night of 1 February, the loss of hydrogen added unforgiving stresses to the duralumin structure and L 19 broke her back, collapsing into the sea. The floundering Zeppelin was now almost in the middle of the North Sea, about half way between Ameland and Spurn Head, the prominent sand spit marking the entrance to the River Humber about 110 miles to the west. Unless someone came to their rescue they were doomed.

In the early morning of 2 February a Grimsby trawler, the *King Stephen*, was out in the North Sea. Her mate, George Denny was on watch and saw a twinkling light in the far distance. After altering course and steaming for 10 miles, Denny realised what they had found, a half-submerged Zeppelin.[36]

The skipper, William Martin, and the seven other members of the crew joined Denny. Martin took in the scene.

> I could see about 15 men in the top hamper... others in a ring with their heads through the companion way... I shouted, 'What is the matter?' 'Send us a boat and I will give you £5,' answered one, and he took off his coat... I knew him at once for a naval officer and the captain of the ship. When one or two of his crew who spoke English tried to butt in he shut them up pretty smart. He was a gentleman and behaved as one. He was nice and polite, and spoke good English too.

Denny, on the other hand, was not so well disposed to Loewe.

> His manner was suave and oily. He said that if we would put off in our small boat and take them off he would reward us with gold. He repeated his offer of money so insistently that it irritated us.

The crew now faced a dilemma as Denny explained: 'For us it was not a question of money or humanity, but one of prudence.'

There were 16 men aboard L 19, although those on the *King Stephen* thought there were about 20 and, reasonably, presumed them to have weapons. The unarmed crew of the fishing boat numbered just nine. Martin made up his mind and told Loewe his decision.

> 'Well, if there weren't so many of you I would take you off, but there's too many.' The officer straightened himself up and said there was nothing in that. I thought again, and I said, 'But supposing we take you and you sling us overboard and navigate the trawler to Germany. That will be another decoration for you, but it won't be much for us.' He said, 'I pledge you my word that we will not do anything of the kind'. He took his dying oath that he would not interfere with us, and that I could have plenty of money if I saved them.

Martin again considered his position but came to the same conclusion – the risks to his crew were too great.

> If there had been another ship standing by to help me I could have chanced it, but there was nothing in sight. Besides, I remembered what the Huns have done, and what they might do again.

Since the beginning of the war British newspapers had reported stories of German brutality with gusto, and raids by Zeppelins – termed 'Baby-killers' – had been ongoing for a year while their bombs had claimed numerous lives in Hull, not far from Grimsby, the fishing boat's home port. His mind made up, Martin sailed away at 9.30 on the morning of 2 February.

> Some of the German crew at first shouted, 'Mercy, mercy, save us,' and then shook their fists at us as they saw it was of no use … I went away to find a gunboat or a patrol vessel better provided than we for looking after an enemy crew.

George Denny added: 'As the trawler steamed away they shook their fists and one of them climbed on the rails and shouted 'Gott strafe England'.

During the day a rising wind brought a weather change and by 10.30pm Martin reported 'it was blowing hard'. Battling through rough seas, with waves crashing over the deck of the *King Stephen*, William Martin encountered no ships on the way back to Grimsby and he had no radio. Off the mouth of the Humber he reported all that had happened to a tug[37] and the navy despatched two destroyers to search for the downed Zeppelin.[38] That same morning – Thursday 3 February – a French vessel docked at Hull and also reported a Zeppelin down in the North Sea on Wednesday morning, but she had not approached it.[39]

Once the *King Stephen* disappeared from sight, the crew of L 19, were alone on their makeshift island in the vastness of the North Sea. As the morning passed the weather deteriorated. The desperate men, soaked to the skin and frozen, contemplated the end. They wrote final messages to their families and threw them overboard in bottles. Three weeks later the yacht *Stella,* sailing off the coast of Gothenburg, Sweden, picked up one. Six months later a fisherman at Marstrand, an island just north of Gothenburg, retrieved another. It contained Loewe's final bleak report written on 2 February.

> With 15 men on the platform of L 19. Longitude 3° East. The envelope is floating without any car. I am trying to send the last report. We had three engine breakdowns. A very high headwind on the homeward flight hampered progress and drove us in fog over Holland when we came under rifle-fire. Three engines failed simultaneously. Our position became increasingly difficult. Now, about one o'clock in the afternoon, our last hour is approaching. Loewe.[40]

The two British destroyers found no sign of the Zeppelin. Five months later, on 21 June, the body of one of the crew, Georg Baumann, washed ashore on the Danish coast near Tranum. Two days later the headless corpse of another, identified as Zugmann, beached at Løkken, also on the Danish coast, and in July a third body, that of Heinrich Specht, came ashore at Sonderho on the Danish island of Fanö.[41] The short life of Zeppelin L 19 was over, but the controversy over William Martin's actions would run and run.

Chapter 4

# A New Beginning

In the aftermath of the Midlands Raid, controversy was everywhere. German bombs had claimed more casualties than any previous raid. No Zeppelins had penetrated so far west before and now those living in the regions affected realised just how defenceless they were, while the lack of a coordinated lighting policy, even between neighbouring towns, also caused great consternation. And not a single anti-aircraft gun or aircraft opposed the raiders over the Midlands. Elsewhere, the RFC lost two senior pilots who went up to evaluate flying conditions around London, while others were fortunate to survive bad landings. Yet no Zeppelin had even come close to London. A thorough overhaul of Britain's air defences was imperative. The actions of William Martin, the skipper of the *King Stephen*, also filled newspaper columns already overflowing with controversy.

Widespread reporting of the *King Stephen's* encounter with L 19 appeared in newspapers in the next couple of days. Inevitably the story reached Germany where the press reacted with a 'storm of indignation' and railed at 'the brutality of the British character'.[1]

This indignation exploded into outrage when the Bishop of London, the Right Reverend Arthur Winnington-Ingram, addressed a crowd on 5 February and expressed his support for Martin's actions.

> Had he taken the 22 [sic] Germans into his ship they might have turned upon the crew, and the whole German Press would have applauded their action... Any English sailor would have risked his life to save human life, but the sad thing was that the chivalry of war had been killed by the Germans, and their word could not be trusted.[2]

Somewhat overwhelmed by the publicity, William Martin initially did not return to sea, but any intentions he had to do so later were quashed in late February when the Admiralty requisitioned the *King Stephen* and fitted her out as an armed Q-ship.

The newspaper coverage spawned letters of praise for Martin, but also delivered hate mail that sorely troubled him. It emerged through interviews with the naval authorities that the *King Stephen* was fishing the Cleaver Bank area of the North Sea, which was a forbidden zone and there have been suggestions that because of that, Martin gave a false position for L 19, some 40 miles short of this area. However, descriptions of his position quoted in the press do match the location of the Cleaver Bank.[3]

Another incident was to confirm the strength of ill feeling in Germany against Martin. Operating in its new role as a Q-ship on 24 April 1916, the *King Stephen* unfortunately encountered German naval forces returning from a bombardment of Lowestoft and Great Yarmouth. The torpedo boat *G41* took her crew prisoner before sinking the hated vessel. Despite protestations of innocence, the *King Stephen's* new captain, a Royal Naval Reserve officer, Lieutenant Tom Phillips, found himself on trial in Germany accused of war crimes. It was only after an English newspaper containing a photograph of William Martin appeared at the trial that the prosecution dropped the charges against him. Phillips and his 12-man crew remained POWs for the rest of the war.

The hate mail Martin continued to receive affected him deeply. He died on 24 February 1917, his demise attributed to 'an affectation of the heart'[4], but a report published at the conclusion of the war added more detail.

> He had received a number of anonymous letters containing threats, apparently from Germans in England, and when he became ill after smoking a cigarette from a packet which had been sent to him in the post, he was convinced that the cigarette contained poison. Analysis proved that his fears were unfounded, but he never recovered from the shock.[5]

The raid on the Midlands had completely overwhelmed the limited inland aerial defences and many now feared the start of a more intensive period of far-ranging attacks, while the civilian population's anxiety and lack of faith in the warning system took time to calm. In fact there were no more Zeppelin raids anywhere in Britain for five weeks, but nervousness caused four false alarms in February alone, which saw factories and railways over wide areas of the country plunged into darkness, bringing production to a halt. With the War Office about to take over the responsibility for aerial defence they were under no illusion about the difficulties of the task ahead.

The warning system relied on the telephone network and it became necessary to inform the public, whose use of the telephone system increased dramatically during raids, to restrict themselves to necessary and urgent calls only at these times to keep lines clear for official communications. From 16 February the current lighting restrictions were extended to cover the whole of England except in the most western, south-western and north-western counties, although public concern saw restrictions extend into some of these areas too by April 1916. The issue of warnings required more thought and Neville Chamberlain,[6] the Lord Mayor of Birmingham, voiced the opinions of a delegation of civic leaders in the Midlands who argued for special warnings for the extensive munitions establishments in the region. He called for cordons of observers between the east coast and the Midlands to report the progress of enemy aircraft and warn centres of munition production early enough for the extinguishing of lights. But that wasn't enough for the munitions workers, as the Ministry of Munitions confirmed on 12 February: 'Our position is that workmen are refusing to work at night at all unless guaranteed that warning will be given in sufficient time to enable them to disperse.'[7] Clearly changes were needed to ensure production did not suffer and in the short term Chief Constables were asked to establish a means to inform munitions factories in their areas of approaching raids.

While GHQ, Home Forces prepared for the transfer of aerial defence from the Admiralty, they had been looking at ways of improving the warning system and much of what Chamberlain suggested already featured in their plans. But, as the time set for the transfer approached, the War Office looked to delay matters. Lord Kitchener, Secretary of State for War, had returned from the Dardanelles in mid-January and immediately decided it was a bad time to make such important changes. The Lords of the Admiralty, however, were having none of it and insisted the transfer took place in February as scheduled. Only after two high-level meetings was the new arrangement confirmed, the most important element being,

> The Navy to undertake to deal with all hostile aircraft attempting to reach this country, whilst the Army undertake to deal with all such aircraft which reach these shores.[8]

When Admiral Sir Percy Scott took command of London's anti-aircraft defence in September 1915[9] he planned two gun rings surrounding the capital. Although not yet complete, GHQ, Home Forces adopted this plan. On paper the anti-aircraft defence of Britain required 475 guns but at the time of the handover there were just 295, with 65 defending the London area and 230 (197 Army and 33 Navy) across the rest of the country. A quick inventory, however, resulted in the War Office classing only 80 of these as 'efficient'. More guns were in the process of conversion to an anti-aircraft role and, although the Admiralty agreed to hand over 86 AA guns currently on order, in the end they transferred only 21, the rest diverted to arm merchant ships in the war against the U-boats. Even so, new guns were on order and the aerial defence capability gradually increased.

Plans to increase the number of night or emergency landing grounds available to the RFC resulted in the establishment or preparation of 44 more by the end of February, from Newcastle in the north to Kent and Sussex in the south. The need for the RFC to create new Home Defence squadrons was clear too, but that would take time due to a shortage of aircraft and personnel. In the meantime training squadrons at Norwich (No.9 Reserve Aeroplane Squadron (RAS)), Thetford (No.35 Squadron), Doncaster (No.15 RAS) and Dover (No.20 RAS) received 12 BE2c aircraft to assist with home defence, and six more joined No.5 RAS for the defence of the Midlands. They were in place by 1 March 1916. In addition, three BE2cs that the RFC had moved to Cramlington for the defence of Newcastle in December 1915 now, at the beginning of February 1916, formed the nucleus of the new No.36 (Home Defence) Squadron.[10]

The lack of a co-ordinated response from the reserve squadrons surrounding London was also a concern. To improve the situation, those aircraft were regrouped into a new single squadron on 1 February 1916. Under Major Thomas Higgins, No.19 RAS was to fulfil a dual role, defending the capital and training new pilots.

* * *

The cycle of the moon ensured no Zeppelins threatened Britain while the Army settled into its new role, but the moon had no impact on the opportunistic raiders of Seeflieger Abteilug (SFA) 1 at Zeebrugge. Their stinging hit-and-run raids in 1915 had proved an annoying thorn in the side of the British defences, their sudden appearance and quick departure meant local aircraft were rarely able to get airborne before the raiders had dropped their bombs and departed. And so it continued.

## 9 February 1916, 3.36pm: Ramsgate, Kent

Wednesday 9 February was cold but bright and sunny along the Kent coast and many people were out enjoying the unexpected spring-like weather. At 3.36pm two German floatplanes crossed the coast. A Friedrichshafen FF33e, with Oberleutnant-zur-See Faber and Flugmeister Jacobs on board, peeled off towards Ramsgate, while a Hansa-Brandenburg NW, crewed by Leutnant der Reserve Friedrich Christiansen and Leutnant-zur-See Exner, turned towards Broadstairs.

On the eastern edge of Ramsgate a double-decker tram trundled along Dumpton Park Drive. As it neared Montefiore College, a woman on the tram noticed an aircraft in the sky.

> I jokingly remarked how exciting it would be if they started to drop bombs when I noticed the crosses on the wings denoting that it was a German machine. The next moment about twelve feet behind us the earth seemed to cough up with a splash like a mine exploding at sea and this was followed in quick succession by three other explosions in the field.[11]

A woman and her children living across the field about 150 yards away heard 'a succession of terrific bangs'.

> I at once caught up the baby. Another little girl was sitting close to the kitchen window, and I had only just snatched her away when it was smashed by the concussion. We looked out afterwards and all we could see was a dense mass of brown smoke rising from the field.[12]

Two teenage girls in the fields saw the explosion and ran towards the tram. As they passed through a gap in a hedge one caught her dress and the other stopped to help her. As she did so the other three bombs exploded close to the terrified pair. Both girls fainted. When the first bomb exploded the driver of the tram slammed on the brake and all the passengers abandoned the vehicle, but rather than running away to safety many scrambled into the field to search for bomb fragments while others cared for the two rather shaken girls. And this extraordinary scene got rather more bizarre when a group of roller-skating soldiers emerged from the nearby skating rink and glided down the road towards the tram to see if they could offer any assistance![13]

## 9 February 1916, 3.36pm: Broadstairs, Kent

The aircraft that flew over Broadstairs homed in on three large buildings on the southern side of the town: two convalescent homes and Bartram Gables girls' school. Four small bombs streaked down with one smashing through the school's roof before exploding in an upper room, bringing down the ceiling of the classroom below in which 14 children were studying.[14] The room filled with smoke, dust and plaster but only one child was injured, nine-year-old Hermione Michaels, whose foot was cut. The bomb also slightly injured Alice Eastop, a housemaid working at the school.[15] The other three bombs fell in the school grounds breaking a few windows. The sound of the explosions alerted soldiers at the convalescent homes: 'The children were delighted at the way the wounded men came over the fence, running and hopping along on their crutches anxious to be of service.'[16]

Not far from the school other bombs fell in the grounds of large houses in Dumpton Park Drive and Ramsgate Road but damage was insignificant.[17] The two aircraft penetrated no more than 300 yards inland and departed as soon as they had dropped their bombs. Local estimates evaluated the material damage at £305. Although 19 RNAS aircraft took off as well as five from the RFC, by the time they were airborne the raiders were on their way back to Zeebrugge.[18] Back in Germany the raiders' reports led to the publication of an optimistic press release: 'During the afternoon of the 9th inst. some of our naval aeroplanes dropped a number of bombs on the port and manufacturing establishments, as well as the barracks at Ramsgate.'[19]

Seven days after the raid, on 16 February, the Army officially took command of London's aerial defence, followed by responsibility for the rest of Britain a few days later. The man now ultimately in command was Field Marshal Sir John French, Commander-in-Chief of the Home Forces, a position he had held since 19 December 1915. He had only been in the role a few days when German aircraft made another stinging attack on the coast.

## 20 February 1916, 10.55am: Lowestoft, Suffolk

At 10.55am on Sunday 20 February, two Friedrichshafen FF33e floatplanes appeared over the Suffolk town of Lowestoft. Many people were on their way to church on this bright sunny morning. Although the two aircraft dropped 17 small HE bombs on the town there were no casualties.[20] The line of the inner harbour divides the town and a police report indicates at least 11 bombs dropped north of the harbour. A small fire broke out the Central Station's parcel office but three bombs that fell within 40 feet of the gasworks only damaged a stables and smashed windows. Other bombs caused minor damage at the electric light station in Rotterdam Road and at the domestic waste destructor yard. At 5 Essex Road a bomb smashed through the roof of a workman's cottage and landed in the back bedroom but failed to explode. The fortunate occupants were downstairs in the kitchen at the time. One bomb, which struck Pike's Restaurant, caused considerable damage and destroyed an outbuilding.[21] On the south side of the harbour a bomb struck the quayside and in Belvedere Road one damaged machinery at a timber yard and another detonated in the roadway smashing a number of windows. About 230 yards away a bomb struck the roof of a large house at 107 London Road South, where,

> … fragments of slates and tiles were thrown in all directions, while nearly all the windows were shattered. Considerable damage was done to the interior on the top floor, but here also the occupants were on the ground floor and escaped injury.
>
> The force of the explosion of this bomb blew in all the windows in one side of an adjacent Methodist chapel [in Mill Road]. As the morning service was at that moment starting the chapel was full and the congregation were greatly alarmed. There was no kind of a panic, however, and all left the chapel quietly and without disorder, the service being abandoned.[22]

On the seafront, at 16 Esplanade, the house served as headquarters of 68th Provisional Battalion, 5th Provisional Brigade. A bomb exploding five yards from the building cut the telephone line, smashed a greenhouse and windows while flying glass injured an officer and a clerk. Berthed in the harbour, HMS *Halcyon* fired one hopeful round at the raiders from a 4.7-inch gun while three naval 6-pdr Hotchkiss guns and a 12-pdr at

Lowestoft also engaged, but the raiders were unharmed as they headed back out to sea.

Completely taken by surprise, the Great Yarmouth RNAS pilots were at church when the raid commenced. Despite their valiant efforts to get back to their station and take off, none of the five pilots saw any sign of the raiders and at least one, Flight sub-Lieutenant Egbert Cadbury, regretted his haste: 'It was simply terribly cold – I had no time to get ready and had not got any gloves; I have never been so cold before.'[23]

Although there were no serious casualties in Lowestoft, the Town Council was angry, firing off a strongly worded resolution to the Prime Minister, the First Lord of the Admiralty and the Secretary of State for War.

> This Council protests against the defenceless state in which the persons and property of the inhabitants were found to be; that a full and impartial investigation is called for into the circumstances under which any attempt at resistance proved to be so completely futile.[24]

Lord French's new task was not going to be an easy one.

About half an hour after the attack on Lowestoft, another floatplane, a Hansa-Brandenburg NW, approached the Kent coastal town of Walmer where many people were enjoying a Sunday morning walk.

## 20 February 1916, 11.30am: Walmer, Kent

The aircraft approached from the south-east but estimates of its height varied wildly. At the time a motorboat, *Elsie*, was just offshore with two men on board. A rowing boat was heading back to the beach from the *Elsie*. Those on both boats had a close shave.

> We had just taken in the anchor and started the motor, when three violent explosions occurred barely 50 yards astern, falling between the motor-boat and the rowing-boat… The explosions followed each other in rapid succession, and all three bombs fell practically in line about 20ft to 30ft apart. The explosions caused a great upheaval of water… We also heard further explosions, obviously from bombs dropped on the land.[25]

Two friends, Cecil Pedlar and George Castle, both aged 16, were walking along a road on the seafront. Cecil had recently run away from home to enlist in the Army but his family informed the authorities of his real age and the Army sent him home again. George worked as a grocer's assistant. As people began to point to the sky a cry went up, 'Look out; it's a German. Get under cover.' Seeing the great plumes of water rising from the sea, Cecil turned to George: 'We had better be going, or we shall have a bomb fall on us.' They had gone just a few paces when an explosion burst in front of them. A boatman standing on the beach told how he was knocked off his feet.

> This was the bomb that killed the boy who was walking along the roadway, and terribly injured a man who was walking behind him. I rushed over to give what help I could, but I found that the boy had been killed on the spot, being almost blown to pieces... the bomb fell right at his feet with a blinding flash and roar. The effect was terrible, and it was a fragment from the bomb that wounded the man.[26]

It seems, however, that Cecil Pedlar's wounds were not as serious as first thought. A police inspector described them as a 'wound in the left thigh and shock, condition not serious'. But for George Castle there was no reprieve.[27]

Seconds later a bomb exploded in Dover Road, smashing windows in 25 shops and houses along the eastern side before a final bomb fell at the vast Royal Marines Depot. It exploded in the barracks' Works Department yard, close to the married quarters and the garrison church where a service was underway. The blast damaged a workshop roof and smashed all the windows down one side of the married quarters and at the church. A Marine suffered a cut leg. It is difficult, however, to reconcile newspaper reports of the stoic attitude of the congregation.

> The Te Deum was being sung when a tremendous explosion was heard, which shook the building and caused a momentary pause to the singing. However the service proceeded without the least sign of anxiety on the part of the congregation.[28]

Having spent little more than a minute over land, the raider now disappeared into clouds over the sea. The RNAS despatched 18 aircraft over the next 90 minutes from Dover, Eastchurch and Grain, and the RFC launched five from Dover, but they really had no chance of catching him. That afternoon the Prime Minister, Herbert Asquith, came to see the damage for himself. Unknown to the Germans, Asquith was staying at Walmer Castle, just three quarters of a mile from where the bombs fell.

## 1 March 1916, 6.10pm: Margate, Kent

Another German hit-and-run raid struck the Kent coast on 1 March. The raider, a Friedrichshafen FF29 crewed by Flugmaat Huth and Flugmeister Johann Jacobs, departed from Zeebrugge and approached the town of Margate at 6.10pm. Darkness was falling and reports state that the aircraft was flying low at about 1,500 feet. Lydia Peile was sitting comfortably at home in Norfolk Road in the Cliftonville district when she was shaken by 'an awfully loud explosion, quite close, followed quickly by another – Bombs of course, & we wondered if the next one would come on the house'.[29] That first explosion – at 6.14pm – was a bomb that partially demolished the back of 5 Norfolk Road, causing havoc within the house where a mother and her baby were in a room used as a nursery. The baby, nine-month-old Jack Dodman, was on the floor. When the bomb exploded his shocked mother scooped him up but immediately dropped him again in panic. He landed on his head and died almost immediately.[30] Lydia Peile soon heard what had happened: 'It was hateful seeing the ambulances arrive, but the other people were only suffering from shock.'

Other bombs in Norfolk Road damaged 12 houses.[31] From Cliftonville the FF29 approached the Kingsgate area north of Broadstairs, dropping two bombs between Percy Road and Kingsgate Avenue. A local newspaper reporter was unimpressed, claiming they 'only had the effect of creating momentary excitement, and providing the glaziers with a fine opportunity for plying their trade'. One woman explained what happened at her house.

> All the front windows were smashed – those upstairs being blown across the room and those downstairs falling outwards. A fragment of shell went through a bedroom window curtain, pierced the frame of a mirror and became embedded in the wall at the back of the room. If the raid had happened half-an-hour later all the children would have been in bed, and I don't know what would have happened to the little ones.[32]

The last two bombs dropped on the wide-open spaces of the North Foreland golf course. With no advance warning of the raid and rapidly diminishing light, the commanding officer at RNAS Westgate decided against sending up any of his aircraft in pursuit. The raider, however, did not make it back to Zeebrugge. Running into difficulties on the return flight, the pilot ditched in the North Sea about ten miles off the Belgian coast where French patrol boats located it at 9am the following morning. They recovered the bedraggled pilot, Huth, but it was too late for his observer, Jacobs – he had drowned.[33]

* * *

In Germany there had been ongoing discussions as to whether it was necessary to restrict airship attacks to moonless nights. The Army General Staff carried out a test over Cologne in November 1915 using Zeppelin LZ 77 to determine 'the exact degree of visibility from the surface during the full moon period'.[34] Those observing concluded that at the heights airships could now attain there was no undue risk. But an army airship commander, Ernst Lehmann,[35] felt their findings were flawed.

> The observers had been located too close to the large and densely populated industrial centres. The haze, which is invariably found hanging above such districts at night, had obscured their vision.[36]

Pressure mounted on Strasser to accept the findings for his naval airships but he remained unconvinced. A couple of days before the February full moon he ran his own test over the base at Hage using Zeppelin L 16. Flying at heights between 9,500 and 10,500 feet, the Zeppelin remained clearly visible, 'as a dark silhouette against the moon, or as a light streak away from it'.[37] The Navy remained committed to only raiding on the darkest nights of each month. The Army, however, sent out four airships during the full moon on the night of 20/21 February at the opening of the campaign against the fortress of Verdun. French anti-aircraft fire hit LZ 95 at 10,500 feet and 'some of the Zeppelin's gas cells were torn almost to shreds'.[38] Her commander, Hauptman Friedrich George, had commanded LZ 74 when she bombed London on the night of 7/8 September 1915, but now he was in trouble.

LZ 95 limped back to its base at Namur but hit the ground before reaching safety; she was beyond repair, but George and his crew were the lucky ones. Their comrades aboard LZ 77, commanded by Alfred Horn, had also taken part in that same raid on England in September

56

1915, and were now attacked by a mobile 75mm gun firing incendiary rounds. Set on fire, LZ 77, 'like some fantastic torch... fell writhing to the earth', smashing into the ground at Brabant-le-Roi, near Revigny.[39] There were no survivors. Ernst Lehmann had no doubts as to the cause of the loss: 'We concluded that while LZ 77 had been shot down by the new flaming shells, the fault really lay in a recent order directing moonlight raids.'[40] The Navy Zeppelin commanders were unsurprised by the outcome.

The Zeppelin crews had other concerns too. The 240hp Maybach HSLu engines, first fitted into Navy Zeppelin L 15 and Army Zeppelin LZ 79 in September and August 1915 respectively, had been rushed into service. As a result, fractured crankshafts, broken connecting rods and crank bearings, as well as over-heated dudgeon pins, were causing engines to fail, with dire consequences in the case of L 19. Frustrated, on 4 March Peter Strasser took all five Naval Zeppelins driven by the HSLu engines out of service (L 15, L 16, L 17, L 20 and L 21), shipping the engines back to the Maybach factory at Friedrichshafen and demanding a solution to the problem.

The 4 March also heralded the dark skies of a new moon and a new raiding period. Strasser's decision meant that he could only call on three older Zeppelins, L 11, L 13 and L 14, all fitted with the earlier 210hp Maybach C-X engine. Bruges, the most westerly weather station available to Germany, reported favourable conditions and on the next day, Sunday 5 March, the Zeppelins departed. This time their target was Scotland's docks and shipyards on the Firth of Forth. The weather station, however, unable to predict weather patterns approaching Britain from the north and north-west was completely unaware of a low-pressure system rapidly advancing from Iceland bringing with it snow, sleet and extremely high winds. It was a Zeppelin commander's nightmare.

Chapter 5

# 'This is not war — but ghastly work of Hell'

The Zeppelin sheds at Nordholz and Hage were a hive of activity on the morning of 5 March. The cycle of the moon and the latest weather forecasts all appeared to offer a good chance of success. With Heinrich Mathy commanding L 13, Viktor Schütze in L 11 and Alois Böcker directing L 14, the three Zeppelins took to the air at around midday. British listening stations immediately picked up their departure transmissions. Initially the skies were clear and all seemed well, then the wind freshened from the north and north-west and gradually grew in strength.

The crew of Mathy's L 13 were in for a torrid night. About halfway across the North Sea the crankshaft of the rear starboard engine broke, a problem they could not fix in flight. They were now flying on three engines. To make matters worse L 13 then flew into a snowstorm, which added a considerable amount of excess weight as the wet snow clung to the envelope, forcing Mathy to jettison 590kgs of fuel to lighten the ship. It was clear now that L 13 would never reach Scotland so about 7pm (British time) Mathy changed course for the River Tyne. Thick snow-laden clouds prevented him discovering he had crossed the coast, which he did at 9.14pm south of the mouth of the Humber as L 13 passed over North Cotes in Lincolnshire. For the next four hours Mathy had no idea where he was; at one stage he believed he had found Sunderland, when he was 125 miles south of the city, and even resurrected the plan to head for Scotland for a time before abandoning the idea again.

Having selected the River Humber as a revised target, Mathy was unaware that the wind from the north-west had already carried him far beyond that location. With the wind behind L 13 she moved quickly, but then the port engine failed. The mechanics cobbled together a temporary repair but, weighed down by snow, Mathy needed to lighten his ship a second time. At 11.15pm he released 32 incendiary bombs over snow-covered fields between the village and church at Sproxton in Leicestershire, followed by a single HE bomb in a field at Edmondthorpe. Unaware of the struggles on board L 13, the attack left the local Chief Constable bemused.

> No damage of any kind was done beyond the holes made in the ground. I cannot find that any light was visible. Both parishes are in a very thinly populated part of my County and I have no idea what the probable objective was.[1]

Five miles further on Mathy released 15 bombs over fields alongside the road between Thistleton and Greetham as the crew of L 13 battled on in difficult circumstances, as Pitt Klein, one of the mechanics, explained.

> We were powerless in the face of the strong north westerly wind, which pushed us before it… It was a long and harrowing night… The weight of snow was pushing us lower. Shards of ice were coming off the propellers and shredding the outer cover… For us in the rear gondola the constant strain of trying to get the engines working again was beginning to tell. We were hungry; our limbs were weak and weary from the cold; our hands were covered in oil and petrol.[2]

## 6 March 1916, 1.30am: Isle of Sheppey, Kent

If Klein thought that was bad, things were about to get much worse. At 1.25am the clouds cleared away to reveal a river below. Mathy presumed that they had finally found the elusive River Humber, but in the time it took to cross it, he realised just how far out they were in their navigation. The river below was the Thames, 160 miles south of the Humber. As L 13 passed over Shoeburyness on the north shore at about 9,000 feet, a 3-inch, 20cwt anti-aircraft gun opened fire, but after just two rounds the traversing gear jammed and it fell silent. Determined to gain something from an otherwise failed raid, Mathy attempted to push westwards and attack the naval base at Chatham. With one engine out of action, another operating at less than full power and facing a headwind estimated at 44mph, it was a reckless decision.

At 1.30am L 13 attempted to turn into the wind over the Isle of Sheppey, her ground speed reduced to just 10mph. To help reduce weight Mathy released four HE bombs over marshland north of Ripney Hill Farm. Battling against the fierce wind L 13 was virtually stationary for seven or eight minutes, during which time searchlights held her in their beams and the six 6-pdr Hotchkiss guns defending Sheerness opened a 'heavy, but useless' fire.[3] Even so the noise they created was deafening: 'With so many guns at work in the comparatively small area, the noise was like that of a battlefield and people rushed to their doors and windows to watch the sight.'[4]

With his airship at risk of destruction, Mathy aborted the attack on Chatham and turned away leaving a relieved Pitt Klein to express the views of L 13's crew: 'It was a complete mystery to us how they missed the airship... Their aim must have been terrible.'[5] L 13 came under more fire from a 3-inch, 20cwt gun positioned at Harty Ferry and also, at 1.55am, from a 6-pdr Nordenfeldt at Faversham, and although both crews thought they had hit L 13, she was unharmed and passed out to sea near Deal at 2.25am. However, her problems were still not over. The damaged port engine now finally spluttered to a halt, leaving L 13 with just two working engines. With no improvement in the weather and having jettisoned so much fuel on the outward journey, Mathy concluded he would not be able to coax L 13 back to Germany and sought a safe haven at the Namur Zeppelin sheds in Belgium, which the Naval Airship Division used in emergencies.

Five hours after landing, with fuel, hydrogen and ballast replenished, L 13 began the 280-mile homeward journey to Hage. But two hours into the flight a third engine failed forcing L 13 to struggle back to Namur. Only on 10 March, after new engines arrived by train, was L 13 finally able to return to Germany.

The failure during the raid of the Maybach C-X engines was not limited to L 13; both L 11 and L 14 also encountered problems.

## 6 March 1916, 12.05am: Hull, East Yorkshire

Alois Böcker in L 14 crossed the North Sea in close proximity to L 13 and, like Mathy, he abandoned the raid on the Firth of Forth. He hoped to attack along the River Tyne instead but the wind had pushed him further south than he realised. Böcker crossed the coast near Flamborough Head at 10.30pm, but only when south of Driffield at 11.40pm from where 'the Humber showed up in the snowy landscape as a darker streak', did he pinpoint his position. Five minutes later L 14 was passing blindly over the darkened town of Beverley when a flare shot out from a retort house at the gasworks. Böcker responded with three HE bombs but they overshot by 200 yards, only smashing windows in a terrace of houses, then three incendiaries landed in fields towards the village of Woodmansey.[6] Just 7 miles away in Hull the majority of its residents were already in their beds when L 14 loomed over the north-western edge of the city at 12.05am.

The first bomb smashed windows at Hymers College and in houses nearby, followed by a second on a railway embankment to the east of Anlaby Road Junction. A newspaper described the first as a 'sharp nerve-racking explosion that shook houses half a mile away'.[7] The sub-zero temperature now caused problems for Böcker as water-contaminated petrol froze and blocked the fuel lines feeding two of his engines. While mechanics worked to clear the blockages, L 14 continued to drop her deadly cargo of bombs in Bean Street then Regent Street and Linnaeus Street. In Regent Street the bomb demolished a house, severely damaged six others and killed James Collinson (aged 63) and James Pattison, a 68-year-old chimney sweep whose body they discovered buried in the ruins of his home.

In The Avenue, a narrow terrace leading off Linnaeus Street, 62-year-old widower Joseph Ingamells, a caterer by trade, had gone to bed. His son was also asleep but Joseph's three daughters, Martha (aged 35), Ethel (33) and 28-year-old Lottie, were downstairs. Lottie's sweetheart had been to visit and she was saying goodbye to him at the front door. Hearing a terrific crash from the bomb in Bean Street, Martha and Ethel ran upstairs to warn their father just as a bomb exploded right outside the house. Lottie died instantly. Joseph Ingamells found his two other daughters crumpled on the stairs; one was dead, the other fatally injured; his son escaped unharmed. Lottie's severely shocked and dazed boyfriend had walked off. He stopped at a house in a darkened Selby Street to ask for a glass of water. Only when he stepped into the light did the horrified occupants realise he was covered in Lottie's blood.[8] The bomb caused widespread damage in The Avenue. The couple living next door to the Ingamells suffered serious injuries but their young child sleeping in a pram was unhurt. An elderly widow living in the end house of the terrace had a fortunate escape when the end wall collapsed and debris piled up on top of the bed where she was sleeping. She sustained injuries and suffered severe shock but she survived.

High above, Böcker watched the effect of his bombs: 'The most striking result was the collapse of whole blocks of houses in a street running north and south, and these afterwards showed up against the snow as big black patches.'[9] Other bombs damaged houses in Day Street while a factory and workshops suffered in Walker Street.[10] The last of L 14's explosive bombs dropped close to the edge of the Albert Dock where it wrecked a crane. Nine incendiary bombs also fell but it seems they did little if any damage. With two engines under repair and a fierce wind, it proved impossible for L 14 to turn back and make another run across the city so Böcker headed away down the Humber. At 12.25am four anti-aircraft guns at Killingholme opened fire, which persuaded Böcker to steer away from the river and head overland towards the coast. He dropped a single HE bomb in a field near Burstwick, followed by four HE and two incendiary bombs in fields near the tiny village of Owstwick at 12.40am. The HE bombs caused no damage and the incendiaries failed to ignite. Five minutes later L 14 crossed the coast to begin her difficult journey back to Germany.

In the streets of Hull, the sound of exploding bombs brought back shocking memories for many of the June 1915 raid on the city. Unwilling to become victims, families gathered up a few scant possessions and began to walk out to the country. Marion Large's family was one of them.

> People were urged to get away from buildings and many families, including mine, went trekking along the main roads as far towards the country as they could get. This of course had to be on foot. I remember the famous 'snowy night raid'… when we wandered with countless families far up the Holderness Road, getting colder and colder and tireder and tireder, and unable to find anywhere to rest.[11]

Others were luckier and found shelter during this unofficial evacuation, as a journalist writing for the *Daily Mail* newspaper described.

> 'Save our children!' was the cry which went up out of the midst of this moving, poignant pilgrimage; and presently kindly folk managed to check the exodus and to shepherd shivering mothers and children into a sanctuary more hospitable than the open air on this bitter March night.[12]

## 6 March 1916, 1.05am: Hull, East Yorkshire

While some of Hull's population were taking to the streets, another Zeppelin had the city in its sights. Korvettenkapitän Viktor Schütze, commanding L 11 in action for the first time, came inland over the Yorkshire coast 15 miles east of Hull at about 9.45pm, although Schütze thought he was approaching the coast near Middlesbrough about 80 miles to the north. Thick clouds prevented any glimpse of Hull and, after heading south across the Humber into Lincolnshire, L 11 flew in a great circle battling through snow and hailstorms for two and half hours. Shortly after midnight the clouds parted for a few minutes and the crew of L 11 saw another Zeppelin in the distance attacking a town on a river, then the clouds swept back to shroud it once more – it was L 14 over Hull. Schütze turned the nose of L 11 into the wind and with his engines working at full power held her in the same position for about an hour until the clouds dispersed leaving Schütze with a perfect view of Hull.

> The town though very well darkened, showed up clearly under the starlit sky like a drawing, with streets, blocks of houses, quays and dock basins... During a period of twenty minutes incendiary and high-explosive bombs were dropped on harbours and docks... The first H.E. bomb struck the quay.[13]

It smashed down by Earle's Shipyard, to the east of the city, causing a partly built 3,000 ton steamer to collapse on its stocks the following day. An incendiary fell in the Humber and another by the mouth of the River Hull before a group of HE bombs crashed down in Queen Street between the junctions with Humber Street and Blanket Row.

> Four of the bombs fell into the centre of the roadway, tearing great holes in the solid foundations of the tramlines, and bending and twisting the metals into fantastic shapes. One bomb penetrated so deeply into the road that it blew the top off the main sewers, some 12 feet below the tramlines.[14]

The bombs practically gutted two pubs, the Golden Lion and The Butcher's Arms Inn, smashing their interiors beyond recognition. Similar damage occurred at a large four-storey building opposite and the explosions wrecked a café where rescuers found two bodies. Knocked unconscious, the wife of Edward Slip, manager of the Mikado Café at 23 Queen Street, came to amongst the shattered wreckage of their business to discover her husband's headless corpse buried in the rubble. The other victim, eight-year-old Frank Cattle, 'was killed while being taken to a place of safety by his mother', blasted into the café by the explosion.[15] The bombs also wrecked the offices of the Humber Garrison Artillery on Queen Street. Making their way to the scene a policeman and a special constable reported 'great pandemonium in the neighbourhood – women screaming, men shouting, dogs barking and cats spitting'.

Awoken by his wife during L 14's attack, John Smith, a 30-year-old dock labourer, had left his home off Blackfriargate to see if he could be of help. He was still out when L 11 appeared. He and another man saw the Zeppelin and began to run. Mrs Smith grew concerned when her husband failed to return, then someone came to tell her he had been hurt. She reached him just before he died. He told her: 'I put two little children in a passage and this is what I have got for it.' They were his last words.[16]

Viktor Schütze looked down with interest.

> One hit had a specially far-reaching effect; radiating round the burst more and more houses collapsed and finally showed up, in the snow covered harbour area, as a black and gigantic hole. A similar, bigger dark patch in the neighbourhood seemed to be due to the raid of L 14. With binoculars it was possible to see people running hither and thither in the glare of the fires.[17]

Just over 200 yards further on the next bomb streaked down to explode within yards of the south-west corner of Holy Trinity Church. The church had miraculously escaped serious damage in the June 1915 raid and this time too the outcome could have been worse than it was. The bomb blew a great hole in the roadway sending the wood setts flying in all directions. It also blew down a low stone wall, smashed the great west window 'in a hundred places' and damaged stained glass windows along the south side of the church. Flying debris cut and gouged into neighbouring buildings too leaving enduring marks.[18]

About 100 yards away, in Posterngate, a bomb damaged various business premises and the Trinity House Almshouses, seriously injuring William Jones, an 80-year-old retired merchant seaman. He must have been a tough man for he lingered on for six months before dying on 17 September 1916.[19] A group of six incendiaries then fell around Princes Dock but none caused any damage.[20] The last of them smashed through the roof of a Boy's Club in Roper Street where it came to rest in a bath.

Beyond Princes Dock, Schütze set his sights on Paragon Railway Station. Many observers reported L 11 hovering over the station, whereas the crew were battling a fierce headwind and unable to make progress. Five bombs dropped near the station 'almost with one crash' as part of its glass roof shattered. In Collier Street and James Place they destroyed or severely damaged 20 houses. A police inspector looked on helplessly as one fell on 32 Collier Street, reducing it to rubble. He found the occupier, Mr Naylor, alive but badly injured. Then the real tragedy began to unfold.

> When he reached the spot the woman [Charlotte Naylor, aged 36], who was partly buried in the debris, was apparently dead. The eldest child, a girl [Ruby, eight], was found on top of the wreckage in the ruins of the back bedroom. She died on the way to hospital. The second child [Annie, six] also was alive when found, but she passed away shortly afterwards. The other two children, both boys [Edward, four, and Jeffrey, two], were dead, the baby being at his mother's side.[21]

Schütze also released seven incendiary bombs. These fell on the south side of the station where most landed harmlessly or were extinguished before the fires got out of hand, but that was not the case at the Master Mariners' Almshouses on Carr Lane. On hearing explosions the caretaker began waking the occupants and had evacuated a number of them when a bomb smashed through the roof and into a room occupied by 89-year-old Edward Ledner. Unable to get out of his bed, flames quickly engulfed the old sea captain as desperate staff battled unsuccessfully to save him.[22]

Heading back towards the Humber, Schütze dropped three final incendiaries over the Albert Dock with one landing in a case of oranges where the juice extinguished the burning bomb. As L 11 left the city of Hull behind, 18 people were dead or dying and 51 others injured.

Following the river back towards the coast, the guns at Killingholme that had earlier engaged L 14, now opened on L 11. Unlike Böcker who shied away, Schütze retaliated with four bombs and although none threatened the guns, one claimed a life.

James Beswick, a 39-year-old widower and railway signalman, was on duty when the first bombs had fallen on Hull. Concerned for his six-year-old daughter he went back to his house to check on her. While he stood outside talking with his housekeeper, they heard the drone of a Zeppelin's engines as L 11 loomed out of the darkness. The terrified housekeeper started to run but seconds later a bomb exploded behind her. She called out to Beswick, 'Jimmy, where are you?', but received no reply. She found him lying on the road about 20 or 30 yards from the house. A man who had been talking with Beswick and his housekeeper a few minutes earlier came running back and found him lying unconscious with an obvious wound to his forehead. At the inquest a doctor explained that Beswick had turned towards the bomb and was hit by a fragment on an upwards trajectory which fractured his skull leaving a part of his brain exposed. The doctor donated his fee to James Beswick's now orphaned daughter, Alice.

Schütze continued down the Humber, passing Grimsby and out over Spurn Head at about 1.40am.

When morning came there was disquiet in Hull. After the raid in June 1915 there were 64 casualties; this time there were 69 more. Bad weather in June 1915 prevented any aircraft taking off to defend Hull and no aircraft went up this time either, due to the snow and fierce winds. And the city still had no anti-aircraft guns for its defence. Rather embarrassingly a wooden dummy gun was set up on a foundry roof in July 1915 to reassure the population but this was quietly removed in January.[23] Frustration boiled over in the wake of this latest raid and there are reports of an attack on RFC transport in Hull and of an RFC officer mobbed in Beverley.[24]

Following a meeting with a deputation of local civic dignitaries, Major General H.M. Lawson, commander of the Northern Garrison, immediately took steps to improve the situation. In the short term two 13-pdr mobile guns arrived in Hull for temporary service, and by the end of May 1916 four guns were in position to protect the city: two 3-inch, one 12pdr and a 6-pdr, as well as others to bolster the wider area. It brought the number of guns defending the Humber region up to 17, although five were the generally ineffective 1-pdrs.[25]

Ten days after the raid, T.C. Turner, a local photographer and special constable, mentioned the positive effect of the new guns in a letter to the Intelligence Department at General Headquarters.

> Today we had a further advertisement of the guns by a demonstration in front of Headquarters. (Two mobile guns, searchlights, etc.) The effect on the morale of the citizens is excellent and no doubt the War Office is being favourably

compared with the Admiralty regime. After the first raid 9 months and no guns! After the second raid 14 days and several![26]

\* \* \*

There were no more Zeppelin attacks in the current new moon phase. The moon, however, never influenced SFA 1 when planning their stinging attacks on the south-east coast. They had come to favour attacks on Sundays, believing the defences were less alert, but at least one pilot had noticed this. Flight Commander Reginald Bone, commanding officer at the RNAS station at Detling, felt so sure that the raiders would return on Sunday 19 March that he had his aircraft, a Nieuport 10, prepared for action. He then packed a picnic and flew to RNAS Westgate on the coast, and there he waited. His hunch was right; German aircraft were on their way from Zeebrugge intent on disturbing the peace of another quiet Sunday lunchtime.

## 19 March 1916, 1.50pm: Dover, Kent

Six aircraft made the attack: a Gotha Ursinus WD, a Friedrichshafen FF33b, two FF33e, a FF33f and a Hansa-Brandenburg NW. Flying between 5,000 and 6,000 feet and led by the Gotha Ursinus, three of the floatplanes approached Dover without warning at 1.50pm. The first six bombs all fell harmlessly in the harbour but the three that followed proved deadly, falling in a military camp at Northfell Meadow on the east side of Dover Castle. One bomb obliterated a hut housing men of the 5th Battalion, Royal Fusiliers. Two soldiers, Private Frank Roseberry and Private Walter Venables, both aged 19, died instantly. Two more, Corporal Daniel Dolphin and Private Alfred Greig, succumbed later to their injuries, while 11 others were injured in the explosion.

The Dover anti-aircraft guns burst into action but bombs continued to drop. Three fell around Castle Street, then one in Folkestone Road where 23-year-old housemaid, Edith Stoker, was cycling to visit her parents in Folkestone. The force of the explosion inflicted terrible injuries as she smashed into the doorway of a shop at 131 Folkestone Road; she died later in hospital. Three men in the street sustained injuries and there was one more victim – a little boy. Seven-year-old Francis Hall, had left his home in Winchelsea Street to attend Sunday School. When he heard the guns he turned to run home. His mother also heard the guns and came after him, only to see him cut down in Folkestone Road by the explosion that left him slumped on the pavement against garden railings, dead.

Other bombs caused significant damage to buildings further along Folkestone Road but no one else was killed, although one family who had just shut their front door were fortunate: '[They] were blown by the concussion to the other end of the passage and thrown into a heap. Each got up expecting to find the others seriously injured, but all escaped without a scratch.'[27]

With four aircraft taking off from Dover within a couple of minutes of the first sighting of the raiders and anti-aircraft guns belching fire, it became impossible for observers to follow the course of the raid in any detail. Two bombs fell on a grass bank near the Christ Church Schools followed by one that exploded in a workshop yard in Northampton Street. The premises backed on to buildings in Snargate Street where two women, both standing by windows, caught the full force of the blast. At 41 Snargate Street, Florence Collier had her arm amputated as well as sustaining fractures to the other arm and to her jaw. Next door at No.40 flying debris struck restaurant owner Jane James. Police Sergeant W.A. Mount found the widowed Mrs James, 'lying on the bed, quite dead', adding, 'There was a large quantity of blood close to the window... She was wounded all down the right of the chest and stomach.'[28]

As that raider departed a bomb dropped in the Wellington Basin narrowly missing a gunboat followed by two others that sent towering plumes of water erupting from the Commercial Harbour.

There were other bombs on land. One struck the roof of the convent school of the Sisters of St Vincent on Eastbrook Place, where flying glass injured one of the Sisters, but as the slates clattered down a woman in the street had a lucky escape.

> [They] fell into the roadway right over a lady who was passing. She fell down, and neighbours rushed to her aid, but before they could reach her she jumped up and ran away at a fast pace, much to their astonishment.[29]

Other bombs damaged a storehouse in Church Street, a mineral water bottle store in Russell Street and St James's Church at the junction of Woolcomber and Trevanion streets. On the other side of the church another exploded in the garden of Castle Hill House and two more fell at East Cliff where one smashed the roof of No.8. The final three bombs fell in the sea.[30]

## 19 March 1916, 2.05pm: Deal, Kent

At the town of Deal, about seven miles away, the sound of the Dover guns alerted the townsfolk and numbers of them left their homes to congregate on street corners and at the seafront. One of them was a journalist.

> I had a clear view of the fight... and it was a thrilling spectacle. With help of a telescope it was possible to distinguish a number of machines in a southerly direction. They were twisting and turning and moving rapidly in all directions while shells were bursting all around them.[31]

One of the aircraft then broke away: 'As it passed over Deal I saw something drop from it, and immediately there were a number of heavy explosions.'

At 2.05pm, following a line from south to north, the raider dropped nine bombs. The first three exploded in the garden of Woodbine Cottage at 11 Victoria Road, 'doing considerable damage', while the next struck a garden between High Street and Park Street, smashing windows and damaging the wall of a miniature rifle range. One exploded in Stanhope Road but only broke a window as the raider released the next bomb as he approached St George's Church. It just missed the 200-year-old building, detonating in St George's Road where it smashed down part of the churchyard wall and shattered more windows. Immediately another fell, inflicting 'considerable damage' to a carpenter's workshop at 8 St George's Place and showering horses in a neighbouring stables with splinters of glass. A bomb in Union Street failed to detonate and the final missile caused some damage at an undertakers' in West Street and to St Andrew's Church nearby. Although there were no casualties one man had a narrow escape. He was in his car when he noticed the aeroplane. He quickly pulled up and ran for cover; moments later a bomb wrecked the front of his vehicle. Later that afternoon hundreds of people visited the sites where the bombs fell, many showing 'a keen desire to secure fragments of the bombs as souvenirs'.[32]

## 19 March 1916, 2.12pm: Ramsgate, Kent

Two of the aircraft that had not attacked Dover or Deal now approached Ramsgate, arriving over the town at 2.12pm. Although the sound of gunfire had reached Ramsgate, inexplicably the town's warning siren did not sound.[33] In St Luke's Avenue, Henry Divers, a well-known local businessman, was out for a drive and groups of children were converging from the surrounding roads on their way to St Luke's Sunday School, amongst them the four Ward sisters and three siblings of the Philpott family. As they did so two bombs shattered this peaceful scene.

One struck the passenger seat of Mr Divers' car. He died instantly, an eyewitness describing how 'the whole of the left side of Mr Divers was blown away but the right side had practically escaped injury'. The car's petrol tank exploded sending additional jagged shards of metal slashing in all directions. All around there were bodies. Five of the children were dead or dying, and at least eight others suffered serious injury, which saw them admitted to hospital; many others had their wounds treated there in the bloodstained street. Amongst those killed was 12-year-old Ernest Philpott, but his elder brother George, aged 15, with great presence of mind and razor sharp reflexes, threw his younger sister Lily to the ground and shielded her with his own body. Lily, although injured, survived, but inevitably George was injured too. He became something of a local celebrity and received recognition for his 'pluck and bravery', but his injuries took their toll and he never fully recovered; he died early the following year. Jagged metal fragments tore into three of the four Ward sisters, leaving nine-year-old Grace with her right arm 'hanging by a shred of flesh'. After amputation Grace lived on as an invalid in bad health for 10 years before she died in January 1926, an overlooked victim of the forgotten Blitz. Gladys and James Saxby, aged six and four, both died in the road, as did seven-year-old Frank Hardwick, but two of his brothers escaped with injuries. The final child victim, nine-year-old Herbert Gibbons, died in hospital the following morning. There was one other victim lying unconscious in the road. Recently married Gertrude Bishop 'was very badly injured and her shoulder was bleeding... having been struck in several places by pieces of sharp steel'. She died in hospital two days later.

Other bombs on the town caused damage to buildings but fortunately there were no more deaths or serious injuries. At 71-73 King Street a bomb smashed through the roof of Blackburn & Sons furniture store where it damaged a room and smashed 'hundreds of feet of plate glass'. A little under 500 yards away another bomb struck a turret on the roof of the Chatham House School, given over to serve as a hospital for Canadian soldiers, before one smashed into 25 Chatham Street, a hairdresser's shop and home to Mr Desormeaux. 'My wife and I,' he explained, 'have had a miraculous escape.'

We were together with three other people in the room on the ground floor when a bomb struck the roof of the house and crashed right through two floors and remained in the ceiling of the ground floor. All the windows were blown out and the upper floors entirely wrecked. We escaped without any injury whatsoever.[34]

The fire brigade arrived just a few minutes after the bomb struck and found an inquisitive crowd already gathered around the shattered shop front. Elsewhere in the town two bombs exploded in Dane Park Road. One smashed windows but the other, striking No.31, caused great damage. This may be the bomb reported as destroying the back portion of a house but leaving untouched a family of eight sitting down to Sunday lunch at the front of the house.

Armed drifters in Ramsgate Harbour opened fire on the raiders as they passed and between 1.55 and 2.10pm at least four RNAS aircraft took off from Westgate, just a few miles away, slowly clawing their way up into the air. From Ramsgate, cutting across the corner of Kent, one of the raiders dropped a single bomb on Margate where it found a military target.

The 9th Provisional Cyclist Company had their headquarters at 29/30 Fort Crescent, overlooking the Winter Gardens. The bomb demolished the chimneys, damaged the roof and shattered its windows there and at No. 28, as well as smashing windows at three other houses where 'the streets were soon thronged with people' who came to see the damage.[35]

With the six German raiders heading home there were at least 12 British pilots in the skies too. One of them was Flight Commander Bone, the pilot who had anticipated a Sunday raid. Fixing his gaze on one of the retiring floatplanes he began a 40-minute pursuit, climbing to 9,000 feet before diving down on the Friedrichshafen FF33f crewed by Leutnant Herrenknecht and pilot Flugmeister August Ponater. Bone's first burst alerted the German crew to his presence and Herrenknecht opened return fire. Bone's second burst injured the observer as he closed in to fire a number of six-second bursts. The Friedrichshafen, with engine smoking and propeller stopped, went into a dive. Despite the damage, Ponater skilfully landed on the sea about 30 miles off the Kent coast. An attempt later that afternoon to bomb the downed aircraft failed and that night a German destroyer recovered both crew and aircraft. None of the other pilots sent up from the coastal air stations had any successes against the departing raiders, even so one more was brought down.

At about 1.30pm a FE2b piloted by Second Lieutenant Reginald Collis with Flight Sergeant Alfred Emery as observer/gunner, took off from Lympne in Kent to ferry the aircraft over to France. They saw the attack developing over Dover. Collis fixed his attention on one of the aircraft, the Hansa-Brandenburg NW flown by Leutnant Friedrich Christiansen with Oberleutnant-zur-See Bernhard von Tschirschky und Bogendorff, the Zeebrugge station commander, as observer. Out over the English Channel, Collis swooped down unnoticed to a position about 150 yards behind the German aircraft, allowing Emery to fire a whole drum of ammunition from his Lewis gun. The crew of the FE2b lost sight of the German aircraft as it spiralled away, plummeting down with steam spouting from the engine and von Tschirschky nursing a wounded shoulder. Christensen managed to level out then, incredibly, the wounded von Tschirschky clambered out onto a wing to make running repairs to the engine with his handkerchief and some insulating tape. It kept them airborne for another 70 minutes before coming down on the sea about 20 miles from Ostend. After taxiing slowly for a while, giving the engine a chance to cool a little, with a huge sense of relief it fired up again permitting them to fly back to Zeebrugge.[36]

The British authorities traced 48 bombs: 'about' 24 in Dover, 14 in Ramsgate, nine in Deal and one in Margate. This, however, may be an underestimate and more may have fallen into the sea as German sources state the Gotha Ursinus alone dropped 32 bombs on Dover.

In Britain the raid caused outrage. A local councillor in Ramsgate decried: 'All they hit was private property – and children. This is not war – but ghastly work of Hell.'[37] There was also frustration and anger that the warning sirens in both Dover and Ramsgate had failed to sound until after the raid was over. At the inquests, families stated that their relatives would not have been out in the streets if the sirens had sounded. This was particularly true of the children killed on their way to Sunday School.

While the debate about protection of the exposed coastal towns rumbled on, life on the streets hardly skipped a beat. Within minutes of the deadly bomb blast in the St Luke's area, Captain Johnston of the Ramsgate Fire Brigade noted that excited youngsters were already hunting for souvenirs.

By the roadside there were several large hoardings advertising theatrical and other matters and small boys were already on the spot working with their pocket knives to extract pieces of shell and bullets which were embedded in all directions in the woodwork and on the posters.[38]

The residents of the south-east coast, however, would be free from attack for the next six weeks. For the rest of the nation though, it was time to steel themselves for the return of the Zeppelins.

# Chapter 6

# 'Dante's Inferno'

## February-March 1916, London

In the early months of 1916 the War Office began to focus on the problems of defence against aerial attack. They initially looked to provide anti-aircraft guns for the protection for munitions and explosives factories as well as magazines where munitions were stored. These they grouped into eight main areas: Scotland, Newcastle, Leeds, Sheffield, Liverpool, Birmingham, London and the Thames, and Portsmouth. Other munitions and explosives factories outside these main areas also received guns as did ports and 'certain populous districts specially exposed to attack'.[1]

The War Office adopted the plan for the defence of London prepared by Admiral Sir Percy Scott in the autumn of 1915, with guns defending the central area and two further gun circles, five miles and nine miles out. The outlying centres of Woolwich, with the all-important Arsenal, and Waltham Abbey, home to extensive explosives production, were included within the London defences. By the end of March there were nine guns defending Woolwich where previously there had been just one. London also benefitted from an outer searchlight ring. Previously most searchlights worked in conjunction with the guns. These new lights, known as 'Aeroplane Lights', were assigned to locate and hold targets for the aircraft defending London. There were 18 in position by 6 March with 29 more locations under construction.

Attention also turned to a warning system to alert critical industries and authorities of potential raids. Field Marshal Lord French handed the task to a staff officer, Lieutenant Colonel Philip Maud, who realised that any efficient system must rely on the telephone network. His plan divided England, Wales and part of Scotland into eight Warning Controls, each under a Warning Controller. He was responsible for receiving and passing on information and warnings within his area. These eight Warning Controls were sub-divided into 54 numbered districts (see Map 2), with each of these roughly 30 to 35 miles square. At a generous presumed speed of 60mph, a Zeppelin would take about 30 minutes to cross a district, allowing those in the path to receive timely alerts ensuring work could continue until a raid seemed inevitable. Observers positioned to cover all approaches telephoned information directly to the Warning Controller for the region. He also received information from GHQ, Home Forces, anti-aircraft gun stations and adjoining Warning Controllers, as well as the police, railway officials and any military commands in his area.

A Warning Controller had four distinct messages he could send: 'Field Marshal's Warning Order Only', then three others prefixed with Field Marshal's Order; 'Take Air Raid Action', 'Resume Normal Conditions' and 'All Clear'. The 'Warning Order Only' message advised those on a 'Warning List' when enemy aircraft were 50 or 60 miles away. 'Take Air Raid Action', or TARA, followed when raiders were 15 to 20 miles away and 'Resume Normal Conditions' was issued when immediate danger was over but defences were to remain alert. The 'All Clear' message signified defences could stand down.[2]

To alleviate confusion when information began to flood in over the telephone, individual Zeppelins received names. The first Zeppelin picked up had a name beginning with A, the second B, and so on. Navy Zeppelins received girls' names, with boys' names reserved for Army Zeppelins. As the pressure of a raid mounted this simple idea seemed to help, as the official history recorded: 'Into this atmosphere of tension, the recurrence of the familiar English Christian names brought a touch of the commonplace, even of humour.'[3] An interim arrangement with three Warning Controls was in place by 14 February with all eight in operation by 25 May.

In March, plans to create ten Home Defence Squadrons received approval but this would take time. Then, just a few months later, increasing demands on the Western Front saw this reduced to six. On 18 March the first two designated Home Defence Squadrons, No.33 and No.36, became fully operational in the north and north-east of England respectively. But neither of them saw action when the Zeppelins returned on the 31 March at the start of an unprecedented period of Zeppelin activity with raids launched on five consecutive nights.

On that first night the Naval Airship Division despatched seven Zeppelins to 'attack in the south, main target London'.[4] New instructions to the commanders instructed them to cease sending their standard departure wireless messages, Strasser finally aware that they were liable to interception by British listening stations. Of the seven raiders, L 9 and L 11 turned back early. L 9 narrowly escaped disaster when a bracing wire from an engine gondola detached and became entangled in a propeller. Only expert work by the crew prevented disaster. She limped back to Germany and was out of service for 10 days. The remaining five reached England: L 13, L 14, L 15, L 16 and L 22.

## 1 April 1916, 1.35am: Cleethorpes, Lincolnshire

Martin Dietrich, commanding L 22, encountered strong crosswinds and the ubiquitous engine problems as he crossed the North Sea.[5] He abandoned hopes of striking London and selected the Humber as an alternative target. With the docks and harbour facilities at Hull and Grimsby so close to the coast, Zeppelin commanders considered the Humber one of the easier listed targets to find. At 12.15am a lightship anchored off the south Lincolnshire coast sent news of an approaching Zeppelin. Unfortunately the telephone lines were down in Area 25 of the new Warning District map just when needed. As a result, army motorcyclists carried the TARA order to the police for further transmission.[6] At 1.20am, L 22 crossed the coast just south of the mouth of the Humber and headed towards Grimsby. Fifteen minutes later, when passing the village of Humberston, a searchlight on the southern edge of Cleethorpes found her and the 1-pdr 'pom-pom' at Waltham opened fire. Dietrich reacted to the light by releasing 26 bombs, which fell 'with fierce intensity' in fields around Humberston, but only smashed windows at a farm and killed a sheep.[7]

Flying north, L 22 passed unknowingly over the blackened town of Cleethorpes. As she passed out over the Humber, Dietrich released a parachute flare and, in its intense light, streets and buildings appeared from where moments earlier there had been only darkness. Believing it was Grimsby, he turned over the river before crossing back over the town.

The 3rd (Reserve) Battalion, Manchester Regiment had been associated with Cleethorpes since early in the war. On 30 March, 70 men of 'E' company arrived by train and occupied a temporary billet in the Baptist Chapel in Alexandra Road. In empty neighbouring shops 14 men of 'A' company bedded down for the night. Four of the men in the Chapel sneaked down to the basement to play cards while elsewhere all was quiet. That all changed at 1.35am when the sound of gunfire and bombs woke the men, as Leonard Newsham recalled.

I heard a gun firing and it woke the lot of us up... then I heard the crash come. There was a flash like blue lightning and down went the lot. I knew nothing more until they put me on a stretcher.[8]

At 1.48am, as the soldiers talked in hushed voices, a bomb hit the slate roof of the hall and exploded. The blast ripped away half of the roof, much of which crashed down on the exposed soldiers below. The upper wall collapsed, sending great sections of brick and stone cascading down to crush the roofs of the shops housing the men of 'A' company. The casualty toll was horrendous. The only men to escape injury were those playing cards in the basement.

Before anyone could react, L 22 dropped two more bombs. One struck a wing of the Town Hall in Cambridge Street, seriously damaging council offices, and the other exploded on the pavement in Sea View Street, smashing numerous windows in houses and shops, but there were no more casualties. Three final bombs exploded in fields just to the south of the town.

Back in Cleethorpes all available medical people rushed to the Chapel. Amy Amelia Ellis, who ran the local Red Cross as well as St Aiden's Voluntary Aid Detachment (VAD) Hospital, was one of them and wrote breathlessly in her diary.

Manchester Regiment asking for all available help – bomb dropped on soldiers' billet...proceed to Cleethorpes with what kit we can carry...try to get taxi...too long – proceed. Zeppelin overhead, very cheering. Make way to Yarra House (used as an emergency dressing station) – Dante's Inferno – 3 room floors covered with bodies, dead, dying, and suffering, and hardly any light. Proceed to do what we can – first man I got to was dead.[9]

A woman living in Yarra Road heard the pitiful sounds emanating from the Chapel.

It was like a distant fairground – a jumble of shouts, screams and moans. Myself and other women... were sent to help the wounded. I remember the police and soldiers were trying to match together odd arms, legs and bodies.[10]

Rescuers pulled 27 dead soldiers from the wreckage and another 53 with injuries of all descriptions. Four more died over the next few days. The last of those who died, Private Thomas Stott, hung on to life for nine weeks before he too succumbed to his injuries on 2 June.[11]

Reports of L 22's movements after the attack on Cleethorpes are confusing but it appears she circled around again before heading back out to sea after coming under fire from an armed minesweeper in the Humber.

## 31 March 1916, 8.45pm: Stowmarket, Suffolk

The other four Zeppelins came inland much further south. One of the first was Heinrich Mathy's L 13. The crew had experienced a torrid time during their last raid and hoped for better luck this time, but it was not to be. Having crossed the coast near Leiston in Suffolk at 8pm, atmospheric conditions prevented Mathy gaining the height he needed before striking London, so he decided to attack the explosives works at Stowmarket en route. Lightened after dropping those bombs, he hoped to gain height and continue towards the capital.

The works manager at Stowmarket's New Explosives Company, F.W. Wharton, had switched off all outside lights as normal but had received no warning of a possible raid because phone lines were down. At 8.20pm the police delivered the 'Field Marshal's Warning Order Only' message by hand, which meant he should commence preliminary precautions, but five minutes later a friend arrived and told Wharton that a Zeppelin had been seen two miles away at Needham Market. Concerned, Wharton went outside and was amazed to 'see a bright light hovering in the sky, which illuminated the whole district'.

As Mathy approached the area he had released a parachute flare – Wharton's 'bright light'. Although those on the ground reported it lighting up the district, it did not illuminate the explosive works just over a mile away. It did, however, alert the defences; two badly positioned 6-pdr Nordenfelt guns, just 20 yards from the works' boundary fence. Zeppelins often retaliated against guns and searchlights and any bombs aimed at these might easily strike the works. Now under fire, L 13 turned towards the guns and at 8.45pm attacked. The first four HE bombs steaked down in a line extending towards the searchlight, standing 80 yards in front of the guns. As the bombs came closer the searchlight crew scattered. Wharton believed that if L 13 had continued, its bombs would have hit the nitro-glycerine plant, but Mathy turned away, skirting the northern edge of the works before following the railway line alongside it. He dropped three more bombs over the railway, all within 25 yards of the boundary fence and 100 yards from important buildings in the works. One man, Private Loker of No.2 Supernumerary Company, 1st Battalion, Cambridgeshire Regiment, suffered a bruised arm and torn jacket. Turning away from the railway, Mathy's last five bombs fell about 400 yards south of the works in ploughed fields on Clamp Farm at Creeting St Peter.

Flying in a wide circle, Mathy returned 30 minutes later. The gunners, who fired five more rounds, thought they had hit the target but L 13 appeared unaffected. On board, however, things were very different as engine mechanic Pitt Klein recalled.

> All of a sudden the ship started to descend with worrying speed; the elevator helmsman could barely hold it... What had happened? It didn't take long to find the cause.[12]

Shell fragments had holed two gas cells and L 13 started losing precious hydrogen. With London now out of the question, Mathy set a course back to Germany while the crew worked feverishly to repair the damage.

At 8.10pm, three mobile 1-pdr 'pom-poms' and a searchlight of the Eastern Mobile Brigade of the Royal Naval Anti-aircraft Service (RNAAS) at Lowestoft received information that a Zeppelin had crossed the coast to the south of their position – L 13 on its inward course. The four vehicles headed south and after about 12 miles, as they approached the village of Wangford, the wounded Zeppelin appeared. At the same time Mathy's crew saw the headlights of the vehicles. The guns pulled up and prepared for action as L 13 began to drop bombs. The gun crews estimated that L 13 was flying at between 4,000 and 5,000 feet, demonstrating the effects of the hydrogen loss, but only managed to get off a few rounds before L 13 passed out of range. In the same time 16 bombs dropped in fields around the guns but inflicted no damage.

At 9.55pm, a BE2c flown by Flight sub-Lieutenant Edward Pulling took off from Covehithe, on the coast between Lowestoft and Southwold. The burning flares on the landing field now attracted L 13 and 27 bombs peppered the area (seven HE and 20 incendiaries). Looking down, they appeared to be effective. 'One after the other the bombs exploded,' Pitt Klein enthused, 'causing terrific blasts. Huge columns of garish flames shot skywards.'[13] These 'terrific blasts', however, merely smashed a few windows. A local policeman expressed surprise that a Zeppelin should target such a peaceful spot: 'All I know is... I heard one, two, three, four, five, six bombs drop, and I said to myself, "Well, they are simply shovelling them out."'[14] Pulling had no luck in finding L 13 before she disappeared, but there would be other Zeppelin encounters for Pulling before the year was out.

A chance find of a piece of paper the following morning quickly dispelled any doubts as to whether the gunners had found their target; it was a copy of a radio message sent by Mathy and blown overboard: '10 p.m. Have bombarded battery near Stowmarket with success. Am hit; have turned back. Will land at Hage about 4 a.m. L 13.'[15]

Both L 13 and the explosives works at Stowmarket had fortunate escapes, but in other towns across Suffolk and Essex that night they would not be so lucky.

## 31 March 1916, 11.35pm: Bury St Edmunds, Suffolk

Werner Peterson brought L 16 inland at 10.10pm near Winterton on the Norfolk coast. He headed for London but as he approached darkened Bury St Edmunds at about 11pm, the Chief Constable, Major E.P. Prest, reported that she appeared to hover for some time in the proximity of Cattishall Farm, which lay close to the Great Eastern Railway line running from Bury to Haughley. It was around this time that Peterson picked-up a worrying radio message sent by L 15 to Germany requesting assistance between the Thames and Ostend; there had also been an earlier one at 10.25pm.[16] At 11.35pm, as Prest looked on, L 16 was on the move again, heading west on a course that would have taken her north of the town, but then two mobile 'pom-poms' of the RNAAS which had taken up a position on the Stowmarket Road, about a mile outside the town, burst into action and Peterson reacted.

> Within a very few seconds – it whipped round & came straight for the guns 'showering bombs', the guns continuing to fire, but how many rounds I could not say as the noise was somewhat deafening.[17]

The first five HE bombs fell in a line just to the east of the railway junction outside Northgate Station before Peterson commenced an evasive zig-zag course, dropping two bombs in a field and five near Eastgate Station. Two more dropped near Layhill Covert, then three in a direct line to the guns, but they fell short. Peterson now became aware of the town and as he passed over the guns he turned west and headed straight towards it.

The sound of exploding bombs woke many of those already in bed and memories of a previous raid in April 1915 came flooding back. In Raingate Street, Henry Adams, an employee of the Town Corporation, became concerned for the welfare of the horses under his charge and set out for the stables taking three of his sons with him: 15-year-old twins, George and Ernest, and their younger brother, Willy, aged 13. In Mill Road, 44-year-old Harry Frost went out into the garden while his wife and children remained inside. Herbert Hardiment, a private of 1/4th Cambridgeshire Regiment, was asleep in his billet in Beaconsfield Terrace on Chalk Lane, undisturbed by the noise, but his frightened landlady hammered on his door and woke him. Similar stories played out across the town.

Approaching the south-east corner of the town at 11.45pm, L 16 prepared to release 16 bombs (nine HE and seven incendiary). The first of these, an incendiary, fell on soft ground in Raingate Street then a second flared up in the garden of St Mary's Vicarage, terrifying Henry Adams and his sons as they walked up Prussia Lane alongside the garden. They had little time to react, however, because at that moment a bomb exploded in Prussia Lane. Ernest threw himself down beside the wall and escaped injury while Willy survived with just a shrapnel wound to his leg, but their father and George were dead, killed instantly by the lethal explosion.[18] Damage extended to Raingate Street, the King of Prussia pub on the corner of Prussia Lane and to Southgate Street. Having crossed the town, Peterson turned his airship over Tayfen Meadows and made a second run over Bury St Edmunds. Two bombs fell harmlessly between the Suffolk Regiment barracks and Spring Lane, followed by three more on Spring Lane from where the blast seared across open ground to damage 13 cottages in Cornfield Road and eight villas in Springfield Road, while a horse in a wrecked stable had to be shot due to its injuries.

In Beaconsfield Terrace 19-year-old Private Hardiment, woken by his landlady, told her, 'Don't worry, Ma, I'll go down and see what has happened'. As he reached the back door a bomb exploded in the garden. While rescuers helped the landlady and her children escape through a bedroom window, another ventured inside the house and found the decapitated body of Hubert Hardiment buried under the rubble.

In the garden of 74 Mill Road, Harry Frost was searching the sky for the Zeppelin. When he saw it he called excitedly to his wife Florence just as two bombs crashed down, one smashing into No.75 and the other into Frost's house. With her husband serving in the army, Annie Dureall was alone at No.75, peering through the window while her five children were all in bed. Evelyn, aged six, James, five, and Kathleen, four, all shared one bed, while baby Eileen slept in her cot in the same room. The fifth child, eight-year-old Thomas, was alone in another bedroom. The bomb smashed through the roof and down through the bedroom where four of the five children lay, carrying their bed through the floor as beams, rubble and debris crashed down. Annie and two of her children, James and Kathleen, died instantly. Evelyn survived, although she remained in hospital for nine months. Rescuers pulled baby Eileen alive from her cot where a fallen beam narrowly missed crushing her and Thomas escaped though badly shaken.[19] A newspaper reporting on the tragedy wrote: 'Nothing remains of the house except a heaped mass of bricks, in which are entangled furniture, bed clothing and odds and ends.'

After calling his wife, Harry Frost turned to go inside just as the second bomb exploded a split second after the first. Much of the back of the house collapsed, burying Harry under three feet of rubble, but his groans told rescuers he was alive. They dug him out but he died in hospital two days later. His eight-year-old daughter Vera received cuts from flying glass but two other children were physically unharmed; their aunt, Grace Barnett, lost an eye. At No.73 the Daniels family all escaped with minor cuts but the bomb had wrecked their home too. It also smashed windows and doors as well as damaging ceilings and roofs across an extensive area.

After dropping four more incendiaries on Bury St Edmunds, L 16 headed towards Lowestoft on the coast where, around 1am, it unleashed one final bomb. This exploded within 30 yards of the Tramway Department headquarters on Rotterdam Road. Damage extended across a wide area but no one was hurt. The seven guns defending Lowestoft engaged the departing L 16 as she quickly climbed away and disappeared out to sea at 1.05am.

## 31 March 1916, 10.30pm: Sudbury, Suffolk

The radio operator on L 14 also intercepted the worrying request for help transmitted by L 15 to Germany. The commander of L 14, Alois Böcker, brought his airship inland at 8.15pm over Sea Palling on the Norfolk coast and set off purposefully towards London. At 10.30pm, about five minutes after L 15 sent out her first message, L 14 approached the small market town of Sudbury where soldiers of the 2/6th (City of London) Battalion had billets. On board L 14 for this mission was Peter Strasser. Burning limekilns or lights at the Victoria Works on the east side of the town may have attracted L 14 because the first of the recorded bombs fell in Constitution Hill, a road that ran alongside.[20] Rifleman Robert Wilson was at his billet when the bomb exploded outside in Constitution Hill sending lethal shards of glass slashing into his room. The owner of the house found him lying on the floor with blood oozing from two chest wounds. He died of his injuries on 2 April.

About 100 yards further on, another bomb exploded in East Street, close to the junction with Constitution Hill. John Edward Smith, a 50-year-old silk weaver, had just left a pub, the Horse and Groom, and was crossing East Street to his house at No.58 when fragments of the bomb killed him. At Nos.34 and 35 both houses collapsed. At No.34, Ellen Wheeler, a 64-year-old widow, was dead, as were her neighbours at No.35, Thomas Ambrose and his wife, Ellen. The last recorded bomb, an incendiary, smashed down on Orford House at 22 Melford Road, another billet accommodating soldiers of the 2/6th Battalion. With the building on fire, flames trapped Rifleman Bond inside. Showing great bravery Sergeant J.C. 'Charlie' May entered the fiercely burning building and rescued Bond. May received the Military Medal for his actions, the first awarded for gallantry on British soil. Besides the houses demolished in East Street, the explosion also smashed windows in around 200 others.[21]

## 31 March 1916, 11.05pm: Braintree, Essex

From Sudbury, L 14 resumed its south-west course and at 11.05pm reached Braintree in Essex. Doris Carter, aged six, was asleep in Cressing Road, sharing a room with her sister Margaret. Disturbed by a neighbour's dog, their mother was already awake when she heard 'a steadily increasing roar overhead'.

> Whether it was for comfort or out of curiosity I never knew but she shook Maggie and me awake to look out of the window, which faced across the allotments towards Crittall's [Manor Works] factory... Eventually, dimly outlined against the stars, we became aware of a long black shape way up in

the sky passing from left to right. Almost immediately we saw a flash of light followed by a loud bang which came from the factory direction.[22]

That first bomb had a devastating impact on Coronation Avenue. All 36 houses in the street suffered some damage but at two of them the impact was tragic. The bomb struck No.19 and demolished it, killing the occupant, 70-year-old Ann Herbert. The force of the explosion also partially wrecked No.21 and badly damaged three others. Lying dead under the rubble were Alfred Dennington, aged 31, his wife, Annie, 32, and her three-year-old niece, Ella Hammond. Amongst the rescuers was the chairman of the town council who owned the block of houses. He picked his way carefully through the ruins of No.21 to the bedroom.

> Groping his way, the dead bodies were reached. By the aid of a flashlight the husband was seen lying face downwards on the pillow; the wife on her right side in a position of crouching from fear, and the little baby peacefully lying between the two. The Chairman was so overwrought by this pathetic discovery that he fainted, and had to be assisted by a doctor.[23]

About four miles south-west of Braintree, the Reverend Andrew Clark, rector at the village of Great Leighs, had retired to bed early but awoke with a start.

> At 11 p.m., just as my wife had come up, there were two tremendous explosions… which shook the house, and caused her to call out, involuntarily Oh! Oh! The second call woke me, and I got up to find my daughters disturbed by the great bangs, and the dogs roused and barking.[24]

After the bomb on Coronation Avenue, Böcker's second and third bombs fell close together, no more than 150 yards further on, between Coronation Avenue and London Road.

> One… descended on the edge of the meadow, making a circular hole four feet deep and ten in diameter. The second… was 25 yards further in a garden… Some workshops ten yards away were shattered, and a conservatory was wrecked. The back door of the house was blown in, and all the glass at

the rear broken.[25] … A Sunday School at the rear of a large chapel had about 100 panes of glass broken. The windows of the chapel and a skylight in the vestry were also smashed.[26]

As L 14 moved away, Reverend Clark was scanning the sky for a glimpse of her.

> At 11.10 p.m. I was dressing-gowned and out… By this time the Zeppelin was roaring like a railway train somewhere near by… I tried every way to locate it against the stars, but did not succeed… I went round to the other side of the house, and listened… as it passed over Great Waltham, and so towards London.[27]

Böcker passed Great Waltham at about 11.15pm and then Chelmsford. At 11.35pm, however, as L 14 flew over Doddinghurst, a 1-pdr 'pom-pom' gun at Kelvedon Hatch opened fire. Piqued by this audacity, Böcker circled back and released 11 bombs at the gun, but all missed the target, two falling in fields north of Doddinghurst followed by nine within the parish of Blackmore. The Reverend Reeve at the village of Stondon Massey reported that his rectory windows 'were violently shaken and considerable alarm was naturally caused'.[28]

At 12.10am Böcker returned to Braintree finally rewarding the Reverend Clark with a view of the Zeppelin.

> Just as clock struck midnight, sound was heard of one Zeppelin coming back…it hesitated; hovered about (as if uncertain how to proceed) over N.W. corner of the house, and over the Stokes's cottage opposite the Rectory Gate. It was now distinctly seen – a long, black thing against the stars. About the same time, a window was heard to open in the Stokes' cottage, and Miss Stokes' voice call out shrilly to her mother (who is rather deaf) – 'I can hear the sound, but can't see anything.' Little wonder, since the Zep. was then directly over the cottage.[29]

As in other towns there was a great desire to see the damage caused by these air raids. The bombs on Braintree came late on a Friday night and by Sunday great crowds were on the move. The Reverend Clark noted in his diary, with some irony, that while 'All Braintree had gone to Sudbury (to see the damage there). All Essex came to Braintree'. A case of another man's bomb crater is invariably more interesting than your own.

## 1 April 1916, 1.25am: Thames Haven, Essex

L 14 continued on an uncertain course, first north then back south. At 12.55am Böcker dropped a single HE bomb in a field at Springfield Tyrells on the outskirts of Chelmsford as he appeared to be heading for London again, but at 1.12am, as he reached Brentwood, L 14 made another change of direction. Turning away from the capital, L 14 now headed south-eastwards; Böcker and Strasser had decided to attack the vast oil storage facilities at Thames Haven, about 25 miles downstream from London.

At 1.25am L 14 released a single incendiary bomb over Stanford-le-Hope then, as she approached the target, six 6-pdrs and a 1-pdr gun at Thames Haven, Pitsea and Kynochtown burst into action. They fired 81 rounds but had no appreciable effect as L 14 released two HE bombs and 12 incendiaries, hoping to set the oil tanks burning. In that they failed. Bomb fragments pierced two empty oil tanks, a small fire broke out on a pier and two oil barrels were damaged. Perhaps concerned by the firepower concentrated on the Thames Estuary, Böcker chose not to make his way home along the river, instead he took a north-east course, passing Colchester, Ipswich and Saxmundham before crossing the Suffolk coast near Dunwich at about 3.00am.

There may also have been another reason why Böcker and Strasser chose an overland route for the start of their homeward journey. Those distress messages sent at 10.25 and 11.00pm from Zeppelin L 15, requesting naval assistance, came from the Thames Estuary where clearly she was in trouble. The overland choice was a pragmatic one. But what had happened to L 15?

Chapter 7

# 'Why, haven't you heard – our boys brought the Zeppelin down!'

The raid carried out by the Naval Airship Division on the night of 31 March/1 April had met with mixed results. Having selected London as the prime target, none of the raiders reached it. Instead bombs had dropped on Cleethorpes, Stowmarket, Lowestoft, Bury St Edmunds, Sudbury, Braintree and Thames Haven. But there is one more Zeppelin's movements that night still to reveal – those of L 15.

Joachim Breithaupt, the 33-year-old commander of L 15, had previously made two telling raids. In October 1915 he had flown across central London in what became known as the 'Theatreland Raid'[1] (for which Breithaupt received the Iron Cross, 1st Class[2]), and in January 1916 he had commanded L 15 in the great Midlands Raid. Now he was heading for London again.

## 31 March 1916, 8.20pm: Ipswich, Suffolk

L 15 crossed the Suffolk coast near Dunwich at 7.45pm. Breithaupt, flying at only 7,200 feet, dropped ballast, bombs and a petrol tank to lighten the airship. At 8.20pm L 15 reached Ipswich, which unfortunately was the same time as the chief constable received the 'Field Marshal's Warning Order Only' alert. Breithaupt dropped three bombs over the docks. An incendiary fell harmlessly in the dock but two HE bombs made their mark. The first exploded in Key Street by Common Quay. A newspaper reported that it exploded on a cottage, 'which was wrecked, in addition to which much of the adjoining property comprising offices, a public house, corn merchants premises, etc., was badly knocked about'. David Bishop Cattermole, a 57-year-old labourer, was killed instantly while standing outside the public house – the Gun Inn – and two women died. One, Ester Louisa Olding, from 'cerebral haemorrhage accelerated by excitement caused by the explosion of bombs', while the other, Jane Hopestill Hoff, aged 75, was so terrified that she died after falling downstairs and fracturing her skull. A soldier inside one of the damaged buildings had to have a leg amputated.[3] Heading south over the docks the second HE bomb smashed onto the river bank at the Stoke Bathing Place, the home of Ipswich Swimming Club, where it made short work of the corrugated iron-roofed wooden buildings.

Continuing towards London, Breithaupt approached Colchester and at 8.45pm dropped a single bomb in a meadow close to a number of large industrial buildings in the Hythe district of the town, but damage was limited to broken glass. Changing course, Breithaupt now headed south towards the River Thames, the indelible highway to London. About five miles from the river, at Pitsea, he turned again and, keeping the Thames on his port side, prepared for his second raid on the capital. He was, however, about to enter a hornet's nest.

The anti-aircraft guns along the Thames were on the alert and 17 were ready for action. Intelligence that Zeppelins were over the country had circulated and RNAAS mobile Maxim guns had already engaged L 15 at Ipswich. The RFC sent pilots up too and three from No.19 Reserve Aeroplane Squadron, based east of London, took off between 9.15 and 9.30pm: Second Lieutenant Henry Powell from Sutton's Farm, Second Lieutenant Alfred de Bathe Brandon from Hainault Farm, and Second Lieutenant Claude Ridley from Joyce Green. All three were flying the BE2c armed with Ranken darts, bombs and machine guns firing standard .303 lead bullets.

Designed by Engineer Lieutenant Commander Francis Ranken of the Royal Navy, the Ranken dart entered RNAS service as an anti-Zeppelin weapon in July 1915 before acceptance by the RFC in February 1916. The darts were 12 inches in length, one inch wide and weighed just under 1lb. They contained an explosive charge in the forward section and black powder in the rear. At the rear of the dart three spring-loaded vanes opened when released, the idea being that the iron tip penetrated through the outer fabric of the Zeppelin on which the vanes caught hold. A wire coil provided a delay action allowing the leading section to penetrate about 18 inches inside the Zeppelin before a friction tube ignited the explosive. Held under the aircraft in a tin box containing 24 darts, the pilot could release batches of three or all together.

## 31 March 1916, 9.36pm: Purfleet, Essex

At 9.36pm a searchlight sweeping the sky from the south side of the Thames located L 15 flying at about 8,500 feet near Purfleet on the north side. A 3-inch, 20cwt gun at Dartford, about four miles away, opened up firing 24 rounds over the next four minutes. By the time the gun ceased more searchlights had found L 15 and more of the Thames guns had commenced firing, although some were at very long range. Police Sergeant Swan at Rainham was mesmerised: 'Anti-aircraft guns blazed away at the Zeppelin as she continued Londonwards. She made a magnificent picture in the glare of the searchlights, with shrapnel bursting all round her.'[4]

At Purfleet there were three guns: a 3-inch, 20cwt and two 1-pdr 'pom-poms'. The commander, Captain Joseph Harris, had been confined to bed by the doctor but 'without a moment's hesitation he left his bed, dressed and, wrapping himself in a large blanket, went straight to his gun to take command'.[5] They opened fire at 9.40pm. While the two 'pom-poms' spat out the first of 122 rounds, Harris calmly calculated the range for the 3-inch gun and set the fuzes. The first two rounds detonated short of the target. Harris ordered a change. Of the next two, one was short and the other exploded beyond the target. Harris adjusted the timings on the next three fuzes.

A report submitted by Lieutenant Colonel John W. Reid, commanding the Woolwich area anti-aircraft defences, described the movements of L 15 as the artillery concentrated their fire.

> She immediately appeared to be in difficulties; she first swung round on a circle to the left, apparently making efforts to rise, but failing to do so she then swung back again to the right on her original course, pointing West, but the fire of the guns intensifying she swung further to the right.[6]

To escape the gunfire and rise quickly Breithaupt released 44 bombs (20 HE and 24 incendiary). These smashed a few windows when they fell in open fields at 9.43pm around Rainham and Wennington. Two minutes later, as L 15 passed over the Wennington Road, Captain Harris had completed his adjustments and the 3-inch gun roared back into action. A gunner manning one of the 1-pdrs noted that 'the big gun got busy'.

> Presently a shot from the big gun caught the Zepp. in the stern and a little flame shot out from the envelope… the explosion seemed to throw it round, and at the same time it dropped by the stern with nose in the air.

> Of course we were busy with our gun, but the boys couldn't help making a slight pause to shout 'She's hit!' And then we were busy again. But the next shot from the big one caught it again near the bow towards the centre, and that seemed to paralyse the monster, for it appeared to remain stationary for a couple of seconds before continuing its flight slowly to the north and out of range.[7]

The crew of L 15 scrambled to assess the damage inflicted by the guns; it was bad news. Shell fragments had ripped through one of the midships gas cells which was now empty. One damaged cell at the stern was leaking badly as was one of the forward cells, and one in the bow was all but empty. Breithaupt was now a worried man: 'As soon as I knew the result of the [enemy's] fire I turned about and tried to reach Ostend.'[8] Lieutenant Colonel Reid reported L 15 escaping the searchlights at about 9.50pm.

All this activity attracted the attention of the RFC pilots patrolling to the east of London. Henry Powell saw L 15 but unable to reach her height was busy avoiding gunfire, which he reported was bursting all around him. Claude Ridley also saw L 15 far above him from the other side of the Thames but could only offer an optimistic long-range burst of machine gun fire before L 15 disappeared from view.

At 9.40pm, Second Lieutenant Brandon, patrolling at 6,000 feet as ordered, saw L 15 near Purfleet 'high up on my right'. He started to climb towards her but after five minutes she broke away from the searchlights and he lost contact.

## 31 March 1916, 9.55pm: Brentwood, Essex

For Otto Kühne, the executive officer (second-in-command) on L 15, the situation had become desperate: 'We must get out of range of those guns

– or at least we must get away from those searchlights. Suddenly we find aeroplanes flying over the ship!'[9]

Brandon had found L 15 again. Alfred de Bathe Brandon, a 32-year-old New Zealander, had studied Law in England before returning home to join his father's firm in Wellington. Following the outbreak of war, Brandon came back to England, gained his pilot's licence in October 1915 and in December joined the Royal Flying Corps as a probationary second lieutenant, his rank confirmed early in March 1916. That month he joined No.19 RAS's flight at Hainault Farm.

It was about 9.55pm when Brandon closed on his quarry, flying west of Brentwood. The release of bombs had allowed L 15 to climb to 9,000 feet as the 536-foot-long aerial leviathan headed north-east with Brandon's tiny BE2c, just 27 feet of wood, canvas and wire, in pursuit. Undeterred he climbed until he was 300 or 400 feet above then released a batch of three Ranken darts.

> I heard three reports and thought that I had made a hit. Shortly after this I heard more reports, which probably were from a machine gun, and this made me uncertain whether I had made a hit or not.[10]

Brandon was actually under heavy fire from the Zeppelin, which had an exposed machine gun position on the top of the envelope for just such a situation, as well as others in the gondolas. The machine gunners easily followed his movements because he had forgotten to switch off his navigation lights when he commenced the attack. Brandon attacked again as the Zeppelin neared Ingatestone, noting 'a tremendous amount of machine gun firing', at which point he remembered to switch off his lights.

> [I] got in a direct line with the Zeppelin. I was then about 500 feet above it; I closed the throttle and volplaned towards the Zeppelin... I then got out an incendiary bomb, and in trying to get it into the tube[11] I had to take my eyes off the Zeppelin, and on looking up again I was astonished to find that in a very few seconds I would have passed the Zeppelin, so I quickly placed the incendiary bomb in my lap, and let off No.2 and 3 lots of darts.

Much to his disappointment there were no explosions and at 10.05pm, disorientated by the darkness and the speed of the engagement, Brandon was flying away from L 15 and although he searched for an hour he never saw her again. On landing, an inspection of his BE2c revealed bullet holes in the right aileron, left tail and right elevator.

Although relieved to have escaped this latest attack, Breithaupt's situation remained desperate. Having risen to 9,000 feet near Rainham, the continuing loss of hydrogen meant L 15 gradually descended 'in a slow even curve'. Attempting to halt this, Kühne issued orders to lighten the ship: 'Overboard with every kilo of superfluous weight. Overboard with everything that is not riveted or nailed.' Machine guns, petrol tanks and all manner of spare parts fell at Stock, around West and South Hanningfield and at Woodham Ferrers.

About 10.25pm, L 15 reached the coast at Foulness where she circled at a height of 2,600 feet and Breithaupt transmitted the first message to Germany that he was in trouble, which the other Zeppelin commanders picked up. Then Breithaupt attempted the shortest sea crossing, hoping to reach Ostend. Once over the sea all confidential papers were weighted and thrown overboard but it soon became clear they would never reach Belgium, prompting Breithaupt's second message at 11pm hoping for help from German ships: 'Need immediate assistance between River Thames and Ostend.' After that Breithaupt jettisoned the radio too.[12]

With L 15 now only a few hundred feet above the sea, Breithaupt accepted there was nothing more he could do. He ordered all but two of the crew – the elevator and rudder helmsmen – up into the envelope of the airship where the impact on hitting the water would be lessened, while he awaited the inevitable in the command gondola with Kühne and the two helmsmen.

## 31 March 1916, 11.15pm: At sea off Kent coast

Lieutenant Carey on the armed trawler *Osbourne Stroud*, operating as a minesweeper, reported a Zeppelin at a height between 400 and 500 feet and engaging her with his anti-aircraft gun, after which he lost sight but heard a loud noise. At 11.15pm Otto Kühne described the last moments of L 15.

> An ominous crack resounds through the whole ship. We are in pitch darkness… but one thing I know for certain: our ship is broken in twain. The fracture must be at some spot where there are empty gas-bags.

With its back broken, the Zeppelin hit the water hard, thrusting the command gondola against the body of the airship.

> I find that I am standing in water, in an empty ship. It is pitch dark around me... I feel myself all over – no injuries. But around me I can hear no sound save the plash of waves and the gurgles of eddies. Am I the only survivor of the wreck?

Kühne took a deep breath and dived through a hole, but when he surfaced he saw L 15, 'a spectral outline in the dark night', drifting away. Swimming after her he caught up and found two other crewmen, then they located Breithaupt and the rest near the middle of the wreck.[13] Breithaupt had a fortuitous escape from the command gondola.

> I was… completely under water and was tossed about by the water streaming in, but marvellous to relate suddenly rose to the surface and was pulled, completely exhausted, into the airship by my crew… The elevator helmsman [Willy Albrecht] who was next to me was drowned, the rudder helmsman had all his teeth knocked out and I escaped with slight concussion and various minor injuries. The L 15 was sinking, her back broken, half under water with the nose and stern above water.[14]

Having clambered up to the top of the airship the crew, cold and wet, peered out into the blackness of the night contemplating their fate, all of them aware of what had befallen the crew of Zeppelin L 19 just two months earlier. They hoped they might be close enough to Belgium for German boats to pick them up but they were only 15 miles off the Kent coast north of Margate.

The Admiralty, having intercepted Breithaupt's call for help, knew L 15 was in trouble and alerted its fleet of minesweeping trawlers and drifters at the mouth of the Thames estuary: 'Look out for damaged Zeppelin flying low.' Standing on the bridge of the trawler *Olivine*, the skipper, a Royal Naval Reserve officer, Lieutenant William R. Mackintosh, saw a flashing light and headed towards it, as did others.

## 1 April 1916, around 2am: At sea off Kent coast

Over two hours after L 15 hit the water the first boats appeared. 'Shadows of trawlers loom up out of the night. Dutchmen?' asked Otto

Kühne. 'They slink silently round our wreck. Are they going to rescue us?' Breithaupt reported that four trawlers stopped about 100 yards off. Among them the *Olivine*. The crew of L 15 called out for help but, 'Suddenly a call came quite loudly over the calm water, "go to hell".' Immediately afterwards Mackintosh ordered *Olivine's* gun to open fire. Breithaupt estimated shells flew over the wreck for about two minutes. Kühne claimed the firing only stopped when the howling siren of an approaching destroyer, HMS *Vulture,* cut through the sound of gunfire, but British accounts state the firing 'ceased after a few rounds as there was no resistance'. As rescue appeared imminent, some of the Zeppelin's crew began to slash the undamaged gas cells to ensure the airship would sink and deny the prize to their captors.

As *Olivine* approached L 15 a voice shouted: 'We surrender; have no arms; come alongside.' Macintosh sent a dingy but remained cautious, insisting they came over in groups of three and ordering them to strip first. Breithaupt was indignant.

> This was in cold March weather at 3 o'clock in the morning [2am British time] and besides myself five of the crew had already been swimming for a long time in the extremely cold water. In spite of my refusal to strip I was taken on board the lifeboat.[15]

The *Olivine* took 17 men on board, one was missing, before Mackintosh transferred them to HMS *Vulture*, but Breithaupt remained unhappy with their treatment.

> On board the destroyer I, together with my officers of the watch and the two warrant officers was shut up in a very dirty auxiliary engine room. As... I had swallowed a lot of water and gas I felt extremely ill and for four hours I was forced to remain in this engine room seated on an upturned bucket.[16]

HMS *Vulture* took the crew to Chatham where Breithaupt's dark mood failed to improve.

> The only furniture in my cell was a very dirty plank bed with no covering and a stool. Scraps of food left by my predecessor were scattered about. Wet through and broken in mind and

body broken as a result of the concussion and the depressing feeling of being a prisoner, I sat shivering on my plank bed.[17]

\* \* \*

For the first time the British authorities had access to a Zeppelin of the latest design, but clearly it was in a sinking condition, with the centre section below the water and the bow and stern in the air. At least two men from the destroyer HMS *Electra* clambered aboard L 15 to start making notes on her construction, but by the time they were ready to take the wreck in tow only the tail remained above the surface. During this time many boats crowded around, their crews eager to grab a souvenir or two. Mr Tibbenham from the Kentish Knock lightship, moored a mile away, was quick off the mark and secured pieces of the framework, which he made into brooches for the ladies in his family.[18] Shortly after they began to tow the wreck it sank. Lieutenant Carey on the *Osbourne Stroud* had no doubts why. 'The cause of the rapid sinking of the ship,' he explained, 'was the damage caused by boats round the ship breaking up the framework and cutting the canvas.'[19]

A salvage crew aboard the armed trawler *Seamew*, led by Chief Gunner (T) W.A. Austin, located and buoyed the wreck on 6 April, pulling up the 30-foot tail section from a depth of 90 feet. Despite numerous attempts, many hampered by bad weather, it was not until 28 May that they hauled the tangled mass of wreckage onto Margate Sand, a sandbank lying off Margate and Westgate.[20]

Each day at low tide they sifted through the wreckage and, up to 8 June, Austin had sent in numerous items, 'including 5 canvas bags, one metal case of charts, 2 propellers with shaft and gear boxes, one machine gun, bomb dropping machines, instruments and control and steering gear'. They also recovered the body of Willy Albrecht, the missing crewman, drowned in the control gondola from which Breithaupt and Kühne had escaped. Soon after, however, Austin reported that, 'owing to the shifting nature of the Margate Sand the remains of the wreckage have now disappeared'.

The crew of L 15 remained at Chatham for six days of interviews and questioning. From this information and the wreckage, it was possible to create detailed reports covering construction techniques, design and the airship service. From these it became clear that L 15 had an internal keel, an innovation introduced in September 1913 but unknown in Britain, a fact summarised in the report with the words: 'All the present published drawings of Zeppelins are wrong.'[21]

While still at Chatham a group of journalists received permission to talk to the prisoners.

> All the men looked strong and healthy…Most of the men were looking very cheerful, apparently glad that they had escaped with their lives from what turned out to be a very dangerous undertaking.

> We asked the men if they could distinguish anything during a raid in dark nights. They were somewhat shy in answering, but declared they could see absolutely nothing – they could only distinguish land from water. One of them said, 'We do not know what our officers may see through the glasses; we could see nothing.' We asked them if it was not a sorry business to kill women and children. Some of the men were quite frank, and said, 'We do as we are ordered.'[22]

When asked the same question, Breithaupt responded:

> You must not suppose that we set out to kill women and children. We have higher military aims. You would not find one officer in the German Army or Navy who would go to kill women and children. Such things happen accidently in war.[23]

On 7 April, with the questioning over, the transfer of the crew to POW camps began. The German officers' camp at Donington Hall, Leicestershire, would accommodate Breithaupt and Kühne.[24] Taken to London they boarded a train for Leicester, guarded by two officers carrying swords and an NCO with loaded rifle and fixed bayonet. At Leicester they had to wait two hours for a train to take them on the final leg of their journey. A newspaper reporter studied the two officers, Breithaupt first.

> He appeared to be quite at his ease as he walked to the first-class waiting room closely attended by his guard, and he seemed rather pleased than otherwise at the curiosity which was shown by the numerous passengers who travelled by the same express from St Pancras. The second officer, however,

appeared to be rather sullen, and his lips were pressed as with downcast eyes he marched along the platform... In spite of the strong feelings aroused by the Zeppelin raids, there were no outward manifestations of hostility.[25]

The rest of the crew, destined for Eastcote camp in Northamptonshire, experienced a slightly different reception.[26]

In Chatham railway station some old women threw some wet bread and eggs at them and at Euston Station in London a crowd was expecting them and they were hooted, else wise all went calm.[27]

* * *

The outcome of the raid demonstrated a clear improvement in Britain's defences. For the first time a British pilot had engaged a Zeppelin over Britain at night and the anti-aircraft guns had put up a spirited defence resulting in the destruction of a Zeppelin. 'It must be acknowledged,' Breithaupt later confided, 'that the enemy's aim was wonderful.' And the embryonic warning system had showed promise too. For his actions Second Lieutenant Alfred de Bathe Brandon received the Military Cross, his citation reading, 'For conspicuous gallantry and skill in dropping bombs on a Zeppelin at night'. But another award also attracted significant interest.

In March 1915, a wealthy businessman and Alderman of the City of London, Sir Charles Wakefield, whose company had developed Castrol Oil, offered a prize of £500 to the first person or persons responsible for bringing down a Zeppelin on British soil.[28] Later that year, in November, Sir Charles became Lord Mayor of London. Although L 15 came down at sea and not on 'British soil', on 2 April an anti-aircraft battery made the first claim for the prize, then others followed. Wakefield was disposed to take a broad-minded view if the War Office would verify the successful claim.

That first claim came from Captain Harris of the Purfleet battery, but the Dartford gunners also claimed the critical hit, while Lieutenant Colonel Reid, commanding the Woolwich area guns, believed a number of guns warranted recognition, but ended his report on 3 April with the following statement.

The most effective hit was by a common shell fired from the Dartford gun which burst on the airship near the top and burst about two-thirds of her length back from her nose.[29]

Harris at Purfleet, however, was having none of this and went out of his way to disprove the Dartford claim. He recovered two fuzes from shells fired by the Dartford gun set to explode well short of the distance of 8,350 yards he calculated that lay between the Dartford gun and the nearest of the craters made by L 15's bombs. He added a cutting remark: 'Possibly this gun was firing at another Zeppelin.' Harris found further evidence nearby as local resident, J.C. Ovenall, living in Sussex Terrace on London Road, revealed many years later. As a boy he witnessed the raid and remembered one shell making a particularly noisy 'whizz' over the house and a big 'plop' on the open field across the road. In the morning his father found a shell fragment weighing 1¾lb. Gunners at a Church Parade in Purfleet heard about this and Harris was quick to investigate and borrow the souvenir.

> At the inquiry which followed it was resolved that the base of the shell was from the Dartford gun, proof that the Dartford shells were falling short of the target, and the credit for bringing down the Zeppelin was given to the Purfleet crew.[30]

There was no doubt amongst the villagers in Purfleet either. A reporter who visited the following day could not help note the joy on the resident's faces: 'If you ask why there are so many smiles and the sound of hearty laughter on all sides, you will be met with: 'Why, haven't you heard – our boys brought the Zeppelin down?'[31]

After sifting through all the evidence, the War Office concluded that the Purfleet gun was most likely to have fired the successful shots and confirmed this in official documents. Awarding Sir Charles Wakefield's prize of £500, however, did not sit well with the War Office and they baulked at the idea of servicemen receiving financial rewards, so publicly attributed the destruction of L 15 to the efforts of all the guns and searchlights along the Thames.

Still keen to provide some form of reward, Wakefield used the prize money to produce medals for all those in action that night. In November he distributed 353 medals made of 9-carat gold, each individually engraved with the recipient's name and rank to mark the night when, for the first time, the British defences had successfully attacked a Zeppelin over British soil.[32] It bore the words 'Well Hit'.

The British public greeted the destruction of a hated Zeppelin with enthusiasm, but the fact that it happened miles out to sea beyond the view of the population diluted some of the impact. And with more raids taking place over the next four nights, the newspapers soon had plenty of fresh copy with which to fill their pages.

# Chapter 8

# A Zeppelin Moon

The loss of Zeppelin L 15 came as a shock to all in the Naval Airship Division but Strasser was determined not to let it disrupt his plans. With a new moon on 2 April the night skies were at their darkest and the weather promised to be in the raiders' favour. While those Zeppelins returning from this latest raid would need time to refit and for the crews to rest, Strasser had two airships available and did not hesitate to send them out on 1 April.

Towards the end of March the Naval Airship Division had 12 Zeppelins. The two oldest vessels, L 6 and L 7, now served respectively as a training ship and a reconnaissance vessel, while two others, L 20 and L 21, temporarily operated in the Baltic. That left eight Zeppelins for service against Britain. With the loss of L 15 that now reduced to seven: L 9, L 11, L 13, L 14, L 16, L 17 and L 22. Having returned early from the previous night's raid, L 11 was ready to go out again along with L 17, which had not been involved.

Strasser gave them London as a target, but over the North Sea the wind became problematical and, following new instructions, Strasser gave them discretion to select targets in the Midlands or north of England. However, the raid did not go well for Herbert Ehrlich and L 17. He arrived off the coast before the sky was completely dark and so held out to sea for about an hour. Then, when he decided it was time to move inland, the shaft of one of the rear propellers broke. He shut down all engines while the crew secured the propeller and dropped 17 bombs at sea to lighten the ship. Running repairs complete, Ehrlich abandoned the mission and returned to his base at Nordholz.

## 1 April 1916, 11.20pm: Sunderland, County Durham

L 11's commander, Viktor Schütze, hoped to find targets on the River Tyne, but the wind pushed him south, beyond the River Wear, and he crossed the coast at Seaham. Schütze changed his target to the important shipbuilding town of Sunderland and as he headed inland to approach from the west, he dropped two bombs over Eppleton Colliery at 11.10pm, aimed at a burning 'fiery heap', but they caused no damage. Two minutes later another pair exploded at Hetton Downs, smashing windows in three houses, damaging pigsties and a hen house, killing a cockerel and nine hens. At 11.15pm a third brace struck the village of Philadelphia. Although smashing windows in 35 homes there were no casualties. Schütze now followed the River Wear towards Sunderland where warning of a possible raid had reached the town.

L 11 flew across Sunderland for two miles in a straight line dropping 21 bombs (14 HE and seven incendiary) that claimed 22 lives and inflicted injury on 128 people. The first bomb landed on the south-western edge of the town in Back Peacock Street but it failed to detonate. From there the course was to the north-east. After that first bomb others to the south of the Wear struck Pickard Street, Milburn Street and Fern Street. A girl named Harriet lived with her grandmother in Pickard Street. After an evening at a picture house they were both in bed when a bomb struck.

> I can remember all the ceiling falling on top of us. To protect me, my grandmother covered me up with bedclothes. If she hadn't gone to bed when she did, she would have been killed. The fireplace had fallen on her chair where she had been knitting.
>
> We had a canary that used to wake us by singing. It was blown across the room and, though it never sang again, it lived another 11 years.[1]

In Fern Street four people died: John Joseph Woodward, Ernest Liddle Johnstone, Hannah Lydon and Thomas, her 14-year-old son. A local newspaper summarised the damage south of the river.

> … about half-a-dozen streets suffered, and in some of them a number of houses were demolished. There were some very narrow escapes. In one house which was blown down there

were five people, but all scrambled from beneath the debris
completely unhurt. Houses around were badly shattered,
and all the glass in the windows for several hundred yards
distance was blown out.[2]

Once L 11 crossed the river, bombs fell in the Monkwearmouth district
causing further significant damage. One exploded at the goods yard
attached to Monkwearmouth Station where the glass roof over the
platforms smashed into countless pieces. Just beyond the station
another exploded in busy North Bridge Street. Thomas Shepherd Dale,
a borough magistrate and leader of the local Labour Party, was on duty
as a Special Constable. They found his body in the street, pierced by
shrapnel and glass, lying about 15 yards from the six-foot-deep crater.[3]
Fred Thirkell was walking along with a daughter on each arm as L 11
approached; his wife was just ahead with two friends. The bomb killed
16-year-old Elizabeth Jane Thirkell, blasting her through a shop's plate
glass window. His other daughter, wife and her two companions all
sustained injuries but, incredibly, Fred Thirkell was untouched.

Teenage siblings Gertrude and Henry Patrick were on their way
home along this main road when the bomb exploded, both dying
from their injuries. Two other victims killed in the street lived
nearby: 68-year-old furniture dealer Robert Garbutt Fletcher lived at
2 North Bridge Street and Alfred Dunlop lived off the main road in
Howick Street. Also in North Bridge Street a No.10 tram had pulled
up in accordance with the local air raid regulations. The passengers
dispersed but the crew remained with their vehicle. The explosion
ripped the tram apart, blasting the conductress, 22-year-old Margaret
Ann Holmes,[4] out into the road where water gushed from a burst
main. Hospitalised for months with a leg injury, although a leg brace
prevented her returning to the trams, the company found her a job in
their office.[5] Henry Dean, an electrician, suffered a fatal injury that
night too in Monkwearmouth. As the trams had stopped he walked
his girlfriend home and was heading back to his lodgings south of
the Wear when bomb fragments slashed open his stomach. He died in
hospital of acute peritonitis.

Behind the buildings on the east side of North Bridge Street stood
the main tramway depot. There a tram inspector, Joseph Thompson,
and another employee took shelter behind a wall. A bomb exploded
behind them and Thompson's colleague saw a bomb fragment zip over
his own shoulder then felt blood on his hands. When he turned around

Thompson lay dead on the ground, the metal fragment having pierced his heart.[6]

The bomb at the tramway depot also smashed windows at the Thompson Memorial Hall in Dundas Street, then another cluster landed close together. They inflicted serious damage to the Thomas Street Council Schools, practically demolished the Workmen's Hall on Whitburn Street and partly demolished St Benet's Roman Catholic Church on Causeway. That last bomb also killed Elizabeth Weldon and her neighbour's five-year-old daughter, Elizabeth Ranson.

Crossing over Church Street North, L 11's next lethal bomb struck a grocer's shop in Victor Street. Despite the late hour the shop, run by brothers Thomas and George Rogerson, remained open. When rescuers sifted through the rubble they recovered the bodies of the two brothers and that of a customer, 17-year-old Florence Johnson. Mr Glasgow, living at 65 Victor Street, heard the bombs and began to shepherd his family downstairs. As he did so, a bomb struck the house wrecking the upper part and killing his 16-year-old son John but leaving the rest of the family untouched. Herbert Chater, another resident of Victor Street died too, as did a plumber, Alfred Finkle, who lived in Dame Dorothy Street, running parallel with Victor Street.

After Victor Street, the final bomb fell at the North Dock at the shipyard of John Blumer & Co., where a fire broke out in the French polishing shop. With the raid over a newspaper outlined the damage inflicted on the town:

> … eight business premises were demolished and two partly demolished, 15 dwelling-houses demolished, and 66 partly so, and 158 houses and 64 shops had windows blown in and other minor damage done. The damage was chiefly confined to houses inhabited by working-class people.[7]

Viktor Schütze, standing in the command gondola of L 11, described how he saw the attack develop from a height of a little over a mile.

> The airship dropped explosive bombs on some works where one blast-furnace was blown up with a terrible detonation… The factories and dock buildings of Sunderland, now brightly illuminated, were then bombed with good results. The effect was grand; blocks of houses and rows of streets collapsed entirely; large fires broke out in places and a dense black

cloud... was caused by one bomb. A second explosive bomb was at once dropped at the same spot; judging from the situation, it may have been a railway station.[8]

Schütze's account is a little more accurate in places than many given by Zeppelin commanders, but his description of anti-aircraft fire appears greatly exaggerated, perhaps wanting to add some jeopardy to the encounter to impress those back in Germany.

> While over Sunderland, the airship was caught by a powerful searchlight and was pelted with shrapnel and fire-balls [incendiary shells], but to no purpose. The concussion from a shell bursting near the airship was felt as though she had been hit.[9]

The reality was somewhat less dramatic. A searchlight briefly illuminated L 11 and a 6-pdr gun at Fulwell Quarry fired a single shell before the light lost the airship and the gun fired no more.[10]

L 11 now headed back to the coast at Seaham from where a Maxim gun opened fire with little hope of success. Most Zeppelin commanders would now have set course for home but Schütze had other ideas and turned south. Having correctly located Sunderland he knew there were other industrial sites within reach.

## 2 April 1916, 12.10am: Middlesbrough, North Yorkshire

Schütze nosed L 11 inland again just north of the mouth of the River Tees with Middlesbrough in his sights. Port Clarence, opposite Middlesbrough on the north bank of the Tees, was first to come under attack at 12.10am but only one bomb fell. It landed in the grounds of Dorman & Long's steel works, contracted to produce artillery shells, where it smashed into a pile of steel ingots and fragments pierced an iron wagon about 100 yards away.

Crossing the Tees, L 11 passed over Cargo Fleet on the east side of Middlesbrough. Lieutenant J.L. Ogilvie, Royal Naval Reserve, saw her from his home in North Ormesby.

> I ran into the house for my sextant, and took the height which I made to be roughly 5500 feet. The airship was travelling fast... I made the course to be from West to East.[11]

Another witness, Reverend Kemm, was on duty as a special constable in Old Ormesby village.

> I saw the Zeppelin over Cargo Fleet, and also saw what I took to be the bombs being released… I then saw a large flash, and smoke, and heard the explosion, about 12.15.[12]

Half an hour after L 11 passed over Cargo Fleet the local Chief Constable, Henry Riches, interviewed Rachel Kirk and her mother at Prospect Place, which faced open ground looking towards the River Tees.

> Both women state that they were standing at the front door, being a little uneasy because all the Works were stopped and the lights extinguished, shortly after midnight when they heard a loud explosion in the direction of Port Clarence…
>
> At the same time a great noise attracted their attention… and they observed a long dark object very high in the sky coming from the direction of Port Clarence…
>
> Almost immediately afterwards two bombs were dropped on the vacant land immediately in front of their house – the concussion from the explosion forcing them up the stairs which is immediately opposite the front door.[13]

While Schütze's navigation had been excellent, L 11's bomb aiming was less impressive. Having passed over numerous industrial sites, Schütze claimed the bombs 'were dropped with good aim on two blast-furnace works', but damage was limited to The Crown Hotel on Works Road, which lost all its windows but sustained little other damage, and 93 workmen's homes and a shop, where similar minor damage occurred. Two men were injured. As the sound of L 11's engines disappeared into the darkness local people heard the faint sound of two more distant explosions.

From Cargo Fleet L 11 headed back to the coast to drop two final bombs on another favourite target, Skinningrove, home to a large iron works; Zeppelin commanders knew exactly where it was because German contractors had helped build the plant before the war. Even so, Schütze's aim was again poor. The two bombs faintly heard at Cargo

Fleet exploded in a field on Cattesty Farm about 250 yards from the iron works' slag heaps.[14] Schütze took L 11 out to sea at 12.30am.

In response to the raid the RNAS sent up four aircraft: a BE2c each from Redcar and Whitley Bay, and a Bristol Scout C and an Avro 504C from Scarborough. The RFC responded with three aircraft: two No.36 (Home Defence) Squadron BE2c from Cramlington and another of No.47 Squadron (temporarily assigned to Home Defence) sent up from Beverley. None of the pilots saw anything and the BE2c from Beverley and the Avro both crashed when landing.[15]

With Zeppelins L 11 and L 17 refitting and L 9 undergoing repairs, Strasser had four airships available on 2 April. Three hours after L 11 returned from the previous night's raid, L 13, L 14, L 16 and L 22 set out for a new rich target, the Firth of Forth in Scotland. There lay the Rosyth naval dockyard, the commercial docks at Leith, the city of Edinburgh and the tempting target of the Forth Bridge – but that required an accuracy of bomb aiming beyond which any Zeppelin could deliver. Shortly after departure Heinrich Mathy's L 13 returned to Hage after developing engine problems.

British ships out in the North Sea radioed back information that Zeppelins appeared to be heading towards northern Britain. At 10pm, before any had reached the coast, a naval force left Rosyth and pushed out into the North Sea hoping to intercept any returning Zeppelins but in this they were unsuccessful.[16]

## 2 April 1916, 11.30pm: Northumberland

Out over the western half of the North Sea unexpectedly strong northerly winds made the crews battle hard to hold their course for the Firth of Forth. Werner Peterson struggled in L 16. He realised he was off course and believed he crossed the coast south of the River Tyne, but he was actually about 20 miles north of it, coming inland at 11pm over Druridge Bay on the Northumberland coast.

Peterson's first command, Zeppelin L 7, had come close to destruction during an air raid on the Friedrichshafen Zeppelin works in November 1914.[17] In June 1915 he took command of L 12, which in August was destroyed by fire in Ostend harbour after earlier damage inflicted by the Dover anti-aircraft guns had forced her down in the sea.[18] Given command of L 16 in September 1915, Peterson had bombed Hertford the following month, East Anglia in January 1916 and Bury St Edmunds at the end of March.

Unsure of his position, the 28-year-old Zeppelin commander followed a southerly zig-zag course over Northumberland for half an hour searching for a suitable target. About 11.30pm what appeared to be a brightly lit angular structure came into view, which Peterson thought could be a blast furnace or factory so he released 23 bombs (12 HE and 11 incendiary). The lights, however, were flares burning at a RFC emergency landing ground at High West Houses just west of Ponteland. The bombs caused no damage of note. Peterson then retraced his route until a similar target came into view. At 11.50pm he released 11 more bombs (five HE and six incendiary); this time the lights were flares burning at Cramlington airfield, home to No.36 (Home Defence) Squadron from where two BE2c aircraft were searching for the Zeppelins. One of the wooden hangars suffered fire damage. Later one of the aeroplanes crashed when landing and caught fire, but the lucky pilot scrambled clear before his bombs exploded.

A local newspaper described how the raid stirred the people.

> The report of the exploding bombs were heard for many miles... and for a distance of fully 12 miles around the windows of houses were shaken. Crowds of people turned out and a good many went to the higher grounds commanding a view of the sea. From these points of vantage the flashes of the exploding bombs were plainly seen.[19]

Peterson took L 16 northwards over the darkened landscape. He reached Broomhill at 12.15am, about 15 miles from Cramlington, where lights betrayed another potential target but in fact there was nothing of consequence below. L 16's seven bombs all fell in fields at Hadston Farm and Togston Barns Farm.

> Close upon midnight heavy explosions and flashes of light were heard, and observed in the direction of Broomhill... About eight reports followed in quick succession near to Togston Hall... Beyond some large holes being torn in the fields, some breakage of glass, and fallen ceilings in the cottages at Togston Barns, no other damage has been reported.[20]

Five minutes later L 16 crossed the coast near the mouth of the River Amble and set course for Germany.

## 2 April 1916, 9pm: Berwickshire

The raid carried out by L 16 had little impact. The same was true of that made by L 22. This latest Zeppelin, commanded by Kapitänleutnant Martin Dietrich, had already carried out the devastating raid on Cleethorpes two nights earlier. Now heading for Scotland, L 22 reached the coast about three miles north of Berwick-upon-Tweed and Dietrich appears, initially at least, to have mistaken the Tweed for the River Tyne. Shortly after 9pm he dropped 11 bombs (six HE and five incendiary) on fields at Lamberton Farm from where, presumably, a light attracted his attention. A few miles away a couple heard what they thought was a 'sharp double knock' on their back door but soon realised it was the sound of exploding bombs.

> Next minute we were upstairs, and carried the children and blankets down to the ground floor, excited a bit, but sufficiently unflurried to resist the habit of lighting a match. One young hopeful, who has been carefully counting up all the aeroplanes he has seen in his short life, took it rather badly that he was not permitted to go out... and see the Zeppelin for himself.[21]

All remained quiet for ten minutes, 'then away to the west several bombs were dropped'.

From the farm L 22 headed inland and approached Chirnside, a village about nine miles north-west of Berwick, where it dropped five bombs (two HE and three incendiaries) – those 'away to the west'. Most fell in a field but one inflicted serious damage at the home of a retired gardener and his wife. The couple were sitting in a room on the ground floor when 'the chimney-stack and about a third of the gable-end and roof were carried away by the bomb'. Fortunately neither of them was hurt.[22]

A minute later and more bombs descended near the next village, Chirnside Bridge. Three HE and five incendiaries landed in fields, seven on East Blanerne Farm and a single incendiary at Lintlaw Farm.

The witness who heard the earlier explosions was in the Chirnside district the following day and took the opportunity to enquire about the bombs.

> Three [incendiaries] had fallen in a field, where they had set fire to a little grass... Other two had fallen into manure heaps,

and a little further along I came across one of these useful depositories. It was close to the hedge, and the manure had been churned up, flung over the hedge, and into the road. It was a pity that when the raider's crew went in for manure distribution they did not distribute it where it would have been of service – in the field.[23]

Dietrich had dropped 14 bombs in the largely rural Chirnside district, which is odd as he reported bombing a big factory in Newcastle. But Dietrich's navigation had been out when he first came inland and contemporary maps reveal a large paper mill at Chirnside Bridge, so it is possible that remote mill became a 'Newcastle factory' to Dietrich although no bombs fell within 600 yards of it. L 22 now turned back, reaching the coast at about 9.45pm where Dietrich released five bombs, probably to lighten his ship, before heading north towards the Firth of Forth.

At about 10.30pm, L 22 came inland again at North Berwick, following the southern shore of the Firth of Forth towards Edinburgh. North of Dirleton, Dietrich released a single incendiary bomb over Archerfield golf course to check his ground speed and any drifting. At 11.05pm, as she passed Gullane, a detachment the 4th (Extra Reserve) Battalion, Argyll & Sutherland Highlanders, part of the Forth Garrison, opened fire.[24] When they did finally reach Edinburgh the crew could see another Zeppelin below them already bombing the city. That other Zeppelin was Böcker's L 14.

## 2 April 1916, 11.30pm: Leith, Scotland

As an officer of the *Hamburg-Amerika* shipping line before the war, Böcker was familiar with the location of Leith docks and the city of Edinburgh. Approaching from the north shore of the Firth of Forth, L 14 passed over the village of Elie at 11.05pm from where a few lights visible about 20 miles to the south-west indicated the target. Böcker knew that the Forth Bridge and Rosyth dockyard lay a few miles beyond Leith.

Earlier, at 9.05pm, the local police received the 'TARA' warning, which resulted in the dimming of lights. Now, as L 14 drew closer, those dimmed lights became dark, but ships lying outside Leith Docks remained brightly illuminated until the first bomb dropped. From Böcker's vantage point, however, everything now became black and featureless and he was unable to locate the Rosyth dockyard. He settled instead on 'the docks and harbour works at Leith and Edinburgh'.[25] The first bomb dropped at Leith at about 11.30pm.[26]

That first bomb[27] sank a pair of rowing boats and smashed skylights on two Danish vessels in Edinburgh Dock. Two incendiaries dropped around Albert Dock but police and others dealt quickly with the small fires. The bombs were falling in quick succession now. One exploded on the roof of a grain warehouse in a narrow thoroughfare between Tower Street and Bernard Street, inflicting 'considerable damage', while another damaged a quay wall at the Inner Harbour and smashed windows all around. Of the two bombs that struck Commercial Street, one claimed the first victim of the raid. It exploded on a tenement block at No.2, smashing into a room at the top of the building where 66-year-old Robert Love lay asleep. He died instantly.

The other bomb in Commercial Street hit a tenement at No.14. On hearing the first explosions an elderly lady went to a window just as an incendiary bomb crashed through the roof, setting fire to some clothes in her kitchen before crashing down to the flat below. Fallen debris prevented the family escaping but the lady coolly gathered everyone in the parlour before returning to the kitchen and pouring water through the hole in the floor onto the burning bomb below. 'In this way', a newspaper concluded, 'she certainly saved the tenement, and probably the lives of several people.'[28]

L 14 continued in a straight line across Leith, parallel to a river, the Water of Leith, that flows into the docks. In Sandport Street three burning incendiaries fell, their descent indicted by a 'blueish ribbon of light'[29]: two fell either side of No.9 without damage while tenants dealt with one that landed on the roof of No.45. The next bomb, however, would bring a tear to the eye of many a Scotsman. It exploded in a bonded warehouse starting a huge uncontrollable fire. The warehouse on Ronaldson's Wharf was packed with bottles of Uam Var Famous Scotch Whisky and in no time the intoxicating smell of burning spirits filled the air. The warehouse had no insurance against aerial bombardment leaving the shocked owners to estimate their losses at £44,000.[30] About 130 yards further on an incendiary smashed through the roof of 15 Church Street, setting fire to the home of a soldier's wife and her three children, before crashing through the floor to a flat below occupied by a couple and their five children. Although the fire did 'a good deal of damage', all eleven escaped unharmed.

L 14 dropped four incendiaries around Mill Lane but the three that fell outside Leith Hospital, in the playground of St. Thomas' school and at a shipyard on Great Junction Street burnt out without causing any damage. The fourth, however, fell on the roof of St Thomas' church manse causing a raging fire. The Reverend Fleming, his wife and their maid had just descended the stairs before flames engulfed the staircase. The police described their escape as 'miraculous'.

The last four bombs on Leith fell in pairs. Near Bonnington Road one landed in a garden doing little damage but the second exploded in an enclosed court about 50 yards away shattering windows and smashing doors. At 200 Bonnington Road, Robert Robb, a warehouseman, was asleep as was his wife and child when the bombs exploded. A 'tremendous crash' woke him and 'the house shook, the windows were broken in, and articles of furniture moved and creaked'. Robb and his wife quickly got dressed intending to find a place of safety but it was too late.

> My wife took the child [one-year-old David] out of the crib, and shortly thereafter made the terrible discovery that it was dead. On examining it we found a piece of a bomb had struck it on the left shoulder and had in all probability penetrated the heart.[31]

The inquest revealed that a bomb fragment had passed through the window 16 feet above the ground then penetrated the cot's one-inch thick wooden headboard and two bedcovers before killing little David as he lay asleep.

The final two bombs both hit the Bonnington Tannery. One struck a section of railway track but failed to detonate; the other smashed through the roof of the tannery into a 'leather manufacturing tank'.

John Macleod, the Chief Constable of Leith, happily reported: 'There were a great number of premises rendered insecure through the breaking of glass in windows, doors, etc... and although goods in many cases were exposed not one case of pilfering has been reported to the Police.' But he expressed his concern that 'thousands' were out in the streets looking for the Zeppelin, where they were at greatest risk of injury.

## 2 April 1916, 11.50pm: Edinburgh, Scotland

The distinction between Leith and Edinburgh would have been indiscernible from the command gondola of L 14, but on a southerly course Böcker's next bombs fell on the Scottish capital. That first bomb exploded on vacant land in Bellevue Terrace where the damage caused was not serious, mainly consisting of broken windows in houses, shops, a school, a church and a printing works there and in several adjoining streets. No one, however, suffered any injury. Keeping to the same course the next bomb, an incendiary, dropped on The Mound, a raised road running along the front of the National Gallery of Scotland and overlooking Princes Street Gardens, where it burnt out. The next, however, claimed the first victim in the city.

The bomb struck the roof of 39 Lauriston Place, in a short terrace of three-storey Georgian houses. It was home to a GP, Doctor John McLaren, his wife, their children, John, Evelyn and Alastair, and two maids. Earlier that evening, when the authorities dimmed the electric lighting, the two boys were reading in bed on the top floor of the building. When his elder brother cheerfully announced, 'Oh, that means there's going to be an air raid!' nine-year-old Alastair was unsettled and his parents let the boys move to a bedroom on the floor below. Evelyn remained on the top floor in her room, the same floor as the maids. While the children slept, their parents were awake, as Alastair explained.

> My father and mother had heard the noise of the Zeppelin engines and had gone up to our top floor bedroom overlooking Lauriston Place and the Castle, and, kneeling at the open window, were calmly watching the Zeppelin overhead when the bomb struck.[32]

It exploded on contact with the roof, sending an avalanche of rubble cascading down the outside of the house to inflict significant damage to the front steps. It also created chaos inside, causing extensive damage throughout the house, particularly to the roof, top landing and staircase, and also blowing out all the windows. The nose cap of the bomb travelled down through the house, only stopped by the stone floor in the kitchen pantry.

Dr McLaren and his wife were untouched by the plaster and rubble that had buried the bed in which the boys should have been sleeping, and were relieved when they found everyone in the house was alive. The maids had dived under their beds, which was a wise move as their door had blasted into the room, but Evelyn was pinned in her bed by a wardrobe. Eventually firemen arrived and brought everyone out, including the family's dog and canary. It was six months before repairs to the house were complete and the family able to return, but with great foresight Dr McLaren had taken out air raid insurance and eventually received payment towards the cost of repairs.

The bomb also damaged the building next door, a special school for children suffering from the fungal infection Ringworm, and smashed many windows in the area. There was a human casualty too. David Robertson, a 27-year-old discharged soldier, was 80 yards from the bomb when struck in the abdomen by a metal fragment as he walked along Lauriston Place. Although quickly taken the short distance to the Royal Infirmary, he later died there of his injuries.

About 150 yards further on a bomb exploded in the grounds of George Watson's College, smashing windows there, at the Royal Infirmary and in Chalmers Street. Archibald Campbell, a 13-year-old student at the College, eagerly went to inspect the damage in the morning. As any schoolboy would Archibald 'mucked about [in] bomb-hole in playground'. After enduring Latin until noon, he returned to the crater and peered through the shattered windows of the damaged part of the school. The first schoolroom he looked into was 'absolutely smashed'.

> Desks, window-frames, broken glass, stones, and piles of plaster, all smashed up filled the room. Other front rooms about as bad... hall an inch deep in fallen plaster and broken glass. Walls all holed by bits of bomb. Picked up two bits of bomb and gave one to [my friend] Main.[33]

At the Royal Infirmary the explosion shattered windows in three wards, damaged side rooms and an operating theatre.[34] An incendiary landed in The Meadows, a public park, after which Böcker changed direction from south to east, with his next bomb, timed at 11.55pm, hitting a tenement at 82 Marchmont Crescent. Although exploding on the roof, a large portion battered its way at an angle through the building to come to rest on the ground floor of No.80. No one in either building was hurt.[35] About a thousand yards further and the next bomb hit a tenement building at 183 Causewayside leaving it 'in a dangerous condition' and injuring six of those inside. Two incendiaries that fell in gardens in Hatton Place and 28 Blacket Place burnt out harmlessly.

After L 14 had turned eastwards it flew a zig-zag course as it headed towards the popular landmark of Arthur's Seat in King's Park, an extinct ancient volcano providing stunning views across the city.[36] But from there L 14 came under machine gun fire. Although Edinburgh had no anti-aircraft guns, when word of the approaching Zeppelin was received, Lieutenant T.C. Noel of the 3rd (Reserve) Battalion, King's Own Scottish Borderers, was despatched with two machine guns to offer some opposition. Noel took up a position at Arthur's Seat and opened fire twice, the first time may have been why L 14 now turned about and headed back towards the centre of the city.

Böcker dropped an incendiary that burnt out on the roof of the Royal Infirmary's boiler house, where staff were now dealing with the casualties caused by bombs dropped on the first pass over the city. L 14 headed towards Edinburgh Castle from where about 40 rifle-armed soldiers of the 4th (Extra Reserve) Battalion, Argyll & Sutherland Highlanders opened an ineffective fire. Although three bombs dropped in quick succession, none hit this iconic symbol of the city. The first exploded a little to the south on the pavement outside the White Hart Hotel in Grassmarket, digging a crater six feet deep. It inflicted 'considerable damage' to the hotel and injuries to four people. Struck in the chest by a fragment of the bomb, William Breakey, a 45-year-old carter who lived in Grassmarket, later died in the Royal Infirmary. The sound of crashing glass filled the air as the second bomb of this trio landed just under 400 yards further on, exploding on Castle Rock, close to the south-west perimeter of the fortification's walls. A hail of stone and rock hurled down by the explosion smashed windows in Castle Terrace, Grindlay Street and Spittal Street directly below. The third bomb fell about 250 yards to the west of the Castle, striking the County Hotel at 21 Lothian Road, opposite Princes Street Station. The explosion destroyed the roof and damaged 18 of the rooms, while Houston's Hotel next door also lost its roof, a gable wall and had three rooms smashed. Surprisingly, only one person – Isabella Ross – was slightly injured.

Continuing on a westwards course, L 14 dropped no more bombs for a mile until it reached the valley of the Water of Leith where she turned over a large building set in its own grounds – Donaldson's Hospital School for Deaf Children. Three bombs dropped as it turned. The first exploded opposite Coltbridge Gardens, the second near Mill Lade and the third close to the school. There were no casualties but the blast shattered a great number of windows in five streets and at the school. Having completed the turn, L 14 headed back to the centre of the city for a third time, passing close to the Royal Infirmary again but Böcker travelled beyond it before he resumed bombing.

All over the city countless people were peering up at the sky hoping for a sight of the Zeppelin while listening to the shocking boom of the explosions. Many crowded into doorways hoping to gain some protection while still having a clear view. Unfortunately it did not work out for those at the entrance to a tenement block at 16 Marshall Street because at about 12.20am Böcker's next bomb exploded on the pavement right in front of them. The powerful explosion ripped through the entrance wrecking homes on the first floor. Six people died instantly, five of them at the entrance, where the force blasted them back against the stairs and buried them beneath falling rubble: David Thomas Graham, aged five, hotel waiter Victor McFarlane, Henry George Rumble (17), tinsmith John Smith (41) and waiter William Smith aged 15. The sixth victim, 23-year-old hairdresser William Ewing, lived at No.33 but was in the street at the time.

The explosion injured seven others in the entrance and five more in Marshall Street. Amongst them was Thomas Donoghue, a soldier of the 3/4th Battalion, Royal Scots, who was visiting his widowed mother at 27 Marshall Street while on leave. When they heard the sound of exploding bombs he went out to 'bring a neighbour woman to keep his mother company'. He then went out a second time to check on another neighbour. That was when the bomb exploded. Rescuers found him in the street under a heavy door with severe injuries to his abdomen and others to his head and right leg. He died in the Royal Infirmary eight days later.[37]

Even before the rubble and shattered glass settled in Marshall Street, the next bomb exploded in Haddon Court on Nicolson Street, where it smashed numerous windows and the premises of spirit merchants D & J McCallum, inflicting damage estimated at £3000.[38] Three people suffered injuries; one of them, 63-year-old Helen Brown, actually lived at 16 Marshall Street and missed the horror there only to be injured by the next bomb. Another of those hurt, 74-year-old James Farquhar, went to the Royal Infirmary where, despite his injuries not appearing to be life threatening, he died from shock after an operation on his right knee.[39]

Böcker now appeared to be heading back towards Arthur's Seat, where Lieutenant Noel and his machine guns waited. But before he reached the park another bomb smashed into a tenement building at 69 St Leonard's Hill. It caused serious damage and on the top floor falling rubble killed four-year-old Cora Bell and injured her mother Isabella and younger sister Alice.[40] These were the last casualties of the raid. Over the southern edge of King's Park, L 14 dropped three more bombs at which point it seems likely that Lieutenant Noel's machine guns opened fire for the second time. Their bullets had no effect while the bombs did little. One managed to damage the roof of a store built adjacent to the park and smash 341 panes of glass, but the other two achieved nothing as L 14 passed about 500 yards south of the machine guns. A final bomb, an incendiary, landed in the grounds of Prestonfield House, about 900 yards from Arthur's Seat, but burnt out without causing damage. The time was now about 12.25am.

While L 14 had passed over the centre of the city three times largely unmolested, L 22, the other Zeppelin that had reached Edinburgh, kept to the south of the city to avoid interfering with L 14. About 12.10am, L 22 began to head eastwards while L 14 continued dropping bombs on Edinburgh. It would seem that the German authorities had good information about military camps in the area because although the British reports suggest the three bombs dropped by L 22 fell in unimportant rural areas, two actually fell in the general vicinity of army camps. The first bomb, however, which fell in a field at Kingsknowle Farm south-west of Slateford, dropped when L 22 came under fire at 12.22am from a detachment of the 3rd (Reserve) Battalion, Highland Light Infantry, positioned about a mile away at Juniper Green. They fired 130 rounds from their machine guns as L 22 climbed and headed away towards the south-east. As she passed between Redford Barracks and Dreghorn Camp a single bomb fell but landed almost a mile beyond them. L 22 was now a little ahead of L 14, which was approaching King's Park for the second time, when her final bomb dropped. This exploded in a field belonging to the Cameron Park Dairy but it seems possible Böcker was looking for Duddingston Camp about a thousand yards to the north. Dietrich crossed the coast at Portobello at about 12.40am and followed the Firth of Forth back out to the North Sea and home. Böcker, having dropped his last bombs, headed eastwards before crossing the coast at Cockburnspath at about 1am.

No British aircraft troubled any Zeppelins that night. Reports of air activity are vague but one, maybe two, aircraft took off from the RNAS station at East Fortune, midway between Edinburgh and Cockburnspath. There was no Zeppelin sighting and one, an Avro 504C flown by Flight sub-Lieutenant G.A. Cox, crashed on landing. It also appears that two Wight seaplanes ascended from Dundee but they failed to spot either Zeppelin, which both returned safely to Germany.

But this was not the only Zeppelin activity that night. While Navy Zeppelins had made their first venture into Scotland, over 300 miles to the south, Army Zeppelins carried out their first raid of 1916, hoping to strike London.

Chapter 9

# 'Such a rain of destruction... so little harm'

The Army Zeppelins' role in the campaign against Britain had been very much a subsidiary one to that of their counterparts in the Navy. While Navy airships had conducted a regular campaign in sync with the cycle of the new moon, the Army demonstrated less enthusiasm for raiding Britain, focusing more on a role supporting the troops at the Front. It was only on the night of 31 March/1 April, the same night that the Naval Airship Division lost L 15, that Army Zeppelins attempted their first raid of 1916.

Three Zeppelins set out to attack London but things did not go according to plan; LZ 81 and LZ 88 both aborted before reaching the British coast.[1] The third raider, LZ 90, commanded by Oberleutnant-zur-See der Reserve Ernst Lehmann, did make it inland but even then her movements puzzled those tracking her. After crossing the Suffolk coast near Alderton, LZ 90 first headed north, then south and was reported circling over Ipswich at 1.19am. The report noted: 'The purpose of this journey is difficult to fathom.' They were unaware that LZ 90's engines were causing concern, as Lehmann explained.

> With only two motors functioning I could not take the LZ 90 over London, so while mechanics worked to make repairs we kept the ship hovering over a line between Colchester and Ipswich... we kept the LZ 90 at about 8,000 feet with only two engines running, and I suppose this made very little noise... because of that we were unmolested. I could not find a landmark or a light, so thoroughly had the British darkened the countryside.

117

When after some two hours the chief engineer reported that
he could not fix one of the motors... I turned homeward.
Thereupon a battery commenced firing at the ship.[2]

The 'battery' was in fact a mobile 1-pdr 'pom-pom' of the RNAAS
Eastern Mobile Brigade on the outskirts of Ipswich, which opened fire
twice between 1.30 and 1.40am.[3]

Engines had long been a problem for LZ 90. Although accepted by
the Army at the beginning of January 1916, Lehmann noted that it was
two months and a change of engines before any level of efficiency was
attained.

The manufacturer, under the urgent demand, had been
compelled by the authorities to release the motors prematurely.
In the vernacular, he had not taken out the 'bugs'. We had to
do it ourselves.[4]

The engine problems he experienced over Suffolk were clearly nothing
new for Lehmann.

## 2 April 1916, 11.57pm: Waltham Abbey, Essex

On the night of 2/3 April, while Navy Zeppelins headed for Scotland, the
Army made another attempt on London with the same three airships:
LZ 81, LZ 88 and LZ 90. The first of these turned back early but both LZ 88
and LZ 90 reached England although neither threatened the primary target.

Lehmann brought LZ 90 overland at the mouth of the River
Blackwater in Essex at about 10.40pm and as he headed inland her
commander reflected on the experience.

The night was very dark... I tell you that one experiences a
peculiar sensation riding high through the sky over enemy
land, knowing that every human being down there on earth
has scanned the heavens before going to bed, hoping that it
will be no fit weather for Zeppelins.

Peering from the window nearest me, I could see few clouds
and little haze. But straight ahead and quite close to the
surface the mist was thicker and I knew it would be difficult
to locate us with searchlights.[5]

That mist, however, was to hinder Lehmann's navigation that night. When he began to drop his bombs he admitted that he could not see the ground below but released them 'where the docks and eastern part of the city must have been'. Lehmann would have been extremely disappointed if he had known exactly where his bombs had fallen.

After passing south of Chelmsford, the sudden appearance of LZ 90 stung an 18-pdr of the Kirkcudbrightshire Territorial Artillery into optimistic action. They fired two rounds, causing the Zeppelin to take evasive action. A few miles on, a 1-pdr 'pom-pom' at Kelvedon Hatch fired 75 rounds at the sound of her engines and, although LZ 90 was unharmed, she deflected from her south-west course towards London and was now heading west towards the towns of Waltham Abbey and Enfield where there were important munitions factories. At 11.50pm, as LZ 90 passed Epping, a searchlight at Chingford pierced the clouds and found her. Other lights then picked her up and soon the Waltham Abbey area anti-aircraft guns opened fire, from Enfield Lock, Farm Hill, Monkhams Hill, Cheshunt, Hayes Hill Farm and Grange Hill. Between them they fired 159 rounds. 'We neared a cluster of searchlights,' Lehmann recalled, 'and a nest of batteries, which were firing with particular fury, and then we prepared to drop our bombs.' This sudden intensity of fire convinced him that they were over London and in particular over the docks of east London whereas he had just passed over Epping Forest, flying at a height of 8,000 to 8,500 feet. At 11.57pm, rather than the London docks, LZ 90's first bombs fell on Woodredon Farm, two and a half miles east of Waltham Abbey.

> Although many bombs were dropped in a few minutes, the only loss of life was that occasioned by the killing of four chickens in a fowl house at the rear of a cottage. Although it is now surrounded by bomb craters, the house was not hit. Every window in the building was shattered, and an unexploded bomb lies buried in the lawn a few feet from the front door… An eyewitness said the occupants of the Zeppelin appeared as if they had suddenly gone mad, and dropped bombs as if they were turning them out of a tip-cart.[6]

Lehmann's bombs fell in a straight line as he headed towards Waltham Abbey, passing close to Upshire Hall. The police later accounted for 90 bombs (25 HE and 65 incendiary), the majority found buried in farmers' fields.

Having released the last of his bombs and facing heavy anti-aircraft fire, Lehmann turned away and climbed to 12,000 feet, not realising that just over half a mile ahead lay the hugely important Waltham Abbey Gunpowder Mills. The searchlights and guns had done their job. LZ 90 passed out to sea near Clacton at about 1am. The RFC had attempted to intercept her with No.19 RAS sending up seven BE2c aircraft from airfields around London: two from Hainault Farm, two from Sutton's Farm, two from Hounslow and one from Croydon. Only one pilot claimed a sighting but was unable to catch her and at least three were damaged when landing.

## 3 April 1916, 12.45am: Ramsholt, Suffolk

The other Army Zeppelin to come inland was Hauptmann Falck's LZ 88, but its impact was no greater than LZ 90's. Pushed off course by the wind, Falck crossed the Suffolk coast near Orfordness at about 11.30pm. He abandoned London and selected Harwich, an important Royal Navy port, as his secondary target.[7] Progress, however, was slow and it was an hour before LZ 88 reached Rushmere Heath on the eastern outskirts of Ipswich, a distance of only 16 miles. There two mobile Maxim guns of the RNAAS and a Lewis gun of the 58th (2/1st London) Division opened fire. Falck followed an anti-clockwise course around Ipswich until he reached the River Orwell, which joined the Stour at Harwich. But close to the river at Levington Green two more mobile Maxim guns of the RNAAS opened fire at 12.45am as Falck crossed over the Orwell heading east. About four miles on LZ 88 crossed another river, the Debden, and moments later rained 73 bombs (10 HE and 63 incendiaries) on the marshy fields between the peaceful villages of Ramsholt and Anderton where they smashed windows at Peyton Hall Farm. It is difficult to reconcile what Falck believed he was bombing, but it may be that the close proximity of three rivers, the Stour, Orwell and Debden, confused him. If when he crossed the Debden and dropped his bombs he thought it was the Orwell, he may have believed he was close to Felixstowe. At 1.16am a final HE bomb dropped at Hollesley before LZ 88 went back out to sea.

After two raids in three days the Army Zeppelins did not undertake any more attacks in this current moon cycle. Strasser, however, planned three more raids on consecutive nights for the Navy Zeppelins. First up, on 3 April, were L 11 and L 17.

# 4 April 1916, 1.40am: Norfolk

Setting out from the Zeppelin base at Nordholz, L 11 and L 17 headed for London but strong winds over the North Sea and a 'considerable mist' enveloping the east coast of Britain prevented this. Herbert Ehrlich was off the Norfolk coast in L 17 at 9.30pm but, unable to make further progress against the wind, he aborted the mission. Viktor Schütze, commanding L 11, persevered and at 1.30am observers heard engines about two miles off the north Norfolk coast. With London no longer possible, Schütze decided he would try for Norwich but the poor visibility prevented even this.

L 11 came inland near Sheringham at about 1.40am with Schütze dropping his first bomb near the village of Hanworth, about 300 yards from Hanworth Hall[8] before continuing towards Norwich, but a number of directional changes indicated that navigation was a problem. About 2.30am he reached the twin villages of Buxton and Lamas on the River Bure about nine miles north of Norwich. There Schütze dropped two incendiary bombs in fields near a farm. Fifteen minutes later L 11 was six miles north-east of Norwich and dropped another incendiary near the village of Salhouse, 200 yards from the nearest dwelling.[9] Unable to find Norwich, Schütze abandoned the fruitless search and returned to the coast, passing out over Caister at 3.05am. Ten minutes later he lightened his ship by dropping nine bombs at sea.

The misty conditions along the coast prevented any of the Norfolk based RNAS pilots getting airborne until Edward Pulling took off from Covehithe at 3.25am, but he saw nothing. Elsewhere Captain Arthur Thomson, a RFC pilot of No.15 RAS based at Doncaster, took off at 11pm when reports announced Zeppelins approaching the coast. No Zeppelins reached his area but when the weather deteriorated, he became lost and with fuel running low he tried to land. Unfortunately his altimeter gave an incorrect reading and he flew into a hillside near Tealby, east of Market Rasen. With great good fortune Thomson walked away from the wreckage with only minor injuries.

While L 11 and L 17 began their refits on 4 April, Strasser ordered out L 13 and L 16 from Hage as well as L 14 and L 22 from Nordholz on the next raid. Bad weather over the North Sea, however, prompted a recall and while the two Hage airships returned safely, it proved something of a problem for L 14 and L 22 as they found their Nordholz base enshrouded in fog. Orders directed L 14 to a vacant Army airship shed at Düren about 230 miles away; she returned to Nordholz on 6 April. L 22 had even further to go to find sanctuary. First directed to Hanover, a distance of about 105 miles, when she arrived fierce thunderstorms prevented a landing so she went on to Dresden, another 195 miles, where she was finally able to find shelter before returning to Nordholz.

With no let up, Strasser ordered the next raid for 5 April. With L 14 and L 22 not yet back at Nordholz he had only three Zeppelins available: L 11, L 13 and L 16.[10] Not long into the mission, Heinrich Mathy, commanding L 13, had to abort again due to engine problems. 'Once again we had to turn back...,' Pitt Klein bemoaned, 'We were having a run of bad luck... All the cursing and swearing was to no avail against a higher force.'[11]

The remaining raiders, L 11 and L 16, with the latter about an hour ahead, approached the Yorkshire coast. With land in sight at 8.15pm, L 16 turned north and, battling against strong winds, headed up the coast for about 80 miles. She only came inland at 11.30pm.[12] By then L 11 had made for the tempting target of Hull where this time her commander had a fright.

## 5 April 1916, 9.17pm: Hull, Yorkshire

Viktor Schütze brought L 11 inland at Hornsea at 9.10pm and took a direct course towards Hull. A month earlier he had made an unopposed attack on the city and this time, choosing to approach at only 4,500 feet, it would appear he anticipated another easy night. Hull's defences, however, had improved since that raid in March and at 9.17pm searchlights at Sutton, Marfleet and Cottingham all held L 11, followed by the beginning of an anti-aircraft barrage from new gun positions in and around the city. Schütze released a single HE bomb over agricultural land at Sutton as he headed south and dropped three more three minutes later. These fell on the eastern edge of the city at East Park, within 300 yards of a searchlight, as L 11 began to climb quickly while turning away from Hull. The bombs smashed windows in Holderness Road and side streets leading from it. The day before, not far away in Barnsley Street, shock caused by a false air raid alarm had caused the death of a two-month old baby, Jessie Matthews. During the raid at least one anti-aircraft shell fell on the city causing the night's only casualties of the raid when it damaged a house at 27 Park Avenue, injuring four of those inside. The guns had done their job, as Colonel H.R. Adair, commanding the Humber Garrison artillery, observed.

The result of the fire was that it was quickly driven off: its behaviour was erratic apparently being taken by surprise, and hardly knowing which way to turn to get out of range of both guns and lights. It finally rose to an estimated height of 10,000 feet and made off in the direction E.N.E.[13]

Schütze took L 11 back across the coast at 9.50pm but, as with his raid on Sunderland a few days earlier, he did not turn for home. Instead Schütze planned to wait for the waxing crescent moon to set and then try again, however, one of his engines broke down and while the crew worked feverishly to make repairs he headed north against the wind, determined to drop his bombs. But four and a half hours later a second engine failed. Other commanders might have given up at this point but not Schütze. He recognised he was close to another favourite target, the Skinningrove Ironworks. A report by the Army's Northern Command states that L 11 circled over Skinningrove three times at about 2.30am. Although there was a 6-inch anti-aircraft gun there it had no accompanying searchlight and the gun crew were unable to locate the target. L 11 dropped 23 bombs (nine HE and 14 incendiaries) over Skinningrove, but six of the latter failed to ignite. Although Schütze claimed they wrecked the ironworks he was wrong. Bombs did smash a laboratory but the rest of the industrial site escaped harm. However, at the village of Carlin How, where many of the ironworkers lived, bombs damaged a school, a Co-operative Society shop and several homes. Estimates put the value of the damage at the ironworks and village at £5,000. Finally satisfied, Schütze took L 11 along the coast to Runswick Bay and headed out to sea at 2.50am.

## 6 April 1916, 12.03am: Evenwood, County Durham

In between the raids by L 11 on Hull and Skinningrove, Werner Peterson, having pushed up the coast in L 16, had made his own attack. He believed he brought L 16 inland north of Scarborough from where, heading south-west, he had dropped his bombs on an industrial area between Leeds and York. He was, however, 50 miles further north than he realised. L 16 came inland just north of Hartlepool at 11.30pm and his south-west course took him across County Durham. Having passed Bishop Auckland he approached Evenwood at about midnight from where Peterson noticed burning below – 'fiery waste-heaps' glowing at Railey Fell Colliery and at Randolph Colliery. In a report, Major E. Barraclough of the Tees and Hartlepool Garrison, explained that the Railey Fell Colliery had no telephone and a verbal warning to shield the fires arrived too late. The first bombs fell at 12.03am.[14]

With the Railey Hill Colliery on its port side, L 16 commenced dropping bombs as it passed over Low Gordon and Evenwood railway station. The sixth of these exploded in Gordon Lane where it caused significant damage to the end of a terrace of houses and injured two people. From there L 16 crossed over a railway line and dropped three more bombs between there and Oaks Bank, including the first incendiary bomb. One of the bombs exploded near Ranshaw School, wrecking a new house where a man and his wife had a narrow escape.

> They had no means of escape except by a shattered window, and, calling for help, they were immediately rescued. In the next bedroom were the son and a visitor, who were precipitated into the basement kitchen and buried in the debris. The visitor was easily extricated, but it took an hour to rescue the lad.[15]

At Evenwood's Randolph Colliery another brightly glowing 'fiery waste-heap' attracted L 16. Peterson ordered the release of eight incendiary bombs but the heaps were a distance from the colliery and the mine was never in danger. Two bombs exploded in fields north of the mine complex and two more detonated on open ground near the village of Evenwood Gate. L 16 had now dropped 23 bombs, (13 HE and 10 incendiary) seriously damaging 15 miners' homes and inflicting lesser damage, such as broken windows, on 70 to 80 others, but although passing close to two collieries no industrial property was harmed. With only two people injured, the area had escaped lightly and it fell to the local vicar, the Reverend G.J. Collis, to summarise the community's experience.

> It is true that they did a certain amount of material damage but not much considering the immense power of the explosives used. One would hardly think it possible that such a rain of destruction could do so little harm. Great gaping holes in the land, broken windows, roofs partially unslated, doors and in some cases furniture damaged was really a small price to pay as the result of such a visitation... But the prevailing feeling is one of thankfulness.[16]

L 16 had been heading on a south-east course but Peterson now turned north-east and at 12.20am he reached Coronation, one of many small mining villages in the Dene Valley, about a quarter of a mile south-west of Auckland Park Colliery. The first bomb of this second attack fell close to the Eldon Lane School at Coronation, exploding just outside the boundary wall. From there L 16 passed over the Auckland Park Colliery and an area packed with coke ovens, but Peterson only resumed bombing when clear of the industrial area. At the village of Close House, Peterson dropped two bombs over Gibson Street. One failed to detonate but the other smashed into No.12, demolishing it and severely damaging those on either side. Helpers gathered to rescue a five-year-old boy buried in the wreckage.

The bomb in Gibson Street also damaged the Post Office, Friends' Meeting House and Co-operative Society shop. Seconds later a bomb damaged Nos.50 and 52 Close House, then another narrowly missed Nos.76 and 78 in the same street, digging a great crater behind them.[17] Just before he reached Eldon, Peterson ordered the release of 10 incendiary bombs. These all fell around Hall's Row, a small terrace of miner's dwellings. Nine of them landed in fields and gardens but one struck No.21, home to the Moyle family.

William Moyle had worked at Eldon Colliery but was now serving in the army. His wife, Hannah, was at home with their two boys, Robert (nine) and his seven-year-old brother. The incendiary bomb smashed a square-shaped hole in the roof and struck Robert as he lay asleep in bed. In the next bedroom, falling debris struck his younger brother fracturing both his legs. His mother escaped unharmed and rescuers brought out the youngest son, but for Robert there was no happy ending, as was revealed at the inquest: 'Another witness stated that he made three attempts to get into the bedroom, but he was overcome by fumes, although he crept on the floor and tried to drag the bed to the door.'[18] Robert's body was 'burned almost to cinders' leading the Coroner to describe the attack as a case of 'devilish barbarism'.[19]

After bombing Hall's Row, Peterson saw more glowing fires – waste heaps at Eldon Colliery. They appeared a significant target and L 16 released 11 HE bombs. The first three landed on a football pitch. In the end house of Office Row, another terrace of miners' homes, eight-year-old Doris Hall woke to the sound of bombs some way off. She got up and peeked through the wooden slats of a venetian blind. She saw 'flickering lights' off to the left – the incendiaries at Hall's Row – before the bombs exploded on the football field. The window glass shattered and a cloud of coal dust filled the room, but the wooden blind preserved Doris from injury.[20]

Six bombs fell amongst the burning waste heaps at Eldon Colliery but again these were at a safe distance from the mine complex. The last two bombs straddled a locomotive shed between the colliery and a brickworks; no bombs had struck any mine buildings. Peterson took L 16 back to the coast and at 12.45am she went out to sea at the same spot as she came inland 75 minutes earlier.

Five aircraft went up to intercept L 11 and L 16. Although the sky was generally clear, fog hung about the RNAS stations on the north-east coast. One RNAS aircraft from Scarborough and two RFC pilots from Cramlington and Beverley saw nothing of the raiders but there was a tragic end for one. Returning to No.36 (Home Defence) Squadron airfield at Cramlington, Captain John Nicol, smashed into a house as he came in to land; his bombs exploded and killed him.

A damage report covering this second part of L 16's raid listed 27 bombs (17 HE and 10 incendiary), which demolished two homes, seriously damaged 11, caused minor damage to 28 more and 18 shops. One child died and there were injuries to a woman and two children.[21] But Peterson had missed four collieries even though passing over or close to them. It was, of course, not the story he told when he got back to Germany. A German press release concluded: 'Furthermore factories at Leeds and environs and a number of railway stations in the industrial district were attacked. Very good results were observed.'[22]

The evening of 6 April brought a change of weather over northern Germany, heralding strong gales from the east, which ended this intense period of raiding. In fact, it proved to be the most concentrated period of Zeppelin activity throughout the war. Between 31 March and 5 April German airships set out on six consecutive days; only on one occasion did bad weather force them to abort. The statistics compiled in Britain state that those raids inflicted material damage to the value of £126,095[23] with 84 people killed and 227 injured. In addition two RFC pilots died in landing accidents. Germany lost one Zeppelin (L 15) with 17 officers and men captured and one man drowned. Although many amongst the Zeppelin crews assumed this pattern of raiding would continue whenever weather permitted, it was not to be. Oberleutnant-zur-See Werner Dietsch, the executive officer (second-in-command) on L 17 during this period, wrote after the war: 'The heady days of 1916, when we would carry out three raids in five days... would never be seen again.'[24]

In Britain the military took stock and expressed a general satisfaction with the gradual improvements in Home Defence evidenced by the guns and lighting arrangements.

> The impunity with which the airships had hitherto generally passed over their objectives, with the possible exceptions of Dover and London, evidently received a rude shock during this week… It may be concluded that the commanders of these airships after 31st March more than once declined to face the risks attendant on the full achievements of their plan… there was also the question as to how far the reduction of lights had achieved its end… The aimless behaviour of other airships during the week under review proves that airship navigation was becoming much more difficult.[25]

The report concluded that the, 'inherent fragility and weakness in face of the increasing powers of our means of defence bid fair to impose a check upon [the Zeppelins'] offensive ability'. In Germany, however, contrary to British observations there was no diminishing in the determination to continue taking the war over the North Sea to Britain.

The next time German airships appeared it formed part of a wider strategy and of necessity took place a little earlier in the moon cycle than usual. In Ireland, Republicans planned a rising against British rule over the Easter weekend and had long sought German support. Now Germany sent 20,000 rifles, ammunition and 10 machine guns. Germany also planned an airship raid on London by naval Zeppelins and hoped to create further confusion by sending out the High Seas Fleet to bombard Lowestoft and Great Yarmouth, hoping to draw out British ships, which they could pick off. HMS *Bluebell* intercepted the arms shipment before it could land and although the rising went ahead in Dublin on Easter Monday, 24 April, British troops crushed it five days later.

Eight Zeppelins prepared for the attack on Britain, while three older vessels, L 6, L 7 and L 9, supported the Fleet. The ships departed late on the morning of Easter Monday, followed in the afternoon by the raiding Zeppelins but both L 14 and L 20 experienced problems and turned back. The other six, L 11, L 13, L 16, L 17, L 21 and L 23, all encountered strong south-west winds that prevented them pushing on to London, leaving them to search for targets of opportunity in a blacked-out landscape, further hampered by heavy banks of cloud, fog and rain. It was another less than successful night for the raiders.

Five of the six appeared over Norfolk and Suffolk with just one, L 17, coming inland over Lincolnshire. Her commander, Herbert Ehrlich, never penetrated more than seven miles. Having crossed the coast at Chapel St Leonards he reached Anderby at about 1.20am where he released a single incendiary bomb in a field, followed ten minutes later by three HE bombs near Alford that smashed a single pane of glass. Struggling to find targets, Ehrlich aborted the raid, turned back to the coast and set course for home.

A few days earlier Kapitänleutnant der Reserve Eduard Prölss and his crew took over L 13 from Heinrich Mathy who was awaiting delivery of a new class of Zeppelin. Prölss had recently commanded L 9. In this, his first raid in L 13, things did not go well, as had often been the case for Mathy's men, a fact unlikely to be lost on any triskaidekaphobic (extreme superstition regarding the number thirteen) members of the new crew. Coming inland near Cromer at about 10.20pm, L 13 wandered over north Norfolk until a 3-pdr mobile anti-aircraft gun at Bacton opened fire resulting in shell splinters splattering the command gondola. They failed to inflict any damage but, having been overland for no more than an hour, L 13 headed back out to sea without dropping any bombs.

## 25 April 1916, 12.30am: Newmarket, Suffolk

Another of the raiders, L 16, came inland five minutes ahead of L 13 and headed south, passing to the west of Norwich and towards Cambridge. When he passed over the famous horse racing town of Newmarket, Werner Peterson circled back to investigate and at 12.30am came under fire from two mobile machine guns at Newmarket Heath. Stung into action, Peterson released 18 HE bombs. These fell in a line across the town from south-west to north-east, from Newmarket Heath to Warren Hill Station. Most of the damage was concentrated in Lowther Street where the bombs damaged five houses, and St Mary's Square where 100 houses suffered lesser damage. Awoken at 12.35am by the sound of exploding bombs, an excited journalist found himself in the firing line for the first time: 'Here it was at last. A real Zeppelin raid, and we were all under fire of the Germans, like the gallant fellows in the trenches… for the moment one seemed to be in the midst of a bombardment.'[26]

He timed the last bomb ten minutes later at 12.45am and then considered what to do next.

Under the circumstances it was impossible to remain in the house. In the streets there were little knots of hurrying, stopping, inquiring people, while a strident voice of command shouted through the stillness of the night: 'Get inside your houses.'... If the voice of command had been enforced by the dropping of a bomb it might have been obeyed, but the lapse of ten minutes had restored everybody's nerves, and curiosity got the better of caution.[27]

Windows and doors were broken, slates ripped from roofs and craters marked the Zeppelin's course, but there were no casualties. 'Nothing had been done that money would not replace,' the journalist concluded, 'and the cash value of restoring the property would be far less than the cost of the air raid to the enemy.'

More bombs dropped near racing stables on the open ground of The Severals as L 16 followed the line of the Bury Road leading out of the town. One killed a valuable racehorse, Coup de Main, favourite to win the Newbury Spring Cup the following week. The only human casualty occurred in a house on Bury Road near Warren Hill Station where Mr Bayliss, a London stockbroker, had committed the basic error of going to a window when he heard the bombs. As he did so, one exploded in his garden sending jagged metal fragments and glass slashing through the air.[28] Mr Bayliss suffered a number of injuries, the most serious to his arm for which, a newspaper reported, 'amputation of the limb will almost certainly have to be made'.[29]

As L 16 left the town Peterson released two final bombs over The Limekilns, another large open area where, unsurprisingly, they inflicted little damage. Heading back towards the coast, Peterson dropped five incendiary bombs at 1.15am as he passed between East Dereham and Norwich. They fell in fields at Honingham Hall, outside the village of Honingham, where one incinerated a large stack of straw. Peterson returned to the coast at Mundesley and set course from there back to Germany.

Kapitänleutnant Otto von Schubert was making his first raid over England when, at 11.50pm, he brought L 23 inland over Caister on the Norfolk coast. L 23 was a new airship, only in service since 16 April. Von Schubert had previously commanded L 7 but his lack of raiding experience saw him penetrate no more than four miles inland and spend less than an hour over England. He dropped three HE bombs near Caister then headed up the coast to the village of Ridlington where von Schubert released nine more. These ripped into farm buildings at Church Farm and smashed windows in the farmhouse. St Peter's Church also had its windows broken and the bombs partly wrecked a cottage. The only casualty was a bullock killed at the farm.

Just over a mile north of Ridlington was RNAS Bacton where landing flares were burning as an aircraft had taken off at 22.55pm. L 23 attacked it with six bombs and although one physically moved a searchlight, the only other damage reported was to two houses close to the airfield where the blast smashed glass and window frames. L 23 then turned out over the coast and began the homeward journey to Germany.

## 25 April 1916, 1am: Dilham, Norfolk

Another of the raiders, Viktor Schütze's L 11, crossed the coast near Bacton at about 12.30am. Schütze, who had already taken part in three other raids in April, set course for Norwich, about 17 miles inland, a journey he would hope to make in less than 30 minutes in normal conditions. He seemed unaware, however, of the strength of the wind he was flying into, because half an hour after heading inland he saw lights and commenced his attack, but L 11 had penetrated only five or six miles. A first batch of four HE bombs fell just north of the village of Honing in the open grounds of Honing Hall, quickly followed by 45 more bombs (19 HE and 26 incendiaries). Rather than bombarding the city of Norwich, they blasted the countryside a little to the north of the village of Dilham where the isolated Dairyhouse Farm found itself in the centre of a war zone. Fortunately no bombs hit the buildings but the blast from those nearby tore off roof tiles and smashed windows there and in four cottages. Three quarters of a mile away, at Hall Farm, the explosions gave 79-year-old widow Fanny Gaze such a shock that she died of a heart attack. Schütze now turned back, reaching the coast at Sea Palling at 1.18am. As was his way, Schütze then followed the coastline north rather than steering for Germany. After about seven miles he reached Bacton where the two 3-pdrs of the Eastern Mobile Section of the RNAAS came into action for the second time that night. The crew fired seven rounds before L 11 passed out of range but it appears that shell fragments ripped open one of her gas cells although she did return safely to Germany.[30]

While other commanders may have struggled with navigation, there was no such problem for Max Dietrich, commanding L 21. Accompanied by Peter Strasser, Dietrich came inland just south of Lowestoft at about 11.10pm and headed directly towards Stowmarket, about 40 miles inland, where an important munitions factory operated.[31] L 21 approached Stowmarket about an hour later but the gunners defending the site were ready. Supported now by two mobile 13-pdr guns at Stowupland and Badley, the two resident 6-pdrs opened fire at 12.16am. It was an unexpected and unwelcome reception. The Zeppelin immediately released water ballast, creating a cloud of vapour, and climbed rapidly as she turned away from the town. Dietrich released nine HE bombs, which fell in ploughed fields at Ward Green, just north of the village of Old Newton, breaking a few windows. He headed back towards the coast, passing around the west side of Norwich, which lay in darkness. A single HE bomb dropped at Witton at about 1.30am before L 21 reached the coast five minutes later near Bacton. However, instead of heading back to Germany, Dietrich and Strasser rendezvoused with the German fleet as it headed towards Lowestoft to commence its bombardment of the town.

Although five RNAS aircraft and one from the RFC were searching for the raiders, only Flight sub-Lieutenant Edward Pulling caught a glimpse of one, but L 23 was about 2,000 feet above him and his slow-climbing BE2c had no chance of catching it. Pulling crashed on landing but walked away unharmed.

At 4.10am, four German battlecruisers began a ten-minute bombardment of Lowestoft before moving on to Great Yarmouth. Shells wrecked 200 houses and two gun batteries, killing three people and injuring 12. The battlecruisers subsequently cut short their bombardment of Great Yarmouth when they received news of the movements of Royal Navy ships, which resulted in them withdrawing to join the main naval force. The subsequent engagement never escalated into anything significant, but one of the casualties is worth noting. It was in this engagement that the former Grimsby trawler, *King Stephen*, so reviled in Germany after the loss of the crew of L 19 and now operating as a Q-ship, was captured and then sunk.

While the German fleet remained within range of the Norfolk coast an incident almost led to the destruction of one of the escorting Zeppelins. Shortly after the bombardment, at 4.38am, two BE2c aircraft from RNAS Great Yarmouth encountered Zeppelin L 9 flying at only

2,600 feet while holding a position between the battlecruisers and the main fleet. The two pilots, Flight Commander Vincent Nicholl and Flight Lieutenant Frederick Hards, both managed to get above her. However, although they were able to drop bombs and Ranken darts, L 9's skilful manoeuvring ensured they all missed the target. What the pilots needed was a more reliable and lethal weapon. The next day there was the first hint that a solution was at hand.

Chapter 10

# Germany's Old Problems —
# Britain's New Weapons

In February 1916, a move to place the Royal Flying Corps' various Reserve Aeroplane Squadrons (RAS) defending London under a more unified control had seen them regrouped as No.19 RAS. Two flights concentrated in Essex, at Sutton's Farm near Hornchurch and Hainault Farm near Romford, although a third flight and the squadron HQ remained at Hounslow on the other side of London while awaiting the acquisition of more land in Essex. On 15 April the squadron changed its designation to No.39 (Home Defence) Squadron, still commanded by Major Thomas C.R. Higgins and operating as part of No.18 Wing (created on 26 March 1916), with Lieutenant Colonel Fenton Vasey Holt at its head having responsibility for all air defence detachments in the London area.[1]

On the night of 25/26 April, 24 hours after naval Zeppelins had made their latest raid, army Zeppelins returned to the south-east corner of England. For the first time as No.39 Squadron, aircraft ascended from Suttons Farm, Hainault Farm and Hounslow. The squadron was to make its name in the war against the Zeppelins – but it was a slow beginning.

That night five Zeppelins set out from Belgium although one, LZ 81, had Étaples on the French coast as its target.[2] Another of them, LZ 87, commanded by Oberleutnant Barth, got no further than Deal harbour on the Kent coast. At 9.55pm, Barth aimed eight bombs at the steamer *Argus*, sending great plumes of water erupting into the air but they all missed the target. As guns at Walmer opened fire, LZ 87 headed north up the coast before turning out over the English Channel and back to her base at Namur.

The attack by LZ 87 had accomplished nothing, yet the 116 bombs dropped on land that night by the three other Zeppelins achieved little more.

## 26 April 1916, 1.20am: North Kent

At 12.30am, about two hours after LZ 87 departed, LZ 88 crossed Kent's north coast near Whitstable. Her commander, Hauptmann Falck, headed south towards Canterbury but engine problems caused him to turn away at 1.05am. After heading east for about seven miles to the village of Wingham, Falck turned north and returned to the coast, dropping 37 bombs (13 HE and 24 incendiaries) as he went.[3] The first batch, nine incendiaries, fell at 1.20am on a line parallel with the road leading to the village of Preston, burning out harmlessly in the countryside. Within five minutes 12 more smacked down onto the saturated Chislet Marshes, followed by one that failed to find a target at the village of Sarre. Approaching the next village, St Nicholas-at-Wade, Falck released his first HE bomb. It exploded 'with terrific force' in the vicarage garden.

> It fell beside a sycamore tree, dug a hole eight feet deep and about twelve feet wide, uprooted the tree, carrying it over a coop of ducklings, all of which escaped injury. The tree in its fall smashed a window in the vicarage, and other windows were destroyed by the concussion, but no one was injured.[4]

Five more bombs exploded in fields between the vicarage and Shuart's Farm, then four on Wade Marsh, but all without inflicting any damage. Falck's last two bombs, both incendiaries, were equally ineffective, the last of them hitting the sea wall at Minnis Bay where LZ 88 left the country at 1.35am.

## 25 April 1916, 10.30pm: Felixstowe and Harwich

Earlier in the evening another of the army Zeppelins, Hauptmann Wilhelm Schramm's LZ 93, approached the Essex coast. No warning had reached the towns of Harwich and Felixstowe, standing either side of Harwich harbour, when the drone of engines alerted the defenders at 10.30pm. Within two minutes searchlights found LZ 93 and the guns of the garrison commenced firing forcing the Zeppelin to climb.[5] From the Felixstowe side of the river, a 6-inch gun mounted on a railway carriage opened fire, joined by two 6-pdrs and a 1-pdr close to Landguard Fort, while on the Harwich side two 6-pdrs engaged from Parkeston; between them they fired 195 rounds. The guns near Landguard Fort, situated on a spit of land south of Felixstowe, attracted the first bombs. Two incendiaries fell in the sea followed by a bomb that exploded just north of the Fort, smashing windows in the magazine. Then the mud on the western side of the spit smothered three that landed close to the shoreline; one of these not far from the RNAS Felixstowe aircraft hangars.

Crossing over the harbour to Harwich, LZ 93 dropped two bombs close to the 18th century Government House on St Helen's Green but both failed to detonate. Schramm then crossed over the River Stour to Shotley, home of a Royal Navy Training Establishment. This attracted seven bombs (three HE and four incendiary) but although reports claim little damage and no injuries, it appears one man was hurt. Albert Edward Redman, a Torpedo Artificer's Mate, was in the Mess when a bomb exploded nearby, a metal fragment cutting his intestine and lodging in his groin. Taken to a naval hospital, the senior medical officer only gave him a 50/50 chance of survival. Redman's strident mother, Kate, however, was not impressed with the diagnosis.

> When he had finished, Kate stood up, and in a voice of cold fury said: 'Lieutenant-Commander, you may know the full details of your patient's innards, but if you think my son is going to go under, you know nothing at all about his guts.'[6]

Kate Redman was right and her son did survive; he returned to light duties before being invalided out of the service in August 1918.

After dropping the bombs on Shotley, LZ 93 crossed back over the Stour. Schramm dropped one more HE bomb, falling on saturated ground between Parkeston Quay Station and Parkeston. Despite a recovery party digging down 12 feet into the mud they never found it. The concentrated artillery fire had ensured LZ 93 did not dwell any longer than absolutely necessary and, after dropping four more incendiary bombs in Harwich harbour, she turned for home at 10.45pm. Despite passing twice over the towns of Felixstowe and Harwich, Schramm had only a few broken windows to show for his efforts.

## 25 April 1916, 10.50pm: Fyfield, Essex

The third of the army Zeppelins was LZ 97, commanded by Hauptmann Erich Linnarz. He had carried out the first raid on London eleven months earlier and was now determined to return. He correctly identified the mouth of the River Blackwater where he came inland at 10pm but London proved rather more elusive as Linnarz confessed: 'Finding London was very difficult as all villages in the area we flew over as well as the capital itself were dimmed excellently.' On a westward course, after passing Chelmsford, Linnarz reached the village of Fyfield at 10.45pm and five minutes later began to bombard the rural landscape between there and Ongar with 47 incendiary bombs: 11 landed around Fyfield, 15 near Shelley, 17 close to High Ongar and four around Chipping Ongar, all burning out in fields although one damaged an empty cow shed.[7] The only logical explanation is that Linnarz wanted to lighten his ship to enable him to gain height before making his attack on London. Linnarz continued towards the capital but, when at 11.08pm a 13-pdr gun near Chigwell Row opened fire as he passed No.39 Squadron's Hainault Farm airfield, he believed he had reached his target and prepared to release his HE bombs. Leutnant Rohde, executive officer on LZ 97, noted: 'We must be right over London. Impenetrable shadows envelop the gigantic city, only pierced here and there by minute pinpricks of light. Yet even so the various districts can be unmistakably recognized.' Despite the confidence of his observation, Rohde was wrong. LZ 97 was approaching the small village of Fairlop.

> At high speed we steer for the city, the Commander standing ready on the bombing platform... His hand is on the buttons and levers. 'Let go!' he cries. The first bomb has fallen on London!... What a cursed long time it takes between the release and impact while the bomb travels those thousands of feet! We fear it has proved a 'dud' – until the explosion reassures us. Already we have frightened them.[8]

The first four bombs fell around Forest Farm, knocking off chimney pots, smashing windows and leaving craters in the fields. Two more exploded either side of Fairlop Station, damaging a gas main, breaking windows at the station and smashing others as well as doors at Railway Cottages, where the six dwellings provided homes for a widow, a railway signalman, a police constable, two railway platelayers and a clerk; no one was injured.

The explosions at Fairlop alerted searchlights near and far which quickly flickered into life. Rohde described how they came 'reaching after us like gigantic spiders' legs; right, left, and all around'.[9] More anti-aircraft guns burst into action. The gun commander for the Woolwich Control, watching from a position seven miles to the south was, however, unimpressed by the light show.

> Another point noticed was the ridiculously redundant employment of the lights. Not less than (I should think) 20 searchlights were trying to illuminate the target at the same time, most of them well out of range of it and doing more harm than good.[10]

And the problem was not restricted to the searchlights. The officer commanding Waltham Abbey Control had problems with at least one of his guns.

> At 23.13 the... gun at Temple House opened fire... The target was far out of range of the gun at the time. The Officer in charge has no reasonable explanation to offer for such a proceeding... He joined the Control from the Anti-Aircraft Training Depot, Shoeburyness, on 16th April, consequently his experience of the work is very small. I expect he will do better in the future.[11]

On board LZ 97 this eruption of gunfire and dazzling illumination forced Linnarz to turn onto a more southerly course as he continued releasing bombs. Two or three fell near Barkingside Station, three at Aldborough Hatch Farm and two at Newbury Park but they caused no damage. Approaching Seven Kings the intensity of the anti-aircraft fire increased as the guns south of the Thames joined in. The Woolwich commander noted much of it was wayward but it was enough to turn LZ 97 away from the capital. Two bombs dropped 50 yards apart at Chadwell Heath where one exploded in a ploughed field on the east side of Grove Road, smashing windows in five houses, while the other caused No.20 Farm Terrace to collapse like a house of cards. Fortunately its occupants, the Chapman family, had ignored official advice and were outside looking for the Zeppelin when the bomb struck and were unhurt.

Linnarz was now heading away from London while the guns along his path kept blazing away and the searchlights continued 'stabbing in the darkness', forcing him to twist and turn on his course. LZ 97 eventually broke clear of the defences and crossed back over the coast near Clacton at 12.34am. Before Linnarz reached his home base at Namur he had to evade an attack by French aircraft close to the Dutch border during which LZ 97 attained a height close to 15,000 feet.[12] As Leutnant Rohde nonchalantly noted: 'On looking at the altimeter we find that we have broken the airship height record.'[13]

While the intense anti-aircraft barrage had worried the crew of LZ 97, it also had an impact on the ground. The more shells fired up into the air meant there were more to fall back to earth. Fred Berris, living at 21 Pelham Road, Ilford, suffered an injured shoulder from falling debris when a shell fell on his house. Superintendent A. Boxhall, Metropolitan Police, also noted two other incidents in Ilford, six in Seven Kings, four in Barking and three in East Ham.[14]

Seemingly unknown to the crew of LZ 97, the airship also came under attack by pilots of No.39 (Home Defence) Squadron in a close encounter that marked the beginning of a new phase in the Zeppelin war. Alerted to a raid, six BE2c took off between 10.30 and 10.50pm. All pilots flew set patrol routes on the north-eastern and eastern approaches to London, some at 5,000 feet and others at 7,000 feet, both well below the height of LZ 97. The two 'A' Flight pilots from Hounslow, to the west of London, both saw the Zeppelin held in the searchlights but it was too far away and too high for them to come into action.

Although LZ 97 passed 'C' Flight's Hainault Farm airfield, neither pilot from there, Alfred Brandon nor Charles Black, were able to reach the Zeppelin, which Black estimated flying at between 12,000 and 13,000 feet.[15]

The two 'B' Flight pilots from Sutton's Farm came closest to success. Second Lieutenant William Leefe Robinson, had climbed to 7,000 feet when he first saw LZ 97 held by a concentration of searchlights. He began to climb towards it.

> When just over 8000 feet, I was in a fairly good position to use my machine gun; this I did, firing immediately under the ship. The firing must have had little or no effect, for the Zeppelin must have been a good 2000 feet above me, if not more…
>
> I fired at the Zeppelin three times (each time almost immediately below it); the machine gun jammed five times, and I only got

off about 20 rounds. When the Zeppelin made off in a E.N.E. direction, I followed for some minutes, but lost sight of it.[16]

While Robinson made his attack, 'B' Flight's commander, Captain Arthur Travers Harris[17], was urging his reluctant BE2c upwards. At 5,000 feet he observed searchlight activity to the north and turned towards it. At 7,000 feet he saw LZ 97 held on the points of the searchlights and, anticipating her movements as she turned east, he manoeuvred into a position to launch a head on attack, albeit from about 2,000 feet below. As the Zeppelin loomed over him he made his move, but it did not go according to plan.

> I opened fire with my Lewis gun and Brock ammunition. The gun jammed almost immediately. I turned again and flew behind and about 1500 to 2000 feet below the Zeppelin, and managed to clear my gun, opening up again. A second jamb occurred almost immediately; while freeing this jamb, I sideslipped and lost sight of the Zeppelin.[18]

Although his attack proved no more successful than Robinson's, it is his troublesome ammunition that is of interest.

* * *

Right from the beginning of the war the question of how to successfully bring down a Zeppelin had proven difficult to answer. The Royal Laboratory at Woolwich had developed 'flaming bullets', an incendiary bullet for use in the .450 Martini-Henry carbine but this was not up to the task. On 17 May 1915, aircraft from RNAS Dunkirk had attacked Zeppelin LZ 39 and although she sustained minor damage from bombs, the machine gun and rifle fire proved ineffective. It led to Commodore Murray Sueter, Director of the Admiralty Air Department, issuing a memorandum which effectively delayed finding a solution to the problem.

> It was very disappointing not to be able to fire the airship with the incendiary ammunition and bombs provided. Probably the exhaust gases from the motors are turned into the ring space. If this is so, the matter of igniting the hydrogen is one of great difficulty.[19]

The feeling was that these exhaust gases pumped into the envelope created an inert layer which prevented incendiary ammunition igniting the hydrogen. The theory was wrong but it ensured official attention looked elsewhere for a solution to the Zeppelin threat.

Besides various bombs, the anti-Zeppelin arsenal included the Ranken dart and fearsome sounding 'Fiery Grapnel', with its explosive-tipped hooks lowered by cable to catch onto a Zeppelin and detonate, but this was never used in action, which for the pilots tasked with deploying it was probably good news. And the problem with all these weapons was that the attacking aircraft needed to get above the Zeppelin to use them, which happened only rarely as German airships could easily outclimb the lethargic aircraft allocated to home defence. A few aircraft carried Le Prieur rockets attached to their outer struts. Designed in France they had been used successfully against observation balloons but, like the grapnel, they never saw action over Britain and so the problem remained unsolved. Although the flammable qualities of hydrogen were well known, it only becomes flammable when mixed with oxygen. While contained within the gas-tight cells inside the Zeppelin framework the hydrogen remained inert. The problem was to find a way to allow the hydrogen to mix with air before igniting it.

While no official work to develop a bullet that might achieve this goal was underway, a number of individuals independently looked to solve the problem. Those bullets fired by Captain Harris against Zeppelin LZ 97 were from a trial batch developed by Flight Lieutenant Frank A. Brock, head of the Admiralty Air Department's Intelligence Section, who used knowledge gained as a director of his family's fireworks company to find a solution to the problem. Aware of Sueter's comment about the possibility of inert gases effectively smothering incendiary bullets, he set out to design one with both explosive and incendiary properties that would detonate between the airship's envelope and gas bags. After trials in 1915 and another in February 1916, the Admiralty placed an order for the Brock bullets. The RFC officially trialed the bullets on 29 April, four days after Harris had used some of an early batch unsuccessfully against LZ 97. On 15 May the RFC placed an order for 500,000 although the final batch was not delivered until the end of the year.[20] The RFC, however, remained unconvinced by the bullet and in 1917 returned 400,000 to Woolwich; instead, the organization favoured the Pomeroy explosive bullet.

John Pomeroy, an inventor from New Zealand, had first put his mind to designing a bullet to destroy a Zeppelin when he saw a picture of one of Count Zeppelin's early airships. He demonstrated his first explosive bullet in 1908 but nothing came of it. In 1914 he was in London when war broke out and on 27 August Pomeroy submitted his 'anti-Zeppelin bullet' to the War Office but, 'was turned down promptly'. The following year Pomeroy went to America and the military there were about to conclude an order for his bullets when he heard news of the first Zeppelin raid on London and, dropping everything, he boarded a ship to England. 'I knew I had a good thing,' he explained, 'and wanted the bullet to be used against the Zeppelins.'

The War Office conducted trials in June 1915 then asked Pomeroy to supply more bullets for a further trial to be conducted in his absence. Pomeroy objected: 'I cannot comply with the request as part of my secret lies in the preparation of the shell as well as the explosive compound, and I have never allowed a shell to go out of my possession.'[21] And so official interest in the bullet waned. But the dogged Pomeroy did not give up. In December 1915 he contacted the Munitions Invention Department (MID) of the Ministry of Munitions and from early 1916 Pomeroy worked closely with the Department to perfect his bullet. At trials in May 1916 it performed well, resulting in the MID ordering a consignment of 500,000 of the experimental bullets but then problems became apparent requiring changes and a further trial in July 1916. The following month the Pomeroy bullet[22] entered service.[23]

Another private individual who recognised the need for a weapon to oppose the threat posed by the Zeppelins was James F. Buckingham, an experienced chemist who owned an engineering works in Coventry where he built engines and small automobiles. He began experimenting with incendiary bullets.[24] Choosing phosphorus as his incendiary compound, his .450 bullet underwent three trials for the RNAS in April 1915 where it did well but then Sueter's concerns regarding inert gas protecting a Zeppelin's hydrogen stifled official interest. With encouragement from individuals within the Admiralty, Buckingham persevered, adapting his idea to a .303 bullet for use in machine guns. He sent 200 of these to the Admiralty for trial on 12 October 1915 and eleven days later they placed a large order for the RNAS with deliveries commencing on 4 December 1915. Buckingham continued to improve the design and on 27 April 1916 the Ministry of Munitions placed an order for the RFC. Further improvements were implemented until Buckingham registered a new patent in June of that year.[25] Both France and America made orders too and by the end of the war some 26 million Buckingham incendiary bullets were delivered.

Prior to the war, the Royal Laboratory at Woolwich had considered the need for a tracer bullet, but the bullet available in 1914 proved unsatisfactory. When the Buckingham incendiary bullet first appeared, the smoke trail it left made it suitable as a tracer too and it was employed in those dual roles until a new tracer was developed. Early in 1916 the Ministry of Munitions took over part of the factory of Aerators Ltd, a company that made the Sparklet Soda Syphon.[26] At the time, Aerators were engaged making copper bullets for the French Lebel rifle. Using the bullet as a base for a new tracer, extensive experiments resulted in an effective trace visible for 1,000 yards. In July 1916 the RFC placed an order for the new bullets, known to everyone as the 'Sparklet'.[27]

All these bullets showed promise but none stood out above the others. When supplies of the Brock and Pomeroy, as well as the Buckingham or 'Sparklet' incendiary/tracers, had been received by the RFC and RNAS, the pilots received instructions to load them alternately in the 97-round Lewis gun ammunition drum – Brock/Pomeroy/Buckingham or 'Sparklet' and so on. It was hoped a combination of types would offer the best chance of success.

\* \* \*

The raid by army airships on the night of 25/26 April, when the Brock bullets were fired for the first time, proved futile with estimates of damage to property reaching only £568. Undaunted, Zeppelin LZ 93 returned again the following night, her commander, Wilhelm Schramm, making his third raid in consecutive nights.[28] He fared no better this time as engine problems cut short his visit to Kent. Appearing off Deal at 10.30pm, 18 minutes later LZ 93 was under fire from two 6-pdr guns at Westgate on the north coast. Although six pilots from No.39 (Home Defence) Squadron and a RNAS BE2c were searching for LZ 93, she made an untroubled escape. No bombs fell on land.

The final Zeppelin raid of this dark phase of the moon took place on the night of 2/3 May. With Scotland as the target again, eight naval Zeppelins had the Rosyth dockyard and the Forth Bridge in their sights. Weather conditions were such that none made it there and their alternate targets were both interesting and varied. The army also sent one Zeppelin out; Ernst Lehmann making his first raid in a new ship, LZ 98, set out optimistically for the long-range target of Manchester. She appeared off the mouth of the Humber at 7.25pm but a combination of anti-aircraft fire, rain and mist prevented Lehmann from coming inland and he abandoned the raid.

## 2 May 1916, 10.30pm: York

The eight naval Zeppelins had made good progress until they were about a hundred miles off the mouth of the Firth of Forth, at which point the wind changed direction. Now blowing strongly from the south, it had the potential to seriously hamper the long flight back to Germany. Even so, three continued on towards Scotland – L 11, L 14 and L 20 – while the rest turned into the wind to search for targets in the north of England. Of these, Max Dietrich believed his L 21 bombed Middlesbrough and Stockton, but he was much further south, crossing the coast north of Scarborough at 9.40pm.

Heading inland, 50 minutes later Max Dietrich found a target, which unknown to him was the city of York. L 21 circled to the south of the city before dropping 18 bombs (five HE and 13 incendiary) over the village of Dringhouses, then set a course for the city centre. Dringhouses bordered the Knavesmire, home to York racecourse, where a large military encampment had been established. The bombs shattered windows in the village, while an officer and a soldier at the camp received minor injuries.

On the north-east corner of the Knavesmire stood Nunthorpe Hall, serving as a VAD Hospital for wounded servicemen. Moments after the bombs fell at Dringhouses, L 21 began its run over the city. An initial batch of seven bombs (three HE and four incendiary) landed close to Nunthorpe Hall where one incendiary struck the roof. A report written for the *Daily Mail* suggests that the invalids, who were quickly evacuated, managed to find humour in their situation.

> The roof of the building at once burst into flames, but there was no panic... Accustomed to Hun frightfulness, the wounded treated the situation with cheerfulness. They forgot the scars of the battlefield and the injunction of the nurses to maintain quietness and as the flames reached higher and higher the heroes sang the tuneful melody 'Keep the Home Fires Burning'.[29]

With L 21 flying on a north-east course over York, the next bomb smashed down just beyond the Hall in Nunthorpe Avenue. Advance warning of possible air raids in York was given by lowering and raising gas pressure, which altered the brightness of the lights. Mrs Chapman, who lived with her family at 6 Nunthorpe Avenue, was out when the pressure fluctuated. Concerned, her husband and their two adult daughters, Emily and Norah, went out to see if they could see her and get her to hurry home. In the street, her husband watched an incendiary bomb fall at Nunthorpe Hall just as his wife came into view. As he shouted to his family to lie down, a bomb exploded in the middle of the street: 'Road material and fragments of the bomb flew in all directions… Every pane of glass near was shattered and the roofs of the houses nearest to the explosion also had their tiles lifted off.'[30] The bomb wrecked three or four houses in the street, including the Chapmans' home.

Five more HE bombs fell in quick succession then, when he felt sure the Zeppelin was moving away, Mr Chapman ran to his family. All had been hit by fragments of the bomb: Emily died within five minutes, Mrs Chapman's left arm was badly injured and at hospital they amputated it, while Norah's injury was particularly grim.

> Norah has had a wound through the top part of her right arm, and out at the back of her shoulder, and it was poisoned, so it had to be scraped out every morning and syringed through, and then filled up with disinfected wadding, they had to keep the wound open until it was perfectly clean.[31]

Even before Mr Chapman reached his family, more lives were lost. Just seconds after Nunthorpe Avenue, L 21 passed over Scarcroft Road and dropped a bomb on a house at 13 Upper Price Road. An elderly couple, George and Sarah Avison, were inside when the bomb struck causing the upper storey of the house to collapse. As rescuers dug through the rubble of the fallen walls they found the couple dead in their bed. Other houses nearby suffered considerable damage. About 60 yards further on, two bombs exploded in Nunthorpe Road, followed by one in Victoria Street and another in Price's Lane, which ran alongside the old mediaeval city walls. Doors were ripped from their hinges and windows and roofs smashed. Wilson Kirby went to see the local damage: 'Nunthorpe Road caught it very severely, particularly about Kettlewells the butchers and right up to St Clement's Church which had a few, perhaps 40, small panes broken. It is a proper wreck about there.[32] At a corner by Victoria Street and Caroline Street, a bomb smashed into the middle of three cottages.

The rather flimsily constructed houses collapsed, and all the inmates were buried amongst the debris. There were 18 persons in the three cottages – a majority of them being young children – but all were rescued from the ruins alive, though some were rather badly injured.[33]

From Price's Lane the next bomb fell just the other side of the city walls in Newton Terrace where the explosion wrecked four houses and injured three people, while a bomb falling in Kyme Street, backing on to Newton Terrace, smashed windows and doors and left one woman injured. Although the preceding 15 bombs between Nunthorpe Hall and Kyme Street had fallen in a line about 950 yards long, Dietrich flew the same distance over the city before dropping his next and final bomb. This exploded at 10.45pm about 450 yards south-east of the city's magnificent cathedral, York Minister, in St Saviour's Place. The road was busy.

William Chappelow, aged 49, and his wife Sarah had been to a picture house and were walking along St Saviour's Place on their way home. Ernest Coultish, the captain of a keelboat, was also walking along the same road as was Benjamin Sharpe. He was on his way home from Leetham's Mill, which had been forced to close for the night when the gas lights dimmed. Sergeant Edward Gordon Beckett, serving in a Royal Field Artillery Ammunition Column, was home on leave with his family in Haver Lane and Susan Hannah Waudby was at 13 St Saviour's Place where she ran a lodging house. When the sound of bombs first reached them, Beckett's mother became very nervous, so he said he would go out and try and find a place of safety for the whole family. He reached St Saviour's Place just as the bomb fell. It was carnage.

Exploding in the street, the bomb opened up a crater, smashing a gas main and wrecking three buildings. An eyewitness saw the bomb fall but after it exploded he was dazed for ten minutes. When he recovered, he found a man lying dead on the ground near his doorway and another a few yards off. William Chappelow, Benjamin Sharpe and Sergeant Beckett all died instantly. The bomb ripped away the lower part of Chappelow's legs and fractured his skull. The back of Sharpe's lifeless body was peppered with wounds while Beckett died after a large metal fragment smashed into his jaw. Coultish was still alive but bleeding heavily from a stomach wound. He died two hours later in hospital. A man who arrived at the scene after the explosion made a search of the shattered houses. He found the body of Susan Waudby amongst the wreckage of her lodging house; she had suffered terrible injuries to her head and right shoulder. From upstairs three lodgers were brought out alive although all were overcome by fumes from the broken gas main. Private Leslie Hinson, aged 18, was serving in the 3/1st East Riding Yeomanry based in the camp on Knavesmire but he was found lying on a sofa amongst the wreckage of one of the houses. He was still alive when rescuers pulled him clear but he also died in hospital. These were the last victims of the raid on York.

Dietrich now turned L 21 back towards the coast, dropping a single incendiary bomb at the village of Kirby Grindalythe at about 11.25pm before passing out to sea near Bridlington 25 minutes later. His bombs had claimed nine lives and left at least 29 people injured.

The other four Zeppelins that headed into the southerly winds after abandoning the attempt on Scotland ran into fierce snow-squalls and thick cloud over north Yorkshire where their raid ended with possibly the greatest wastage of bombs recorded in the entire campaign. But it started with great promise.

## 2 May 1916, 9.45pm: Danby High Moor, Yorkshire

Otto von Schubert brought L 23 inland over Robin Hood's Bay at about 9.15pm then headed inland over the North Yorkshire Moors. As was common practice, von Schubert released a single incendiary bomb, checking the effects of the wind, before turning northwards and heading for the favoured target of the Skinningrove Ironworks. A policeman noted that it fell at 9.45pm near Danby Head on Danby High Moor where it set fire to the heather.[34] Leaving the moors behind, L 23 reached Skinningrove 20 minutes later where the ironworks were in darkness. Von Schubert's 11 bombs (seven HE and four incendiaries) partly wrecked a storehouse while others fell harmlessly in fields or gardens, but three rows of cottages sustained some damage.[35] Coming under anti-aircraft fire from Brotton, L 23 moved away to the east for a couple of miles before dropping six incendiary bombs at 10.10pm over the tiny settlement of Street Houses. One of the bombs set fire to a house where a 12-year-old girl suffered burns. Continuing along the coast to Whitby, von Schubert went back out to sea at about 10.25pm.

As L 23 departed, Zeppelin L 13 arrived, Eduard Prölss taking her inland towards the moors. A half hour earlier Werner Peterson crossed the coast near Scarborough in L 16, about 20 miles further south. Prölss soon became aware of a large fire. To him it appeared that another of the raiders had found a worthwhile target and had bombed it with some success. But he was wrong; the fire he saw was a result of the incendiary dropped about an hour earlier by von Schubert. Fanned by the wind, the fire had caught hold and a large area of heather was now burning fiercely. At about 10.50pm Prölss ordered the release of a number of HE bombs over the raging fire. As he did so Peterson approached from the south in L 16. He saw the other Zeppelin and believed it was attacking the industrial town of Stockton-on-Tees, actually 17 miles to the north-west. He, too, dropped bombs on the remote moor, imagining: 'well-placed hits on buildings at the site of the fire as well as clearly recognisable [railway] tracks and embankments.' After dropping his bombs Peterson turned L 16 over the village of Castleton as the fire on the moor escalated and headed east along the valley of the River Esk for about five miles to Lealholm. There he dropped five bombs at about 10.55pm, which fell between there and Lealholmside. A farm building sustained some damage while the sound of smashing windows filled the air and two men narrowly escaped flying bomb fragments.[36] Peterson now turned north-west, released five incendiary bombs over Moorsholm at 11.15pm without causing any damage before passing out to sea near Skinningrove at about 11.25pm.

After L 13 had added its bombs to the great conflagration on Danby High Moor, Prölss turned south, following a very confused route for nearly two hours before heading out to sea north of Scarborough at 12.50am. During that time he released two parachute flares near Pocklington, an incendiary at Fridaythorpe and another at Seamer.

At 10.50pm, as L 13 and L 16 were both dropping their bombs on Danby High Moor, the final Zeppelin, L 17, approached the Yorkshire coast. At 11.05pm Kapitänleutnant Herbert Ehrlich appeared over the village of Carlin How, alongside the Skinningrove Ironworks, which had been bombed an hour earlier by L 23. Ehrlich ordered the release of 17 bombs (13 HE and four incendiaries) over the tightly-packed terraced streets. They wrecked six houses and caused slates to crash down from the roofs of numerous homes all accompanied by the sound of smashing glass, while a joiner's shop and several outbuildings were also destroyed. However, no one was hurt because the residents, alerted by the earlier attack, had sought shelter at a local mine. From Carlin How, Ehrlich headed over the moors and saw the huge fire engulfing Danby High Moor. With visibility limited, like the captains of L 13 and L 16, Ehrlich concluded that the inferno marked a major target and so L 17 became the fourth Zeppelin to waste its bombs on the wild and remote moorland.

His bombs released, Ehrlich turned away from the conflagration and went out to sea about three miles north of Whitby.

The police concluded that following the single incendiary dropped on the moor by the first Zeppelin (L 23), the attack at 10.50pm (L 13 and L 16) resulted in the explosion of at least 39 bombs, with the final attack (L 17) seeing at least six incendiaries added to the total.

It seems likely, however, that some bombs failed to explode and remained undetected, increasing the total as Superintendent Rose of the police at Guisborough later concluded.

> Seeing that this moor is very boggy it is quite probable there are bombs still buried in the bog. Some of the holes have water in them and are very deep consequently bombs dropping in such places as these and failing to explode will be difficult to recover.[37]

While the Zeppelins were threatening Yorkshire, the RNAS launched aircraft from Redcar (a BE2c), Scarborough (a BE2c and an Avro 504C) and Whitley Bay (two BE2c). Only Flight Lieutenant Bruno de Roeper from Redcar saw a raider but was unable to close. No.15 RAS at Doncaster sent up two BE2c, while two pilots from No.33 Squadron at Bramham Moor and others from No.36 Squadron at Cramlington were also in the air but they had no luck finding the raiders.[38]

Peace now settled over this remote part of the North Yorkshire Moors, the traumatised sheep and grouse the only victims of one of the most intense aerial bombardments of the Zeppelin war. But the raid was not over. Much further to the north the Zeppelins that continued towards Scotland were still seeking targets, while one embarked on a long-range odyssey from which it would never return.

Chapter 11

# The Coming of the Super Zeppelins

When strong southerly winds interrupted the progress of the eight Zeppelins towards Scotland on 2 May, five turned away to seek targets in northern England, leaving three to continue with the original plan. One of these, Victor Schütze's L 11, gradually drifted away from the other two and at 8.40pm, when about ten miles off St Abb's Head, came under fire from two armed vessels, the trawler *Semiramis* and yacht *Portia*. L 11 escaped by turning back eastwards but Schütze appears disorientated by the interruption. At 10.20pm, L 11 came inland 16 miles further south, at Goswick near Holy Island on the Northumbrian coast, where Schütze dropped two incendiary bombs. The first landed in a field between the North Eastern Railway tracks and the sea, the second on the sands between Holy Island and the mainland. Inevitably they caused no damage. Schütze was now heading south, keeping inland but parallel with the coast. Unsure of his position he dropped a parachute flare as he passed Alnwick but low rain clouds and ground fog made matters impossible and Schütze abandoned the mission, going out to sea at Amble at about 11.15pm having dropped no more bombs.

Kapitänleutnant der Reserve Alois Böcker had made the successful attack on Edinburgh at the beginning of April. Now, a month later, he hoped to repeat his achievement but the strong winds disrupted his plans, pushing him beyond the Firth of Forth. At 10.50pm, Böcker reached Lunan Bay, north of Arbroath. Here he circled for about 45 minutes in atrocious weather before coming to the conclusion that he was still over the sea and, seeing two small groups of lights below, he dropped five bombs on what he believed were 'two big warships'.[1] In fact Böcker was about two miles inland and south-west of the village of

Arbirlot. Rather than targeting warships, his first three bombs landed in a field on Bonhard Farm. A huge upheaval of earth left holes about 14 feet in diameter and over four feet deep and although too far from any buildings to cause damage, a young horse in the field took fright, jumped a fence and injured its hind legs. The other two bombs exploded about a mile further on in a field of potatoes at Panlathie Farm. Through rain and snow clouds Böcker headed to the south, passing Carnoustie and across the River Tay east of Monifieth, unaware that Dundee and its docks lay in darkness less than six miles upstream. At 12.07am, L 14 passed over Tayport on the south bank of the river before dropping bombs in St Andrew's Bay prior to heading back out over the North Sea.

At first light the next morning army officers collected up all the bomb fragments they could find and took them away.[2] The bomb craters quickly became a tourist attraction and two enterprising youngsters at Bonhard Farm cashed in on this curiosity by breaking up an old iron cauldron and selling the fragments to unwary day-trippers as pieces of the bombs.[3] Having encountered adverse weather, both Schütze and Böcker took a pragmatic approach and aborted their raids while still close to the coast. Their comrade, Franz Stabbert, however, remained determined to carry out his orders and attack the docks at Rosyth. It did not end well.

## 2 May 1916, Midnight: Loch Ness, Scotland

Stabbert and L 20 crossed the Scottish coast at Lunan Bay at about 9.55pm, an hour before Böcker. Wireless bearings he received, which were inaccurate, convinced him the wind had veered to the north-west and was retarding his progress, whereas it continued to blow from the south pushing him forwards. Clouds formed a solid layer and, with no ground reference available, he planned to steer west, estimating that a north-westerly wind would edge him south towards Rosyth. Instead, the southerly wind pushed him further away from his target and into the Scottish Highlands. At 10.30pm, L 20 passed over Glen Clova where the Reverend R.M. Watson reported he could see nothing of the Zeppelin through the mist but that 'there was no mistaking the sound of its motors'. Others in this remote region of Scotland thought that 'the very air was vibrating with noise' as L 20 battled on through heavy rain and snow squalls.[4] Stabbert passed near Aviemore at 11.30pm, heading ever deeper into the Highlands. Further requests for wireless bearings failed due to ice coating the aerial. At about midnight the clouds parted and for the first time since crossing the coast Stabbert had a view of the ground. Consulting his maps he made the shocking discovery that the great body of water below was Loch Ness, which placed him about 90 miles north of Rosyth. Villagers on the west side of the loch heard the sound of L 20's engines as she turned and set a course to the east, passing Aviemore again and proceeding over the Cairngorm Mountains. At 1.45am, much to Stabbert's surprise, a bright light appeared in the endless blackness below. He thought it might be a mine pithead and prepared to release six bombs on this unexpected target. There was, however, no mine.

Standing equidistant between the villages of Rhynie and Lumsden, 16th century Craig Castle was home to William Penny Craik, the Laird of Craig. He had a dynamo producing hydro-electricity and had a habit of leaving the lights on all night.[5] It was not an area regulated by lighting restrictions because no one ever anticipated Zeppelins raiding the region. Stabbert's bombs exploded with a shattering noise. Roused by their boom and the crash of glass, the Laird cut the electricity and herded his family down to the castle's dungeons. One of the bombs exploded within 40 yards[6] of the castle, others in the farmyard, but the impact was not significant. Besides some damage to the castle's roof, the bombs smashed 167 small panes of glass.[7]

Stabbert continued east from Craig Castle and, when north of Insch at 2am, he released four bombs that exploded in a field at Knockenbaird and an incendiary in another at Scotstown. Three miles on and three more bombs exploded in a field at Freefield House, about two miles north of Old Rayne. About 2.40am L 20 reached the coast south of Peterhead. Stabbert's journey over Scotland had covered about 200 miles and achieved nothing but crucially had used up a significant amount of fuel.

## 3 May 1916, 10am: Norwegian Coast

At about 5am (British time), on the morning of 3 May, L 20 made contact with Germany for the first time since heading inland and received wireless bearings. An hour later L 20 descended close to the water and Stabbert got confirmation of his position from a passing steamer – the bleak news placed him 300 miles north-west of his home base at Tondern, a flight he had to make into the face of a 40mph wind. Stabbert was under no illusions; L 20 would never make it. At 6.49am (British time), he transmitted a message: 'Require immediate assistance as I cannot reach my base.' The response instructed him to head for the northern tip of

Denmark where ships would rendezvous, but even that proved beyond L 20 due to a lack of fuel and engine problems.[8] Rather than be lost at sea Stabbert took the decision to land in neutral Norway, about 95 miles away. At 10am, with just two hours fuel left, L 20 crossed the coastline about 20 miles south of Stavanger.

Approaching Gandsfjord, a fjord that runs south from Stavanger, Stabbert attempted to land near the southern end. Downdrafts from the mountains, however, caused severe turbulence, thrusting the bow of the Zeppelin down into the frigid waters and almost ripping away the command gondola. Stabbert and his executive officer, Leutnant-zur-See Ernst Schirlitz, along with six men jumped overboard but, lightened by this reduction in weight, L 20 soared upwards and was carried by the wind towards the west side of the fjord. Stabbert and another man swam ashore at Holmavik, while a local fisherman, Jeremiah Bykle, pulled the other six frozen crewmen into his boat. For the eight men left onboard their situation looked bleak.

As L 20 just cleared the high ground on the west side of Gandsfjord, the rear gondola smashed into a rock, ripping it away and throwing out five more of the crew. The three desperate men left inside slashed the remaining gas cells and she finally came down at the southern end of Hafrsfjord, between Grannessletten and Liapynten, where she broke in two. A torpedo boat picked up the three relieved men. A company of Norwegian soldiers took charge of the wreck, tying it down as best they could, but rising winds overnight carried it across the fjord. The following day, after being blown to the northern end of Hafrsfjord, she beached at Sør-Sunde. Concerned for the damage that could be caused if L 20 broke free again, the military decided to destroy it. With no other means available, a 12-man firing squad formed up 120 metres from L 20 and opened fire. At least one of the bullets must have hit a metal girder and caused a spark because the leaking hydrogen instantly ignited in a great pillar of flame while the pressure blast knocked over some of the soldiers and destroyed nearby boathouses. Zeppelin L 20, the bomber of Loughborough, Ilkeston and Burton, was no more. But what of her crew?

As a neutral country, Norway now had to decide what to do with them. The logical step was internment but Norway took a more open-minded view, interning ten and repatriating six of the men, individual fates determined by the actions of Jeremiah Bykle. Norway decided that the six men pulled from the water by Bykle, a civilian, were shipwrecked mariners and sent them home, the rest, who landed on Norwegian soil by their own means or were rescued by the military became subject to internment. Stabbert, one of the internees later escaped and, making his way through Sweden, eventually returned to Germany where in December 1916 he took command of Zeppelin L 23.

The destruction of L 20 on the afternoon of 4 May coincided with the loss of L 7 earlier that morning. After a failed seaplane raid by the Royal Navy on the Zeppelin base at Tondern in Schleswig-Holstein in the early hours of 4 May, Zeppelin L 7 set out from there at 7.50am on scouting duties. Two hours later her crew observed elements of the Royal Navy's 1st Cruiser Squadron that had been escorting the seaplane carriers, *Vindex* and *Engadine*. In the ensuing engagement, shells fired by HMS *Galatea* and HMS *Phaeton* damaged L 7, and although the two light cruisers abandoned the chase at 10.20am, ten minutes later the Zeppelin broke in half and fell into the sea. At 11am, the British submarine E.31 opened fire with her deck gun and the wreck of L 7 burst into flames. Only seven of the 18-man crew survived. The day had been a particularly bad one for Franz Stabbert. Not only was it the day that the Norwegian Army destroyed his L 20, but L 7 had been his first command in November 1915. Then, the next day, 5 May, the German Army lost a Zeppelin too when the guns of HMS *Agamemnon* crippled LZ 85 before she crashed in marshes near Thessalonica in the Mediterranean. The loss of three Zeppelins in three days was a costly blow to Germany.

The raid of 2/3 May brought to a close the current round of Zeppelin attacks. By the time the next new moon appeared the shorter nights of summer would deny the raiders their valued cloak of darkness. But the seasons of the year had little impact on Zeebrugge's floatplane flyers of SFA 1. While the rest of the country would be free from attack for the next three months, those living close to the Kent coast had no such respite.

## 3 May 1916, 3.30pm: Deal, Kent

While the wreckage of L 20 still lay under guard on the shores of Hafrsfjord on 3 May, a single Hansa-Brandenburg NW appeared over Deal at about 3.30pm. It circled for a couple of minutes while the pilot searched for a target.

The first bomb[9] smashed down alongside Tar Path leading to the railway station. Bomb fragments zipping through the air in all directions struck Mr Potnell, a railway ticket inspector, on his way to work.[10] Badly wounded, he later had a leg amputated. Another exploded in a roadway digging a great hole and smashing windows, followed by one that obliterated the upper floor of a house nearby in Albert Road and severely injured an invalid woman inside. 'Roofing, rafters, beams and slates, and broken glass littered the roadway beneath and a large part of the roof fell in the middle of the road and stopped the traffic.'[11] A young milkman, Charles Hutchins, tried to calm his horse when the first bomb exploded but fragments from one of the others struck him. Doctors managed to save his leg.[12] Only one other bomb inflicted any damage. That fell just under a mile away on the Admiral Keppel pub[13] in Manor Road. The bomb damaged the roof and outer walls, while just across the road at St Leonard's Church, the blast damaged walls and smashed windows. The raider then made off out to sea. Twelve aircraft took off from local RNAS stations but with no advance warning of the raid they were only airborne after the raider had departed.

## 20 May 1916, 2.05am: Broadstairs, Kent

The next stinging attack from Zeebrugge took place 16 days later, and for the first time the raiders on 20 May attacked in the dark early hours. Seven aircraft participated in the raid on the Kent coast: a Gotha Ursinus WD (30 bombs), three Hansa-Brandenburg NW (ten bombs each) and three Friedrichshafen FF33 types (10 bombs each) although it is not clear if all came inland. These raids were always difficult to counter as the aircraft arrived with little or no warning, and this time the confusion caused by a raid commencing a little after 2am made matters worse. British reports account for 59 bombs of which nine fell into the sea, but many more may have been lost beneath the waves.

The first anyone knew of the raid was when 15 bombs rained down over the St Peter's district of Broadstairs on a southerly path towards Ramsgate. There were probably two aircraft involved. The first five bombs fell in fields between the Whitfield monument and Victoria Avenue, punctuating the ground with craters and smashing 15 windows. Other bombs pitted the ground south of Victoria Avenue near the Electric Tramway Depot and Rumfields Waterworks. Towards West Dumpton a bomb killed a chicken.[14] It is likely that five other bombs dropped in the sea opposite Small Downs Coastguard Station.

Another of the raiders dropped nine HE bombs in the parish of Sholden, north of Deal. The first landed about 300 yards from the sea near the Chequers Inn. The rest followed at intervals of about 50 yards on a line across open fields.[15] The last attack in this area saw ten bombs fall around the village of Ringwould at about 2.25am where the impact was negligible.[16] In Dover, however, the raid had a more serious impact.

## 20 May 1916, 2.15am: Dover, Kent

The first of two aircraft to attack Dover approached from north-west of Dover Castle and dropped a bomb at a garden nursery on Barton Road. The next struck the steps of a house in Maison Dieu Place and made a 'peculiar hole' about three feet in diameter in the side of the house as well as smashing many windows in the locality and terrifying patients in a hospital, before an explosion in Effingham Crescent caused limited damage. As the raider approached Dover College, a second aircraft appeared, the first passing over the college north to south and the second east to west. They dropped four bombs in the college grounds and one outside 12 Saxon Road, damaging iron railings at the front of the house. One report thought the tremendous noise from the explosions sounded 'more like a quick-firing gun than a bombing raid'. The shockwaves from the bombs smashed countless windows and gave the resident boys at the college 'a very alarming experience'.[17]

The first of these two aircraft continued on its course, and 100 yards on dropped a bomb on the gravel path leading to Christ Church on Folkestone Road, followed seconds later by one that exploded on Military Road, injuring Mrs Bridges Bloxham as she stood in her bedroom. On the south side of the road, a bomb struck a grass bank looming over the Christ Church Schools – also hit during the raid on 19 March. The pilot now turned on to a south-east course and dropped two more bombs as he headed back to the sea; one damaged gravestones in the old Cowgate cemetery and the last, which failed to detonate, was recovered from Albany Place on the east side of the cemetery. The pilot who crossed over Dover College on a westerly course, turned south and over the Western Heights dropped a bomb in the ditch of the Drop Redoubt. Three more followed. The first exploded by a stable at Grand Shaft barracks inflicting serious injury to Private Henry Frederick Sole, 3rd (Reserve) Battalion, East Surrey Regiment, as he opened a door. He died in hospital later that day. A hundred yards on, a bomb streaked down to smash into a public house, The Ordnance, at 120 Snargate Street. The upper part of the pub's frontage and the roof collapsed as tons of rubble cascaded into the street.[18] The landlord, William James Taylor, had a narrow escape.

> The landlady and her grandchild had been sleeping in the kitchen to be safer in such attacks, and they escaped untouched. The landlord was at the top of the house, looking out of the back window, when the bomb struck the coping

of the front of the house... The slates slid over the landlord's head without touching him.[19]

Even as the rubble tumbled down into the street, the next bomb exploded on the roadway at Commercial Quay where a fragment badly injured James Hervey, a deckhand on the armed drifter *E.E.S.* More bombs dropped in the sea as the raider left the damaged streets of Dover behind and headed back to Zeebrugge.

From first to last the raid lasted no more than 30 minutes. Taken by surprise, the first of the RNAS aircraft to take off in response was a BE2c from Westgate at 2.12am, followed by a Bristol Scout C from Eastchurch and a Short Type 827 floatplane from Grain at 2.25am. By the time any of these aircraft had climbed to an effective height the raiders were gone. And although official figures state only one person was killed in the raid – Private Sole – there was another who lost his life. While carrying orders through the darkened streets, Lance Corporal Victor George Parsons, a 19-year-old Royal Engineer despatch rider, smashed his motorcycle into the back of a searchlight lorry at the foot of Castle Hill and died.[20]

## May – July 1916: War Office, London

Free from Zeppelin attack throughout June and most of July, those summer months provided a welcome opportunity for Home Defence pilots to gain more night-flying experience. There was, however, friction over their responsibilities.

The War Office insisted that pilots combined their defensive duties with 'advanced instruction to pilots under training'[21] and at the end of May stipulated that half of all Home Defence aircraft should also be available for training. Forming part of No.6 (Training) Brigade, the commander of No.18 Wing, Lieutenant Colonel Fenton Vasey Holt, voiced his concerns that the rough-handling experienced during training in the daytime could negatively impact on aircraft required to defend the skies at night, and that the efficiency of his pilots, training others during the day then flying patrols at night, would suffer. The War Office listened. On 25 June, Holt's squadrons established No.16 Wing, divorced from any training responsibilities – their sole task to intercept and destroy enemy aircraft over Britain. Urgent demands for more pilots on the Western Front, however, initially restricted the Wing to six squadrons: No.33 (Bramham Moor), No.36 (Cramlington), No.38 (forming at Castle

Bromwich), No.39 (London area), No.50 (Dover) and No.51 (Norwich). At the end of July No.16 Wing became Home Defence Wing.

As pilots gained experience in night flying they had learnt to land safely at unfamiliar airfields, undertaken far-ranging patrols and returned safely from long distance Zeppelin pursuits. Previously, official advice had encouraged pilots not to venture too far from their landing grounds due to the perceived danger inherent in night flying.[22]

With this new confidence, airfields used by flights near to such places as Birmingham, Sheffield and Leeds were relocated as part of a plan to create 'a barrage-line of aeroplanes and searchlights parallel with the east coast of England' that would 'prevent the enemy getting through in normal weather'.[23] This 'line' running from Dover to Edinburgh placed airfields about 20 miles apart, supported by a line of double searchlights every three and a half miles, stretching from around London to Blyth in the north-east (see Map 5). In addition, searchlight barrage-lines positioned in Kent, Essex and Norfolk covered the main approach routes favoured by Zeppelins intent on attacking London. The line was not complete by the end of the war but the conviction to complete it remained constant throughout the period.

While great steps were being taken in Britain to offer a more effective response to the Zeppelin raids, in Germany a new type of Zeppelin was about to join the naval airship fleet.

## May – July 1916: Friedrichshafen, Germany

Since May 1915 the 'p-class' Zeppelin had carried the threat from Germany across the North Sea to Britain. They had a length of 536 feet 5 inches (163.4 metres) and diameter of 61 feet 4 inches (18.7 metres) with a capacity of 1,126,400 cubic feet of hydrogen (31,896 cubic metres) contained in 16 gas cells. This gave the 'p-class' a 'useful lift' (crew, fuel, oil, ballast and bombs) of between 14.7 to 15.6 tons (15,000 to 15,900 kgs). (See Map 4).

Even before the Zeppelin works at Friedrichshafen had completed the first 'p-class', the naval authorities discussed plans for a new type and in July 1915 requested a far larger design. It would have six engines instead of four and required extending some existing Zeppelin sheds and redesigning new ones already under construction. While this work was underway the next batch of 'p-class' Zeppelins were altered, starting with L 20. Lengthening by 49 feet allowed the inclusion of two more gas cells, which increased the 'useful load' on this interim 'q-class' to about 17.8 tons (18,000 kgs).[24]

L 30, the first of the all-new larger Zeppelins – the 'r-class' – left Friedrichshafen on 30 May 1916. Command of it went to Oberleutnant-zur-See Horst von Buttlar. The vital statistics were impressive. With a length of 649 feet 7 inches (198 metres) and a diameter of 78 feet 5 inches (24 metres), the envelope contained 19 gas cells holding 1,949,600 cubic feet of hydrogen (55,206 cubic metres), a massive 73 per cent increase on the 'p-class'. This additional hydrogen gave the 'r-class' a useful lift of 27.7 tons (28,114 kgs), enabling it to carry a bomb load of anything between two and a half to four tons, depending on the amount of fuel/ballast required. But this new design did not significantly alter the operational height. The 'p-class' generally operated at heights between 9,500 and 11,000 feet, while the 'r-class' flew at up to 13,000 feet. At the time altitude did not appear to be an issue but it would come back to haunt the Zeppelin crews. This overall leap forward in Zeppelin design had the British dubbing the new class as the 'Super Zeppelins'. After the Navy took delivery of L 30 at the end of May, a second airship, L 31, was ready on 14 July. This one went to Kapitänleutnant Heinrich Mathy. The Army did not receive its first 'r-class' airship until February 1917.[25]

While Strasser and other senior officers excitedly anticipated the arrival of L 30 at Nordholz, things did not go according to plan on the day. With Strasser and his entourage out on the landing field, von Buttlar realised L 30 was too heavy and coming down too quickly. To remedy this, he released a deluge of water ballast that engulfed the observers below in a great flash flood. When von Buttlar stepped down from the command gondola a dripping Strasser commented wryly, if not dryly, 'You came in like a watering cart'.[26]

Throughout June and most of July, L 30 undertook test flights and scouting patrols over the North Sea. There had been no raids over Britain of any sort since 20 May and if anyone in Britain had begun to think that German raiding had ceased, on 9 July they had a rude awakening.

\* \* \*

## 9 July 1916, 11.50pm: Dover, Kent

The south-east corner of England received its early warning that air raids were not a thing of the past on Sunday 9 July. On that night the first bombs to fall on Britain for three months struck Dover. Five aircraft of SFA 1 set out from Zeebrugge heading for Harwich and Dover but three had to abort. Of the other two the crew of Gotha Ursinus No.120

(Flugmeister Klein and Flugmeister Seeländer) claimed they bombed coastal installations near Harwich but there is no record of any bombs in that area so it seems likely they all dropped in the sea. The final aircraft, Friedrichshafen FF 33h, No.599, crewed by Leutnant-zur-See Rolshoven and Leutnant-zur-See Frankenburg[27] came inland at 11.50pm west of Dover.

The FF 33 kept very low, approaching Dover over St Radigund's Abbey and Buckland. As they neared the imposing outline of Dover Castle, Rolshoven and Frankenburg began to release eight 10kg bombs along a half a mile line straight towards the sea. The first of these exploded behind Castlemount Cottages in Castlemount Road, followed in quick succession by two in the grounds of the VAD hospital at Castlemount School. The next detonated on the roadway at the top of Laureston Place, then two on the lawn behind the houses in Victoria Park. The penultimate bomb smashed against the cliff behind houses in Trevanian Street where it wrecked an old stable just seconds before the final bomb exploded in the garden of a house at 1 Douro Place where the blast uncovered a long-forgotten well in the yard at the back.[28] Other than the destruction of the stables, these bombs smashed windows in 20 homes. From first bomb to last the raid was over in 30 seconds.

Before the month of July was out the Zeppelins returned. But any great hopes Strasser had for this opening raid of the second half of the year were dashed by the weather.

Strasser detailed ten Zeppelins for the raid on the night of 28/29 July but various problems forced four to turn back early.[29] The remaining six found the east coast swathed in a protective blanket of thick fog. Five of those that reached land spent little more than an hour searching through the gloom before abandoning the mission.

## 29 July 1916, 12.45am: River Humber, Yorkshire

Two Zeppelins approached the River Humber. The first, Herbert Ehrlich's L 17, followed the southern shore of the Humber but was caught by a searchlight at North Killingholme at 12.45am and responded by releasing 11 or 12 bombs. One fell on a road, the rest in fields. Three minutes later four bombs fell at East Halton. They set fire to a large straw stack, damaged two farmhouses, demolished a granary and stables, killed a calf and caused minor damage to six cottages. At one of them the bomb damaged the roof, windows and scullery, while the shocked occupier, Mr A. Harvey, had to extinguish an incendiary that landed just outside his door. Ehrlich then took L 17 across the Humber and passed out to sea between Hornsea and Withernsea about 1.10am. Five minutes later Ehrlich aimed three bombs at the mast lights of a P&O steamer, SS *Frodingham*, but they all landed about 100 feet behind the ship.[30]

The second Zeppelin, L 24 commanded by Kapitänleutnant Robert Koch, appeared over the Humber at 12.50am and 20 minutes later was at Immingham. Some activity spotted through the fog resulted in Koch releasing six HE bombs. These fell on Stallingborough Marsh where they broke some electric wires and smashed windows in a railway hut. A 12-pdr gun near Immingham Halt Station fired two rounds before losing L 24 in the fog. Frustrated by the weather, Koch crossed the Humber and headed back to the coast at Withernsea, which he reached at 1.25am. Guns at Withernsea Station and Waxholme each fired a single round as Koch pushed up the coast hoping to find clearer weather. He moved inland again at Bridlington Bay, but continuing poor visibility forced him to abandon the raid and he went back out to sea again near Hornsea at about 3am.

## 29 July 1916, 12.50am: East Anglia and Lincolnshire

The three raiders that made landfall over East Anglia fared no better against the fog than those on the Humber. Commanding L 16 for the first time, Kapitänleutnant Erich Sommerfeldt crossed the coast over Brancaster Bay at 12.50am. He exited again about an hour later having dropped a flare at Ringstead and two incendiary bombs at Snettisham.

Heinrich Mathy, in his first raid commanding L 31, one of the new 'Super Zeppelins', intended striking Dover but was way off target. Pitt Klein, recalled their dreadful journey through the fog.

> For eighteen hours we flew around in the murk. Finding Dover was impossible. Even when we tried to descend through it, we found it went down to the surface of the sea.[31]

In fact L 31 was about 90 miles north of Dover when she crossed the coast at 1.15am, just north of Lowestoft. Through heavy fog Mathy steered inland for about 12 miles towards Bungay but seeing nothing he gave up. He departed without having released any bombs over land.

L 11, the third Zeppelin, commanded by one of Strasser's more determined captains, Viktor Schütze, also had little luck. Schütze came inland over Weybourne at 2.40am, dropping a bomb in a field close to the cliff edge where it killed a cow and damaged roof tiles at a farm. Heading south-west, Schütze released a parachute flare over Holt then a bomb at 2.45am over Sharrington, followed by another a mile further on at Gunthorpe; neither caused any damage. At this point it seems likely that Schütze decided there was little point in continuing and made his way back to the coast, dropping a bomb at Paston at 3.20am followed by two more at Mundesley, all with no effect.[32]

Of the six Zeppelins that reached England that night only one attempted to push deep inland and drop a significant number of bombs. The result, however, was no more effective than that achieved by any of the other raiders.

Eduard Prölss brought L 13 in near North Somercoates on the Lincolnshire coast at 12.37am and followed a south-west course towards Lincoln, but found it difficult to find targets. At 1.10am he dropped an incendiary and a HE bomb that broke windows in a house and at a chapel in the village of Fiskerton, but passed darkened Lincoln without seeing it. Continuing, an incendiary burnt out harmlessly at Bassingham but with Newark also effectively darkened, L 13 passed to the south of the town before dropping an incendiary at 1.30am over Long Bennington. The lights of a moving train on the Grantham to Newark line then attracted Prölss and following it he released six bombs close to the railway where it passed between Dry Doddington and Stubton but only a few broken cottage windows resulted. Circling at 2am, L 13 approached the station at Hougham where Prölss dropped 21 bombs (four HE and 17 incendiaries). All landed within 200 yards of the station but failed to damage the buildings. From there L 13 headed east and went out to sea over The Wash about 2.30am, around ten miles north-east of Boston.[33]

The raid was over. The first Zeppelin raid for three months saw six airships blinded by the fog tentatively feeling their way over eastern England to record damage estimated at just £257.

As ever, the German version of the evening's events was a little different – and inaccurate.

A naval airship squadron attacked the English east coast, dropping bombs on the railway depot at Lincoln and industrial establishments near Norwich, the naval bases of Grimsby and Immingham, and on advance-post vessels off the Humber. The lighthouse at the mouth of the Humber was destroyed.[34]

Reports of this nature ensured the public in Germany continued to believe that the Zeppelins, the perceived embodiment of German technical superiority, were striking a heavy blow against Britain. No one would have believed the truth.

Despite the negligible damage inflicted by the raid, many a sleepless night ensued. From Hartlepool in the north to Brighton in the south and as far west as Birmingham, most of this area was subject to the 'Take Air Raid Action' order.[35] And there would be a further week of broken sleep to come.

Chapter 12

# A Fruitless Summer

The day after the raid of 28/29 July was generally quiet over Britain but in Germany the Zeppelin ground crews were busy preparing their charges for the next raid, while the flight crews grabbed some welcome rest.

There were, however, a couple of alarms on the night of 30/31 July, which saw 14 RNAS aircraft out over the North Sea searching for Zeppelins. One of the pilots, Flight sub-Lieutenant J.C. Northrop flying a BE2c from Covehithe, submitted a detailed report of an encounter with a Zeppelin in the early hours of the morning. He describes firing two mixed drums of the new explosive and incendiary bullets from about a 1,000 feet below the target before a third drum flew off and struck him in the face. When he regained his composure the Zeppelin had disappeared in a cloud. His style of attack was one that would later pay dividends for Britain's pilots, but on this occasion Northrop had nothing to show for his actions. There is, however, no German record of a Zeppelin being out that morning. The encounter remains a mystery, but it confirms the new bullets were reaching front line pilots.

## 31 July/1 August 1916, 10.30pm – 3am: Lincolnshire and East Anglia

On 31 July the naval Zeppelins returned. The weather conditions in Germany seemed promising enough for Strasser to despatch ten Zeppelins but the raid proved disappointing. Two of the raiders, L 21 and L 30, turned back before reaching England while three trawlers out in the North Sea radioed in news of the others' approach. Unknown to the raiders, low-lying mist lingered over eastern England.

163

The Zeppelin that came inland furthest north was Erich Sommerfeldt's L 16. Crossing the Lincolnshire coast near Skegness at 11.35pm, Sommerfeldt followed a slightly erratic course in the general direction of Newark, about 50 miles inland. Having passed the village of Caythorpe at 1.15am, something must have caught his eye because Sommerfeldt returned to it twenty minutes later and dropped two incendiary bombs. Five minutes later another landed at Skinnand before L 16 resumed its course towards Newark. Sommerfeldt circled the blacked-out town without locating it, dropping a fourth incendiary over Langford Common at 1.55am before heading back towards the coast with an almost full bomb load. He exited near Mablethorpe at 2.45am having dropped single incendiary bombs at Metheringham and West Ashby. The mist had prevented Sommerfeldt finding any worthwhile targets; it was a problem shared by every Zeppelin commander that night.

Between 10.30pm and 2.15am five Zeppelins were over East Anglia, before a sixth came inland for an hour between 2 and 3am. Their impact was negligible.

After crossing the coast near Lowestoft at 10.30pm, Martin Dietrich's L 22 pushed inland for about 50 miles before dropping a first incendiary bomb over Poslingford at 11.45pm. Then, in the 15 minutes between 12.20 and 12.35am, L 22 dropped 16 bombs (10 HE and six incendiaries) in the area around Haverhill. Four of these exploded at West Wickham airfield where a hurricane lamp was burning brightly in an otherwise darkened landscape. A police report succinctly described the result: 'No damage except for the holes made in the ground.' The incendiaries landed in a field near Haverhill gasworks and five bombs exploded at Withersfield resulting in broken windows at four houses before a final HE bomb dropped at Great Wratting but proved a dud.

An hour later L 22 dropped three HE bombs over Snarehill airfield near Thetford after which a parachute flare released over Croxton set fire to heathland. Three miles on, eight bombs fell harmlessly near the tiny village of Stanford.[1] At 2am L 22 released ten bombs near the village of Hevingham where an injured horse was the only casualty. The final bomb, an incendiary, burnt out at Burgh-next-Aylsham as L 22 passed out between Mundesley and Happisburgh at 2.10am.

Hauptmann Kuno Manger, an army officer transferred to naval airships, approached over The Wash in L 14 and at 12.10am came inland near Sutton Bridge. Heading south, glaring lights drew him towards extensive railway marshalling yards on the northern outskirts of March. At 12.33am four bombs crashed down at Whitemoor Junction. The two incendiary bombs 'lit up the neighbourhood considerably' but the two HE bombs, besides digging large craters merely cut some telegraph wires and smashed a few windows. Turning east into Norfolk, L 14 dropped an incendiary at Hockwold, but about nine miles ahead Manger observed a fire. Presuming another Zeppelin had found a target, Manger dropped eight bombs as he passed. These fell on Croxton Heath around 1.30am, just minutes after L 22's flare had started a heath fire, repeating the Danby High Moor incident back in May. Heading towards the coast now, L 14 dropped two incendiaries at Bunwell and another east of the station at Buckenham. Following the railway line, Manger's last four bombs exploded at Reedham at 2.05am before he crossed the coast south of Great Yarmouth ten minutes later. Other than the minor damage at March, L 14's bombs had little impact.

About 15 minutes before Manger had passed Sutton Bridge, Eduard Prölss had preceded him in L 13. Prölss, however, restricted his probing to north Norfolk where, unable to find any targets of note in the mist, he remained for little more than an hour. Between 12 and 12.25am single incendiary bombs landed at Walpole St Peter, West Newton and West Rudham, followed by an explosion in open country at Guist and at 12.40am by three bombs near Cawston. Prölss passed out to sea near Cromer at 1am, his seven bombs having caused no damage.

Zeppelin L 23 spent even less time overland than L 13. Otto von Schubert crossed the Suffolk coast near Kessingland at 11.15pm but after heading inland for about five miles and seeing nothing through the mist he gave up. Returning to the coast, von Schubert dropped his only bomb, an incendiary, on Southwold Common. It was almost a very lucky shot, the burning bomb falling just 20 yards from an army ammunition store.

Herbert Ehrlich, commanding L 17, arrived near Great Yarmouth at about 11.45pm and appeared to be heading towards Norwich but, effectively darkened, he failed to find the city. He passed around the south of Norwich drawn towards landing flares burning at No.51 Squadron's Mattishall airfield, laid out between the villages of Mattishall and East Tuddenham and about nine miles west of the city. As L 17 approached, a searchlight at neighbouring Honingham flickered into life. It was enough activity in an otherwise darkened landscape to draw a response. Ten HE bombs dropped around East Tuddenham, with seven more and five incendiary bombs streaking down between there and Honingham. Not one of them hit or damaged anything. Ehrlich passed to the north of Norwich and departed the coast between Mundesley and Bacton at 1.40am.

The last of the East Anglian raiders, Viktor Schütze's L 11, crossed the north Norfolk coast near Cley-next-the-Sea at 2.04am. After dropping an incendiary bomb on the sands at Warham Hole, Schütze headed inland to the south-east but clearly had problems, releasing three parachute flares in his search for targets even though he was over Norfolk for less than an hour. Single incendiary bombs released over Binham and Gunthorpe achieved nothing but at 2.25am two bombs dropped at Thurning caused the only damage of Schütze's raid. At a farm owned by James Gay of Thurning Hall an explosion dislodged roof tiles, broke glass in a cottage door and injured two bullocks, one of which had to be slaughtered. Schütze now abandoned the raid, dropping single incendiaries at Wood Dalling, Cawston, Wroxham, Hovetown St John and Neatishead as he returned to the coast near Winterton at 3am.

There was one more Zeppelin over England on the night of 31 July/ 1 August. Some 95 miles south of the action in East Anglia another raider was tasked with striking London – Heinrich Mathy's new L 31. The official German communique issued after the raid announced an attack on the capital: '...several naval airship squadrons successfully attacked London and the Eastern Counties of England. They dropped numerous bombs on the coast works, anti-aircraft batteries, and industrial establishments.' On board L 31, Pitt Klein gave a graphic account of their attack on London.

> The first of [the bombs] rained down. The terrific crash and powerful blasts combined with great columns of fire told us they had hit home... The space between heaven and earth was filled with the horrific explosion of bombs, the rapid fire coming from the gun batteries, the sharp crack of exploding shrapnel, the blood red glare of flames and the swirling beams of searchlights... The blazing light of fires lit up the City.... London that night was a gruesome sight.[2]

Klein's account, however, is fantasy. No bombs fell anywhere near the capital.

The sound of L 31's engines was heard at 11.10pm as she approached the north-east corner of Kent where the sky was clear. Observers recorded 12 bombs exploding in the sea off Kingsgate as L 31 followed the coast around to Margate and Westgate where she came inland at 11.25pm. As searchlights swept the sky, L 31 headed across this corner of the county towards Ramsgate while two anti-aircraft guns at RNAS Manston

Freepost Plus RTKE-RGRJ-KTTX
Pen & Sword Books Ltd
47 Church Street
BARNSLEY
S70 2AS

# DISCOVER MORE ABOUT PEN & SWORD BOOKS

**Pen & Sword Books** have over 4000 books currently available, our imprints include; Aviation, Naval, Military, Archaeology, Transport, Frontline, Seaforth and the Battleground series, and we cover all periods of history on land, sea and air.

Can we stay in touch? From time to time we'd like to send you our latest catalogues, promotions and special offers by post. If you would prefer not to receive these, please tick this box. ☐

**We also think you'd enjoy some of the latest products and offers by post from our trusted partners: companies operating in the clothing, collectables, food & wine, gardening, gadgets & entertainment, health & beauty, household goods, and home interiors categories. If you would like to receive these by post, please tick this box.** ☐

We respect your privacy. We use personal information you provide us with to send you information about our products, maintain records and for marketing purposes. For more information explaining how we use your information please see our privacy policy at www.pen-and-sword.co.uk/privacy. You can opt out of our mailing list at any time via our website or by calling 01226 734222.

Mr/Mrs/Ms .....................................................................................................

Address .............................................................................................................

Postcode..................................... Email address.............................................

**Website: www.pen-and-sword.co.uk  Email: enquiries@pen-and-sword.co.uk**
**Telephone: 01226 734555  Fax: 01226 734438**
**Stay in touch: facebook.com/penandswordbooks or follow us on Twitter @penswordbooks**

fired 16 rounds. Three bombs streaked down, smashing windows in ten cottages at Northwood on the outskirts of Ramsgate. Two guns at Ramsgate now joined in but both were out of action after firing a single round. Meanwhile, the sound of guns and bombs had alerted the residents of Ramsgate and many 'streets and promenades were soon thronged with people, many half dressed'. Off Ramsgate and Sandwich the sea again bore the brunt of the attack as more bombs dropped into the water, after which Mathy turned for home, his 'London' raid over.

The misty weather conditions elsewhere affected the British response and although the RNAS flew 11 sorties from Killingholme in the north to Manston in the south, and one RFC fighter took off from Mattishall, none of the pilots saw anything and two crash-landed leaving one pilot injured.

Despite eight Zeppelins reaching England and reporting great successes, the raid was a complete failure. Damage estimates compiled by the police were even less than the raid two nights previously – just £139. In the German press, however, the raids were a continuing success story: 'Contrary to the assertions of the British Government the general conviction reigns in London that the attack on August 1st was the most serious which London has ever been through up to the present.'[3]

## 2 August 1916, 7.30pm: the North Sea

Keeping up the intensity of the attacks, Strasser ordered six Zeppelins out again on 2 August, five of which had only returned on the previous morning. As early as 7.30pm British tracking stations had established the number of incoming Zeppelins, their identifications and locations over the North Sea. It meant a number of RNAS aircraft from Felixstowe, Killingholme, Great Yarmouth and Bacton were searching for the raiders before they neared the coast. Also out was the seaplane carrier HMS *Vindex*, which additionally had a short flying-off deck for a Bristol Scout landplane, and the smaller seaplane tender, HMS *Brocklesby*. However, even before any Zeppelins approached the coast a RNAS Sopwith Schneider floatplane, which had taken off from Yarmouth at 7.15pm was in trouble. Her pilot, Flight Lieutenant Christopher J. Galpin, had spotted a Zeppelin some distance away and gave chase but eventually lost it in cloud. With his petrol running low and the light fading, Galpin saw a ship and decided to land near it to seek help. He immediately regretted his decision: 'As I alighted alongside the vessel, a guttural voice hailed me from the bridge in some unknown but apparently teutonic language.' There had been rumours that German merchant ships guided Zeppelins by showing lights and now Galpin was convinced he had landed alongside one of them. While part of the ship's crew manned rowing boats and battled the strong currents to come alongside, Galpin disconsolately made ready.

> I hastily undid my various flying garments and destroyed every paper... and prepared myself for capture and imprisonment... I was standing rather dismally in a dishevelled flying-suit when they came up with me and at that moment one of the boat's crew, moved by my miserable appearance, cried heartily, 'Good Lord! It's Charlie Chaplin'. My relief knew no bounds.[4]

By a stroke of good fortune the ship was Belgian and took Galpin and his aircraft back to England.

Four of the six Zeppelins to attack England that night focussed their attention on Norfolk again. When about 50 miles off the coast, at 7.50pm, the seaplane carrier HMS *Vindex* observed distant raiders and launched its sole landplane from the 64-foot flying-off deck. The armament of Flight Lieutenant Charles Freeman's Bristol Scout comprised two boxes of Ranken darts. Despite a number of technical problems, Freeman managed to coax his aircraft above Zeppelin L 17 and release all his darts while under machine gun fire, but skilful manoeuvring of the airship meant the giant target escaped. Freeman did note a puff of smoke and felt that one had hit, but as there was no explosion, the smoke may have been the black powder component burning off without completing the ignition sequence. Shortly after turning back, Freeman's engine gave out. He made a good landing at sea – for a landplane – before passing an uncomfortable 90 minutes in the dark clinging to its tail. He was picked up by another Belgian ship, which landed him in Holland from where he was repatriated as a shipwrecked mariner.[5]

While Freeman had been engaging L 17, about 40 miles away HMS *Brocklesby* launched her two floatplanes. The pilots both made brief attacks at long range on what appears to be L 13 but failed to inflict any damage.

## 3 August 1916, Midnight – 2.15am: Norfolk

At 11.55pm Zeppelin L 21, commanded by another army airship officer transferred to the navy, Hauptmann August Stelling, crossed the north

Norfolk coast near Wells-next-the-Sea and followed a course to the south. He penetrated about 40 miles inland before dropping his first bombs at 12.45am, attracted by flares burning at Snarehill airfield near Thetford, as had happened during the 31 July raid. The five bombs failed to inflict any damage. From there Stelling turned L 21 east, dropping no more bombs for 40 miles until he neared the coast. There four bombs fell close to Covehithe airfield but caused no damage of note; a further eight dropped in the sea.

At 11.52pm Eduard Prölss brought L 13 inland at Happisburgh after a brief encounter with two mobile 3-pdr guns at Bacton. L 13 headed south on a meandering course as far as Earsham, near Bungay, dropping 16 bombs en route: an incendiary at Panxworth, three HE at Mundham (breaking windows at Grange Farm), five HE and three incendiaries at Ditchingham (breaking 70 panes of glass at Ditchingham Hall) and four incendiary bombs at Earsham. Other than the broken windows they caused no further damage.

From Earsham, Prölss changed course north-west towards Wymondham, dropping 16 bombs over the next 15 miles to little effect. Three bombs at Shelton at 12.45am smashed windows at Shelton Hall and other property nearby, but seven bombs at Tacolneston detonated harmlessly, while two incendiaries at Fundenhall fared no better. At Silfield explosions from three bombs smashed roof tiles and broke 20 windows at two farmhouses and a pair of cottages, but an incendiary at Wymondham burnt out without effect. From Wymondham Prölss changed course again, this time to the east. When about six miles south of Norwich he circled as though searching for the elusive darkened city but at 1.25am he gave up and returned to the coast, L 13 passing out to sea at 2.10am between Mundesley and Bacton.

The other two Zeppelins that raided Norfolk that night, L 16 and L 17, reached the coast together at about 12.30am near Ormesby St Mary and headed south-west across the county. The commander of L 16, Erich Sommerfeldt, penetrated about 25 miles inland before he dropped his first three bombs at 1.10am near Long Stratton. Ten minutes later he turned back, making for the coast at Great Yarmouth. When about seven miles south-east of Norwich he released seven bombs over Ashby St Mary. As they exploded or burned they shattered nearly all the windows at Ashby Lodge and at two cottages close by, but no one was hurt. L 16 passed out over the coast at 2.10am.

Having earlier brushed off the attack over the North Sea by Flight Lieutenant Freeman, L 17 came under attack again shortly after crossing the coast. Frustrated by jammed machine guns and reloading difficulties, Edward Pulling, flying a RNAS Yarmouth BE2c, had to settle for firing ineffective bursts at long range as L 17 drew away. Keeping south of L 16, Herbert Ehrlich held L 17 on a south-west course for almost 35 miles, dropping three bombs at Pulham Market before crossing over into Suffolk. The police did not discover those bombs for 16 days due to them 'falling in secluded places and into growing crops'. Reaching the town of Eye at 1am, Ehrlich doubted the value of continuing on his current course and, after releasing a single incendiary bomb at Mellis three minutes later, he commenced an erratic journey back to the coast.

Between 1.15 and 1.20am L 17 released nine bombs. Three explosive bombs at Billingford killed six horses and injured two others but the other six (three HE and three incendiary) that fell at Brockdish only damaged a farmhouse. At Hardwick five exploded at 1.30am damaging farming implements then seven minutes later L 17 dropped two more at Long Stratton, the village attacked by L 16 half an hour earlier and where fires may still have been burning. An incendiary bomb at Forncett St Mary narrowly missed a railway signal before Ehrlich headed back towards Pulham Market and released two bombs at Starston at 1.45am, which killed three more horses and injured another. A single HE bomb at Redenhall and six incendiaries at Denton inflicted no damage before Ehrlich released his final three incendiaries over the village of Broome at 1.55am where, as with so many others dropped over Norfolk that night, they proved ineffective. L 17 crossed the coast near Southwold at 2.15am to commence the long journey home.

The paths of Zeppelins L 13, L 16 and L 17 crossed and re-crossed throughout the raid while L 21 largely followed its own course. Despite dropping about 100 bombs the impact of the raid across the rural communities of Norfolk was negligible; a few windows and roofs damaged, a few farm animals killed. A British press release described the damage as 'astonishingly small', but in Germany the press claimed another successful raid with hits 'on railway works and on industrial establishments in the county of Norfolk, important from the military point of view'.[6]

## 3 August 1916, 1.54am: Felixstowe and Harwich

Further south Viktor Schütze, commanding L 11, appeared off the Suffolk coast near Hollesley just before 1am, intending to attack Harwich harbour at the junction of the rivers Stour and Orwell. Initially, however,

Schütze followed the River Debden upstream by mistake. When he turned back at 1.20am, a searchlight at Kirton caught L 11 and Schütze responded by dropping a parachute flare and three bombs that blasted houses in Kirton. They caused serious damage to six cottages, smashed windows in 12 others and inflicted minor injuries on a boy – the only human casualty of the night. Five minutes later, back at the mouth of the Debden, L 11 dropped three more bombs of which two fell in the river near the Bawdsey Ferry.[7]

At 1.30am Sub-lieutenant Slee, RNVR, commanding a mobile gun at Shingle Street on the coast, saw L 11 at a height he estimated at 6,000 feet and opened fire. L 11 moved out over the sea to begin a game of cat and mouse with the defenders of Felixstowe and Harwich that lasted an hour. At 1.54am L 11 dropped a parachute flare over Landguard on the Felixstowe side of Harwich harbour, but when a gun opened fire she retired. At 2am L 11 appeared over the harbour entrance but veered away over Landguard Fort when the guns commenced a heavy fire, dropping five bombs of which four fell in the sea. The other bomb exploded on the fort's parade ground sending metal splinters slashing through a few tents and smashing hut windows, but no one was hurt. L 11 approached again, this time towards Dovercourt on the south side of Harwich, but as soon as the guns fired, Schütze retired. At 2.25am L 11 passed over Harwich and Landguard for the final time but dropped no bombs. With L 11 held in the beam of a searchlight, Slee's mobile gun at Shingle Street fired a few rounds to send her on her way back to Germany.

Philip Hewetson, a soldier of 3rd (Reserve) Battalion, Loyal North Lancashire Regiment, based at Felixstowe watched the raid. He blamed the 'beastly Zepps' for regularly getting him out of bed, but was thrilled by L 11's appearance, although he thought there was more than one Zeppelin due to the separate approaches.

> We got a splendid view twice as the searchlights found them & they showed as plain as anything. They had a nasty time as all the guns strafed them from all around, it was quite a battle!! shells and bombs bursting, though not so very near to us, but tremendously exciting.[8]

One more Zeppelin reached England that night, Heinrich Mathy's new L 31. As with his raid two nights earlier, Mathy claimed a successful attack on London, but again he ventured no further than the Kent coast. Lying off Deal, the captain of the armed boarding vessel, *Duchess of Devonshire*, observed L 31 at 1am after which the ship's searchlight immediately illuminated her. Commander M.B. Sayer, Royal Naval Reserve, opened fire with two rounds of night tracer from his 6-pdr Hotchkiss gun. As the first tracer arced up into the sky, Mathy responded by '[dropping] 20 bombs in quick succession which caused a tremendous sound, throwing up huge columns of water'. Mathy moved away to the south and at 1.10am was off the coast near Dover where more searchlights opened and the guns of the Dover Garrison roared into action, sending 125 rounds of night tracer cutting bright streaks across the sky. The crew of L 31 felt they were in a 'fearsome battle'. A local reporter agreed.

> The bursting shrapnel was plainly seen by many of the inhabitants who had hurriedly left their houses and run on to the sea front... shells bursting all around the airship, which continually manoeuvred to escape from the beams of the searchlights... Numbers of 'tracer' shells, which have the appearance of rockets in their flight, were being fired, and with the bursting of shrapnel and other shells around the airship the scene was a striking one.[9]

Although the crew of L 31 claimed they released their bombs over London, other than those aimed unsuccessfully at the *Duchess of Devonshire*, any others dropped by L 31 must have fallen unobserved into the sea. With L 31 safely back at Nordholz, Pitt Klein reported that Peter Strasser personally addressed the crew after their two consecutive 'London' raids to 'express his heartfelt thanks and recognition of our achievement'.[10] This erroneous acknowledgment no doubt added to the esteem by which all within the Naval Airship Division had come to regard Heinrich Mathy. In reality, for the third time in six days they had little to show for their considerable efforts.

## 9 August 1916, 12.30am: Dersingham, Norfolk and Kelso, Scotland

The new moon had risen on 30 July so it was unusual that Strasser should announce a raid for the night of 8/9 August, just five days before the full moon. He did, however, keep clear of London and chose the less well-defended north-east coast as the target. Few of the eight raiding Zeppelins penetrated far inland, while two strayed off course, one appearing over Norfolk, the other Scotland.

Erich Sommerfeldt's time over Norfolk was brief. L 16 crossed the county's north-west coast at Brancaster at about 12.30am. Heading south-west, a RFC machine gun at Sedgeford landing ground opened fire, forcing L 16 to climb out of trouble. At 12.43am Sommerfeldt dropped 20 bombs (10 HE and 10 incendiaries) near the village of Dersingham. At Wellswill House and at 36 other dwellings the bombs smashed windows and brought ceilings crashing down. L 16 dropped 15 more on the heathland of Sandringham Warren, between Dersingham and Wolferton, where fires broke out but local people were quick to respond. Sommerfeldt then followed the coastline of The Wash to the north, going back out to sea at Hunstanton at 1.09am.

The other wayward strike saw bombs falling over the sparsely populated Borders region of south-east Scotland. Kuno Manger brought L 14 inland over Berwick-upon-Tweed at 12.25am and pushed 20 miles across the border into Scotland. Unsure where he was, Manger released a parachute flare over Greenlaw[11] before dropping an incendiary bomb on a farm at Fallsidehill. Moving south of Kelso, L 14 dropped three HE bombs in fields at Grahamslaw, an incendiary near Kersknowe and two more on a hillside near Clifton, a mile north of Morebattle, which set thistles burning. Crossing back over the Cheviot Hills into England, Manger dropped one more futile incendiary bomb about half a mile south of Southern Knowe before he headed back towards the coast, which he reached at 2am near Alnwick.

The main group of six Zeppelins came inland on an 85-mile-wide stretch of the north-east coast between Whitley Bay and Flamborough Head. The regular targets of Hull and Skinningrove came under attack again and tragedy struck ordinary working families once more.

## 9 August 1916, 1.20am: Hull, Yorkshire

Robert Koch's first command had been Schütte-Lanz 3 (SL 3) but in May 1916 he took command of L 24, the last of the navy's 'q-type' Zeppelins to join the fleet. He had reached the River Humber during the raid of 28/29 July and now he returned. He came in just south of Flamborough Head at 12.15am and positioned himself to approach Hull from the west, following the north bank of the Humber towards the city. At 1.18am, as he passed between Hessle and Swanland, Koch released ten bombs that broke several windows but nothing more serious. Hull had received warning of a possible raid and those in the city could now hear the sound of exploding bombs just a few miles away. Some went out to seek more secure shelter.

At 1.20am, L 24 approached the western districts of Hull, dropping three bombs on a golf course followed by four over the railway at Spring Bank Junction but they caused no damage. L 24 then crossed to the south of the Anlaby Road where she dropped seven HE bombs on the residential streets below.

John Broadley, his wife and their three-year-old son, John Charles, left their home to seek safety elsewhere. With their child in a push-cart they turned up a passageway between Sandringham and Granville streets but huddled in a doorway when the monstrous Zeppelin loomed overhead. Razor-sharp metal fragments struck all three as a bomb exploded in a garden: little John was dead, his mother and father both injured.[12] As houses crumbled nearby, at 32 Granville Street 86-year-old retired clergyman, Arthur Wilcockson, shocked by an explosion so close, called out to his daughter, 'What gun is that?', before he fell to the floor and died.

Emma Louisa Evers, aged 46, and her sister Gertrude were standing outside their house in Brunswick Avenue, alongside the railway, when they heard bombs. Panicking, they ran to the end of their road and into Walliker Street. Seeing the two women and the Zeppelin a man shouted a warning, 'They are on top of us!', and pushed them into the doorway of 61 Walliker Street, just where a bomb exploded. Gertrude was against the door and shielded by her sister Emma who died instantly. The explosion also killed 64-year-old Charles Lingard who lived at No.61, the building wrecked by the blast. On the other side of the street the explosion demolished William Solly's fried fish shop. When news of a possible raid came through Solly had closed the shop and taken his family to a friend's house.[13] It may have saved their lives.

L 24 then crossed over the railway at the southern end of Walliker Street, the next bombs landing in Selby Street. Albert Edward Bearpark, a stevedore, was standing outside with his wife, Mary Louisa, his son and two teenage daughters, when a bomb exploded not far away. Florence, aged 15, remembered her father desperately calling out, 'Are you all there?' as she saw him holding her mother in his arms. Mary was already dead, the others all injured. The youngest daughter, 14-year-old Emmie had laceration wounds to her thigh, leg and another in her back. She died in hospital. Also out in the street were the Hall family. They suffered terribly too. Their father was away serving in France but the explosion caught Rose Alma Hall, aged 31, their son, William, 11, and two daughters, Elizabeth, nine, and Mary, aged seven: 'A constable ran to the spot and found the child [Elizabeth] upon the footpath with part of her head blown

Fregattenkapitän Peter Strasser was appointed to command Germany's Naval Airship Division (Marine-Luftschiff-Abteilung) in September 1913, becoming the driving force behind the development of the division. Despite setbacks during 1916, he never lost his belief that airships could effectively take the war to Britain. (David Marks Collection)

The Zeppelin base at Hage in East Frisia. The four sheds were completed by June 1915. As was normal practice, each shed was given a name with the first letter the same as that of the base, hence the sheds at Hage were Hanne, Hannibal, Harald and Hasso. Similarly, the sheds at Nordholz, for instance, had names beginning with N. (Author's Collection)

A Friedrichshafen FF33e floatplane. Aeroplanes of this type regularly made hit-and-run raids on Kent coastal towns. They arrived without warning and as such local defence aircraft struggled to intercept them. (Phil Jarrett Collection)

The BE2c (BE = Blériot Experimental) was built by the Royal Aircraft Factory and became the mainstay of the Britain's Home Defence squadrons. Outclassed on the Western Front, at home it eventually proved to be an ideal Zeppelin night-fighter. This example flew defence flights with No.50 (Home Defence) Squadron and is now part of the Imperial War Museum collection. (Author's Collection)

The first Zeppelin raid of 1916 caused terror over a large area of the Midlands. This is King Street, Wednesbury, where a bomb dropped at 8.20pm on 31 January and killed at least eleven people, including Joseph Smith and four members of his family. (Author's Collection)

The ruins of the Christ Church mission rooms in Burton-upon-Trent, with the bomb crater in the foreground. A meeting was in progress when the bomb exploded with 'a blinding flash'. Six of those at the meeting died, with many more injured. (Author's Collection)

A German postcard showing the crew of Zeppelin L 19 left to their fate by the British trawler *King Stephen* after the raid on the Midlands on the night of 31 January/1 February 1916. The original caption says '*King Stephen*, you are cursed'. (Author's Collection)

The damage in Queen Street, Hull, after four bombs dropped around 1.00am on 6 March 1916. An eyewitness reported 'great pandemonium in the neighbourhood – women screaming, men shouting, dogs barking and cats spitting'. The tram tracks in the roadway have been ripped up by a bomb. (Author's Collection)

The wreck of Zeppelin L 15 on the morning of 1 April 1916, about 15 miles north of Margate. Having been damaged by anti-aircraft fire over Purfleet, L 15 tried to make it back to Germany but this proved impossible. Attempts by British boats to tow the wreck to shore failed, but later a salvage team brought up a significant amount of the wreckage. (Author's Collection)

Around midnight on the night of 2/3 April 1916, Zeppelin L 14 attacked the Scottish capital, Edinburgh. This image shows crowds gathered opposite the White Hart Hotel in Grassmarket. All the windows appear blown out and one man there, William Breakey, died of his injuries. (Author's Collection)

On the night of 2/3 May 1916, Zeppelin L 20 ventured over the Highlands of Scotland in error and, having used up precious fuel supplies, was unable to get back to Germany. The commander decided to land in neutral Norway but it did not go well. Although the crew survived, L 20 suffered severe damage before coming to rest in Hafrsfjord, where the Norwegian Army destroyed the wreck. (David Marks Collection)

The command gondola of L 16, a 'p-class' Zeppelin, in a shed at Hage. From here the airship's rudder and elevators were controlled, the electronic bomb releases were positioned and a small radio room operated. The rear section of the gondola housed a single engine, its propeller just visible in the image. The rear gondola on the 'p-class' held three engines. (Author's Collection)

L 31, one of the new 'r-class' Zeppelins, known to the British as the 'Super Zeppelins', flying over the battleship *Ostfriesland*. Navy Zeppelins undertook regular scouting flights over the North Sea. Commanded by Heinrich Mathy, L 31 joined the Naval Airship Division on 14 July 1916. (Author's Collection)

In the early hours of 25 August 1916, Zeppelin L 31 dropped numerous bombs over south-east London. An inquisitive crowd gather in front of 32 Southvale Road in Blackheath, close to the corner with Tranquil Vale. The bomb killed 70-year-old Emma Vane while asleep in a room at the top of the house. (Steve Hunnisett Collection)

RFC ground crew dig out one of the engines of SL 11, deeply embedded in the ground at Cuffley in Hertfordshire. As Schütte-Lanz airships were built of wood there was very little in the way of significant debris at the crash site – the fire having consumed most of the framework. (Author's Collection)

Lieut. W. L. Robinson, V.C.
Cheered by his fellow airmen after destroying Zeppelin, Sept. 3rd 1916.

William Leefe Robinson became an instant celebrity after shooting down SL 11 in the early hours of 3 September 1916; the first airship destroyed over British soil. Five days later he received the Victoria Cross from the King at Windsor Castle. (Author's Collection)

William Leefe Robinson's successful attack on SL 11 spawned a wave of souvenirs, including a great number of postcards. There are portraits of Robinson, views of the crash site, artistic images of the attack on SL 11 and others depicting the burning airship falling to earth. At the time, he was probably the most famous man in the country. (Author's Collection)

A bomb crater somewhere in East Anglia after the raid of 2/3 September 1916. Despite extravagant claims of successful attacks by some Zeppelin commanders, in 1916 a great number of bombs did little more than dig holes in farmers' fields, creating photo opportunities for local people. (David Marks Collection)

On the night of 23/24 September 1916, Zeppelin L 17 attacked Nottingham. A bomb that exploded on 32 Newthorpe Street killed Alfred and Rosanna Rogers. Rescuers found Alfred's body buried in the wreckage, while the blast threw Rosanna out into the street, depositing her body on a pile of rubble. (Author's Collection)

During the raid over East London by L 33 on the night of 23/24 September 1916, one bomb exploded in Wrexham Road, the blast wrecking six houses in Old Ford Road and injuring three women. It is surprising there were not more casualties given the extent of the damage as shown in this image. (David Marks Collection)

On the night of 23/24 September, Zeppelin L 31 caused significant damage as it passed over South London. This image shows the rear of 19 Baytree Road, Brixton, the home of Music Hall artist, Jack Lorimer. The explosion killed his 4-year-old son and the nanny/housekeeper. Two other sons were pulled alive from the rubble. One of them, Maxwell, later earned fame as the entertainer Max Wall. (Author's Collection)

Damaged by anti-aircraft fire over East London and losing hydrogen, L 33 was intercepted over Essex by 2nd Lt Alfred de Bathe Brandon of No.39 Squadron. The engagement was frenetic and the pilot was unaware that his bullets had pierced the Zeppelin's fuel tanks, compounding L 33's problems. She would not make it home. (Author's Collection)

The looming skeleton of L 33 under guard at Little Wigborough. The cottages are on Copt Hall Lane and lay about 25 yards from the nearest part of the airship. The intact framework of this latest Zeppelin was analysed in detail and influenced the designs of the later British airships R33 and R34. (Author's Collection)

After being picked up by Special Constables and arrested at Peldon, the crew of L 33 were kept overnight in the Church Hall at West Mersea before being taken to Colchester. Here they are shown arriving under guard at Hyderabad Barracks, Colchester on 24 September. One man has a bandaged head. (Author's Collection)

Zeppelin L 32, one of the new 'r-class' Zeppelins, was a major step forward in Zeppelin design and it was felt that this new type would allow Germany to dominate the skies over Britain. The introduction of this new class, however, coincided with the development and issue of both explosive and incendiary bullets to Britain's Home Defence squadrons. (Author's Collection)

Destroyed by the new explosive and incendiary bullets on 24 September 1916, L 32 smashed into a field just south of Billericay in Essex. In this image, army and navy personnel search through the twisted wreckage, which en eyewitness described as 'like the skeleton of a monstrous prehistoric reptile'. (David Marks Collection)

The original caption is 'Impression made in ground at Billericay by Commander falling from burning Zeppelin'. At the time the executive officer of L 32, Leutnant-zur-See Karl Brodrück, was named in error as the commander by the British authorities. It may therefore be his body that left this mark. (Author's Collection)

The wreckage of Zeppelin L 31 piled up around an oak tree at Oakmere Park, Potter's Bar, the third 'Super Zeppelin' lost in a week. Her commander, Heinrich Mathy, chose to jump to his death. The crew were buried in the same cemetery as the crew of SL 11, shot down a month earlier. (Author's Collection)

The Zeppelin fighters of No.39 (Home Defence) Squadron. Top left: William Leefe Robinson, awarded the Victoria Cross for shooting down SL 11. Top right: Frederick Sowrey, awarded the Distinguished Service Order (DSO) for shooting down L 32. Bottom left: Wulstan Joseph Tempest, awarded the DSO for destroying L 31. Bottom right: Alfred de Bathe Brandon, awarded the Military Cross for his attack on L 15 and the DSO for his actions against L 33. (David Marks Collection)

Naval Zeppelin commanders. Top left: Joachim Breithaupt, L 15, brought down and made POW, 1 April 1916. Top right: Werner Peterson, L 32, shot down and killed, 24 September 1916. Bottom left: Alois Böcker, L 33, brought down and made POW, 24 September 1916. Bottom right: Heinrich Mathy, L 31, shot down and killed, 1 October 1916. (Author's Collection)

Top: An artistic impression of the RNAS attack on L 21 off the Suffolk coast in the early morning of 28 November 1916. L 21 was the last Zeppelin shot down in 1916. Bottom: Flt sub-Lt Edward Pulling standing by the cockpit of his BE2c. Although he only fired two rounds at L 21, he received credit for its destruction. (Top: Author's Collection/ Bottom: David Marks Collection)

Pilots in action on the night of 27/28 November 1916. Top left: Ian Pyott, RFC, awarded DSO for shooting down L 34. Top right: Egbert Cadbury, RNAS, received the Distinguished Service Cross (DSC) for his attack on L 21. Bottom left: Edward Pulling, RNAS, awarded the DSO for his part in destroying L 21. Bottom right: Gerard Fane, RNAS, received the DSC for his attack on L 21. (Photo top left, courtesy of Collen Cumming and Ivor Markman, others are Author's Collection)

away. He placed the body in a perambulator and took it away.'[14] A bomb fragment had struck Mary in the back as she stood beside William and their mother lay in a fast-spreading pool of blood where the blast had ripped away a leg. Both Rose and Mary died in the infirmary a few hours later. William had lost his family in an instant but the resilient 11-year-old still gave evidence at the inquest the following day.

Ground mist prevented all but one of Hull's guns coming into action. The 3-inch, 20cwt gun at Harpings took five minutes to locate the target then fired eight rounds as L 24 began to rise and turn on to a northerly course. Koch now switched to incendiary bombs, the first of these setting alight a haystack in Arnold Street as L 24 passed between West Park and Anlaby Road Junction on the railway. Others landed in Wyndham Street, Derringham Street, Louis Street, Princes Street, Clumber Street and Belvoir Street. 'The bombs fell in couples,' a newspaper explained, 'sometimes not more than a dozen feet apart, but the damage done was insignificant.'[15] The final bombs were in Park Avenue where four fires broke out, and in Victoria Avenue. There a bomb smashed through the roof of Mr and Mrs Jones' home. They were in the garden watching the Zeppelin.

> The incendiary fell with a prodigious clatter of slates right through the roof and ceiling, and damaged the floor. The bedroom was wrecked and fired, and the flames mounted fiercely, but were put out by willing 'specials', two plucky youngsters from school, and neighbours generally.[16]

Having dropped his last bomb, Koch took L 24 back to the coast and departed over Hornsea at 1.47am. Back in Hull the death toll mounted.

Elisabeth Jane Bond, aged 76, awoke to the sound of exploding bombs. After the raid she went outside and fell, hitting her head. She died in the infirmary the next morning. Esther Stobbart, the 21-year-old wife of a sergeant in the East Yorkshire Regiment also died. Esther had recently given birth and shared a home with another soldier's wife. Esther had been feeling unwell and became very unsettled by the raid. The next morning she seemed cheerful but at 5.30pm she had a fit on the stairs and died. The Coroner attributed the deaths of Esther Stobbart, Elisabeth Bond and the Reverend Wilcockson to shock brought on by the raid.

The police reported that 12 HE and 32 incendiary bombs fell on Hull, with casualties given at the time as 10 killed and 11 injured.[17] And while

Hull had experienced its fourth raid, 60 miles to the north Skinningrove was under attack for the fifth time.

## 9 August 1916, 1.20am: Skinningrove, Yorkshire

As August Stelling headed L 21 towards Skinningrove it survived an encounter with the armed trawler *Itonian* about 12 miles north-east of Scarborough and another with the armed yacht *Miranda* at 12.45am about two miles north-east of Skinningrove. At 1.17am L 21 crossed overland at Hummersea Scar, immediately bombarding an old quarry with three bombs. Three minutes later L 21 released seven bombs over the Skinningrove Ironworks. As on previous occasions, however, they had little effect, the explosions destroying a small office and damaging several tanks, pipes and pumps.[18] Stelling turned back out to sea where he dropped three more bombs. But L 21 had not been alone, as the fire of an anti-aircraft gun confirmed.

About 12.50am Martin Dietrich and L 22 came inland near Hartlepool, about 15 miles along the coast from Skinningrove, and set course towards the ironworks. About half way to the target Dietrich released ten bombs at some lights below. They were flares burning at the RNAS station at Redcar where an elderly BE2c has taken off at 12.15am to search for the raiders. Six of the bombs cratered the airfield but caused no other damage and four overshot, falling in fields at Wheatlands Farm where there was an army camp, but there the result was the same. A gun near Saltburn fired a single round at L 22 at 1.12am as Dietrich pushed on to Skinningrove, but five minutes later he saw L 21 commencing her attack so turned back. The Saltburn gun fired again before Dietrich took L 22 inland over the North Yorkshire Moors. After about ten miles Dietrich dropped a single incendiary at Howlsyke, between Danby and Lealhom, then returned to the coast, passing out to sea between Whitby and Robin Hood's Bay at 1.45am.

The pilot who had taken off from Redcar, Flight Lieutenant Bruno de Roeper, carried only bombs and grenades. He appears to have seen both L 21 and L22 at different times but was unable to coax his 1914-vintage aircraft above them to make his attack.[19]

## 9 August 1916, 12.58am: Seaton Carew, County Durham

A third Zeppelin also appeared off Skinningrove. The engines of Kapitänleutnant Horst von Buttlar's L 30, the first of the 'Super Zeppelins', were heard off the coast but when a searchlight briefly caught her in its beam, von Buttlar turned away to the north, dropping as many as 15 bombs at sea as he climbed rapidly. At 12.50am von Buttlar came inland, unaware he had passed over darkened Hartlepool, before a glimpse of light to the south caught his attention. With little time to react he dropped nine bombs at 12.58am. The light came from chimneys and furnaces at Seaton Carew Ironworks where three bombs exploded close to slagheaps and smashed windows in ironworkers' homes in Bellevue and Longhill, but the others landed beyond the target in cornfields east of Seaton Carew Station. A similar glow from the ironworks at Seaton Snook drew a single incendiary bomb a minute or so later. At 1.05am a searchlight at Port Clarence on the River Tees found L 30 and von Buttlar needed no further persuasion to turn east over the river mouth and set course back to Germany, having been overland for little more than fifteen minutes.

Another raider came inland at Denemouth, just north of Hartlepool. Commanded by Eduard Prölss, L 13 crossed the coast at 1.30am and headed west towards a major coal mining area. About ten minutes later Prölss dropped a single explosive bomb in a field near Wingate Grange colliery, smashing windows in 10 houses. From Wingate, L 13 headed towards East Hetton colliery, dropping nine bombs over burning slag heaps, followed by 17 more over limekilns at Quarrington Hill and another colliery at Bowburn. The bombs at East Hetton wrecked a length of railway track and those at Quarrington Hill smashed windows in 40 houses and a shop; Bowburn escaped undamaged. Prölss then headed back to the coast, crossing it near Easington at 2.05am.

The other 'Super Zeppelin', Heinrich Mathy's L 31, which so far had made a couple of half-hearted raids on the Kent coast, had little more to show for this raid on the north-east; this time Peter Strasser accompanied Mathy.[20] After dropping a number of bombs at sea, Mathy came inland at 1.42am between South Shields and Sunderland. Heading west, L 31 only penetrated about four miles to Bolden before swinging around to the north-east and returning to the coast. Passing over Marsden, Mathy released six bombs as L 31 approached a large isolated house on the coast. The bombs missed Salmon's Hall, a former mansion house now providing homes for mineworkers, but exploding nearby they damaged the end of the Hall, smashed windows in a number of homes and ripped tiles from roofs. The bombs also killed a horse but no one was hurt, although Mrs Miller, one of the residents, had a narrow escape: 'When the air raid was on I was so frightened I ran outside. It was amazing that

I was not killed.'[21] Passing over darkened South Shields, L 31 reached the fog-shrouded mouth of the River Tyne at 2am and headed out to sea.

## 9 August 1916, 2.30am: Whitley Bay, Northumberland

The last of the raiders to reach England was Viktor Schütze's L 11. It was about 2.30am when he crossed the coast about three miles north of the mouth of the River Tyne at Whitley Bay. Schütze released a parachute flare as he headed towards the railway station and commenced dropping a line of seven bombs, meticulously recorded by the police as extending for 223 yards. The first exploded at the rear of 111 Whitley Road wrecking the premises and causing serious damage to adjoining properties; in one of them falling rubble buried three men in a bakehouse but they emerged uninjured. Two bombs in Albany Gardens caused extensive damage. In one house the explosion ripped the staircase away and to reach two of his children in an upper room the father hauled himself up by seizing hold of carpets hanging down before passing the two boys through a hole in the roof.[22]

By now the crew of a 3-inch, 20cwt gun had spotted L 11 and fired four rounds. This may have persuaded Schütze to terminate his raid because after the next four bombs all fell close together he changed course. The first of this quartet landed at the junction of Clarence Crescent and Algernon Road, smashing a water main and numerous windows, then another damaged a wall after detonating on waste ground. The final two bombs of this line of seven both landed just east of the station buildings, one close to the tracks and the other just beyond in an allotment garden damaging a fence and a hen house. Other damage around the railway included two signal posts, telegraph and telephone wires, fencing, brickwork, an illuminated sign for the 'Gents' toilet and the station's glass roof, as well as many other windows.

Schütze turned over the allotments, crossed back over the railway and across the close-packed streets, dropping six incendiary bombs as he headed towards the sea. Two of these landed in Burnfoot Terrace setting fire to a house but firemen quickly brought it under control. Two in Lish Avenue, striking Nos.24 and 41, were dealt with quickly as the final two landed in Carlton Terrace on Whitley Road. One fell behind No.7 with minimal effect but the other smashed through the roof of No.3, on the corner with Marden Crescent, where a major fire broke out. By the time the fire brigade had it under control it had practically destroyed the house and its contents. Fortunately the occupants were not at home. Despite the bombs causing significant material damage in this part of Whitley Bay, no one was killed and only five people received treatment for minor injuries with others reporting cuts and bruises.

The total material damage inflicted by the eight Zeppelins that raided on 8/9 August drew estimates of £13,196 and while this was more than that recorded in the previous raids that summer, it was still an incredibly poor return for the massive financial investment Germany was making in its airship programme. But in Germany press releases continued to feed the people stories of highly successful raids inflicting widespread damage across Britain, the stories fuelled by the crews' own embellished reports.

The north-east of England would not be troubled by Zeppelin attack again for sixteen weeks, and when they did return the air war over Britain had turned dramatically against the raiders.

# Chapter 13

# The Return to London

After a three-month hiatus due to the short summer nights, the Naval Airship Division had anticipated striking a heavy blow against Britain when it resumed raiding at the end of July 1916. Strasser now commanded a fleet of 11 Zeppelins able to take the war right to the doorsteps of the British people, yet those raids failed to deliver the desired results. Between 28 July and 9 August, airships raided Britain on four occasions. The 29 individual missions[1] resulted in at least 436 bombs falling on Britain but their effect was negligible with material damage estimated at just £14,388.[2] Considering that the cost of building an early wartime Zeppelin was about £50,000, rising to £150,000 for later models, and then factoring in the great cost of building the sheds to house them, the poor return is clear.

So far the first of the new 'r-class' Zeppelins had failed to demonstrate any significant improvement over the earlier models and it seems noticeable that the increasing effectiveness of both guns and searchlights was affecting the determination of the Zeppelin commanders to press home attacks over well-defended locations. Home Defence aircraft, however, were still having little impact, but all the time Britain's defences were improving.

On 8 August, Strasser took delivery of L 32, a third 'Super Zeppelin', taking his fleet to 12 airships. Command of the new vessel went to Oberleutnant-zur-See Werner Peterson, who had commanded L 16 until 31 May.

With an eye to the next new moon period and increasing the pressure on Britain, Strasser had two Schütte-Lanz airships transferred from the Baltic: SL 8 and SL 9. They arrived at Nordholz on 18 August. Now with 14 airships available, Strasser still wanted more, suggesting 22 as the ideal number to Admiral Scheer, commander of the High

Seas Fleet, insisting optimistically that 'airships offer a certain means of victoriously ending the war'. The sanguine reports submitted by his subordinates convinced Strasser of the effectiveness of the raids, as he outlined to Scheer on 10 August.

> The performance of the big airships has reinforced my conviction that England can be overcome by means of airships, inasmuch as the country will be deprived of the means of existence through increasingly extensive destruction of cities, factory complexes, dockyards, harbour works with war and merchant ships lying therein, railways, etc.[3]

Scheer, however, remained unconvinced.

Yet despite Strasser's confidence, after the raid on 8/9 August, one of his commanders, Heinrich Mathy, admitted that he was finding command difficult.

> The raids of July 31-August 1, August 2-3, and today's show that it is dangerous to fly for long periods at night over solid cloud ceilings, because winds that cannot be estimated and which are often very strong can produce significant and even serious drift errors unless wireless bearings are used freely.[4]

Yet wireless bearings produced their own problems. British listening stations could intercept the signals, giving away the Zeppelin's position. Keeping requests for bearings to a minimum meant Zeppelin commanders were often quite literally in the dark as to where they were over Britain.

## 12 August 1916, 12.27pm: Dover, Kent

While the Zeppelin crews waited for the moon cycle to favour their next series of attacks, a pilot of Marine Landflieger Abteilung 1 mounted a stinging hit-and-run attack on Dover. The explosion of a bomb near a shed on the RNAS Guston Road airfield at 12.27pm announced the arrival of a single aircraft flown by Walter Ilges. Within a very short time ten aircraft had taken off but it was already too late as Ilges only dropped four bombs before departing.

He passed over the military camp on Northfell Meadow on the eastern side of Dover Castle and released his second bomb. The camp housed the 5th (Reserve) Battalion, Royal Fusiliers. Five months earlier a bomb there had caused 15 casualties, this time Ilges' bomb injured six more.[5] The third bomb struck the cliff face behind a public house, The Prince Alfred, at 55 East Cliff, sending a shower of stones flying in all directions; one injured Private Bowden of the 61st Protection Company, Royal Defence Corps, who was chopping wood. The final bomb landed in the sea in front of East Cliff. Such had been the speed of the attack that many people were still enjoying the beach when this last bomb exploded. Considering the frequency of attacks on Dover, the choice of the town for a summer holiday seems odd, but the Toope family from Worcester were unconcerned and their 12-year-old son was paddling in the sea when the bomb fell.

> Immediately on contact with the sea, it exploded with terrific force, throwing up a large volume of water and covering him with spray. His relatives moved further along the beach, fearing that further bombs might be dropped, but by this time the hostile airman had made away.[6]

* * *

Before the Naval Zeppelins resumed raiding, eight were out scouting for the High Seas Fleet on 19 August, which almost resulted in the loss of von Buttlar's L 30 after a surprise encounter with the armed trawler *Ramexo*. As von Buttlar observed, 'Heavens, it was a close shave!'

> A terrible concussion threw us all to the floor, the whole car shook, and smoke rose up on all sides. Scarcely thirty feet below the control car a high-explosive shell must have burst. When I came to my senses again... I cast my eyes quickly round. The engines were working, thank God! No one was hurt. And when I looked at the body of the ship I could see nothing wrong... We had escaped death by a hair's breadth![7]

## 23/24 August 1916, Midnight: Trimley, Suffolk

Army Zeppelins had been absent from Britain for four months when LZ 97 set out on 23 August from the base at Namur with London as its target. Her commander, Oberleutnant Helmuth Weidling, had taken command from Erich Linnarz in June.

News of an approaching Zeppelin reached the Harwich garrison at 11.33pm; 25 minutes later LZ 97 was off the mouth of the River Debden. Rather than pushing on for London, Weidling dropped all his bombs over the countryside between the Debden and Felixstowe.

Initially appearing to head for Felixstowe, Weidling dropped his first two bombs in fields, one north of the village of Old Felixstowe and the other at Cow Pasture Farm, 600 yards north of the church at Walton. Moments later, over Blofield Hall, Weidling changed direction and heading north dropped five HE bombs between the Hall and Trimley Station, followed by an incendiary bomb which narrowly missed the station buildings. From the station, LZ 97 passed over Trimley St Mary, dropping four incendiary bombs as it headed towards neighbouring Trimley St Martin. There Weidling released 11 more incendiaries: one fell at Street Farm and ten in the grounds of three large houses. At one of them, The Limes, a bomb broke through the roof of an outbuilding and fell into a bath of water. This was the only damage recorded during the raid. The residents of the village, aided by the rain, soon put out any other fires. 'The Zepp had come and gone,' one farmer said, 'and the whole thing was over before you could dress and get downstairs.'[8]

Heading off to the east, LZ 97 dropped a single HE bomb over Mill Farm on the edge of Trimley St Martin then, just after midnight, Weidling dropped a line of 11 more across waterlogged fields and marshes between Hill House and a stretch of water known as King's Fleet. So saturated was the ground that the exploding bombs made little sound when they detonated. Heading up the coast, LZ 97 departed near Orford Ness. A press release succinctly summed up the effectiveness of the raid: 'No damage and no casualties have been reported.'

Peter Strasser would no doubt have dismissed the efforts of a single army Zeppelin as a waste of time, because the following day, 24 August, he committed 13 of his 14 airships to attack 'England South', which meant London if possible. However, matters beyond his control meant that only four battled through to reach England: L 16, L 21, L 31 and L 32 with Strasser on board. Having intercepted radio messages, the British concluded a raid was underway and a number of Royal Navy ships put to sea hoping to intercept them. High winds and rain hindered some of the raiders while at least six reported coming under fire from the navy ships and one, L 13, had an extraordinary escape when a shell passed right through one of her gas cells only to explode when above the fortunate vessel.

## 24/25 August 1916, Midnight: Ipswich area, Suffolk

Erich Sommerfeldt brought L 16 over the coast of Suffolk at Aldeburgh at 11.05pm but struggled with navigation as low cloud blanketed much of the countryside. He only released his first bomb at midnight, an incendiary at Woodbridge, before dropping a HE bomb at Martlesham followed by six more and three incendiaries at Kesgrave as L 16 headed towards Ipswich. Broken telephone and telegraph wires, smashed windows at Bracken Hall to the north of the Woodbridge-Ipswich road and cratered fields marked Sommerfeldt's progress.[9]

Although hindered by low cloud, the crews of two searchlights north-east of Ipswich switched on their lights shortly after midnight searching for the source of the clearly audible engine noise. Seeing the lights Sommerfeldt turned away from Ipswich and prepared to attack them. At about 12.15am he released nine bombs as L 16 approached one of the lights near the twin villages of Great and Little Bealings.[10] One exploded just 20 yards from the searchlight and another severed the telephone line linking it to an anti-aircraft gun. After this incident Sommerfeldt terminated the raid, returning to the coast at Aldeburgh at 12.30am.

## 25 August 1916, 2am: Little Oakley, Essex

About 45 minutes after L 16 had begun its homeward journey, L 21 was off Harwich and heading south. Oberleutnant-zur-See Kurt Frankenburg, previously the executive officer on L 14, had taken command of L 21 just ten days earlier.

L 21 came inland about seven miles south of Harwich at 1.43am. Once he crossed the coast Frankenburg turned north, passing over Walton-on-the-Naze, and at about 1.55am crossed Hamford Water, flying over the low-lying uninhabited Pewit Island, completely unaware that he was little more than a thousand yards from the Great Oakley Explosive Works on neighbouring Bramble Island. Crossing a small channel to the mainland, Frankenburg released seven bombs most of which landed between 500 and 1,000 yards from Little Oakley Hall although one fell in the grounds. Frankenburg released his next six bombs as L 21 passed south of Little Oakley and towards Foulton Hall. Explosions smashed windows in Little Oakley and seriously damaged a granary and a cow shed at the Hall's farm. At 2am a searchlight at Dovercourt located L 21 and guns at Great Oakley and Ramsey opened fire, soon joined by others at Dovercourt, Shotley, Landguard Fort and Felixstowe Golf Club. Seeking safety, Frankenburg returned to the coast, dropping five more explosive bombs in fields and a single incendiary on the mud flats at Crabknowe Spit. Now heading north up the coast, L 21 ran the gauntlet of fire from the Harwich Garrison and Royal Navy ships in the harbour before turning out to sea off the mouth of the River Debden at 2.15am. Back at Nordholz, L 21 made a bad landing, the damage to her hull and gondolas requiring six days to repair.

## 25 August 1916, 2.10am: Folkestone, Kent

The two other Zeppelins to reach England, L 31 and L 32, were two of Strasser's newest airships. They followed an overland route via Belgium but both experienced delays while making in-flight repairs. Heinrich Mathy and L 31 made good progress after the delay and began to cross the English Channel at about 10.15pm. Werner Peterson in L 32, however, encountered unfavourable winds at a higher altitude, which delayed him further, and it was 2am when the sound of L 32's engines was first heard off the Kent coast. Too late for London, Peterson came inland at Folkestone but immediately came under fire from two 6-pdr Hotchkiss guns at the village of Capel-le-Ferne, which fired 70 rounds. Peterson headed back out to sea, but as he followed the coast northwards, seven guns of the Dover Garrison bombarded him with 205 rounds. It is hard not to imagine that this proved uncomfortable for Peterson. A year earlier, anti-aircraft fire from Dover had damaged his L 12 after which the Zeppelin came down in the English Channel and was towed into Ostend harbour. Peterson released three or four bombs at 2.20am as he pulled away from Dover. 'The bombs were very heavy ones,' a newspaper reported, 'and as they burst in the sea with a crash masses of flame sprang up, followed by cascades of water.'[11]

Peterson continued on his northward course keeping about two miles off the coast. Just before 3am a searchlight at Deal located L 32 and an anti-aircraft gun fired 11 rounds. Peterson reacted by dropping 18 bombs on shipping and, although he claimed that 'a square hit on one ship caused a devastating explosion', none were hit.[12] A few minutes later a searchlight and gun at Ramsgate joined in but Peterson turned away from the coast and the searchlight lost him.

At the same time two BE2c pilots of No.50 (Home Defence) Squadron were stalking the raider. They took off from Dover about 2.15am and immediately had L 32 in their sights as they began their slow climb; the BE2c could take 40 minutes to reach 10,000 feet. Both pilots entered cloud at 4,000 feet but when they emerged only one, Captain John Woodhouse, still had L 32 in sight. He got into a position below his target, still 2,000 feet from it, when he fired a drum and a half of the new Pomeroy explosive ammunition, but when the searchlight lost L 32 so did Woodhouse. As became clear later, 2,000 feet was too great a distance for the new bullets to carry a serious threat and on board L 32 the attack had passed unnoticed by the crew.

Shortly after 3am, when north-east of Ramsgate, L 32 fell in with her sister ship L 31. Mathy's L 31 was also on its way home after completing its mission. This time there was no doubt as to where she had been – this time it really was London. A Zeppelin had reached the capital for the first time in ten months.

## 25 August 1916, 1.30am: Isle of Dogs, London

The sound of L 31's engines was earlier heard off the north-east corner of Kent at 11.17pm but her progress along the county's north coast was slow at first, as though she was waiting for the delayed L 32. At 12.30am, however, Mathy crossed the Thames from the Isle of Sheppey to the Essex shore and followed the river towards London. The 'TARA' order had alerted the guns and searchlights defending the capital but mist and heavy clouds prevented them locating L 31. Keeping close to the Thames, L 31 passed between the impotent searchlights at Beckton and North Woolwich before reaching Blackwall from where Mathy saw enough through the clouds to know he had reached the unmistakeable great horseshoe bend of the river around the Isle of Dogs. Below lay two of London's great shipping destinations, the West India Docks and Millwall Docks. Mathy turned south and dropped his first bombs at 1.30am.

Following the line of the West Ferry Road, L 31 had already passed the West India Docks when his bombs detonated just south of the entrance to Millwall Dock. Two HE bombs and an incendiary struck the Cyclops Works of tube makers Edward Le Bas & Co. on land between West Ferry Road and the river. The bombs wrought severe damage to half the premises with the rest of the industrial site requiring the fire brigade's hoses to bring the inferno under control. Damage extended to

Winkley's Wharf alongside the river and to the rear of homes and shops along the west side of West Ferry Road from Nos.134 to 186.

At the same time another bomb exploded on the other side of West Ferry Road inflicting some significant damage.

> [The bomb] fell into some gardens at the rear of a row of workmen's cottages. It dug a hole about ten feet deep, smashed the brick walls of two or three gardens, blew in one of the side walls of an institute [St Mildred's House] a few yards away, and damaged somewhat the rear walls of several of the cottages. The concussion shattered the majority of the windows of the cottages over an area of about 200 yards, and also some of the wire-protected windows of [St Paul's] Presbyterian church.
>
> Some of the debris was flung into the rooms of a number of cottages, in three of which, let in two floors, some twenty-five children were sleeping. Pictures and furniture were scattered about indoors, some of the pieces falling on the children's beds, but not a single child, so far as can be ascertained, was injured.[13]

The damaged houses included all those between Nos. 237 and 303 West Ferry Road and others in Claude Street and Crew Street.

A single incendiary then crashed through the roof of the Providence Iron Works at 192 West Ferry Road but damage there was negligible, and another landed on a barge lying at Ferguson's Wharf as L 31 crossed over the Thames. The London Fire Brigade estimated the damage at the Cyclops Works at £55,000, significantly more than the previous eight Zeppelin raids combined.

## 25 August 1916, 1.31am: Deptford, London

Three bombs fell in the Thames before Mathy reached the Deptford side of the river. There the Army Service Corps' No. 1 Supply Reserve Depot occupied 27 acres of the former Foreign Cattle Market site. A bomb smashed into 'G' store and exploded amongst 8,000 sacks of flour each weighing about 140lbs (63.5kgs) and boxes of tea. A second bomb detonated in a garden behind the office of the Divisional Officer, Royal Engineers, causing considerable structural damage and injury to an officer. Assessors estimated the losses here at £9,524. Damage extended beyond the depot to Watergate Street and Butchers' Row. Another bomb, in Deptford Green alongside Deptford Dry Dock, demolished or severely damaged workshops, offices and stores with the effects of the blast spreading to six neighbouring streets. Here estimates valued the damage at £17,528.

Between Deptford Dry Dock and Deptford Creek, the London Electric Supply Corporation had a large generating station at Stowage Wharf. The assistant foreman engineer lived on site and awoke to the sound of exploding bombs. As he went outside there was a terrific explosion. A few minutes later a bloodied, limping figure appeared.

> We met [Richard Turner] coming along, his face covered with blood. He put his hand on my shoulder and said: 'I have copped the lot.' His face was badly lacerated in several places, and he had a nasty scalp wound over the left ear. I bathed his face and put on a dressing, and asked if he was prepared to walk to the hospital, and he replied, 'No, I am too bad.' So I said, 'Don't worry; we will put you on the ambulance.'[14]

Turner, aged 34, worked as an electrical switchboard attendant at the generating station and had been close to the bomb when it exploded. He died in hospital a few hours later leaving a wife and two very young children.[15] A doctor attributed his death to 'shock and haemorrhage'. Estimates of damage at the electricity station reached £16,643.

The last bomb in Deptford, an incendiary, fell on a barge at Wood Wharf but caused no damage. Still shielded from the searchlights by the low clouds, Mathy turned away from the river to commence laying a trail of destruction across south-east London from Greenwich to Plumstead.

## 25 August 1916, 1.33am: Greenwich, London

About 150 yards south of Wood Wharf, two incendiary bombs set fire to a coal merchant's offices in Norway Street, and another struck a house in Straightsmouth. Then three HE bombs and an incendiary fell in the space of 100 yards. The first of this group exploded outside Greenwich Station causing a significant amount of damage and wrecking a public house, The Prince of Orange.[16] The following day a journalist met the stationmaster, Edward Huish, who bore a 'wonderful black eye'.

'I was looking out of the window of my house over there,' he told me, 'when a bomb struck the street just in front. Up came a shower of stone and shell fragments, and one chip caught me under the eye, while minute particles struck me all over the face and made these.' He pointed to scores of minute cuts about his face.

The front wall of the station was pitted with holes... while at other places the glass and stonework had been shattered, evidently by jagged fragments of shell.[17]

The second of the three bombs fell in a garden behind the Queen Elizabeth's College Almshouses.

The old couples were pitifully scared. They had had warning... and had gone into one another's houses to sit waiting in the dark. Some more infirm had to wait in their beds. Then came the crash outside. In flew windows and doors... Apart from a few cuts, none of them is actually injured very badly, but some received such a shock that they are now quite ill.[18]

The third of this group exploded at the top of South Street, the roadway lined with shops and homes.

A carter on his way to market with a van and two horses had pulled up at a coffee-stall in the street, and was talking with the keeper of the stall when the bomb burst with terrific uproar not many yards away.[19] When the men recovered their senses they found themselves lying amid the ruins of the stall and its crockery, but only slightly hurt. The two horses were killed... On every side was a scene of wreckage.[20]

Properties between 15 and 23 South Street took the full force of the blast with doors and windows smashed and the walls pockmarked by bomb fragments. Inside five people sustained injuries.

Switching to incendiary bombs, Mathy passed over a mainly residential area of Greenwich where fires broke out at 86 King George Street, 52 Croom's Hill and at Hillside House on Croom's Hill. Another burned itself out in the roadway as L 31 approached Blackheath and dropped an explosive bomb at the rear of 8 The Grove[21] shattering numerous windows.

## 25 August 1916, 1.35am: Blackheath, London

Next in the path of L 31 was a large encampment at the north-west corner of Blackheath where the Army Service Corps had established No.2 Reserve Horse Transport Depot. At least three bombs exploded at the camp.

> One bomb fell at a point between one hut and some other fenced in huts in which some soldiers were sleeping. 'Down went the fence,' said an eyewitness, 'as though a hurricane had hit it. In went windows and side like – well, the place might have been put in a big nutcracker.'[22]

The bombs injured 15 soldiers, smashed wooden huts, wrecked corrugated iron storerooms, damaged four ammunition wagons and destroyed a large YMCA recreation room.

As L 31 crossed the open space of Blackheath, Mathy's next bomb blasted a crater in Eliot Place, smashing windows in 24 homes. Seconds later, just off the inappropriately named Tranquil Vale, another crashed through the roof of 32 Southvale Road. Elizabeth Emma Vane, aged 70, was asleep at the top of the house when a sister-in-law and her daughter on the ground floor awoke to the sound of loud booms.

> I said to my daughter, 'There are the guns!' My daughter said, 'Nonsense!' but she jumped out of bed. Then the crash came, and I was surrounded by bricks and debris, but was not touched in any way.
>
> My daughter and myself crawled over the bricks, but when we went to go to the assistance of my sister-in-law upstairs we found that the staircase had gone.[23]

The explosion sent Elizabeth Vane crashing down to the drawing room where a fallen beam pinned her in her bed. When firemen reached her, although terribly injured, she managed to gasp, 'Thank God you have come'.[24] It took an hour to extricate Elizabeth from the wreckage of her home but she died of her injuries in hospital. The houses either side, 31 Southvale Road and 51 Tranquil Vale, both suffered severely and the crash of shattered windows sounded in both roads and in Camden Row, Royal Parade and Collins Street.

## 25 August 1916, 1.37am: Eltham, London

From Blackheath, Mathy dropped two bombs along Manor Way in Lee then no more fell for a mile and a half until L 31 reached the Progress Estate in Eltham, built in 1915 to house skilled workers employed at Woolwich's Royal Arsenal.

Two bombs exploded with terrific force in Dickson Road. One landed squarely on No.33, severely damaging the house and its contents as well as smashing roofs and windows in 19 other houses in the street and more in neighbouring Sandby Green and Phineas Pett Road. The second detonated in the street, bursting a gas main and damaging houses from Nos.4 to 20 on one side of Dickson Road and Nos.5 to 27 on the other. Bomb fragments injured seven people who were outside looking for the Zeppelin but only one required hospital treatment.[25] Roofs and windows in Cobbett Road also felt the impact of the bomb.

Seconds later a bomb tore through a house at 210 Well Hall Road, where engineer Frederick Thomas Allen lived with his family.[26] The house collapsed, killing Frederick, his wife Ann, their daughter Gladys, aged 11, and Ellen Funnell, the wife of a corporal in the Life Guards who lived with them.

At 2.45am a corporal in charge of a lorry from the 2nd London Division Demolition Section, Royal Engineers, received orders to go to Well Hall Road.

> I set my squad to work clearing away the wreckage, lifting the heavier portions of the debris with our tackle. I called upon some members of the Police and Special Constables to assist.

> Several bodies were extricated and on recovering the last body I received instructions from the London Fire Brigade at 5.20am to return to Headquarters.[27]

Newspapers reported the findings of the inquest in gory detail.

> The medical evidence showed in the case of the man [Frederick Allen] both legs and the right arm were fractured, and the spinal column broken. The lower jaw was smashed, and there

191

was a large wound on the body and another on the chest. The woman [Ann Allen] was practically cut in two, and all her limbs were fractured.

In the case of the child [Gladys Allen] both legs were severed below the knee, the left thigh was broken, the right arm was cut off, and the head was smashed.

The younger woman [Ellen Funnell] had a broken nose, contusions about the mouth, and evidence of pressure by a heavy body on the forehead and parts of the limbs.[28]

From the shattered neighbouring houses, where 'furniture was left hanging in all kinds of ungainly and curious attitudes,' everyone escaped without injury.[29]

There are reports that the family's dog followed the ambulance carrying Frederick's body to the mortuary and then returned to lie forlornly on the pile of debris that had previously been its home. About a thousand mourners attended the Allen's funeral.

Another 220 yards and the next bomb crashed down on No.1 Brome Road where by good fortune the family were away on holiday. The houses from Nos.1 to 9 suffered as did six more in Lovelace Gardens, with minor damage extending to Arsenal Road and Prince Rupert Road. The final bomb of this group exploded just beyond the Progress Estate, at 215 Grangehill Road. It demolished the house, more or less wrecked those on either side and damaged others all along the road and in both Granby Road and Westmount Road. Incredibly there were no reported injuries.

L 31 now approached the high ground of Shooter's Hill, where Special Constables on duty at Severndroog Castle had a close shave. The castle, not a castle at all, rather an 18th century folly in the form of a triangular tower, offered uninterrupted views across London and was one of the best points south of the Thames for observing hostile aircraft on their way to and from the capital. L 31 appeared to be heading straight towards the tower and as it drew closer two bombs streaked down to explode in woods on either side.

No great damage was done, and there was no break in the service. The Special Constables stuck to their work, and

192

continued faithfully to telephone the results of their scrutiny to the Central Observation Station at Spring Gardens.[30]

From Severndroog Castle, Mathy's course took him towards Plumstead and now, at last, the first searchlight located the lone Zeppelin. About two and a half miles to the east, the light at Danson Park had a clear view of L 31 and others soon joined it but the low cloud layer holding at 1,000 to 1,200 feet 'rendered the view of the Zeppelin intermittent and hazy'. Six guns of the Woolwich Sub-Command of London's gun defences opened fire joined by the North Woolwich gun across the Thames; they fired 119 rounds in four and a half minutes before L 31 was lost to view. All the shells appeared to fall short of the target.

## 25 August 1916, 1.40am: Plumstead, London

While under fire, L 31 passed a mile and a half south-east of Woolwich Arsenal and approached Plumstead where two bombs exploded in Swingate Lane, digging up allotments and smashing a great number of windows there and in Kirkham Street. Two bombs in Kingsdale Road partly demolished two houses with the inevitable accompanying broken windows there and in Melling Street, Bassant Road and Heathfield Terrace. Four more wrecked plant nurseries, a house and cottages on the eastern side of Plumstead Common while others caused damage around King's Highway, at Woolwich Cemetery and at many other properties in the area. Mathy was now heading north towards the point where Plumstead High Street joined Bostall Hill.

The house at 3 Bostall Hill was home to two families. On the top floor munitions worker Walter Pearce lived with his wife Ellen and their two children, Winnie, aged four and 22-month-old Elsie. Earlier that evening the family had gone to a party on the ground floor at the home of the Allam family to celebrate the 70th birthday of Mrs Allam's mother. In the house next door everyone was asleep except six-year-old Eva. A 'buzzing noise in the sky' woke her and she whispered to her brother, 'The "Zepps" are coming'. Hearing a bomb explode in the distance he woke their parents and the whole family trooped down to the basement as three bombs exploded.

The place seemed to be struck like an earthquake. The roof and upper floor crashed in, pictures and ornaments fell, and

even in the basement the refugees were shaken. The light
went out but all were alive. Not one was harmed.[31]

Next door at No.3, however, the story was very different. Ellen Pearce was
up very late when she heard the sound of exploding bombs. Carrying
baby Elsie she decided to go downstairs to warn the Allams. Just as she
reached the second flight of stairs a bomb smashed into the house.[32]
A police sergeant found it practically demolished: 'Only the side wall
and centre partition between the front and back rooms on the ground
floor remained.' Picking his way through tons of rubble he found the
bodies of Walter, Ellen and Elsie.[33]

A police surgeon described their injuries.

> The dead man had very many scalp wounds and injuries
> to both legs but his death was due to asphyxia from being
> crushed by debris and also to shock.

> Witness next described terrible injuries to the child, which
> included a bad fracture of the skull, a wound in the left leg,
> fracture of the left thigh, two wounds on the left arm, and
> one on the right arm. A severe fracture of the skull would
> probably cause instantaneous death.

> Later he saw the body of the women, who had a large wound
> on the body, which was the cause of death.[34]

Buried under an accumulation of furniture and beams the Pearce's other
daughter, four-year-old Winnie, was alive.

> When the firemen came they saw her imprisoned… 'Now you
> be a good girl and keep quite still till we get to you,' said one
> worker, 'and you will be alright.' 'I've got dust in my eyes,'
> said the child, beginning to cry. 'Well,' said the tender-hearted
> fireman, 'you be good and I'll buy you a nice dolly.' Soon
> they led her off to the infirmary, where she received kindly
> treatment. But she did not realise that her father, mother and
> baby sister had gone.[35]

The other family in the house, the Allam's, all survived. Mrs Allam's
mother was unhurt, 'but her daughter, who was pinned by both legs

amidst the debris, refused to be assisted until the rescuers were able to assure her that her mother was safe'.[36]

Two more bombs had fallen at almost the same moment. One behind 3 Bostall Hill demolished the back of 78 Cordite Street[37], with resulting damage to many others homes, but the other landed on an allotment. There were no more casualties.

Mathy now crossed back over the Thames, dropping a single bomb at Rainham at about 1.45am where it smashed a few cottage windows. Benefitting from a tail wind L 31 reached the Essex coast near Shoeburyness about 2.15am and rendezvoused at the north-east corner of Kent with Peterson and L 32 a little after 3am. Together they headed back to Germany. For Mathy, however, the journey did not end well. Carrying excess weight through an accumulation of rain on the envelope and having used all the water ballast, L 31 hit the ground hard, the impact inflicting significant damage. She was out of action for a month, but the 43 bombs (35 HE and eight incendiary) she dropped on London inflicted damage estimated at £130,000, the second highest amount by a single Zeppelin in the war.[38]

Although Woodhouse of No.50 (Home Defence) Squadron had tried to engage L 32 off the Kent coast, no other pilots had any luck. Seven RNAS aircraft were searching fruitlessly for Zeppelins as were five from the RFC's No. 39 (Home Defence) Squadron. Their flight based at Hounslow had recently transferred to a new airfield at North Weald Bassett, concentrating the squadron's three flights in Essex on the eastern approaches to London. One of its pilots, Second Lieutenant James Mackay caught a glimpse of L 31 but another, Lieutenant William Leefe Robinson, patrolling from Sutton's Farm failed to see L 31, which must have passed close by when Mathy crossed the Thames to Rainham. But Robinson's day of destiny was fast approaching.

Chapter 14

# A Bright Flare of Light

After Heinrich Mathy's raid on London on 24/25 August, Strasser was keen to try again. He sent out an eight-Zeppelin raid on 29 August but changing weather conditions resulted in an early recall. When he received a prediction of good weather four days later, Strasser authorised a raid on 'England South, chief target London' for the night of 2/3 September. In this enterprise four army airships joined 12 from the navy, making it the largest airship raid of the war. Both fleets included a wooden-framed Schütte-Lanz in their number. The naval airships would approach over Norfolk and Lincolnshire while the army vessels would come in over Kent and Essex.

Waiting for them in England was an improving air defence organisation. The warning system had been operating for three months, helping to ensure the timely transmission of information regarding approaching airships, which improved the chances of locating the raiders. And there was a belief amongst pilots that the new bullets they were receiving would give them an advantage in future encounters – if only they could get close enough to use them effectively. Some pilots reduced the weight of their aircraft by removing the boxes of Ranken darts, allowing them to climb a little higher and a little faster.

An important part of the air defence organisation were the listening stations on Britain's east coast, where both the Admiralty and the War Office had established their own networks, yet there was little in the way of co-operation between them until early 1917. On 2 September these stations intercepted increased wireless transmissions and by 5pm it became clear that a raid was underway. Both organisations had their own codebreaking sections, which deciphered these transmissions. The Naval Intelligence Division's 'Room 40' is well known,[1] but the

Directorate of Military Intelligence's M.I.1b (and later M.I.1e) was a far more shadowy organisation.[2]

Out over the North Sea the anticipated good weather failed to materialise. Heavy rain, snow and ice weighed the raiders down and a dramatic change of wind direction, now blowing from the south-west, further hindered progress. The commanders of the navy's L 17 and the army's LZ 97, did not find things easy. Oberleutnant Weidling on LZ 97 bemoaned the impossibility of getting wireless bearings to confirm his position, and Kapitänleutnant Hermann Kraushaar aboard L 17 reported the headwind reduced his ground speed to 22mph.[3] Both commanders reported dropping their bombs and Kraushaar claimed an attack on Norwich, but British trackers placed them both about 30 miles out to sea when they turned back. In fact four other raiders also claimed to have bombed Norwich that night and two others reported attacks on Nottingham, however, not a single bomb dropped on either place.

Three of the raiding Zeppelins came inland over the coast of Lincolnshire between 10.40 and 10.56pm. The county received its first warning at 9.20pm, with the TARA order following at 10.29pm.

## 2 September 1916, 10.50pm: Boston, Lincolnshire

The first to come inland was Kapitänleutnant Wilhelm Ganzel's L 23; he had relinquished command of the old L 9 only three weeks prior. He crossed the coastline of The Wash at 10.40pm about five miles from Boston. He had earlier dropped a number of bombs at sea to lighten his ship.

The Grand Sluice in Boston, controlling the flow of the River Witham, lies by a railway bridge and is crossed by Fydell Street. John Thomas Oughton, employed by the Witham Drainage Commissioners, lived in a house on Haven Bank just a few yards from the Sluice, and as a member of the Town Guard was just about to go on duty. In a signal box where the railway passed the Grand Sluice, signalman Beeton was at work as Zeppelin L 23 approached from the east.

At first a dull subdued hum caused concern. 'Louder and louder the whirring became,' an eyewitness recounted, 'gradually increasing in volume until it exceeded many times the noise of a railway train.' On the other side of the river two couples scanned the sky then one of them exclaimed, 'Why, it's right above'.

Before one could hardly realise what was happening there was a flash of light in the sky and above the roar of the Zeppelin engines... a shrill whistling... heralded the fall of the first bomb. There was a vivid flash of light, a deep intonation, and Boston had received its baptism of fire.[4]

Mr Oughton heard the Zeppelin's engines as he left his house. His two sons were standing in the doorway as he called to them, 'There it is'. Thomas, aged 19, shouted to his brother, 17-year-old Horace, 'Run for your life. There's a bomb coming.' Thomas ducked into the house but Horace stood transfixed as the bomb exploded just yards away. Their father was on the ground stunned and wounded, but Horace had suffered terrible injuries with half of the left side of his face blown away and a large gaping hole in his back. Astonishingly he was still alive but died 15 minutes after arriving at the hospital.[5]

Beeton, the signalman, had just stepped back into his signal box when the bomb exploded shattering all the windows and damaging the parapet of the sluice. He lay on the ground bleeding profusely from 32 separate cuts to his back, legs and arms.[6]

About 60 yards along Fydell Street and just a few yards from the gasworks, an incendiary bomb fell into the garden of a house. Perhaps no more than a second or two later another bomb exploded at the entrance to the gasworks, destroying the gates, damaging the fitter's shop, the stores and the boardroom as well as the house where the incendiary bomb was burning. At another house the occupiers were thrown about by the blast and it seemed as if 'the concrete foundations were indiarubber'. The family left their home and walked towards the Grand Sluice.

> As we got outside... I was feeling my way up to the bridge... and then we went on the Haven Bank, and practically walked on to Beeton, a railwayman, who was injured. He said, 'Missus, take your apron off and tie my leg up. I believe it is off'.[7]

Beeton's leg was still attached but when he got to hospital the doctors had no choice but to amputate.

The next bomb exploded in a garden about 100 yards further along Fydell Street, smashing windows in all directions but there were no injuries. The following day nearly every house bore some mark of the

Zeppelin's visit 'in the way of boards, pieces of corrugated iron, sacking, paste boards, nailed up to hide the bareness of the empty window frames'.

The fourth and final HE bomb fell in Mrs Belton's garden at her house in Carlton Road. Mrs Belton, an elderly lady of 86, was sitting by a window with two friends when the bomb exploded, 'and instantly the room was brought to a state of chaos'. Fortunately for the three ladies the blast sucked the glass out and not into the room. The concussion of the explosion spread from Carlton Road to Albert Street and Granville Street, smashing countless windows there and in Argyle Street, while apples from fruit trees in Mrs Belton's garden were hurled for a great distance.

Leaving Boston behind, Ganzel initially headed west before commencing a wide anti-clockwise circle with a bomb damaging farm buildings at Kirton Fen, but the four incendiaries at Kirton Holme, Swineshead and Gosberton failed to cause any harm. At 11.25pm L 23 was at Tydd, near the Lincolnshire/Norfolk border, although Ganzel believed he was much further into Norfolk at the time. Deciding he had little prospect of reaching London against the wind, Ganzel decided on a north-east course which he thought would take him to Norwich where he reported bombarding the city and surrounding area, although he added: 'The effect of the dropped bombs could not be observed because of the clouds.'[8] In reality there was little to see. Trackers recorded L 23 out over The Wash at 11.55pm when his 22 'Norwich' bombs fell in the sea.[9]

The other two Zeppelins that crossed into Lincolnshire, L 13 and L 22, did so about five minutes apart on the coast between Cleethorpes and Donna Nook shortly before 11pm. Kapitänleutnant Martin Dietrich, with one of L 22's engines out of action, quickly abandoned any idea of raiding London and selected Nottingham as a secondary target. Inaccurate wireless bearings placed him north of the Humber but he was south of the river at Humberston when he released five bombs over searchlights at about 11.10pm. An hour later and in atrocious weather conditions, L 22 was south of Goole when Dietrich gave up on Nottingham and chose Hull as his third target. He crossed the Humber near Killingholme at 12.35am but thick cloud prevented him finding the city. Seven minutes later, guns to the east opened fire as L 22 moved towards the coast at Aldebrough, having dropped three bombs in fields at Flinton. Dietrich reported dropping 27 bombs on an industrial site near Hull but had passed over the coast at 12.55am without making an attack. These 'Hull' bombs may be those recorded falling at sea at 1.35am.[10]

# 3 September 1916, 1am: East Retford, Nottinghamshire

Kapitänleutnant der Reserve Eduard Prölss came inland in L 13 with Martin Dietrich's L 22 and also abandoned the attempt on London, selecting Nottingham as his secondary target. Heading west, L 13 passed Market Rasen and at 11.40pm dropped a single incendiary bomb at Caenby, no doubt to check ground speed and drift, and as he moved further inland the skies began to clear. At 12.15am L 13 dropped four incendiary bombs over Morton Carr and ten bombs on East Stockwith, opposite the industrial site of Morris' Chemical Works where lights were showing as the TARA warning had not been received. The bombs at Morton Carr fell on farmland but at East Stockwith they demolished two houses, smashed many windows and injured an elderly woman. Across the river at West Stockwith, 16 homes lost their windows but the chemical works escaped untouched. At 12.40am L 13 reached Bawtry where Prölss observed a train running from Doncaster and followed it to the outskirts of Retford, which he believed was Nottingham. That city was actually 27 miles further south.

Veering eastwards away from the railway, Prölss began dropping the first of 13 bombs along the line of Hallcroft Road at 12.56am. Most fell on open ground but not far from the Mayor's residence, a glue works, a dye works and a laundry. Despite the violence of these explosions, as one newspaper reported, 'No material damage was done so far – only great shell holes 16 feet across and 5 feet deep – were left to mark [the Zeppelin's] course'.[11]

Crossing the River Idle and now over East Retford, L 13 passed the close-packed homes on Moorgate to drop a bomb in fields at the back of Wellington Street. A few seconds later the next exploded at the bottom of Spital Hill demolishing a fruit warehouse, smashing water and gas mains and damaging properties all around. 'The roof was torn off in many places,' a newspaper reported, 'windows and doors blown in, and the furniture upstairs and down exposed, but here again there was no serious injury to the person.'[12]

At the gasworks on Grove Street the sound of exploding bombs woke the family of the site manager who lived within the grounds. They made their way quickly to the basement which they reached just as a huge explosion shook the house and lethal glass shards sliced into still warm beds. After the bomb on Spital Hill the next had exploded on open ground to the north of Grove Street smashing windows at the Methodist Chapel and Wesleyan school, but it was followed almost immediately by another that blasted an orchard next to the gasworks. Jagged bomb fragments pierced the three gas holders as an incendiary bomb ignited the escaping gas in an eruption of volcanic proportions. In the intense heat 'apples baked on the trees and roosting birds were roasted alive'. With some satisfaction Prölss noted: 'First some fires started, but suddenly a big factory blew up. The fire it caused was so strong that the streets of the city were clearly visible for a while.' An eyewitness on the ground thought it 'a weird and wonderful spectacle'.

Less than 150 yards away another bomb exploded at 1 Grove Lane, just across the Chesterfield Canal, ripping away one side of the house leaving a bedstead and other furniture exposed. Four people in the house emerged uninjured from the wreckage and into the glaring light of the burning gasworks.

Continuing on his course for another 200 yards, Prölss released his final HE bomb. It exploded in Trent Street, smashing gas and water mains as well as drainage pipes. The blast destroyed windows, ripped tiles from roofs and sent showers of glass into the houses. In one of those closest to the explosion, bomb fragments struck two sisters lying in bed with a little Belgian girl asleep between them. Both sisters were removed to hospital but their companion escaped injury. The girls' parents were lucky as bomb fragments zipped about their bedroom without hitting them.[13] Across the street another young woman was injured by flying glass. The last incendiary bomb burnt out in a field between Trent Street and the railway. As Prölss departed, he noted that L 13 remained 'lit up bright as day' by the burning gasworks, unaware that he had caused the most significant damage of any of the raiders that night.

Prölss dropped just two more bombs before he reached the coast at 1.30am near Donna Nook, at Lea, south of Gainsborough and at Aylesby, west of Grimsby. Neither caused any damage.

## 2 September 1916, 11.10pm: Earsham, Suffolk

Of the eight Zeppelins that arrived over East Anglia, L 30 and L 24 spent as little time as possible over land. Commanding L 30, Horst von Buttlar filed another of his 'enthusiastic' reports. Not for the first time he claimed a successful raid on London that did not happen.[14] Crossing the coast at Southwold in Suffolk at 10.40pm he pushed inland but as he approached Pulham Market a searchlight pierced the clouds and found L 30. Without hesitation von Buttlar turned away from the light onto a north-east course towards the historic market town of Bungay positioned by a dramatic bend in the River Waveney.[15] As the clock showed 11.10pm von Buttlar began his 'London' raid. About three quarters of a mile west of the village of Earsham he dropped a line of 21 bombs across agricultural land with only two making any impact on the communities below. One damaged buildings at Earsham Park Farm, while at Hill Farm another injured a man, partly demolished the farmhouse and damaged other buildings. Over Bungay Common, located within the grand sweeping turn of the Waveney, von Buttlar released nine more bombs, killing two cows and injuring three more. Maintaining the same course L 30 released six bombs north of Ditchingham but damage was again limited. At Ditchingham House, home of the novelist Sir Henry Rider Haggard (who was overseas at the time), explosions shattered windows. Similar damage occurred at another large house, The Grange, and at St Mary's church and a reformatory, the House of Mercy. Four bombs achieved similar results at Redhouse Farm north of Broome.[16]

Von Buttlar's 40 bombs, dropped along a perfectly straight line four and a half miles long had achieved little. As he returned to the coast near Great Yarmouth at 11.25pm, L 30 encountered the defences. Two mobile 3-pdr anti-aircraft guns at Fritton opened fire and two pilots, Flight Lieutenant Egbert Cadbury from RNAS Yarmouth and Flight sub-Lieutenant Stanley Kemball from RNAS Covehithe, both saw L 30 and gave pursuit for about 10 minutes before losing her in the clouds.[17]

## 3 September 1916, 1.30am: RNAS Bacton, Norfolk

Robert Koch in L 24 also made only a brief stay over East Anglia. Battling foul weather, Koch believed he came inland over The Wash and had penetrated as far south as Cambridge before giving up on London and targeting Norwich instead. The reality was quite different. British trackers recorded L 24 crossing the Norfolk coast between Cromer and Bacton at 12.30am. Twenty minutes later L 24 was at Briston, a village some 12 miles south-west of Cromer, where he dropped two bombs. Briston may have been Koch's 'Norwich' because in his report he states the crew were blinded by a searchlight at Norwich and dropped two HE bombs in the hope other lights would illuminate and pinpoint the city for him. Unsurprisingly, this did not happen and Koch gave up any hope of finding Norwich (which was 18 miles to the south) and headed back towards the coast at Bacton, dropping an incendiary at the village of Plumstead on the way.

A 75mm mobile gun north of Bacton fired five rounds at 1.05am but visibility was severely hampered by the clouds, then, as L 24 headed up the coast, a mobile 3-pdr at Mundesley briefly opened fire too.[18] Koch retaliated and, circling round, dropped five bombs on the gun positioned by the cliff edge. They all missed but were close.[19] Turning over the sea L 24 returned, attracted by a patch of diffused light illuminating the clouds which, combined with the gunfire, convinced Koch he had found a target and concluded it was Great Yarmouth (actually about 20 miles to the south). He dropped two incendiary bombs over the village of Trunch around 1.30am as L 24 headed towards the patch of light over which he released 40 bombs (13 HE and 27 incendiaries). He reported hitting a 'train station, gas-works and batteries' at Great Yarmouth, as well as an airfield. He was correct about an airfield. Some of the bombs fell close to RNAS Bacton, where the landing flares had illuminated the clouds, but all had fallen on open ground between the airfield and the village of Ridlington. L 24 passed out to sea over Bacton from where a mobile 3-pdr and two French 75mm guns fired 19 rounds to send her on her way.[20]

## 3 September 1916, 2.25am: Haddenham, Cambridgeshire

Norfolk saw much airship activity on the night of 2/3 September but little of it had a significant impact on the rural landscape. The commander of SL 8, a Schütte-Lanz airship recently transferred from the Baltic and on its first raid over England, was one. Her commander, Kapitänleutnant Guido Wolff, claimed to have bombed Norwich but like others who made a similar claim he was wrong.

Wolff never saw the Norfolk coastline when he crossed it near Holkham at 11.05pm, and after dropping two incendiary bombs at Burnham Thorpe ten minutes later he headed south-west, into the wind. Three hours later, at 2am, SL 8 had progressed only 67 miles and was east of Huntingdon having earlier dropped an incendiary at Littleport and six more on Oxlode Fen, north of Ely. As the weather cleared, Wolff observed the subdued glow of London on the far horizon but realised it would take too long to reach the city in the face of the strong wind and turned away onto a north-east course. At 2.20am SL 8 passed Haddenham but a few minutes later the crew saw an unexplained bright flare of light far to the south. With the wind now pushing him forward at 60mph, at 2.55am Wolff believed SL 8 was approaching Norwich and prepared to attack. He was, however, 34 miles west of the city and his bombs fell on a line from the village of Congham to Cley-next-the-Sea. At 3am six bombs at Congham broke windows and roof tiles in a couple of cottages, followed by 11 bombs dropped at Harpley Dams, Fitcham, East Rudham, Helhoughton, Syderstone and South Creake, but only at the last village was any damage recorded: four cottages had their windows smashed. Wolff then released a single bomb at 3.15am over Great Walsingham and two at Wighton. A final bomb landed at Cley-next-the-Sea before Wolff dropped eight in the sea as he set course back to Nordholz. His four hours over Norfolk had resulted in six cottages losing their windows and a few smashed and dislodged roof tiles.

## 3 September 1916, 2.25am: Harwich Harbour, Essex

An hour before SL 8 crossed the coastline, the usually determined Viktor Schütze was off Great Yarmouth in command of the old L 11. He identified the town through the clouds but facing strong headwinds he gave up on London. At 10.10pm Schütze dropped a number of bombs at sea before coming inland.

> 'There it is,' exclaimed spectators, and there it was sure enough, distinctly seen as it passed across the stars. Gradually lessening, the drone and thud of the engines appeared to indicate that the aircraft was going inland. It had not gone more than a few hundred yards in that direction when it dropped two or three bombs on marshes, doing, however no damage at all worth speaking of. Suddenly it turned, as if its crew had found their position precarious; it retreated rapidly over town and sea; and in a few minutes had passed out of hearing.[21]

The two bombs fell close to the marshy banks of the River Yare before Schütze turned back to the sea where more bombs fell. He reported dropping 20 bombs on the town, its batteries and on warships in the harbour, so he may have lost sight of the coastline due to the clouds.[22] Heading south and having brushed off anti-aircraft fire from the Lowestoft area, Schütze reached Harwich and its harbour. He had attacked there a month earlier and, mindful of its defences, now waited for just over an hour for cloud cover to aid him. At 2.20am he made his move, dropping four bombs in the harbour, which although exploding in the water still broke a few windows. With searchlights occasionally picking up the airship through the clouds and guns of the Harwich Garrison opening fire, L 11 turned away and went out to sea north of Aldeburgh at 2.50am. Shortly after leaving Harwich, however, the crew, like those on SL 8, saw a flare of light in the sky about 60 miles away in the direction of London. It was disconcerting.

Before the crews of SL 8 and L 11 had seen that flare of light, one of the army Zeppelins had come and gone, claiming a raid on London and having left a unique souvenir for the British authorities.

## 3 September 1916, 12.40am: Wixoe, Suffolk

Hauptmann Charles la Quiante, commanding LZ 90, came inland just north of Clacton, Essex, at about 11pm. Once overland he battled the fierce wind until he reached Mistley, about 10 miles from the coast, where he remained for at least 25 minutes. A local man, Robert Grimwade, thought the Zeppelin shut down its engines, but it was more likely a case of throttling them back because, in an attempt to lighten his ship, La Quiante decided to jettison his *Spähkorb* (sub-cloud car). The crew winched it down about 5,000 feet before cutting the cable. Grimwade heard a thud as it hit the ground at 11.45pm. When the abandoned *Spähkorb* was found in a field the following morning there was some concern that a man had landed in it but this was soon dismissed.[23]

The *Spähkorb* was an observation car lowered by winch from where an observer could communicate by telephone with the command gondola while the airship remained unseen above the clouds. There was no standard design, the one that fell at Mistley had the shape of a miniature Zeppelin, made of wood and covered with thin duralumin sheeting. Inside it the observer lay on a mattress while looking through small windows. It measured 4.35 metres in length and weighed between 50 and 60kgs.[24] While army airship commanders valued the *Spähkorb*, the navy officers did not share their view. This may be due to a rather unsettling experience suffered by Peter Strasser while personally testing one.

About 300 feet down, while the winch was allowing the cable to unwind slowly but steadily, the tail of the car became entangled with the wireless aerial.

It caught the car and tilted it upside down. The cable meanwhile continued unwinding from the winch above and was beginning to dangle in a slack loop below Strasser, who only saved himself from being tipped out by clinging to the sides of the car with a deathlike grip.

Suddenly the aerial gave way, sending the car and Strasser plunging down until it brought up at the end of its own cable with a sickening jolt. It was not a propitious introduction for a new device.[25]

Leaving Mistley behind, LZ 90 headed north-west and dropped two incendiary bombs at the village of Foxearth near Sudbury from where La Quiante reported a bright spot on the horizon, which he concluded was London. Over Poslingford he jettisoned the now superfluous winch that carried the *Spähkorb's* cable to lighten his ship further[26] and at 12.40am prepared to attack as he could 'clearly see that a densely built-up area of London was below us'.[27] He reported dropping 50 bombs but only 37 (21 HE and 16 incendiary) were discovered. Although cloud cover made observation difficult, La Quiante confidently reported that 'two sources of fire were clearly identified and a loud explosion followed by a strong fire'. In fact, La Quiante never even got close to London, his bombs landing around the tiny village of Wixoe, three miles south-east of Haverhill in Suffolk and about 45 miles from the capital. The only damage amounted to a few broken windows at the school and in two other buildings. Taking advantage of the south-westerly tailwind, La Quiante sped homeward across East Anglia before exiting between Caister and Great Yarmouth at 1.45am.

While other Zeppelin commanders abandoned plans for London, at one point four navy Zeppelins appeared close to achieving their goal. Those four raiders, L 14, L 32, L 21 and L 16, all crossed over a 25-mile stretch of the north Norfolk coast between 9.50 and 10.40pm and, despite flying into the fierce headwind, all were closing on London when plans dramatically changed.

## 3 September 1916, 2.25am: Thaxted, Essex and Tring, Hitchin and Essendon, Hertfordshire

The first of these, Kuno Manger's L 14, crossed the coast near Wells-next-the-Sea at 9.50pm, dropping an incendiary bomb there and a HE bomb at Ringstead, but he struggled to make progress against the wind, snow and hail. Circling to the south of King's Lynn, Manger believed he had found Boston,[28] which was 30 miles away, and dropped six bombs around 11.30pm, two at Gayton, one on Wormegay Fen and three on the wooded Shouldham Warren. No damage was caused by any of these. Heading south-west, at 12.40am Manger passed north of Kimbolton, having dropped an incendiary at Upwood, a village between Yaxley and Huntingdon, but could not make further headway. Slowly flying in a wide circle L 14 progressed to the south-east and at 2.25am was between Thaxted and Dunmow, with the north-eastern outskirts of London just 30 tantalising miles away. But that is as close as L 14 got. Matters elsewhere made Manger immediately turn away from London.

Werner Peterson commanded the second of this group of four Zeppelins to threaten London. L 32 crossed the coast at Sheringham at 10.03pm. Battling against the wind, Peterson headed south-west covering only 23 miles in the first hour. At 11.10pm L 32 dropped six bombs on farmland between the villages of Ovington and Saham Toney where explosions smashed windows and damaged a ceiling at Woodhouse Farm, north of Ovington. Peterson, however, was uncertain of his position and requested wireless bearings three times in forty minutes, the first at 11.27pm. At 11.45pm he dropped two incendiary bombs at Two Mile Bottom and at 12.30am, when near Newmarket, he headed into the wind, taking 80 minutes to reach Sandy in Bedfordshire, just over 30 miles away and where L 32 crossed paths with L 21. At Woburn L 32 changed course to the south and about 2.25am, after nearly four and a half hours over England, Peterson inexplicably believed he had reached Kensington in the heart of south-west London and prepared to turn east and bombard the city. But L 32 was not over London; Peterson was at Tring in Hertfordshire, almost 30 miles to the north-west. As he made ready, Peterson, like Manger in L 14, saw something that caused great concern to him and his crew. And they were not alone.

Kurt Frankenburg in L 21 crossed the coast at Mundesley at 10.20pm and followed a similar course to L 32, although keeping a few miles south of Peterson's airship. Frankenburg was south of Newmarket at 12.20am, requesting wireless bearings at the same time as Peterson who was on the northern side of the town. With ground speed reduced to 10mph at times, Frankenburg reached Biggleswade in Bedfordshire at 1.35am and, changing direction to the north-west, crossed paths with L 32 at Sandy at 1.50am. A couple of course changes later and L 21 reached Hitchin at 2.25am with the north London suburbs a little over 20 miles away. But just as Frankenburg prepared to make his approach, the situation changed dramatically and, as with Manger and Peterson, it meant a sudden change of plan.

The fourth in this quartet of navy Zeppelins, L 16, crossed the Norfolk coast at 10.40pm about five miles west of Sheringham. Heavy with rain and ice, Kapitänleutnant Erich Sommerfeldt took 48 minutes to cover the first 25 miles to the village of Kimberley, about 10 miles south-west of Norwich, where an incendiary bomb caused no damage. At 11.45pm Sommerfeldt reported attacking a train 'south-west of Norwich' with three bombs. These were probably the bombs that fell at Little Livermere close to the Bury St Edmonds to Thetford Line on the Great Eastern Railway. No damage was done. Keeping to a south-west course, L 16 reached Hitchin at 12.45am where Sommerfeldt sought wireless bearings after which problems with the forward engine delayed him further and it was not until 1.30am that L 16 passed between Redbourn and Harpenden where it dropped six bombs. These exploded in open country near a Midland Railway branch line where one smashed windows in cottages on the outskirts of Harpenden.

At 1.50am L 16 reached South Mimms from where it must have been clear to Sommerfeldt that another airship was close by as bombs were exploding and burning about six miles away. Strangely, Sommerfeldt turned away from London and headed slowly north but at 2am numerous searchlights began concentrating over north London and one after another, anti-aircraft guns began to bark at the sky. Sommerfeldt changed direction again and, heading south once more, reached Potter's Bar in Hertfordshire at 2.15am. The intensity of the fire aimed at another airship left Sommerfeldt unsure what to do next, but as that fire edged north and concentrated on an area about six miles away from L 16, Sommerfeldt decided his next move. There was a searchlight sweeping the sky just four miles to the north of his position and it appeared unprotected by anti-aircraft guns. Sommerfeldt decided to attack it. The light was probing the skies from the village of Essendon.

At the home of the village blacksmith in Essendon, his eldest daughter, 26-year-old Frances Bamford was awoken by the sound of engines. On looking out of the window she saw the searchlights and realised it was a Zeppelin she could hear. Frances, who worked as a telephonist at the Hatfield telephone exchange, woke her parents and told them she thought she would be needed at work. As they roused the other four children, the first of L 16's bombs exploded nearby and Frances' father ordered everyone out into the paddock. Sommerfeldt released 25 bombs (16 HE and nine incendiary) and as they rained down, crashing and burning in and around the village, one burst in the paddock. In the chaos another of the Bamford daughters told her father that 12-year-old Eleanor was badly hurt. He found her lying on the grass terribly injured and carried her unconscious body into the house which was untouched by the blast. Already distraught, a neighbour than told Mr Bamford that he had found Frances dead in the paddock, killed instantly when a fragment of the bomb sliced right through her body. Doctors amputated Eleanor's leg but it failed to save her and she died later that day. Elsewhere in the village, a bomb exploded on the roof of the church vestry smashing the ceiling above the altar, blasting a hole in the south wall of the chancel, wrecking the organ and smashing windows. Others wrecked homes in the village, injuring a man and a child. Fortunately, two thirds of the bombs landed in fields outside the village.

Having released most of his bombs Sommerfeldt had no intention of continuing towards London, but even if he had, what happened next would have made him change his mind. An intense blinding light suddenly illuminated L 16, lighting up the control gondola as though it were a sunny day. The source of that light was just four miles away. Everyone on board L 16 knew what they were witnessing. While his horrified crew looked on, Sommerfeldt gave the order to head away from the light as fast as possible.

\* \* \*

Far away to the north-east army Zeppelin LZ 98 was approaching the Suffolk coast at the end of her raid. Her commander, Ernst Lehmann, was checking his maps before heading back out over the North Sea on the homeward leg of his journey when his executive officer, Baron Max von Gemmingen, 'let out a scream'. Lehmann looked back in the direction from which they had come and saw the same shocking sight that had halted Manger, Peterson, Frankenburg and Sommerfeldt in their tracks; 'far behind us, a bright ball of fire'.

> We knew that the blazing meteor on the further rim of the city could only be one of our airships... The flaming mass hung in the sky for more than a minute; then single parts detached themselves from it and preceded it to earth. Poor fellows, they were lost the moment the ship took fire.

> We remained silent until it was all over, and then realized how easily the same fate could have overtaken us.[29]

Lehmann had no idea just how true those final words were.

## Chapter 15

# 'One Glowing Blazing Mass'

A TARA warning was issued at 10.51pm, alerting Area 42 (covering Essex) that Zeppelins were over Britain. Three pilots of No.39 (Home Defence) Squadron allocated night patrol duty were standing by when HQ at Woodford Green relayed the order to the airfields at North Weald Bassett, Sutton's Farm and Hainault Farm on the eastern approaches to London. Standing orders required a pilot from each airfield to spiral up to 10,000 feet then follow a set patrol line for two hours looking for Zeppelins before commencing his descent. Two hours after the despatch of the first patrols a second patrol would ascend to take over from those descending. Once in the air they were on their own, there were no radios to guide them to a target.

'A' flight at North Weald Bassett patrolled between there and Hainault Farm from where 'C' flight continued the line to Sutton's Farm. 'B' flight flew the most southerly leg from Sutton's Farm to Joyce Green airfield on the south bank of the Thames near Dartford. The patrol lines extended for about 18 miles. At the three airfields, aircraft engines spluttered into life as ground crew and pilots rushed to complete final checks. Lieutenant William Leefe Robinson, commanding 'B' flight, was first to get his BE2c airborne at 11.08pm. Three minutes later a BE12 piloted by Lieutenant Clifford Ross took off from North Weald and only another minute passed before Alfred de Bathe Brandon bounced along the grass runway and coaxed his BE2c up into the air from Hainault Farm.

Designed before the war as a two-seater reconnaissance aircraft, the BE2c saw service on the Western Front in 1915 where, although this extremely steady aircraft was ideally suited for its role, it became an easy target for nimble German fighters. In a Home Defence role, however, its steady reliability proved ideal for pilots embarking on the challenge of night flying. Flown as a single seater, the pilot occupied the rear seat with the front cockpit covered over to reduce drag. Although now armed with a Lewis machine gun, British engineers were still working on an efficient interrupter gear to allow the gun to fire through the propeller, so the gun fired upwards at an angle of 45 degrees through a cut-out at the rear of the upper wing. To make a successful attack the pilot had either to fly under the target Zeppelin or tilt over while flying alongside, not an easy feat while avoiding 'friendly' anti-aircraft shells and enemy machine gun fire. The BE12 flown by Lieutenant Ross was in essence a single-seat version of the BE2c with a more powerful engine.

William Leefe Robinson was born in India in 1895, where his father owned a coffee estate, and was educated in India and England. He did well in his school's Officer Training Corps and in August 1914 entered the Royal Military College, Sandhurst. On 16 December 1914 he was posted with the rank of second lieutenant to the 5th (Reserve) Battalion, Worcestershire Regiment in Cornwall where the boredom and drudgery of training recruits quickly wore Robinson down and he looked for a way out to 'do his bit'. In March 1915 his application for transfer to the Royal Flying Corps received approval and by the end of the month he was in France as an Observer with No.4 Squadron where he fell in love with flying. On 8 May, however, a wound in his right arm saw him return to England for a month's recuperation during which time he applied for flying training. After gaining his 'wings' and completing a military flying course, he joined No.19 Squadron forming at Castle Bromwich in September 1915. Having shown an aptitude for night flying, Robinson had a number of 'loan' postings to assist in the defence of London until he arrived at Sutton's Farm at the beginning of February 1916 to join No.19 Reserve Aeroplane Squadron, which in turn became No.39 (Home Defence) Squadron.[1]

When Robinson took off from Sutton's Farm it took him 53 minutes to climb to his patrol height of 10,000 feet, emphasising the importance of the early warning system. Once at the required height he headed south and began patrolling back and forwards between Sutton's Farm and Joyce Green, all the time scanning the darkness for raiding airships. Lieutenant Ross completed his patrol having seen nothing of the enemy and crashed when landing back at North Weald but was unhurt. Brandon also had no luck in his search, returning to Hainault Farm at 1.38am.

At 12.01am, at exactly the same time that Robinson reached 10,000 feet over Sutton's Farm, Ernst Lehmann brought Zeppelin LZ 98 inland over the Kent coast between Dymchurch and Dungeness. He made steady progress north-west and at 1.09am neared the village of Hartley, five miles south-west of Gravesend, from where a searchlight found him. Searchlights from Southfleet and Dartford also located the intruder and guns burst into action from both places. At 1.20am LZ 98 escaped the grip of the lights and the guns fell silent.[2] Lehmann had handled his airship skilfully.

> Finding several single clouds floating about two miles high, I decided to use them in escaping the searchlights…. It had taken us about an hour… to come up to the position best suited for the attack. Again the cloud and haze made it exceedingly difficult to spot definitely the surface objectives, but finally we recognised the familiar bends of the Thames.

> We went in from the south, taking a zig-zag course and jumping from one cloud to another until LZ 98 was over the docks. There we dropped our bombs. Three times before this the ship had been picked up by the lights and on each occasion they had lost her as we entered cloud.[3]

While Lehmann's skilful use of cloud cover and his identification of the Thames is not disputed, his bombs did not fall on the London Docks. Most of his bombs fell as he approached Gravesend, aimed loosely at the searchlights at Hartley and Southfleet. His first six bombs, incendiaries, fell in a field west of Longfield, then 12 more landed in fields either side of the road from Westwood to Southfleet, setting fire to a stack of wheat, before three HE bombs descended near the Southfleet searchlight. One failed to detonate, another smashed windows in Church Street and at Cook's Cottages in the neighbouring hamlet of Red Street, and the third exploded on a brick-built outhouse at Northfleet Green Farm where the farmer had a fortunate escape.

> The farmer was looking out of a window overlooking the outhouse, and there was a horse in the stable: the former was driven backwards from the window uninjured and not even thrown down as he hung on to the sill, the horse was quite uninjured. The whole force of the explosion appears to have expended itself forward through the door giving on to the lane, and vertically upwards. The house and stable are very little damaged.[4]

About a mile on, LZ 98 dropped two more bombs while skirting Gravesend; both fell on the golf course. Across the Thames, searchlights on the Essex side of the river now picked up LZ 98 and at 1.20am the 12-pdr gun at Tilbury opened fire, causing Lehmann to climb rapidly to 14,000 feet and head north-east with a strong tailwind aiding his escape. In a report on the action the officer commanding the Woolwich area guns concluded: 'The Zeppelin was not seen to be attacked by our aircraft.' A dangerous hunter, however, had been stalking LZ 98.

As William Leefe Robinson neared the end of his patrol, like Ross and Brandon he had seen no sign of Zeppelin activity. At 1.07am Second Lieutenant Frederick Sowrey took off from Sutton's Farm to take over Robinson's patrol but three minutes later, when he should have commenced his descent, Robinson saw a Zeppelin held by searchlights; it was LZ 98 at Southfleet. Robinson made his move.

> The clouds had collected in this quarter, and the searchlights had some difficulty in keeping on the aircraft.
>
> By this time I had managed to climb to 12,900 feet and I made in the direction of the Zeppelin which was being fired on by a few anti-aircraft guns... I very slowly gained on it for about 10 minutes – I judged it to be about 800 feet below me, and I sacrificed my speed in order to keep the height. It went behind some clouds, avoided the searchlights and I lost sight of it. After 15 minutes fruitless search I returned to my patrol.[5]

Lehmann had evaded the hunter he never saw.

LZ 98 dropped 15 bombs as Lehmann flew across Essex and Suffolk. The first two fell at Corringham at 1.30am, then two at Fobbing, eight at Vange and one at Great Waltham before the last two fell at Rushmere and Playford near Ipswich at 2.10am. None of these caused any damage. LZ 98 passed Saxmundham at 2.21am and just a few minutes later, as she neared the coast, her crew saw that unmistakeable 'bright ball of fire' far behind them that denoted a terrible fate had befallen another airship. It could so easily have been them.

Frustrated after his failed encounter, Robinson searched for the Sutton's Farm landing flares in the blackness of the Essex countryside and located them at 1.50am. Frederick Sowrey had orders to shift his patrol south of the Thames, along a line from Joyce Green to Farningham, reacting to reports of the progress of LZ 98, but he returned to his airfield at 1.20am following engine failure. The pilot flying the second patrol from Hainault Farm, Second Lieutenant Basil Hunt, took off in a BE2c at 1.22am, also receiving orders to patrol south of the Thames. The only pilot now operating north of the river was James Mackay. He took off from North Weald Bassett at 1.08pm to cover the whole line to Joyce Green.

Robinson was also still flying north of the Thames but he was already long overdue back at Sutton's Farm. However, at the same time that he spotted his airfield's landing flares, he also noticed a red glow in the sky north of London. Forsaking the beckoning flares, Robinson turned to investigate and at 2.05am, as he headed towards the glow, he saw another Zeppelin held by searchlights. Mackay, who was near Joyce Green at the time, saw it too and in his own words 'gave chase'. Five minutes later Hunt joined the pursuit of a Zeppelin that appeared to be threatening the capital. In fact the airship was not a Zeppelin, it was the army's wooden-framed Schütte-Lanz, SL 11, but the finer points of airship design meant little to those now in pursuit.

SL 11 had crossed the Essex coast at Foulness at 10.40pm. Commanding her was 30-year-old Hauptmann Wilhelm Schramm. He joined the army in 1905 but in 1910, gripped by the wave of enthusiasm sweeping the country, he transferred to airships. Surprisingly, Wilhelm Schramm had been born in London. His father was a director of the German engineering firm Siemens and Wilhelm's parents lived in Victoria Road, Charlton, when Wilhelm was born in December 1885. Before his fifth birthday, however, Wilhelm's father suffered a stroke and the family returned to Germany. Perhaps even more surprising, Schramm had come close to bombing the house he had once lived in. A year earlier, on 7 September 1915, when serving as executive officer on SL II,[6] that airship bombed south-east London with one bomb exploding on Fossdene Fields in Charlton. It smashed windows in 40 houses on Victoria Road but Schramm's old home was untouched. Since then Schramm had spent time on the Eastern Front but more recently had attacked Harwich on the night of 25 April in command of LZ 93 and was over Kent the following night.

In August 1916 he and his crew transferred to the new SL 11, one of eight airships of the 'E class' (SL 8 to SL 15). Although Peter Strasser did not have a high opinion of Schütte-Lanz airships, the 'E class' compared favourably with both the 'p' and 'q-class' Zeppelins. Alongside Schramm on board SL 11 were his executive officer, Oberleutnant der Reserve

Wilhelm Vohdin, and 14 other members of the crew. Taking off from their home base at Spich, about 12 miles south-east of Cologne, it was the first flight to England for this new airship.

After coming inland SL 11 made a wide sweep across Essex and Suffolk, around the capital's defences, towards Hertfordshire. Schramm reached Royston at 12.30am, 23 miles north of North Weald Bassett, far beyond No.39 Squadron's patrol lines. After careful manoeuvring Schramm was near St Albans at 1.10am and well positioned to launch his attack on the capital from the north-west. Ten minutes later he released 10 bombs, probably to gain height before approaching London. Six fell in fields south of the village of London Colney and four north of South Mimms, two of those close to Ridge Hall Farm and two by the edge of Mimmshall Wood.

The anti-aircraft guns defending London formed a number of geographical Sub-Commands. North-West Sub-Command HQ at Wembley received a message at 1.23am that a Zeppelin was approaching from the north, helpfully adding, 'exact whereabouts unknown'. Their report highlights some of the problems encountered that night.

> The weather was very foggy, and the lights were very bad. From 1.30 to 2.00, various guns on the Eastern side of the Sub-Command reported that the sounds of a Zepp. could be heard, apparently within range, and asked for their lights to be uncovered. This was done, and in each case a report was received that the lights did not penetrate the heavy mist, and they were therefore covered again.[7]

## 3 September 1916, 1.28am: Little Heath, Hertfordshire

One of those lights was at the village of Little Heath, just north of Potter's Bar. The beam failed to penetrate the mist but the effect of the diffused light drew the attention of SL 11 and at 1.28am three bombs dropped. Two incendiaries fell north of the village at Bolton Park and a bomb that exploded in Heath Road smashed a water main and damaged roofs. A minute later another exploded in the grounds of Northaw House. Turning on to a more easterly course, SL 11 headed towards the Enfield Branch of the Great Northern Railway from where its continued course resembled a reversed letter 'S'. About this time the Temple House searchlight (Waltham Abbey Sub-Command) tried to come into action but things did not go according to plan.

At 1.27 sounds of aircraft were reported West of Temple House Gun and Light Station. Three minutes later... orders were given to the light to train on the sound. In doing so the back of the projector came away in the hands of the operator.

A bomb was then dropped about a mile West of the Gun Station followed by another about three quarters of a mile South of the first.

It took a few minutes to rectify the problem but by then the airship was heading south and out of range. The two reported explosions were those at Northaw House and another to the south of the position, dropped after SL 11 had crossed the railway at Crews Hill Station. Schramm had dropped an incendiary bomb on a golf course west of the tracks, and five more and the HE bomb on the east side at the Glasgow Stud Farm. An ensuing fire in a stable block killed three racehorses. Having circled around, SL 11 followed the railway south for about a mile before dropping another incendiary in a field next to The Chantry, a large house on The Ridgeway. A mile on and another incendiary fell in Bell's Field on the east side of World's End Lane and just north-east of the Enfield Isolation Hospital. Then, commencing one of the curves of the 'S', three more burning bombs fell in a field on Oak Lodge Farm at Southgate. Now heading north-west, after about two and a half miles, Schramm dropped two more in fields on Greenwood Farm at Hadley Wood, close to where the main line of the Great Northern Railway emerges from a tunnel to head towards London. Having crossed the railway SL 11 made another change of direction around to the south-east, once more on course for the capital. The time was now about 1.50am. It was at that moment that William Leefe Robinson observed a red glow to the north of London, that glow the result of the fires ignited by SL 11's incendiary bombs.

## 3 September 1916, 2am: Finsbury Park, London

As SL 11 approached the outer suburbs, those men operating the searchlights of the North-Eastern Sub-Command could plainly hear the sound of engines but the fog and mist made observation extremely difficult. Lieutenant W.H. Moffatt commanding the 3-inch, 20cwt gun in Finsbury Park thought the sound was coming towards him. At 1.53am he ordered the searchlight switched on but a minute later he cancelled the order as the diffused light was 'clearly illuminating the

Gun Station and giving our position away'. The sound of the engines became louder and more distinct until, at a time precisely recorded by Moffatt as '1.58½', he caught a fleeting glimpse of the airship as it passed a gap in the clouds. At 2am Moffatt's searchlight caught SL 11 as it passed west of Finsbury Park and his gun blasted into action as two more searchlights – from Victoria Park and Clapton – locked-on, then more followed.

The three pilots, Robinson, Mackay and Hunt, saw the lights converging and headed towards them. Then came the gunfire. By 2.05am guns at Victoria Park, Clapton, West Ham and Deptford Park had joined Finsbury Park. Within another two minutes the guns at Wanstead, Beckton, Paddington, Green Park, King's Cross, Honourable Artillery Company grounds, Meath Gardens and Tower Bridge were also thundering across the city, with Regent's Park joining in at 2.08am. At this point SL 11 became visible at the Waltham Abbey Sub-Command, but for now their guns waited in silence. For Schramm the situation had suddenly deteriorated and, when south-east of Finsbury Park, he turned east and away from central London. At about this time the crew working the Clapton gun felt sure one of their shells had damaged SL 11. An officer observing for the Clapton gun agreed.

> I can only say for certain that Clapton got one shell into her. It burst so close that it illuminated the envelope and seemed to burst absolutely on it. The ship gave a very decided tilt and rocking motion for some seconds afterwards.[8]

An officer of the Royal Army Medical Corps based at the German Internment camp at Alexandra Palace, Captain R.N. Moffatt, appears to confirm this observation.

> [The airship] appeared to be stationary for a few seconds and one or two shells seemed to burst rather near it. It then tilted its nose a little and turned to a more northern direction after which it put out smoke of its own, and it entered a thicker belt of clouds for it disappeared from view.[9]

The 'smoke' Moffatt reported was a cloud of water ballast released by SL 11 as Schramm tried to climb rapidly away from the guns.

A shell may have detonated close to SL 11 and caused consternation to those on board but it did not interfere with her progress. However, the rising cacophony of gunfire over the capital did have an extraordinary effect on the population of London. No German airship had disturbed central London for almost a year but when the London guns burst into action in the early hours of Sunday 3 September it created a tumult impossible to sleep through. From bedroom windows and gardens across the capital, Londoners stared up into the sky and saw one of the hated airships pierced by light beams and bombarded with bursting shells. They watched spellbound, seeming to recognise that this powerful response was very different from anything that had happened in the past and that they were witnesses to a great event. Many parents dragged sleepy children from their beds to share the moment. Some estimates say hundreds of thousands were watching, all desperately willing the guns to find the target and for a raging inferno to illuminate the sky.

Having turned away from central London, Schramm was heading north keeping the great reservoirs of the Lea Valley on his starboard side, passing Stamford Hill, Tottenham Hale and Northumberland Park, towards Edmonton. As he did so SL 11 began to break free from the searchlights and the gunfire had ceased by 2.13am.

## 3 September 1916, 2.12am: Edmonton, North London

But the reduction in fire was only momentary because the searchlights of the Waltham Abbey Sub-Command now uncovered and the guns opened fire at 2.15am from Enfield Lock, Temple House and Warlies Park as SL 11 drifted in and out of view through the mist and fog. Three minutes earlier Schramm had released six bombs over Edmonton, the first since Hadley Wood. One landed at Eley's Cartridge Works in Angel Road, which produced rifle ammunition, but it failed to explode. One did explode at the North London Ballast Works but without causing damage, while it was a similar result for three at a sewage works between Montagu Road and the Great Eastern Railway line. The final bomb in Edmonton landed on allotments on the west side of Montagu Road but, like the first, failed to detonate. Two minutes later SL 11 reached Ponders End where two bombs exploded in the High Street. The first damaged seven houses but the second, which exploded by the junction with Southbury Road, broke a water main as well as tram and telephone wires, smashed windows and tore roof tiles off 56 homes. Two more bombs fell close by, on allotments and at Rochford's Nursery near Durant's Park. The area was home to a large number of horticultural nurseries and inevitably the explosion of a bomb so close ravaged the great commercial greenhouses. Then in Green Street, just to the north of Durant's Park, another broke apart as it hit the ground and failed to explode.

From Green Street, Schramm travelled another half a mile before releasing three more bombs. One shattered more greenhouses at Smith's Nurseries on Hertford Road, another damaged an old coach-house in Old Road along with 14 other houses, and the third caused a little damage at Rainer's brickfield. Edging north-west, SL 11 passed within a mile of the Enfield Lock gun and at 2.17am dropped about a dozen bombs between the settlements of Turkey Street and Bull's Cross. Two or three at Turkey Street damaged the backs of three houses and eight more fell amongst the lettuces and potatoes on a market garden on Bullsmoor Lane, Bull's Cross, with the last landing in a river. Relieved of the weight of the bombs, SL 11 climbed again as Schramm distanced himself from the gun at Enfield Lock but was now heading towards the Temple House gun; the guns were two and a half miles apart.

It is surprising that Schramm did not turn north-east at this point, using the tailwind to speed him between the two guns, away from London and back towards the coast. Instead he headed north-west, passing within 350 yards of the Temple House gun. But could he have thought he *was* heading north-east?

All German airships carried a compass, relying on the liquid magnetic type as they weighed less than a gyro compass. Although the liquid element contained alcohol as an anti-freeze, these compasses could still freeze due to the long hours spent at sub-zero temperatures. If the compass on SL 11 had frozen, Schramm would have relied on observation of landmarks to ascertain his course, but the weather was foggy and misty, restricting close scrutiny. After the first guns opened fire, did Schramm catch a glimpse of large body of water and, presuming it to be the Thames, steer towards it and, keeping it on his starboard bow prepare to drop his bombs on what he presumed was central London? That body of water he may have seen, however, was not the Thames, it was a line of great reservoirs running up the Lea Valley from Edmonton in the south to Enfield Lock in the north. This was not a mistake without precedent; the commander of Zeppelin L 10 had made exactly the same error just over a year earlier on the night of 17/18 August 1915.[10] Schramm's bombs never fell more than a mile west of the reservoirs; if it had been the Thames, then these bombs would have hit the heart of London. It is impossible to know what Schramm believed but if that north-west turn at Turkey Street was made while alongside the Thames, SL 11 would have been heading across East London, out into Essex and home. Schramm may have believed he had succeeded in bombing central London but the reality of the situation saw SL 11 heading deeper into danger.

## 3 September 1916, 2.15am: Temple House Gun, Hertfordshire

The 3-inch, 20cwt anti-aircraft gun at Temple House stood on the north side of South Osiers Wood with the searchlight about a quarter of a mile away on the west side of Home Wood. The commander, Lieutenant C.M. Brown, had been following SL 11 in the searchlights for eight minutes before he came into action.[11] The gun's fifth round came close; Gunner A.J. Hoare reported that the airship 'quivered but did not otherwise seem affected'. At about the same time, Lieutenant Brown heard machine-gun fire. Some of the crew thought the twelfth round burst close to the tail but Gunner Hoare disagreed, reporting that it exploded 'rather low without apparent effect'. Continuing on its north-west course, SL 11 dropped three bombs at Burnt Farm, Goff's Oak, but as their nineteenth round arced across the sky the gun crew unanimously agreed that it hit the rear of the airship and shortly afterwards she began to burn.[12] There is strong evidence that a shell fragment damaged the rear engine but that shell did not destroy SL 11. Lost to onlookers in the darkness, others had closed in for the kill.

As soon as the pilots Robinson, Mackay and Hunt had seen SL 11 in the searchlights they headed towards it with all speed, each unaware of the others. Mackay had closed to within a mile of SL 11 when it began to burn, slowly at first but then the flames took hold of the stricken airship. Hunt was even closer; he was just about to engage when fire engulfed SL 11, the helpless wreck passing within 200 yards of him as the intense glare briefly blinded him. They had both been close to earning enduring fame as the first man to shoot down a German airship over Britain, but that honour went to 21-year-old Lieutenant William Leefe Robinson.

After his earlier unsuccessful attempt to close with LZ 98, Robinson changed his tactics.

> Remembering my last failure I sacrificed height (I was still 12,900 feet) for speed and made nose down in the direction of the Zeppelin. I saw shells bursting and night tracer shells

flying around it. When I drew closer I noticed that the anti-aircraft aim was too high or too low; also a good many some 800 feet behind – a few tracers went right over.[13]

Having overtaken SL 11, Robinson turned back and flew directly towards the airship, his tiny BE2c dwarfed by the overpowering bulk of the great aerial monster. 'I flew about 800 feet below it from bow to stern,' he explained, 'and distributed one drum along it (alternate, New Brock and Pomeroy).'[14] With some frustration he added: 'it seemed to have no effect.' Undaunted, he loaded a second drum of mixed ammunition and tried again. This time he tilted his aircraft over so his upward-firing machine gun could rake the flank of SL 11, but he was to be disappointed again, the new bullets the RFC had put much faith in were hitting the target 'without apparent effect'. Robinson loaded a third drum and noted that the anti-aircraft guns had fallen silent as he moved into position. By trial and error he had found the most effective method of attack.

> I then got behind it (by this time I was very close – 500 feet or less below) and concentrated one drum at one part (underneath rear). I was then at a height of 11,500 feet when attacking Zeppelin.
>
> I hardly finished the drum before I saw the part fired at glow. In a few seconds the whole rear part was blazing.

Above him the uncontrollably burning airship began to fall as Robinson squirmed out of its path then in his excitement he 'fired off a few red Very's lights and dropped a parachute flare'. In a letter to his parents he described his feelings.

> I hardly know how I felt as I watched the huge mass gradually turn on end and – as it seemed to me – slowly sink, one glowing blazing mass. I gradually realised what I had done and grew wild with excitement.[15]

In a more candid moment Robinson admitted: 'I was so pleased that in my excitement I pulled the 'joystick' and looped the loop several times.'[16] That would certainly have met with disapproval had it appeared in his official report.

One of those manning the Temple House searchlight thought SL 11 was over Soper's Farm when fire broke out. The farm stood just over half a mile south of the village of Cuffley in Hertfordshire.

In the great flare of light Basil Hunt caught a glimpse of another Zeppelin but, dazzled by the glare, he quickly lost sight of it. It was L 16 at Essendon, about four miles away.

Numerous eyewitness accounts of the last moments of SL 11 filled the nation's newspapers. A particularly descriptive one published by the *Morning Post* appeared in a number of provincial papers later in the week.

> We watched fascinated, the terrible death of the Zeppelin. The blazing airship swung around for an instant, broadside on, as though unmanageable; then the burning end dipped, the flames ran up the whole structure as her petrol tanks one after another caught fire. In another second or two the Zeppelin, now perpendicular, was falling headlong to earth from a height not much short of a couple of miles, a mass of roaring flame. So tremendous was the blaze and so intense the light that she seemed to be an immense incandescent mantle at white heat and enveloped in flame, falling, and illuminating the country for miles around... With ever-increasing momentum she sped down until at last she struck the earth with a crash that could be heard for miles. A dull red glow brightened the heavens for a few seconds, and a distant mass of still burning wreckage was all that was left of the Zeppelin. The people watched the attack on the Zeppelin in silence, but when she was seen to be on fire cheer upon cheer was raised and repeated again and again.[17]

Those countless onlookers across London and in the surrounding counties had indeed watched in silence, but when she fell from the sky the cheers grew reaching a peak as SL 11 hit the ground. A brief pause and then realisation set in that after 25 months of war one of the feared and hated 'Baby-killers' had been destroyed before their eyes. This was different to the destruction of previous airships far out to sea or over Europe, this was a moment in history witnessed by the masses.

> The Zeppelin took quite two minutes dropping to earth, but during those two minutes mad, deafening cheers rose out of the night on all sides. Hooters from works and from

vessels in the Thames and railways shrieked and whistled and screeched, all joining in the general pandemonium of joy. For a full half-hour the cheering continued, echoing and re-echoing from all sides.[18]

Despite the hour – SL 11 hit the ground shortly after 2.25am – vast crowds congregated to celebrate, seemingly oblivious to the fact that many were only 'half dressed'. But while people joyously caroused, few gave a thought to where the burning wreckage had fallen or to the damage it might have caused.

Mr Grow, who lived on Cuffley Hill, had woken to the booming of the guns and was looking out of his bedroom window when SL 11 began to burn.

> The flaming mass was so near me that I thought it was going to drop on an old hostelry [The Plough] only a few score yards away, but it glided on and fell with a fearful crash on to a field about 150 to 200 yards from that house. I had watched the whole spectacle, enthralled with the magnificent sight. Immediately the flaming mass crashed to earth I ran across the field to witness the final scene. The only other person there at the time, so far as I could see, was a special constable, and together we watched the wonderful and historic spectacle.[19]

When Special Constable Moore and Mr Grow arrived at the field on Castle Farm, Cuffley, the heat from the burning wreckage was so intense that it prevented them from getting too close, as did the machine gun bullets 'popping-off' in the fire. Eventually, when others arrived, they organised a chain of buckets to douse the now smouldering remains with water.

The crews of the four Zeppelins nearest to London could not mistake what they had just witnessed. (See Map 6). Sommerfeldt, commanding L 16 over Essendon, watched in horror as 'it caught fire at the stern, burned with an enormous flame and fell'.[20] With the wind behind him Sommerfeldt moved quickly. He dropped just two incendiary bombs on his way back to the coast, one at the village of Aston, eight miles north of Essendon, and another at West Stow, north of Bury St Edmunds, before crossing the coast near Great Yarmouth at about 4.20am.

The Zeppelin furthest to the west was Peterson's L 32 at Tring. He looked on helplessly as, 'A great fire… lit up the surroundings within a large radius and then fell to the ground slowly'.[21] From his claimed position over Kensington, Peterson reported heading east towards the City of London dropping his bombs as he went. But from Tring as he headed east his 'London' bombs fell near Hertford at 2.54am. At the village of Hertford Heath 16 bombs resulted in the deaths of two horses and the 24 that rained down around the neighbouring village of Great Amwell managed to kill a pony and smash the windows in three houses. L 32's final two bombs exploded in countryside east of Ware causing no damage. Peterson reached the Suffolk coast near Lowestoft at about 4.15am.

Kuno Manger was just south of Thaxted when he saw the flames and immediately turned away from London. On his journey to the coast the military authorities attributed 18 bombs to L 14. Two dropped almost immediately at Little Bardfield and Finchingfield, then no more for 18 miles until L 14 reached Lavenham. From there to the village of Haughley, about 10 miles away, Manger promiscuously dropped 16 more bombs across Suffolk: two at Lavenham, single bombs near Thorpe Morieux and Brettenham, two at Drinkstone, five near Buxhall and five more around Haughley. The only damage was to some crops at Buxhall. Manger reached the coast at Bacton at 4.05am.

The last of the raiders approaching London when SL 11 burst into flames was Kurt Frankenberg's L 21. Although at Hitchin, 18 miles from Cuffley, Frankenberg saw two aeroplanes attacking SL 11 through binoculars and turned away from London without hesitation. In the next hour L 21 released eight bombs: two incendiaries at Dunton near Biggleswade, one at Huntley Park near Gamlingay, an incendiary and two HE bombs on the Cambridgeshire fens south of Chatteris, which damaged a few crops, and two bombs at Tilney St Lawrence, about seven miles south-west of King's Lynn. In his report Frankenberg planned to attack Norwich on this return journey but struggled to find the darkened city. He dropped bombs to try to force a reaction from the city's defences. He was in fact 50 miles west of Norwich when, at 3.40am, he dropped two bombs as he passed to the west of King's Lynn, which shattered greenhouses at a horticultural nursery and windows in a house, followed by two incendiaries north of the town. These did elicit a response and Frankenberg believed like others that night that he had finally found Norwich. But the gun that opened fire was a 75mm mobile gun protecting the Royal Estate at Sandringham. As the gun boomed into action, Frankenberg dropped an incendiary bomb over the village of Wolferton, to the west of Sandringham, followed at 3.47am by nine bombs around Dersingham to the north of the Royal Estate. The exploding bombs shook the unsuspecting villagers from their slumbers and the Norfolk police reported serious damage to six houses and other damage to eight more.

The words 'serious damage' do not adequately relay the cost to one family. George Dunger and his wife, Violet Ellen, lived at the hamlet of Doddshill, on the east side of Dersingham. The couple were awake but their three daughters slept on. At the inquest Mr Dunger explained that he and his wife 'were standing outside their cottage door, when he saw a Zeppelin in the sky lit up by two searchlights'.[22] An explosion threw them to the ground and sliced off the gable end of their cottage. Although Mr Dunger sustained an injury to his thigh, his wife had suffered far worse, although the children were unharmed even though their bedroom now lay exposed to the night air. Unfortunately Mrs Dunger never recovered from her injuries and died in hospital on 21 September.[23]

Continuing his attack on 'Norwich', Frankenberg dropped seven bombs around Snettisham and ten at Sedgeford, none of which caused any damage, then a final incendiary bomb landed at Thornham before L 21 passed out over the coast at 4am. The mobile gun at Sandringham claimed a hit on L 21 but she showed no reaction and, although struggling with engine problems on the journey back to Germany, reaching Nordholz after a mission lasting almost 27 hours, there is no suggestion that this was the cause. But unknown to the crew of L 21 and in a strange twist, as far as the British public was concerned they were dead, their charred and broken bodies lying amongst the smouldering wreckage in a farmer's field at Cuffley.

# Chapter 16

# 'Mother, they have got me this time'

Amongst the countless thousands watching the drama unfold in the sky in the early hours of Sunday 3 September were the ground crew at Sutton's Farm. They shared the excitement of everyone when fire engulfed SL 11 but there were worries too. William Leefe Robinson should have returned from his patrol by 1.30am and was now an hour late. But when the sound of an aeroplane reached the airfield that tension evaporated. As Robinson brought his BE2c to a halt, eager faces gathered around to ask the question on everyone's lips.

> I was greeted with, 'was it you Robin', etc. etc. 'Yes, I've Strafed the beggar this time', I said, whereupon the whole flight set up a yell and carried me out of my machine to the office – cheering like mad.[1]

As darkness gave way to dawn a vast pilgrimage was already underway to Cuffley. Thousands who had watched the demise of SL 11 now descended on the tiny village by train, car, cart, bicycle or on foot, eager to be part of the story. The press named it 'Zepp Sunday' and filled their columns with vivid accounts of Robinson's deed. Here at last was a 'good news' story, an antidote to the depressingly endless casualty lists from the Battle of the Somme.

While huge crowds flocked to Cuffley, a copy of Robinson's report landed on the desk of Sir John French, Commander-in-Chief, Home Forces. On 4 September French's office contacted Sir David Henderson, Director-General of Military Aeronautics, to ask if he recommended any reward. Henderson replied immediately: 'I recommend Lieut. W.L.

Robinson for the Victoria Cross, for the most conspicuous gallantry displayed in this successful attack.' Just five days later, Robinson received the award from the King at Windsor Castle. Now arguably the most famous man in Britain, Robinson's picture appeared in newspapers and on the covers of magazines, numerous photographic postcards depicted him and the crash site, as well as artistic renditions of the demise of SL 11 and souvenirs of all descriptions bore his image. All this to honour the man who shot down a 'Zeppelin'. Yet a decision taken behind the scenes had changed the facts.

When the authorities sifted through the wreckage it quickly became clear that the absence of any significant amount of metal and the great quantity of charred and burnt wood denoted that the wreckage was a Schütte-Lanz airship and not a Zeppelin. And here was a dilemma. The British public hated the Zeppelins, while few of the population were aware of the name Schütte-Lanz, and the destruction of one would not have the same boost to morale as that resulting from the loss of a Zeppelin. A press release published on 4 September added a smokescreen to explain the lack of metal in the wreckage: 'The large amount of wood employed in the framework of the Zeppelin is startling, and would seem to point to a shortage of aluminium in Germany.' Three days later at the burial of the men, it was stated that they were the crew of Zeppelin L 21, an airship that the authorities had tracked leaving the country. While the real crew of L 21 relaxed back at Nordholz, most people in Britain believed they lay buried in a mass grave at Potter's Bar. This misinformation remained firmly entrenched even though secret documents produced in November 1916 refer to SL 11 throughout.[2] The authorities were also particularly keen to keep the new bullets a secret to prevent the information reaching Germany.

The destruction of their latest Schütte-Lanz airship was a significant blow to the army's airship service. At the beginning of September the army had eleven front line airships: nine Zeppelins and two Schütte-Lanz. Mainly due to accidents as well as enemy action, these numbers quickly reduced and by November just six remained: LZ 93, LZ 98 and LZ 103 in the west and LZ 97, LZ 101 and SL 7, in the east. New airships were on order but the mood in army headquarters was changing.

Ernst Lehmann, commanding LZ 98, had returned safely from the raid of 2/3 September but his fellow army airship commanders were concerned by the loss of SL 11. They met and agreed that a height of 15,000 or 16,000 feet was needed when attacking London, only achievable by dramatically reducing the bomb load. 'That, of course was undesirable,'

Lehmann admitted, 'so for some time to come we were to remain away from the capital and visit other places where the defence was weaker.'[3]

In fact Army airships never returned to Britain. Weaknesses exposed in the German Army air arm during the campaigns of 1916 over Verdun and the Somme, had resulted in the need for a greater unity of command. In October 1916 all flying and support services came together as the Luftstreitkräfte (Air Force), a branch of the Army under the command Generaleutnant Ernst von Hoeppner; he soon concluded that the risks in sending airships to attack Britain were too great.

> Successful attacks were possible only when especially favourable conditions prevailed and these were seldom present and we had to reckon on the chance that in each large attack a ship would be shot down and would fall into the hands of the enemy as a trophy.[4]

But von Hoeppner did not end the army's air raids on Britain, he looked instead to the new bomber aircraft that were due to be ready in early 1917 to take on the task, and gradually dismantled his airship fleet.

The navy, however, did not share his views and Peter Strasser remained as determined as ever to prove the effectiveness of his airships in carrying the war to Britain. To Strasser, the loss of the Schütte-Lanz airship merely confirmed his own negative views of the wooden-framed airship design and he, unaware of the new bullets that had brought her down, felt that must have been a factor in its destruction. Strasser also firmly believed that the new 'r-class' airships were the weapon to confirm Germany's superiority in the air war over Britain.

The army, however, did not have all the bad luck. On 16 September a fire at broke out during hydrogen filling at Fuhlsbüttel, Hamburg, and the flames destroyed L 6 and L 9, two of the navy's older Zeppelins.

## 22 September 1916, 3pm: Dover, Kent

Strasser now waited for the next moon cycle, the new moon rising on 27 September. While the Zeppelins waited, carrying out engine tests, test flights and mine searching operations over the North Sea, on 22 September a single unidentified German aeroplane approached the Kent coast at about 3pm in another of the series of sudden stinging attacks. Aided by cloud cover the first anyone knew of the presence of the raider was when the first of three bombs exploded in the grounds of the Duke of York School, which provided barracks for the 6th (Reserve) Battalion, Royal Fusiliers. This alerted the Dover anti-aircraft gunners and RFC pilots of No.50 (Home Defence) Squadron at Dover's Swingate airfield. The bomb smashed windows and cut telephone wires while the remaining two bombs exploded in a field between the school and the airfield. As the Dover guns opened fire, two RFC pilots climbed after the raider. Guns from Deal opened fire too and eight RNAS aircraft took off but it was all to no avail. A reporter based at Deal watched the action.

> All around the enemy machine shrapnel was bursting, as the intruder dodged and manoeuvred... Not only was there firing from all directions, but British aeroplanes... also went up... For five or eight minutes spectators had the aircraft in view, and shrapnel burst very near it... There was no option but to bolt to sea... as it scurried outwards it rose to a still greater altitude, eventually becoming as a mere speck in the sky.[5]

The next day, Saturday 23 September, Peter Strasser deemed the weather promising for a raid and ordered 12 of his Zeppelins to prepare. Eight of the older 'p' and 'q-class' vessels would approach over the North Sea while four of the new 'r-class' Zeppelins took their routes over Belgium to approach England from the south-east. Strasser hoped to strike London but if the wind created difficulties, the raiders could redirect to the Midlands. Two of those approaching over the North Sea (L 16 and L 24) both turned back early and L 30 did not appear over Britain, although once again von Buttlar issued a dramatic report, this time of an attack on east London and Gravesend. In all likelihood L 30's bombs fell in the sea. That left nine Zeppelins to attack England, whose air defences had now proven to be far more formidable, even deadly.

## 23 September 1916, 10.39pm: Stowmarket, Suffolk

The first of the Zeppelins to come inland on 23 September was L 21. Her commander, Kurt Frankenburg, thought he crossed the Essex coast at Foulness and intended to attack Colchester but reported that searchlights found him as he neared Chelmsford. In fact he came inland at 9.40pm, about 50 miles further north, and followed a rather tortuous course across Suffolk as L 21 struggled to climb above 8,000 feet. At 10.25pm he jettisoned a couple of empty fuel tanks to reduce weight; one of these fell at Stonham Parva, just over three miles east of Stowmarket where an explosives plant had been the subject of previous unsuccessful attacks. A searchlight flickered into action and caught L 21 – the light Frankenburg believed was at Chelmsford. He circled around to the south, dropping a single bomb ten minutes later at Coddenham then another at Needham Market before following the railway line towards Stowmarket. At 10.39pm two bombs exploded at Badley ripping down telegraph wires alongside the tracks and damaging windows, doors and the roof at Doveshill Farm. These bombs stirred the explosives works' defences into action and the two 3-inch, 20 cwt guns opened fire.

Frankenburg dropped 26 bombs around Creeting St Peter and six more as he neared Stowupland, the bombs falling on the line Creeting Hall, Pound Lane, Brazier's Hall and Crown Hill at Stowupland.[6] Some of them fell within 500 to 600 yards of the guns, cutting the telephone line between gun and searchlight, but the explosive works was never in danger. At Creeting Hall Farm bombs killed five pigs and damaged buildings. Lightened by the release of the bombs, Frankenburg coaxed L 21 up to 9,500 feet and returned to the coast at 11.20pm. While the British authorities concluded this had been a determined attack aimed at the Stowmarket explosives works, Frankenburg never knew how close he had come to making a devastating attack on an important target.

## 23 September 1916, 10.45pm: Washingborough, Lincolnshire

The other five Zeppelins that crossed the North Sea criss-crossed the skies over Lincolnshire but only one pushed beyond the county borders. Reports state L 14 and L 17 crossed the coastline between Mablethorpe and Skegness at 10pm with both approaching Lincoln at 10.45pm. It seems more likely, however, that this was L 23 with L 17.[7] At the village of Washingborough, south-east of Lincoln, a searchlight caught L 23 in its beam and moments later a 12-pdr gun south of the city at Canwick opened fire. While the unseen L 17 continued on its way, Wilhelm Ganzel swung L 23 to the north, identifying the gun and light as defending Lincoln. He released 17 incendiary bombs, which all fell in fields near the village of Heighington and had no effect. Switching to HE bombs, 12 of these fell around Washingborough as L 23 followed a course just to the east of Lincoln: 'The windows of many houses in the village were broken, a joiner's shop was partly wrecked, and four fowls were killed.'[8] They also badly damaged an orchard. Crossing the River Witham, 15 more bombs fell around Greetwell where the explosions tore down telegraph wires and killed a sheep. Ganzel now turned back to the coast, which he crossed near Sutton-on-Sea just after 11.30pm. L 23's bombs caused no human casualties, but two people were to lose their lives the following day as a result of the raid.

On Sunday morning large excited crowds came out from Lincoln to see the Washingborough bomb craters. Many crossed the River Witham on an old chain-operated ferry. At 4.30pm a large number crowded on board to head back to the Lincoln side, dangerously overloading the ferry. Ignoring the pleas of the 69-year-old ferryman George Moore to disembark, someone pushed the ferry out. Moments later it tipped dramatically to one side. In high spirits, those crammed on board cheered and tried to counter-balance the 6-foot-wide ferry, at which point it turned over, throwing everyone into the river where tragically two people drowned: 17-year-old Ernest Robinson and young George Melson, aged seven.

## 24 September 1916, 12.34am: Nottingham

While Ganzel made his attack, Hermann Kraushaar continued on a south-west course in L 17, having already dropped a bomb at Waddingworth, 15 minutes before passing Lincoln. Kraushaar had taken command on 10 August and was leading a Zeppelin over England for the first time. At 11.50pm he reached Newark in Nottinghamshire, from where he observed bright lights 16 miles to the south-west, believing them to mark Sheffield. The lights, however, were shining from Nottingham. Kraushaar dropped an incendiary in the River Trent at North Muskham where it fizzed and bubbled as he aligned L 17 on the lights.

At 9.28pm Nottingham received the TARA order and lighting went off across the city – but not on the railways. To ensure that the numerous false alarms did not interfere with important work, the railways had permission to keep working until it was clear a raid was imminent. Nottingham's goods yards were busy – and brightly illuminated. About 12.15am reports started to come in that a Zeppelin appeared to be heading towards the city from the north-east.

At 12.34am six bombs dropped on open ground close to the vast Colwick Sidings on the Great Northern Railway. Explosions damaged track and broke windows in six houses in Netherfield at the junction of Cross and Dunston streets. The crew of the anti-aircraft gun at Sneinton, on the south-eastern edge of Nottingham, waited anxiously as their searchlight failed to penetrate the ground mist and the throbbing sound of the Zeppelin's engines drew nearer. Between

Colwick and Sneinton L17 dropped six more bombs and at 12.39am an explosion severed the telephone line connecting the searchlight with the gun. On the southern edge of Nottingham a searchlight at Wilford was also blinded by the ground mist. Directly ahead the lights at the Great Central Railway depot, north of Wilford Bridge, and those at the Midland Station were still glaring, identified as 'brightly lit industrial plants' by Kraushaar.

The first bomb in the city exploded about 50 yards south of the Midland Railway's London Road Junction signal box, shattering the windows and damaging Ashworth & Kirk's timber yard on London Road. A second bomb fell in the Eastcroft Sanitary Depot's yard where the explosion 'scattered an immense heap of material'. Just how unpleasant this 'material' was is not clear. L 17 now approached the more densely populated working class area of south Nottingham where a bomb wrecked buildings and lives.

The bomb smashed into No.32 Newthorpe Street. A family with four children lived next door and all awoke to a chaotic scene of falling masonry and breaking glass. The explosion was responsible for 'blowing in the wall of the sitting room, obliterating the scullery and reducing everything made of wood to splinters'.

'As soon as I got out of bed,' the father explained... 'I could hear a woman's voice from next door screaming for help. The floor gave way under me, but I got the child out of bed and made for downstairs.'

His wife was thrown out of bed with one of her babies, but she too, managed to reach the street in safety, and her husband at once began to assist in the attempt to extricate their neighbours from the pile of debris caused by the explosion of the bomb.[9]

Next door, No.32 was home to Alfred Taylor Rogers, a tailor's cutter, and his wife, Rosanna. They had two sons serving in the army. Buried in the rubble, Alfred was dead when rescuers found him, while the explosion had blown Rosanna out of the house, leaving her lifeless body sprawled on a pile of rubble. After many hours delicate work, rescuers pulled eight people alive from the ruins of other broken houses. Groans from the rubble alerted them to one victim. Bewildered by his terrifying experience, he simply asked: 'Where am I; what am I doing here?'[10]

Leaving the residents of Newthorpe Street reeling from the shock of being attacked in their beds, L 17 followed the line of Carrington Street northwards towards the Midland Railway Station. Kraushaar dropped three bombs on the goods yard shed, two shattering the glass roof and injuring two men while the third exploded at the entrance on Carrington Street. It dug a deep crater, shattered windows all around and damaged the clock in the tower over the station entrance opposite. A foreman at the goods yard, Alfred Harpham, was within 30 yards of all three bombs and, although not physically injured, it affected him mentally. Harpham, a father of six children had worked for the Midland Railway for 21 years, was of good character and had an unblemished record at work, but after this incident he became 'careless and reckless'.[11] Three years later he appeared in court charged with petty theft, but friends testified that Harpham had not been the same since the raid. The Court dealt with his case sympathetically.[12]

Leaving the Midland Station behind, L 17 now headed towards lights still showing at the Great Central Railway's Victoria Station. Before he got there Kraushaar released two bombs that struck the Canaan Street Primitive Methodist Chapel. One smashed down through the roof and floor but failed to detonate as it buried itself several feet deep, as the other bomb set fire to a gallery and the organ. Together they caused extensive damage but firemen controlled the blaze.

As those flames were taking hold, another incendiary bomb smashed through the roof of a house on Chancery Place, a group of about a dozen three-storey dwellings in a yard off Broad Marsh. It struck No.3 where an elderly male lodger occupied the top floor, the first floor being home to a recently married couple, 21-year-old Harold William Renshaw and his wife Ethel, while Ethel's mother lived on the ground floor. Harold was serving in the army, based at the Sherwood Foresters (Notts. & Derbys. Regiment) Depot.

The bomb, described by witnesses as 'a ball of flames', crashed through the roof of No.3 before smashing through the upper floor and bursting into Harold and Ethel's bedroom. The terror caused by these burning bombs is clear in Ethel's own words.

> I must have been awakened by the noise of the raiders, and I had just said to my husband, 'They must be near, for they are firing guns.' He opened his eyes to answer me when a bomb came from the ceiling... setting him on fire. I rushed from the

room, got a bucket of water, and did my best to put out the flames, but when I returned the second time, I could not get to him for fire and smoke. And I could see him trying to crawl from the bedroom onto the landing.[13]

The helpless Ethel escaped injury, but when a neighbour arrived, she found Harold lying on the landing, his head and shoulders in flames. Harold died before he reached hospital.

In the meantime another bomb dropped behind 18 Low Pavement as L 17 swung to the west and dropped three or four more bombs, all close together. Damage occurred at the rear of a pub, the Sawyer's Arms, and to business premises around the junction of Greyfriars Gate, Lister Gate and Castle Gate. There were no casualties in this commercial area but newspaper reports described how dislodged heavy stonework smashed into other buildings and into the street. These bombs had an effect over a wide area.

A strong wooden beam was hurled a distance of some 70 yards, on to the roof of another building, and a small hall, used for religious purposes, was practically destroyed... It indicates the force of explosion to explain that, as the result of not more than three or four bombs, the windows of practically every shop and building for a distance of close upon 300 yards, were more or less shattered.[14]

Kraushaar swung L 17 back on to a more northerly course as he headed towards Victoria Station. A bomb in Bridlesmith Gate had little effect then a single bomb hit the station exploding on Platform 7. It made a crater over four feet deep, damaged a section of track and inflicted other damage inconsequential in nature. Observers recorded L 17 steering away to the north-east at 12.49am. A final bomb exploded in the suburbs at Mapperley, damaging a house on Hickling Road and smashing windows in the area. From there L 17 returned to the coast, receiving anti-aircraft fire from a gun at Spurn Head at around 2am.

Incredibly, at the Midland Railway Station on Carrington Street, the lights still remained an issue ten minutes after L 17 had departed. It was only after Company Sergeant Major J.H. Wright of 18 Protection Company, Royal Defence Corps, arrived and following what he described as, 'a lot of shouting', that the lights were finally extinguished. In the inquiry into the raid the railway lights featured strongly.[15]

But before the inquest took place vast numbers of sightseers flooded into Nottingham the following morning to see the damage. Dick Cheetham, a 16-year-old miner, was one of them. The site of so many people left a lasting impression: 'The Market Place and all down Wheeler Gate and Greyfriar Gate was just like Goose Fair. People were trying to dig pieces of shrapnel out from among the cobbles in the street.'[16] Another witness, Emma Cupitt, wrote to a friend: 'You ought to have seen the thousands of people looking at the damage. Nearly every shop from here to the market place has broken windows.'[17]

Later, Cheetham, like many others walked to Newthorpe Street to view the wrecked houses there. Others went to look at the burnt chapel in Canaan Street, where an enterprising man started a restoration fund by charging the inquisitive a fee to look inside.

The casualties amounted to three deaths – Harold Renshaw and Mr and Mrs Rogers – and 16 injured: 9 men, 4 women and 3 children.

At the inquest into the deaths the railway received much criticism but the coroner pointed out that they had not breached Home Office regulations. In his summing up, however, he added some damning comments.

> The Jury are of the opinion that the City was exposed to the risk of attack by Airships entirely by the action of the Railway Companies in keeping their premises lighted until the first bombs had been dropped.[18]

Taking up the matter, John Godfree Small, Mayor of Nottingham, sent a strongly worded telegram to the Home Secretary. It concluded: 'The city authorities and citizens demand that measures be taken by Government to ensure that the railway lighting shall be so arranged as not to endanger the lives of the people.'[19]

While this rumbled on there was still the matter of burying the victims of the raid. Sadly this became a public sideshow. After Alfred and Rosanna Rogers' burial on 28 September a local newspaper reported under the headline – 'Revolting Burial Scene'.

> Their progress through the streets was marked by scenes of reverence and sympathy but at the cemeteries there were large crowds of idle sight-seers mainly composed of slatternly women, many with children in their arms and at their skirts.

In their morbid curiosity these women showed neither respect for the feelings of the bereaved nor for the graves of others.

They pushed their way as close to the burial-places as the authorities would allow, trampled on graves ... and clambered onto tombstones in a disgusting effort to secure a 'good view'.[20]

As Nottingham began to return to normal, the passions ignited by the railway were to gradually dim and never flare up again – no Zeppelin ever returned to the city.

## 23 September 1916, 10.25pm: Lincolnshire

At 10.25pm, about 25 minutes after L 23 and L 17 had come inland, Zeppelin L 22 appeared off Kilnsea, just north of Spurn Head, but spent little more than an hour overland. Her commander, Martin Dietrich, approached the instantly recognisable spit of land from where a searchlight was sweeping the sky. Three bombs fell in the sea before Dietrich dropped five more hoping to disrupt the searchlight and a 3-pdr Vickers anti-aircraft gun that had opened fire. One landed within 100 yards of the gun. Crossing the mouth of the Humber, Dietrich targeted Grimsby with three bombs but they all fell in the sea followed by three more off the coast at Donna Nook where he crossed into Lincolnshire. Dietrich took L 22 about 20 miles inland, dropping 11 incendiary bombs, but he was unable to find any worthwhile targets and none of his bombs caused damage. Two landed at North Somercotes, five at Grainthorpe, one at Fulstow, two at Utterby and one at Caistor, this last bomb recorded at 11.10pm. Dietrich then returned to the coast, reaching Donna Nook at 11.35pm having achieved nothing.

At 10.30pm another Zeppelin came inland just north of Skegness. The British report identified this as L 13, but again, when comparing timings with German reports it appears probable that this was Kuno Manger's L 14, which the British had mistakenly reported attacking east of Lincoln.[21] Twenty minutes after coming inland the Zeppelin was located between Boston and Sibsey, but Manger appeared uncertain as to his whereabouts and half an hour later he remained only four miles from Boston. By 11.50pm L 14 had pushed westwards and was south of Sleaford from where she came under fire from two mobile 6-pdr Nordenfelt guns at Rauceby. The guns defended the RNAS station at

Cranwell from where five minutes later a BE2c took off, but L 14 was gone before the pilot could reach its altitude. In response to the guns Manger dropped five incendiary bombs. One landed at the village of Silk Willoughby and four around Holdingham but none caused any damage. He then released 13 HE bombs over Rauceby where damage was restricted to a house and some farm buildings. Passing north of Sleaford, L 14 released seven incendiary bombs over Leasingham, again causing no damage, before Manger returned to the coast, going out to sea at 12.15am near Wainfleet.

## 24 September 1916, 12.35am: Scartho, Lincolnshire

The last to come inland over Lincolnshire was Kapitänleutnant Franz Eichler's L 13.[22] It was the first time he had commanded a Zeppelin over Britain and like others that night he struggled to find a target. L 13 headed inland from Mablethorpe at about 11pm, travelling for about 30 miles before Eichler manoeuvred around northern Lincolnshire, dropping an incendiary bomb at Glentham at 11.45pm and two more at Kingerby, only three miles away, 40 minutes later. Eichler eventually decided to attack Grimsby on the Humber.

At 12.35am, as L 13 neared Grimsby, anti-aircraft guns at Scartho Top and Cleefields burst into action. Due to poor visibility the guns only fired seven rounds but Eichler described it as an 'extremely violent bombardment' to which he responded with 'an attack on two batteries'. His 30 bombs (19 HE and 11 incendiary) fell between the villages of Scartho and Weelsby. 'A dozen or more bombs fell in meadows,' a newspaper reported, 'scooping out great circular holes at regular intervals in a straight line across country.'[23] But there was damage at Scartho where the first bomb exploded in a field on the south side of Carr Lane (now Springfield Road), about 80 yards west of the junction with Waltham Road.[24] The next half-wrecked a cottage on Penfold Lane, opposite the village school and close to the junction with Louth Road. Fortunately the two elderly occupants were in the undamaged part at the time. The school suffered too, but not the pupils. One of them, Charles Cocking, later expressed the views of many a schoolchild: 'A near miss by a Zeppelin bomb closed the school for a short period whilst broken windows and fallen plaster were repaired, much to our delight. We even loved Zeppelins after that.' From there L 13 passed over St Giles Church. A bomb exploded in the churchyard about 25 yards from the church, another just beyond the boundary hedge, then a third about

237

80 yards further on in a field, 'scattering sods and [bomb] fragments in all directions'. There was minor damage recorded at the rectory but more at the church.

> The vibration smashed the windows of the church, falling fragments broke many slates, and wrecked part of the roof of the building, and a tombstone was cut cleanly in two by the impact of a bomb fragment.[25]

Other bombs fell near Scartho Hall and alongside the Great Northern Railway as L 13 made for the coast. The only casualties were four dead chickens.

## 23 September 1916, 10.45pm: Kent coast

While these six Zeppelins had been in action, three 'Super Zeppelins' were on their way across Belgium to attack London. They were Heinrich Mathy's L 31, Werner Peterson's L 32 and Alois Böcker's L 33. The first to cross the coast, L 33, did so over Foulness in Essex at 10.40pm while the other two approached the Kent coast near Dungeness around five minutes later. Mathy dropped 10 bombs as he crossed the coast to lighten his ship, hoping to hit the Dungeness lighthouse but only four exploded on land.[26] They wrecked two cottages, one unoccupied but the other home to Mr and Mrs Austin and family. Six people were in the kitchen at the time, the only room untouched by the explosion. Following a north-west course, Mathy was south of Tunbridge Wells at 11.35pm.

While Mathy headed inland, Peterson appears to have had problems. He manoeuvred L 32 for 45 minutes within a few miles of the coast and only moved off at 11.45pm.

L 33 had joined the airship fleet on 2 September. Her experienced commander, Alois Böcker, and his crew had previously served on L 5 and L 14 and now proudly manned the very latest Zeppelin to emerge from Friedrichshafen. Böcker, however, had a new executive officer, Leutnant-zur-See Ernst Schirlitz, one of the six men repatriated after the crash of Zeppelin L 20 in a Norwegian fjord back in May. At 11pm Böcker dropped an incendiary bomb over South Fambridge and a parachute flare south of Brentwood at 11.35pm. She was now only seven or eight miles east of No.39 Squadron's airfields.

The aircraft defending London were in for a busy night. Four pilots of Kent based No.50 Squadron took off between 9.30 and 11.30pm but failed to locate the raiders. At 11.30pm the three flights of No.39 Squadron received orders to commence patrolling. They followed the same routes as the night William Robinson shot down SL 11, but this time, much to his frustration, he was unable to take part, his value to the public morale considered too great to risk.[27] Lieutenant Clifford Ross went up from North Weald, Alfred Brandon from Hainault Farm and Frederick Sowrey from Sutton's Farm. At 12.20am James Mackay replaced Ross who had returned early with engine problems. But with L 33 so close, none of the pilots had time to climb and intercept the raider before she had passed on her way to London.

After his delay at the coast, Peterson reached Tunbridge Wells at 12.10am, about 30 minutes after Mathy had left there and progressed to Caterham. From there he saw another Zeppelin about 17 miles away over London. Mathy reported: 'At [12.15 a.m.] the attack by another ship was observed, followed by two raging fires.' Pitt Klein, on board L 31, looked on with concern.

> We could see our comrades over the urban sprawl, already under heavy fire… My heart was literally pounding, watching our friends in action over this inferno. They were illuminated as bright as day by searchlights. Curtains of anti-aircraft fire closed in around them, forming a great dome of fiery trails.[28]

They were watching Böcker's L 33.

## 24 September 1916, 12.11am: East London

From Brentwood L 33 released bombs over Upminster Common and others aimed at landing flares burning at Sutton's Farm airfield but all failed to hit anything of importance. At 11.55pm Böcker was south of Chadwell Heath and four minutes later the Thames appeared off the port bow; Böcker made a turn towards the river knowing it would guide him to London. Passing between the silent guns at Beckton and North Woolwich, Böcker was about to poke his head into a wasp's nest.

At 12.11am searchlights of London's North-East Sub-Command at Victoria Park and Wanstead found L 33, followed a minute later by West Ham. Then three lights from the Central area locked on as did four from the Woolwich area. With L 33 illuminated the guns opened fire, from Wanstead, Beckton, Clapton, West Ham, Victoria Park, Tower Bridge, Blackwall, Deptford Park, Meath Gardens and Shooter's Hill.[29]

The gunners found the atmospheric conditions difficult as smoke deflected the searchlight beams but the consensus was that L 33 was flying at about 11,000 feet. While the gunners adjusted their fuzes, Böcker ordered the release of his bombs. The first seven all dropped within a 90-yard radius of a point where St Leonard's Street crosses the Limehouse Cut, a canal connecting the River Lea navigation with the Thames.

The first bomb landed with deadly impact, killing at least five people as it wrecked houses from 130 to 136 St Leonard's Street. Amongst the dead were Harry Brown, a French polisher, 71-year-old widow Mary Lunnis and George Jones, a porter at the Poplar Casual Ward. He was standing outside, about 160 yards from the bomb, when a metal fragment struck him in the face and killed him. The houses closest to the bomb came tumbling down with other buildings in the locality suffering to a lesser extent. Two incendiary bombs caused small fires at the Sun Flour Mill on St Leonard's Street and on a barge moored on the Limehouse Cut, before four fell in Bell Road causing a major fire at a timber yard. A girl living with her family in St Leonard's Street had been unable to get to sleep due to a noisy party a few houses away and witnessed the aftermath of the explosion.

> I was listening to the music when there was an enormous crash, the house shook, and [mother] and I were hurled from our bed and down the stairs, amidst falling bricks and plaster and a cloud of dust. Neither of us was hurt. My mother placed me in the cellar. She ran upstairs to get my brothers, who were all safe.[30]

When L 33 moved on, the family went to their door and looked on horrified as the woman who had hosted the party was standing beside the ruins of her house while rescuers extricated the 'terribly mangled' body of her unconscious daughter.

Böcker had turned onto a westward course, as though intending to attack the City, but was under intense gunfire, which also affected those on the ground. One anti-aircraft shell smashed down in Victoria Dock Road. Discharged from the army in March 1916 due to ill health, Frederick Monk told his family to go to the kitchen when the guns started. Moments later, as his mother remembered, the shell exploded just outside the house.

The next thing there was a terrible explosion, falling of glass, screaming and moans and cries… With the aid of a policeman and his lantern, what was the first thing I should see but my soldier son lying in the washhouse?... His eyes glanced at me, and he said, 'Mother, they have got me this time'; and so he died. Shrapnel had penetrated his lungs.[31]

Five other people suffered injuries and a man living next door, Edward O'Brien, a 43-year-old stevedore, died when shell fragments fractured his skull.

In Hoxton, five miles away, another anti-aircraft shell exploded outside a house in Myrtle Street, killing Alfred Fletcher, and injuring two men and a child.

The next group of five bombs fell within the space of 200 yards. In Empson Street two incendiaries caused limited damage and a HE bomb struck a business premises. An incendiary bomb started a fire at 7 Gurley Street and another fell in Brickfield Road. At about the same time, some eight miles away, Alfred Brandon, who was patrolling between Hainault Farm and Sutton's Farm, caught a glimpse of L 33 in the searchlights before losing her again. But L 33 was in trouble.

Anti-aircraft shells were now bursting all around her, then one passed right through a gas cell behind the command gondola. It did not ignite the hydrogen but it did fracture one of the main ring girders, while other shell fragments slashed into gas cells and one damaged a propeller. Böcker turned back to a northerly course and dropped more bombs helping to counter the loss of hydrogen. Directly below him lay the London & North West Railway goods yard and the huge North London Railway Loco and Carriage works. Buildings suffered, railway carriages and trucks smashed and tracks ripped up. Damage at the first site extended into Violet Road, Devons Road and Shephard Street, where four people sustained injuries, and at the second site two men were hurt as the effects of the blast spread down Burdett Street, Campbell Road and Swaton Road.

While the crew battled to prevent further hydrogen loss, L 33 progressed another 500 yards before releasing the next bomb. Falling at the corner of Botolph Road and Eagling Road, it ripped through a Baptist Chapel, damaged 20 houses in Botolph Road, six in Devons Road and the Devons Road School.

Lieutenant W.G. Roberts, an army officer home on leave, reported the next bomb exploded 'with an awful roar which seemed to rock our house on its foundations'. The blast ripped open the front door and smashed all the windows.

> After making sure my family were safe, I went to Bow Road, a few yards away, where a large public house, the Black Swan, had been wrecked. Only the carcase of it was left standing, and a heavy pall of black dust hung over the ruins.[32]

The Black Swan stood at 148 Bow Road, on the corner with Bromley High Street, and was home that night to the landlord, Edwin John Reynolds, and eight members of his family. Lieutenant Roberts joined in the rescue.

> I and others groped our way amongst the debris, searching for any victims who might be alive. Lifting some flooring, we discovered the wife of the licensee, Mrs Reynolds, lying in the cellar, where she had been blown by the bomb. It had struck the house dead in the middle, taking all the floors to the basement.

As well as saving Mrs Reynolds, the rescuers pulled out her husband, their two sons, aged 11 and nine, and son-in-law, Henry Adams. But Mrs Reynolds mother, Mary Potter, was dead, as were her two daughters, Queenie Reynolds (aged 19) and Sylvia Adams (20). Firemen found Henry and Sylvia's baby daughter, also called Sylvia, hanging from a rafter by her nightdress. She died shortly afterwards. The explosion also wrecked the house next door, killing four-year-old Henry Taylor.

Continuing northwards for about 350 yards, Böcker released the next bomb. It exploded on the footpath in Wrexham Road, at the junction with Old Ford Road, injuring three women, destroying a gas main, wrecking six houses from 746 to 754 Old Ford Road and smashing many windows. From there L 33 crossed the River Lea, dropping a bomb on Cook's Soap Works on Cook's Road, but it failed to detonate. Then, passing over the Midland Railway's Bow Goods Yard, a bomb at the Home Light Oil Company's works set a huge fire blazing. Four bombs exploded amongst industrial buildings on Marshgate Road and Carpenter's Road[33] causing damage to factories, a laboratory and offices, while a large fire destroyed the greater part of Judd & Bros. match factory. Four other bombs lay undiscovered on Stratford Marshes for a week. As L 33 drew away from the guns she dropped a final bomb on waste ground at the Great Eastern Railway marshalling yard at Temple Mills. Böcker released a cloud of water ballast to lighten his ship further, whereupon the guns lost sight of the Zeppelin. The bombing run had only lasted about four minutes but caused the deaths of 11 people, in addition to the three killed by anti-aircraft shells, and injured at least 39 (13 of these by AA fire).[34]

At 12.19am, L 33 passed Buckhurst Hill, her engines emitting a pounding noise, possibly due to the damaged propeller. But Böcker was not yet clear. Four minutes later the searchlight at Kelvedon Common found L 33 and a 13-pdr, 9cwt gun opened fire, estimating her height at 9,000 feet. The gun fired four rounds as Böcker released more water ballast to escape. Any respite, however, was temporary because at about 12.30am, Alfred de Bathe Brandon of No.39 Squadron spotted L 33 again. Brandon, who had attacked L 15 almost six months earlier but failed to bring her down and was unable to locate LZ 97 during a raid in April, now had the ailing L 33 in his sights. Once more, however, his attack did not go according to plan. Free of the searchlight, darkness shrouded L 33 as Brandon struggled to keep her in view while both manually pumping fuel because his automatic pump had failed and working the cocking handle on his Lewis gun. The ensuing engagement was frenetic.

> I came up behind the Zeppelin and on raising the gun jerked it out of the mounting, the gun and the yoke falling across the nacelle. I managed to replace the gun but in the meantime had passed under and past the Zepp. I turned and passed along it again, but from the bow, but we passed each other too quickly for me to aim. On turning I came up from behind and fixed a drum of ammunition. The Brock ammunition seemed to be bursting all along it but the Zepp did not catch fire. I was using Brock, Pomeroy and Sparklet. I turned again and put on a fresh drum and came up from behind and fired again. The gun jambed [sic] after about 9 rounds.

With his Lewis gun out of operation, Brandon, who had retained his Ranken darts, attempted to get above L 33 but lost her in the clouds before he could get into position. His attack, which had lasted just three or four minutes, was over. While L 33 escaped to the east, for her crew a bad situation just got worse; bullets fired by Brandon had pierced fuel tanks and Böcker noted that 'fuel flowed out in the gangway'.[35] And with no more water ballast to jettison to lighten the ship, Böcker feared the end was in sight.

Watching from far away and with no telltale fireball in the sky, the crews of L 31 and L 32 could only conclude that L 33 had completed her attack on London, avoided the intense anti-aircraft fire and escaped. It was now time for them to make their own attacks, unaware of the predicament their comrades in L 33 now faced.

# Chapter 17

# 'They are all someone's sons'

After L 33 had made her attack on London, the capital's defences remained on the alert. Those tracking the intruders knew she had not been alone and information that two other Zeppelins had come inland over Kent suggested a possible dash for the capital. Three Zeppelins over London on one night would be a first and those on duty, manning the guns, searchlights and aircraft, remained vigilant and ready for action.

Peterson had headed north-west from Tunbridge Wells at 12.10am, dropping an incendiary bomb twenty minutes later as L 32 passed over Ide Hill, about three miles south-west of Sevenoaks, but at 12.50am a searchlight at the village of Crockenhill held the Zeppelin in its beam. It drew the standard response, with Peterson releasing seven bombs in an attempt to disrupt the light. They smashed a few windows and uprooted some trees in an orchard but none exploded within 200 yards of the target.[1] A ground mist south of the Thames ensured this was the only searchlight to hold L 32 before she crossed the river just east of Purfleet at about 1am.

## 24 September 1916, 12.35am: Streatham, London

Further to the west, Mathy and L 31 continued towards London. Over Kenley he released a parachute flare and at 12.25am, in the glare of its light, quickly released four bombs on a 130-yard line along Hall Way between Kenley and Purley. Three exploded in gardens, smashing windows and roof tiles, while the last wrecked a post box. A searchlight at Croydon now found L 31 but Mathy immediately released two more parachute flares that effectively blinded its crew. When they found her again, L 31 had reached Streatham with the 4-inch gun at Croydon firing two

245

rounds before another flare blinded the searchlight crew again. Prior to reaching Streatham, Mathy dropped two HE and two incendiary bombs over Longmorton Farm, Mitcham, smashing windows in nine buildings. Mathy was now about 1000 yards south of Streatham Common Station where his main bombing run began, although Mathy's navigation was out and he believed those first bombs near Kenley were dropped over Clapham, nine miles further north. It affected his orientation for the rest of the raid and led him to believe his main bomb run was north of the Thames from Chelsea, through Pimlico to the City, whereas it ran south of the river from Streatham through Brixton to Kennington.

Mathy's first string of bombs fell around Streatham Common Station. The first, an incendiary, landed in Mr Tomlin's vegetable patch at the rear of 50 Ellison Road, followed seconds later by three bombs at the station's goods yard, which set fire to railway trucks, ripped up track and damaged a couple of buildings as well as houses in Ellison Road. An incendiary in Greyhound Lane caused only minor damage before a bomb exploding on a house at 11 Estreham Road, opposite the station entrance, struck a devastating blow. Nos.10, 11 and 12 collapsed with Nos.13 and 14 left in a bad way. The first casualty of Mathy's raid, 74-year-old Mary Chadwick, died in her bed at No.12; rescuers managed to extricate her daughter, Maud Chadwick, aged 31, who was pinned under a wall and buried by rubble. At No.11 the Meggs family escaped from the wreckage of their home, as did seven others from the affected houses, although dust-covered and suffering from shock. At the station the blast ripped through the booking office and damaged the roof over the platform with less significant damage extending to other houses in Estreham Road, Pathfield Road, Barrow Road and Greyhound Lane. The final two incendiary bombs of this first string fell in back gardens at 17 Pathfield Street and 33 Barrow Road.

Mathy began to release a second string of bombs half way between Streatham Common Station and Streatham Station. A fire at the back of 56 Lewin Road was quickly dealt with but another, in Walter Drayson's back garden at 64 Natal Road, was only prevented from getting out of control by Prince, the family's prized Old English Sheepdog. His terrified barking as a shed caught alight and flames scorched his kennel alerted Walter who saved his dog and extinguished the fire as it threatened a neighbouring property. In appreciation, neighbours presented a handsome collar bearing the inscription, 'Awarded to Prince by grateful neighbours for services rendered during Zeppelin raid on September 23rd 1916'. But traumatised by his experiences, Prince, previously a friendly, intelligent and much-loved dog, became nervous and at times uncontrollable. Reluctantly Walter and his wife had Prince put to sleep.[2]

Seconds after the bomb in Natal Road, one exploded on the railway embankment just south of Streatham Station, smashing windows along Gleneagle Road while station staff battled to extinguish a fire at the goods yard. A huge explosion wrecked flats in nine buildings between 19 and 35 Babington Road where three people were injured, then another tore through a building occupied by a wine merchant at 294 Streatham High Road causing great destruction there and to neighbouring homes and shops. A chemist, an upholsterer, a bootmaker, the Geisha tearooms all suffered and, perhaps most unfortunately, so did glass merchant Frank Cox, who no doubt missed a business bonanza as a sea of broken glass frosted the High Road and Mitcham Lane.

For the next 700 yards L 31 passed over residential streets without dropping more bombs, then two exploded at Streatham Cricket Club at the end of Pendennis Road, the only open space in that area, where they killed a grazing donkey. Four incendiary bombs at Leighton Avenue and Leighton Court Road had a minimal effect but L 31 was now approaching the third of Streatham's railway stations, Streatham Hill. Flying at about 12,000 feet, Mathy released a huge 300kg bomb.

Earlier that evening Edgar Tilley, an air mechanic in the RNAS, had arrived at London's Victoria Station and caught a tram to his parent's home by Streatham Hill Station. At Victoria he bumped into an old school friend, Roger Shaw, who was getting the same tram with his fiancée. The couple alighted at the stop on Streatham Hill by Telford Avenue and Edgar remained on board. A little later, when safely at home, Edgar heard 'a terrific explosion'. He went out and found a shattered, wrecked double-decker tram in the middle of the road.

The 300kg bomb had fallen in front of two large houses at the corner of Streatham Hill and Sternhold Avenue, directly opposite the station. Both houses were empty at the time but for those on board the tram the explosion had tragic consequences. John Fenton, a Special Constabulary sergeant, had just boarded and was climbing the stairs when the bomb exploded like an earthquake about 25 yards away. The motorman, conductor and the four other passengers did not stand a chance as jagged bomb fragments and razor sharp shards of glass cut through the tram. Only Sergeant Fenton remained standing, shielded by the stairs he was climbing. The conductor, Charles Boys, was lying motionless at the foot of the stairs; the motorman, John Gaynor was dead too. Fenton did what he could for the injured until medical help arrived – he then reported for a night's duty as a Special Constable. For his courage and devotion to duty that night, Sergeant Fenton received the British Empire Medal.

A fleet of military ambulances arrived but the sight of the bodies shocked a corporal with them. 'One we found,' he recalled, 'so terribly mangled that we had to put the poor remains in a sack: he was either the driver or conductor; I don't know which.'[3] Also found amongst the carnage was 55-year-old Henry Bloomfield and Edgar Tilley's friend, Roger Shaw. After seeing his fiancée to her house he had boarded the next tram to take him home. Now he was lying in a pool of blood, 'his head nearly blown off'.[4] Elijah Wade and William Wood both sustained terrible injuries from which they did not recover, and only one passenger, Jessie Le Britton survived, although injured.

Following Streatham Hill, Mathy dropped six incendiary bombs close to the junction with Telford Avenue where they all fell in gardens, followed by a bomb in Tierney Avenue that ravaged the houses at Nos.25 and 27. A family who had taken shelter in the cellar emerged shaken and covered in dust but unhurt. The final bomb in Streatham, an incendiary, damaged a house at 12 Streatham Hill.

## 24 September 1916, 12.40am: Brixton, London

Mathy continued to follow this main road leading into London as Streatham Hill became Brixton Hill, then Brixton Road and Kennington Park Road. His 17 incendiary bombs dropped along this route caused three serious fires, at 37 Fairmount Road, 81 Brixton Hill and at 433 Brixton Road.

A tramway official standing outside the Town Hall on Brixton Hill heard the sound of distant engines but initially could see nothing.

> A second or so later there was a great burst of flame in the sky followed by a tremendous explosion, which nearly threw me off my feet. At first I could hardly realise what had happened, but turning around I saw behind me a cloud of dust and people pouring out of their homes and rushing down a side street.[5]

The first of six HE bombs that fell on Brixton struck 147 and 149 Brixton Hill, which were both unoccupied. The explosion caused much damage, with windows shattering all along the road and in Upper Tulse Hill and in a maze of small streets running off it. The eyewitness followed the people 'rushing down a side street', to Beechdale Road where the second of the bombs exploded on a house at No.19, home to Alfred Ward, a C.I.D. Inspector at Scotland Yard, and his family. The explosion demolished the house, blasting Alfred out through a front window and into the street where a police constable found him. Despite his considerable injuries he assisted the constable in bringing out his injured wife and daughter Grace, a clerk at the Foreign Office. All three went to hospital but Grace died ten minutes after arrival from injuries sustained to her spine. Inspector Ward survived an operation and rallied briefly before dying the following day; only Ward's wife, Ada, survived.

The next bomb landed about 340 yards beyond Beechdale Road, smashing into a builder's premises at 87 Brixton Hill. It destroyed workshops and stores, damaged four taxis parked outside No.93, inflicted some damage to the Scala Picture Palace and in Josephine Avenue. In Baytree Avenue, about 470 yards further north, Mr Davis was in bed when he heard the sound of approaching explosions.

> After a few seconds the most terrific explosion I had ever heard shook the house to the foundations and blew out all the windows.
>
> Rushing out, I found a house three doors away razed to the ground and the debris right across the road. I climbed over the ruins shouting as loud as I could 'Anyone alive?' [6]

The house was home to a music hall artist, Jack Lorimer. Lorimer and his wife were away on tour so the 'nanny-cum-housekeeper' Betty Hobbs was looking after their three young sons, Alex (aged nine), Maxwell (eight) and William (four). Alex and Maxwell were sharing a bed in one room and William and Betty in another. The force of the blast turned over the bed in which Alex and Maxwell were sleeping and landed on top of them. It saved the lives of the terrified children.

Mr Davis' desperate shouts finally got a reply.

> I heard a thin little voice crying, 'Save me, save me!' I went frantic; after pulling away part of the roof, and broken furniture, I saw the moonlight shining on the white flesh of a little boy. I gathered him into my arms and carried him to my house.

249

Mr Davis returned to the ruins to continue his search but a falling beam struck his head and he lost consciousness. After treatment he returned home in time to see ambulance men carefully carrying away two bodies.

Those bodies were the youngest boy, William, and Betty Hobbs, both suffocated under the rubble. But the boy Mr Davis pulled from the wreckage and the brother who had shared a bed with him were both safe. One of them, Maxwell, later earned enduring fame in the world of entertainment under the stage name Max Wall.[7]

Damage extended into neighbouring streets, then two incendiary bombs followed, falling either side of Brixton Station, where one of the serious fires took hold at 433 Brixton Road, the home and shop of a tailor, S.H. Messent. About 330 yards north of the station, the next bomb exploded outside 337 Brixton Road, severely damaging the home of a doctor, John Robertson, and injuring him in the process. The last of the Brixton HE bombs exploded with tragic consequences in the roadway opposite Nos.263 to 269 Brixton Road. A man working at a taxi garage described what happened.

> Standing at the top of the yard leading into the garage, I heard
> the firing of guns… Suddenly there was a great burst of flame,
> a terrific explosion, and I was thrown to the ground. When
> I picked myself up the air was filled with dust and glass was
> flying in every direction.[8]

The previously empty street suddenly filled with people, many of whom sought shelter at the garage but they quickly turned away when told of the large store of petrol there. The eyewitness, untouched by the bomb, was a lucky man. 'The bomb fell about thirty yards from where I was standing,' he explained, 'blowing a great hole in the roadway several feet deep.' Others were not so fortunate. Gaston Leonard, a shipping clerk from Belgium, had been visiting a friend but the 32-year-old's body was now lying on the pavement with severe injuries. He died in hospital. An employee at the *Daily Telegraph* newspaper, Walter Archer, aged 68, had heard the sound of exploding bombs and went to look for his two daughters who had gone out for the evening. He told a policeman who found him lying in the road, 'I do not feel very much hurt,' but he died of his injuries in hospital an hour later.[9]

William Hogg managed and lived above a tobacconist shop at 269 Brixton Road, with his wife, Florence and their two children. Alerted by distant rumblings, William and Florence were standing by the side door of the shop. With nothing in sight, William told his wife, 'I will pop up and see how the children are.'

> I went upstairs and the crash came just as I was leaning over the first child's bed. The ceiling came down on us. I went into the back room and got the other boy. I then went out of the front window along... some ledges, over another shop, downstairs, and left the children at another shop.[10]

William explained to the coroner that fire and debris prevented him using the stairs. 'Everything went down,' he added, 'the whole place was wrecked.' Having brought his children to safety, William went to find his wife but she was nowhere to be seen. Later the police informed him they had found Florence's terribly mutilated body in the street. William could only identify her by the coat she was wearing.

Mathy continued his course for about a mile before he dropped his final bomb south of the Thames. Passing 400 yards from The Oval cricket ground and its neighbouring gasometers, the bomb exploded on the open space of Kennington Park, inflicting limited damage to the Kennington Theatre on the northern edge of the park, and smashing windows in Kennington Park Road, Kennington Road and in St Agnes Place.

A newsagent living above his shop on Kennington Park Road heard the sound of explosions and went to the window, the exact opposite to what the public were instructed to do during a raid.

> The window in which I was standing was shattered, and the force of the explosion blew me across the room and flung me on the bed. I was stunned, but otherwise uninjured, and speedily recovered. But, as all the electric bulbs in the house were broken, there was naturally a good deal of confusion... Shop fronts and the glass in the houses in the neighbourhood were shattered. Mine is an old house, and we found later that the force of the concussion had raised the roof fully four inches.[11]

## 24 September 1916, 12.47am: Leyton, London[12]

Mathy now ceased dropping bombs for just over seven miles. He crossed the River Thames between London Bridge and Tower Bridge and passed right over the City of London, heading north-east towards Leyton. Mathy stated that after dropping the majority of his bombs between Chelsea and Pimlico, he released 12 bombs over the City and Islington in quick succession. No bombs landed in any of those places, but 10 HE bombs did drop in Leyton.[13]

At 12.47am Mathy turned to follow the line of the Lea Bridge Road and dropped his first bomb of this final string. Former baker George Sexton and his wife, Virginia, had woken earlier to the sound of gunfire that accompanied L 33's attack and were still at the door of their house, Richmond Villa, at 495 Lea Bridge Road, looking for Zeppelins when Mathy's bomb exploded just yards from them. Together in their doorway the couple stood no chance. The next bomb struck a building at 503 Lea Bridge Road, at the corner with Shrubland Road.

> A family of five, who occupied a house at a corner opposite a police station, had a remarkable escape. A bomb fell and tore away one side of the house, and, although they were inside, they were uninjured.[14]

In fact the explosion inflicted significant damage to the police station, section house and stables, and affected 189 other houses and shops, leaving five people injured.[15]

The next bomb detonated on waste ground on the corner of Russell Road before one exploded with great force between Westerham and Bromley roads, an area previously bombed in August 1915.[16] A Salvation Army hall stood on the corner of Bromley Road and Lea Bridge Road where an officer of the organisation, H.V. Rohu, manned a First Aid Post. He reported serious damage to the hall and that Bromley Road was almost in ruins. He joined others in searching for the injured.

> Upstairs in the first I found... nothing but the floor of a bedroom the furniture of which had been blown to pieces. In the back kitchen were two families, including eight children. One mother was a cripple, and both mothers had tiny babies. Covered with blood and plaster... they looked a pitiable sight.

He got the families out and arranged shelter for them but what he later saw outside moved him.

> I shall never forget the sad procession up that street, about 2 a.m., one of the poor mothers crying and exclaiming 'What

have we done to the Germans that they should have destroyed our home?'[17]

After thoroughly checking the wrecked houses, rescuers accounted for one man dead and eleven people requiring treatment for their injuries, among them a bus conductor with lacerations to his face and his wife who lost her sight.[18] Mathy continued on his course; the next bomb fell on 831 High Road. It destroyed the home of a well-known local doctor, Harold Everett Price, but he and his family escaped physical injury. L 31's next bomb exploded in St Heliers Road, causing damage but no casualties, but that changed with the next bomb.

William Webb, a 25-year-old bus driver, had just finished a shift and was walking home up Leyton Green Road with a conductress from the bus garage.[19] When the bomb exploded 300 yards away in St Heliers Road the conductress ran, but ten seconds later the next one exploded at the corner of Leyton Green Road and Knotts Green Road and a lethal fragment cut into William Webb's brain, killing him instantly. Five seconds later another exploded on waste ground between Essex Road and Lea Bridge Road injuring four women and a child. Mr H. Burdon, who lived nearby, went to see what had happened.

> Pieces of the iron shell were still hot when I reached this spot, and heard how a man who lived near had gone to his door to see which direction the Zeppelin took and was killed.[20]

Mathy now had just two bombs left. They landed either side of Halford Road, close to the West Ham Union Infirmary.[21] At 25 Halford Road, eight-year-old Violet Wade was at home with her family when 'the building' caught between the two blasts, 'was crushed inwards like a concertina'.

> I was flung out of bed amid a mass of broken glass. My grandfather was terribly cut about the head, and my grandmother lost her right eye. To add to the horror, voices shouted to us not to strike matches, owing to the fear of explosions from burst gas mains.[22]

The groans and shrieks of the injured haunted Violet for the rest of her life. Some of those came from next door. A grandchild of the Wade's neighbours, the Stonehams, lived on Lea Bridge Road where she was listening to the 'fearsome, doom-like, destructive noises' with her terrified family, when a neighbour brought them dreadful news.

> A bomb had fallen in front of Grandfather's house in Halford Road. His head was almost blown off. My uncle had pieces of bomb (or shell) in his spine, and was carried screaming towards the hospital: he died before he got there.[23]

The two victims were Henry Stoneham, aged 47, and his namesake 13-year-old son. Henry's wife was badly injured and had to have her right arm amputated. And tragedy extended to the next house too, where 50-year-old Charles Rogers lived. When he heard the bombs he lay down in his hallway but the explosion tore off one of his legs and he died soon after.[24]

Mathy's raid was over. From Kenley to Leyton the authorities traced 74 bombs (33 HE and 41 incendiaries), which claimed 22 lives and injured 74 people. Now he set a course across East Anglia, exiting just south of Great Yarmouth at about 2.15am. But there was no celebration on having completed a successful raid. An hour earlier, when about five miles east of Bishops Stortford, Heinrich Mathy observed another Zeppelin about 20 miles to the south and it soon became clear it was in trouble as Mathy's unemotional report concludes:

> The ship was very heavily attacked and seemed to have taken refuge after dropping its bombs, when again searchlights flashed in front of it, and after a short, violent bombardment, the destruction occurred. The ship crashed at [1.15 a.m.], burning as it fell to the ground.[25]

The question for Mathy and his crew was which Zeppelin was it? Was it one of their sister ships, L 32 or L 33?

## 24 September 1916, 1.00am: Purfleet, Essex

Zeppelin L 32 had crossed the River Thames just east of Purfleet at 1am. Once across the river the ground mist melted away and within a minute or two Purfleet's Beacon Hill searchlight, followed by the Tunnel Farm light at West Thurrock found her. Almost immediately the guns began to thunder: from Tunnel Farm, from Belhus Park and from Tilbury. Guns south of the Thames joined in too but with tragic results for one. The two guns positioned at Southern Outfall, Crossness, came into action but after three rounds the breech of one blew out, killing Gunner John McDougall of the Royal Garrison Artillery, and injuring three others.

The situation was getting hot for Peterson and his crew. Commanding the Beacon Hill searchlight, Second Lieutenant R.W. Corbett, Royal Engineers, was convinced one gun had scored a hit.

> I noticed that Tunnel Farm, soon after opening fire… scored a direct hit which, as the target was receding, appeared to be very near the nose of the Zepp. The shell itself appeared to go as close to the Zepp's body as it was possible to do without actually touching it, then exploded.
>
> The Zepp was then seen to point its nose directly downwards and rushed down at a very great speed to a very much lower altitude when it regained a horizontal altitude and proceeded in a N.E. direction.[26]

Peterson dropped 15 bombs over Aveley, midway between the guns at Tunnel Farm and Belhus Park. Released in emergency, they caused no damage but countered some of the height loss. Moments later Peterson dropped his main bomb load, with 44 bombs (23 HE and 21 incendiary) falling on a line from South Ockendon towards North Ockendon. They broke a few windows at Belhus Park House and in houses at South Ockendon, where they also killed two horses. More lights now found L 32 and other guns opened fire as she moved beyond the reach of those first guns. The crews manning the gun at Shonks, a farm near Vange, and the two at Shenfield Common, believed they hit L 32 but it was not just the guns at work in the sky.

After his unsuccessful attack on L 33, Alfred Brandon remained on patrol. At 1.03am he saw L 32 held by searchlights over Purfleet and turned towards the beleaguered Zeppelin but, unseen in the darkness, other hunters were closing in too: James Mackay had seen her, as had Frederick Sowrey. Earlier in the month Mackay had been about to attack SL 11 when William Leefe Robinson set it on fire. This time he saw another aeroplane fire two drums of ammunition before he tried a few rounds himself at long range. When Brandon approached he spotted 'Brock bullets bursting', and it appeared to him that, 'the Zepp was being hosed with a stream of fire'. Frederick Sowrey had beaten them both to it.

## 24 September 1916, 1.15am: Near Billericay, Essex

Sowrey, now aged 23, had joined the Royal Fusiliers in August 1914, but after receiving a wound at the Battle of Loos in 1915 he recovered in England and transferred to the Royal Flying Corps. He joined No.39 Squadron in June 1916 and became great friends with William Leefe Robinson.[27] Patrolling between Sutton's Farm and Joyce Green, he was in an ideal position when the lights north of the Thames found L 32. 'I could distinctly see the propellers revolving,' Sowrey reported, 'and the airship was manoeuvring to avoid the searchlight beams.'[28] He opened fire with his Lewis gun.

> The first two drums had apparently no effect but the third one caused the envelope to catch on fire in several places; in the centre and front. All firing was traversing fire along the envelope. The drums were loaded with a mixture of Brock, Pomeroy and Tracer ammunition.[29]

An eyewitness described L 32's final moments.

> The shrapnel fire had ceased, and then suddenly at one end of the Zeppelin a brilliant point of light appeared as though a piece of magnesium ribbon had been ignited. As the light spread with marvellous rapidity and developed into flame a boyish voice exclaimed triumphantly, 'Got him!' By this time the whole of the envelope seemed a mass of liquid fire.... and after retaining her horizontal position for a few moments longer the giant vessel threw up her head in despair and as she rapidly disintegrated... she dissolved into what looked like a cascade of liquid lava.[30]

Once the fire took hold there was no way to save the ship and those on board had a simple but terrible decision to make: to jump to their death or stay with the ship and be burned alive.

In Shenfield, 16-year-old Leslie Goddard, had watched silently with his mother as the drama unfolded.

> As we continued to gaze upwards at the crumbling blazing monster, we could clearly see the airship's crew climbing on to the railings of the gondolas and jumping to their deaths;

clearly they preferred to meet their end that way than by being roasted alive. My mother turned to go back to her bed and as she slowly crossed the room, I remember her saying, 'Oh Les, they are all someone's sons.' I think that remark of hers remains my chief recollection of that astonishing experience.[31]

L 32 was destroyed at about 1.15am, parts of the disintegrating ship falling over a wide area of countryside, but the main body smashed into a field on Snail's Hall Farm, South Green, about a mile south-east of Billericay. The race was now on to reach the burning wreckage. Inspector Allen Ellis of the Essex County Constabulary cycled from Billericay. When he arrived he found six local men at the wreck and others running across the fields towards it as flames illuminated the scene, the bulk of the crumpled wreck lying across a line of trees and bushes. When Special Constables began to arrive at around 1.30am, Ellis formed a cordon around the wreckage to keep back the gathering crowd. In Brentwood, where the Southern Army (Home Forces) had its Headquarters, troops received orders to march to Billericay. At 2.15am the Army took over the protection of the site. Once the fire brigade had doused the flames, the smouldering bodies of the crew were dragged clear and those who had jumped were located a short distance from the wreckage. Major Myddleton Gravey, senior medical officer of the Southern Army, had the unpleasant task of examining the 22 burned and broken bodies.

> With the exception of 3, the 22 bodies were all very much burned. In many cases the clothing of them consisted only of a few charred remnants, several had had their hands and feet burned off, nearly all had broken limbs. The burning in most cases appeared to be after death but in a few instances it was evidently before this happened.[32]

The eyewitness who earlier heard the boy shout 'Got him!' when L 32 began to burn also reported cheering from the surrounding villages. But there was more excitement still to come.

> About ten minutes after the airship had been brought down we heard a dull explosion from another quarter. 'Well, Dad,' cried the boy in joyful accents, 'it looks as if they'd bagged a brace.[33]

257

He was right. About 20 miles away a second Zeppelin had hit the ground in extraordinary circumstances and left a tale long remembered in that remote part of rural Essex.

## 24 September 1916, 1.20am: Little Wigborough, Essex

After his earlier encounter with Second Lieutenant Brandon, following his attack on East London, Böcker had continued eastwards but L 33 was in trouble. Damaged by anti-aircraft fire and with fuel leaking from holed petrol tanks, it was a struggle to keep her aloft, as her commander recalled.

> Due to loss of gas the ship fell 1000 metres in four minutes, and I realised the ship could not be saved, so I had dropped overboard all fuel and oil except for one hour supply, machine guns and ammunition, spare parts and equipment, and finally the entire wireless apparatus.[34]

The last of the jettisoned items fell near the village of Tolleshunt Major about 1.05am. Even so, Böcker could only keep L 33 in the air by flying nose up with engine power alone keeping her in the air, but that was not sustainable. The end was approaching.

L 33 briefly passed over the sea near Mersea Island but, recognising his dire situation, Böcker turned back inland where a gust of wind battered his ship down from a height of 150 metres. The great wounded airship came to rest across Copt Hall Lane at Little Wigborough, just 25 yards from a pair of isolated cottages; inside were the families of farm labourers Thomas Lewis and Frederick Choat. Böcker called his men together, all had survived the landing although one had cracked his ribs. Piling all documents and papers into one of the gondolas in preparation for setting fire to the wreck, Böcker sent some of the crew over to the cottages where, hammering on the doors, they tried to warn the occupants. Unsurprisingly those inside did not respond to what appeared to be the vanguard of a German invasion right on their own doorstep. Frederick Choat later gave an interview to the press.

> All that blessed crew came to my cottage and started knocking at the door. I never answered, and I heard the commander cursing. He spoke English and said something about the

'b[loody] house'. I put my wife and three children in a back room and made myself scarce too.[35]

The crew started a fire with a flare gun, the flames from a burning pool of petrol causing three small explosions as escaping hydrogen ignited. The heat from the fires blistered the cottage's paintwork.

> It didn't hurt any of us, but it smashed the front windows of my house and those of my neighbours. I found afterwards that all the hair was singed off the back of my dog, which was in a kennel outside.[36]

Much to Böcker's frustration, the fires burned away the envelope and gas cells but the metal skeleton, with the bow and stern tilted upwards, remained intact. With nothing more he could do, Böcker formed his men up and marched off down Copt Hall Lane towards the Wigborough Road.

Just over a mile away, at Maltings Farm, just north of the village of Peldon, Edgar Nicholas had awoken to the sound of the Zeppelin's engines, which he described as circling around the district. Nicholas served as a Special Constable.

> For a while I stood in my garden, listening and looking for the ship. Suddenly the sound of its engines ceased, and a few minutes afterwards there was a loud explosion about a mile from my house.
>
> A neighbour agreed to stay with my wife while I went to see what had happened.[37]

Nicholas noted that the explosion occurred at 1.20am then, mounting his bicycle, he set off to investigate. Pedalling through Peldon, he followed the glow of the fire, until he reached the turning to Copt Hall Lane. There, appearing from the darkness, he saw a body of men marching towards him. He estimated there were 20 (actually 21) and with remarkable coolness, Edgar Nicholas dismounted and walked up to the leading man. Then followed a remarkable conversation as Nicholas asked Böcker:

> 'Is it a Zeppelin down?' He said, 'How many miles is it to Colchester?' I replied, 'About 6.' He replied, 'Thank you.' I at

once recognised [a] foreign accent and from their clothing and conversation knew they were Germans. I received no answer to my question.[38]

Colchester was a well-known garrison town and it appears Böcker intended to march there and surrender. With the direction pointed out the Germans set off again, marching towards Peldon, while Special Constable Nicholas joined the rear of the column where one of the men spoke a little broken English.

> I asked this man if he was hit by gun-fire. He answered, 'Zeppelin explode, ve crew prisoner of war.' Later he remarked 'What people tink of war?' I replied 'I hardly know.' He said 'Did I tink nearly over?' I replied 'It's over for you anyway.' He answered 'Goot, Goot' offering me his hand to shake which I did. After this he gave me his lifesaving vest... with regard to the vest, he said 'Schwim Schwim' extending his arms in swimming fashion and added... 'I learn English at School.'[39]

As the column approached Peldon another Special Constable, Elijah Traylor, appeared and with him was Ernest Arthur Edwards, an Essex Constabulary police sergeant there on holiday. They escorted the crew to Peldon's little post office where there was a telephone. The local police constable, Charles Smith, had already telephoned information about a low-flying Zeppelin to Home Forces Headquarters and was awaiting a response when Sergeant Edwards entered the Post Office and advised him that the Zeppelin's crew were outside! Smith contacted the nearest army post, about four miles away at West Mersea. In an interview many years later, Smith added, '[Böcker] asked to use the telephone and I refused, telling him that he and the crew must be handed over to the military authorities, to which he agreed.'

Smith arrested the crew then he and an escort of seven 'Specials' set off to meet a detachment of the 83rd Provisional Battalion on the road from West Mersea. By this time Sergeant Edwards had slipped away to return to the house where he was staying, for which he later received an official rebuke for leaving the scene when he was the senior police officer present. Nicholas meanwhile had returned to guard the crash site but had no concerns about the intentions of the Zeppelin crew: 'So far as I could see the prisoners seemed thoroughly glad to be on firm ground, and in fact only too anxious to be placed in the hands of the military.' Once the army picked up the prisoners, however, it created a new problem – where to keep them until morning? But help was at hand.

At about 1.45am, the Reverend Charles Pierrepont Edwards[40] had woken to raised voices in the street at West Mersea, and seeing a fire in the distance quickly concluded what had happened. He and his wife mounted their bicycles and set off towards the light.

Along the road they encountered the prisoners and escort. Informed of the problem of where to hold the men, the vicar offered the Church Hall and he and his wife cycled off to make the necessary arrangements. But the Reverend noted that the mood was changing: 'In the short time that had elapsed before I got back the news had spread rapidly, and the street was full of people… The people were naturally very excited.' The atmosphere was, in fact, turning hostile as the Germans, the 'Baby-killers', marched into West Mersea. The Reverend Edwards, however, turned the mood of the crowd.

> 'Three cheers for the King,' I cried. And so, although it was dark, we ran up our Union Jack to the top of the mast… we were satisfied it was the right thing to do in honour of such an occasion… And when the party arrived… I can assure you we gave those cheers for our good King George as they had never been given in this place before.[41]

The Reverend studied the crew as they filed into the Church Hall.

> The commander is a big man, about 5ft 11ins in height, and looked extremely stout as he came into the hall. But I fancy that was due to padding, as he never opened his coat, and they had a good deal of clothing on. The crew, with one or two exceptions, were really decent chaps and looked clean and smart and well cared for. Many of them were extremely friendly.[42]

Any minor injuries received attention and a doctor attended the man who had broken a rib. The Reverend Edwards, however, thought Böcker 'surly' and a 'typical Prussian'; after some tea and food he complained about being kept with his men. They made up a bed for him behind a screen but he refused to use it as it was still in the same room.

The crew first moved to Colchester then on to London for interrogation before transfer to prisoner of war camps: Böcker and Schirlitz to Donington Hall, Leicestershire, and the men to Stobs at

Hawick, Scotland. And so ended the war for one of the most experienced Zeppelin crews. Flying first in L 5, then L 14 and finally L 33, they had bombed Lowestoft, East Dereham, Lympne, East Croydon, Derby, Hull, Sudbury, Braintree, Leith, Edinburgh and London, amongst other places. Their attacks resulted in the deaths of 87 people, and on this their final raid there was to be one more death attributable to their presence.

At Grove Farm on Copt Hall Lane, 500 yards from the wreck of L 33, Alfred John Wright set off on his motorcycle to alert the military at West Mersea. He did not get far, however, smashing into another vehicle driving with blacked out lights. Taken to hospital in Colchester, Wright had a leg amputated but never recovered, eventually dying in November. But there was new life too.

About a mile west of the crash site, at a cottage at Abbot's Hall, Great Wigborough, Emily Clark went into labour and gave birth to a daughter. When the doctor suggested they name her to mark the special night, Emily and her husband, George, agreed to one that would forever link her with this incredible story. Mr and Mrs Clark named their daughter Zeppelina.[43]

There were now two Zeppelin wrecks to attract the thousands of sightseers who made their way to the crash sites the following morning, but the specialist military and naval teams were on their way too. For the first time they had a virtually intact Zeppelin framework to pore over and the opportunity to sift through the wreckage of another searching for valuable documents and papers. Both L 32 and L 33 had much to reveal.

## Chapter 18

# 'A scene of woebegone desolation'

The loss of two of the very latest 'r-class' Zeppelins within a few minutes of each other was a serious blow for the Naval Airship Division. These new vessels were supposed to give Germany the upper hand in the air war over Britain, but the country's defences had progressed too and were a match for these latest Zeppelins. And British engineers now had direct access to the largely intact frame of L 33 just three weeks after its maiden flight, and her crew to interrogate.

Before that could get underway it was necessary to clear the other site where L 32 had come down. At first the bodies of the crew were removed to a small barn close by. One of those who appeared to have jumped to his death was the executive officer, Leutnant-zur-See Karl Brodrück, initially named as the Zeppelin commander.

Michael MacDonagh, a journalist working for *The Times*, took a train from London to Billericay to visit the wreck but saw the congested roads before reaching his destination.

> On leaving the railway station I avoided the town... and, taking to the fields, walked with thousands of others to the farm. Vendors of mineral waters, fruit and cake, who put up stalls in the fields, did a roaring trade, as we say, for refreshment was not to be had elsewhere and the weather was oppressively hot. In the distance I could see the huge aluminium framework of the wrecked airship gleaming brightly in the sunshine.[1]

The military cordon around the site prevented the public from getting too close, even so, what lay inside the cordon clearly impressed MacDonagh:

'The enormous length and spread of the airship astonished me. It is like the skeleton of a monstrous prehistoric reptile, the aluminium girders, corroded by fire, suggesting its bleached bones.'[2]

MacDonagh then received permission to view the bodies in the barn.

> They presented a ghastly spectacle... I could see that the crew had been dressed in heavy warm clothing – thick overcoats, mufflers and long felt boots...They are the first invaders of England I have seen, and they are – defeated and dead... But I confess my uppermost feeling in the barn was sympathy for these ill-fated young fellows... sent, and no doubt gladly accepting the service on an abominable mission and meeting what many will say is a just and ironically fitting end. As the frightfully disfigured bodies lay huddled together on the floor of the barn, smelling foully, I saw in them nothing of the majesty of death; only its gruesomeness and its terror in the most abominable shapes.[3]

There were no burned and broken bodies to inspect where L 33 had crashed at Little Wigborough, 22 miles away, instead the crew were alive and available for interrogation. Some were prepared to talk freely, although at least two of the men impressed the interrogators as they remained 'loyal to their officers, and showed a proper reticence in replying to questions'. Others did not.

> Certain members of the crew were clearly not enthusiastic about their work, owing to its trials and discomforts, and many seemed unaffectedly pleased at the thought that their participation in the war was over. One prisoner in particular... appeared convinced of the futility of Zeppelin raids and stated that the value of the airship, as a weapon, was greatly over-rated in Germany... Most of the members of the crew appear to be very conceited and advantage was taken of this fact to extract information from them. It is evident that they were regarded in Germany as heroes and encouraged in every way to consider themselves as persons of consequence.[4]

And while the interrogators drew much useful information from the crew of L 33, specialists from the Royal Corps of Naval Constructors pored over every inch of the wrecks, which in the case of L 33 lasted some months before the removal of the last remnants of the framework. When they studied the fuel tanks they found bullet holes, confirming that Brandon's attack had been more successful than he thought. He subsequently received the Distinguished Service Order (DSO) to go with the Military Cross awarded for his spirited attack on L 15 earlier in the year. Frederick Sowrey received the DSO too, for shooting down L 32. Like L 33, the burned wreckage of L 32 also had secrets to reveal – a charred but readable copy of Germany's latest codebook, the *Allgemeinefunkspruchbuch* (AFB). This had replaced the *Handelsverkehrsbuch* (HVB) in early 1916, but which had been in British hands since 1914. Military codebreakers remained well informed of German naval communications throughout the war.[5]

While the destruction of two of the latest Zeppelins, just three weeks after the shooting down of SL 11, caused celebration in Britain, the mood amongst airship crews in Germany was understandably sombre. L 31 and L 32 had both operated from the base at Ahlhorn and Mathy's men had witnessed L 32 fall in flames to her doom. Pitt Klein recalled: 'We were all haunted by the terrible spectre of fire; the dreadful sight of our colleagues and their ship going down in flames was etched deep into our minds.' The day before this latest raid Klein had sat in the canteen with members of L 32's crew discussing that very subject – fire.

> I could still picture some of their faces, and hear their voices. One man had said: 'Death will come so quickly that there won't be time to think or even act instinctively.'

> Another had observed: 'It's pretty obvious that because of the enormous fire we'd all instantly be rendered unconscious and wouldn't know anything more about it.'[6]

Mathy had become good friends with Peterson and was shocked by the loss of his comrade. In a letter to Peterson's wife he tried to console her, assuring her that her husband had not suffered.

> Your husband has found a beautiful quick death. In the instant his ship was hit he was already no more... High in the clear air Werner met his end, an end whose reality his consciousness could probably not comprehend, so suddenly did it happen.[7]

For Peter Strasser too, the loss of two of his latest Zeppelins and their highly experienced crews was a major setback. Unwilling to show any doubts or weakness, he ordered another raid for 25 September, just a day after the return from the most disastrous attack to date. The older Zeppelins were to focus on the Midlands and industrial North, while the two surviving 'thirties', L 30 and L 31, received orders to attack London, with Strasser urging von Buttlar and Mathy to show caution if the sky was clear of clouds.

Nine Zeppelins set out but two returned early, while L 23, commanded by Wilhelm Ganzel, hovered around the Norfolk coast without coming inland. That left four Zeppelins, L 14, L 16, L 21 and L 22 to carry out the more northerly raid.

Both L 14 and L 16 came inland at 10.05pm, about five miles apart, over Bridlington Bay on the Yorkshire coast. The commander of L 16, Erich Sommerfeldt, had little to show for his foray and appears to have dropped only five incendiary bombs. Heading west he passed south of Driffield and at about 10.30pm dropped his first bomb over Middlebridge Farm at Warter. Changing course, L 16 now headed north-west, dropping another bomb 20 minutes later in a hedge at Whitwell-on-the-Hill and a third at Ampleforth before Sommerfeldt turned back towards the coast.[8] At 11pm a further bomb burnt out in a field at Langtoft, about five miles north of Driffield. From there L 16's wanderings make little sense, moving back and forth within ten miles of Driffield for almost an hour, with a final bomb falling in a field at North Burton (now Burton Fleming) at 11.30pm. Approaching Bridlington on the coast, the crew of an anti-aircraft gun at Bessingby heard L 16's engines and at 11.40pm fired a single round towards the source of the sound. Sommerfeldt turned away from the gun, headed north and eventually crossed back over the coast at Speeton at 11.55pm.

## 25 September 1916, 10.45pm: York

Kuno Manger's L 14 ventured further inland than L 16 but also achieved little. Having crossed the coast, Manger followed a course towards York, approaching the city from the north-east. At 10.45pm, L 14 arrived over Heworth, just a mile from the city centre, where Manger began to release his bombs. The first smashed a few windows after exploding in a field behind Elmfield College on Malton Road.[9] Two or three others dropped harmlessly on a golf course and in fields as L 14 headed south, keeping to the east of the city, until seven bombs (two HE and five incendiaries) dropped at Fulford.[10] As the first of these fell, a searchlight at Acomb found L 14 and a 3-inch, 20cwt gun opened fire on the now illuminated target. The first shell burst too high but the second was close enough to convince Manger to head back the way he had come, with three more shells bursting before the searchlight lost contact. Free of the light, Manger dropped more bombs. One exploded on vacant land at the back of James Street in the Layerthorpe district, smashing windows in nearby homes.

In one of them a couple had heard the sound of explosions and gone downstairs. The wife, who had a history of heart problems, was tying the laces of her boots when the bomb exploded outside. She fell forward and died. Just beyond James Street, two incendiary bombs set fire to a timber stack at St Lawrence's brick and tile works, but eager helpers quickly dealt with the conflagration. The next fell close to Layerthorpe Station where the soft ground absorbed the violence of the blast. Returning to Heworth, Manger released three more bombs. The first exploded on open ground alongside Main Avenue, smashing the windows in all 21 houses there and in First and Second Avenues, which led to East Parade. The second of these bombs exploded with terrific force between East Parade and the western end of Holy Trinity Church, the blast ripping off the gable end of the home of Dr Lyth and his family and shattering windows at the church.

The final bomb exploded in a garden at the end of Chestnut Terrace, smashing windows in the row of small cottages. Manger now took L 14 away to the north. The gun at Acomb, allocated to the city's defences after the raid back in May, had proved its worth. Reaching Stillington at 11.15pm, L 14 commenced a wide anti-clockwise circle, dropping an incendiary bomb at Pilmoor, then a HE bomb in a field at Newby-with-Mulwith, south of Ripon. Moments later, at 11.49pm, four bombs exploded at Wormald Green, three on the army's rifle ranges and one at Monkton Mains Farm. The range commandant reported the limited damage to a workshop with due brevity: 'All glass broken, some of contents knocked about.'[11] Manger passed within a mile of blacked out Harrogate, attracted instead to flares burning at Dunkeswick where No.33 Squadron had an emergency landing ground. Four bombs cratered the airfield but caused no other problems.

A mile and half beyond Dunkeswick, L 14 approached Harewood where a VAD hospital at Harewood House cared for recuperating servicemen. A light must have been visible because Manger dropped 11 incendiary bombs in the grounds: 'When day broke most of these were pulled up out of the damp soil like ripe turnips and formed a most interesting exhibition in the coach-house of the Harewood Arms.'[12] In the village, close to the entrance to the estate, another incendiary bomb smashed through a cottage roof falling into a water cistern that flooded the bedroom below. A newspaper reporter was not impressed: 'Such damage can hardly be said to be worth even the cost of the bomb.' The last of this group struck an empty hen-house.

At this point the darkened city of Leeds lay just six miles ahead, but about four miles to the east a mobile searchlight at Collingham switched on and Manger changed course towards it. As he did so a mobile 13-pdr gun fired nine rounds; Manger replied by dropping three HE bombs. They missed both gun and light but one cut the telephone wire connecting the two. At 12.55am L 14 passed close to Stillington, completing the circle begun at 11.15pm, then on to the coast at Scarborough and back across the North Sea to Hage.

Earlier, at 9.45pm, Kurt Frankenburg's L 21 came inland near Mablethorpe on the Lincolnshire coast and embarked on a journey that saw her penetrate further into north-west England than any other Zeppelin before, although Frankenburg was not aware of this.

As he headed west his progress triggered the TARA order in Yorkshire where in cities like Sheffield steam hooters on the numerous steelworks, known as 'buzzers', alerted the population. At a house in the Highfield district, like many others throughout the city, a family nervously gathered together, as Maggie recounted in a letter to her aunt.

> About 10.45pm the alarm buzzers went and within half an hour the streets were empty... I think we all realised it was more serious than ever before as the soldiers, police and specials worked like Trojans... Suddenly we heard a droning sound overhead, which came stronger every minute... and Elsie clutched hold of Harry's arm and screamed out 'they are here' – she trembled like a leaf.[13]

But L 21 by-passed the city and those fearing the worst could breathe again – at least for an hour anyway.

Twenty minutes after the TARA order, two BE2c aircraft took off from the No.33 Squadron airfields at Coal Aston and Bramham Moor hoping to intercept the raider, but the foggy skies around Sheffield made that impossible and one pilot smashed his aircraft on landing but walked away unhurt.

## 26 September 1916, 12.05am: Rossendale Valley, Lancashire

About 11.15pm, L 21 had skirted to the north of Sheffield, heading west and passing over the sparsely populated Peak District to reach the Lancashire town of Bacup at midnight where Frankenburg prepared to commence bombing as he neared the Rossendale Valley. Two miles from Bacup, Frankenburg dropped an incendiary that landed on Hill Top Farm to the east of Lumb. Heading south-west, L 21 released two bombs over Newchurch but neither detonated: one landed in the grounds of Height Side House[14] and the second near Lea Bank House. Just under a mile further on a bomb exploded close to Hall Carr Road where it gouged a large crater but there were no casualties. Crossing the River Irwell, L 21 turned from its westerly course to the south, heading towards Ewood Bridge, dropping a HE bomb in a field on the north side of Green's Lane and an incendiary on a golf course to the south of the road. A large sewage works occupied the area between Ewood Bridge and Irwell Vale and Frankenburg released perhaps as many as nine bombs over it. Three fell amongst the filter beds and another damaged the railway track running alongside the sewage works, exploding just before the track crossed a viaduct over the River Irwell. Across the river another detonated in a field close to a row of cottages on Hardsough Road, blasting a field wall and smashing cottage windows and doors. Unperturbed, one of the residents stoically told a reporter: 'That can soon be mended and at least we are still alive.'

From Irwell Vale, L 21 headed south towards Ramsbottom where three bombs exploded on the outskirts of the mill town: two expended their energy in fields and one exploded on the driveway of a large house off Dundee Lane. Then L 21 veered towards the neighbouring village of Holcombe. 'Five or six shells exploded almost at once,' villagers explained, 'It was just like thunder. And then you could hear the windows smashing everywhere. The concussion did the damage.'[15]

Passing over the church in Holcombe, three bombs fell in fields around the village school. The first exploded adjacent to its eastern end and shattered the field wall, 'scattering the big stones… like chaff', pitting the gable end of the school and smashing all the windows. The shock wave stopped the clock in the church tower about 75 yards away. To the rear of the school another destroyed a chicken run, scattering the carcasses of the occupants up the hillside, and one landing on the west side of the school knocked down a wall on Moor Road and smashed the windows and roof tiles of cottages lining Holcombe Road. The last bomb

269

exploded in the road between the village post office and The Shoulder of Mutton, an inn and farm. Mr and Mrs Hoyle, who ran the post office, had quite a shock as shattered furniture flew around their house like matchwood, leaving Mrs Hoyle as the only casualty in the village with a cut to the back of her head. Across the road a barn and an empty cow shed suffered badly, while the inn lost its windows and the main door.

Now over the southern outskirts of Ramsbottom, L 21 dropped two bombs in fields between Holcombe and Bolton Road West before a third struck cottages in Regent Street housing a mineral water works. It caused considerable damage there, wrecked the company's two delivery lorries and left one particular lasting memory for those who lived nearby.

> The most phenomenal feature was a joist from the damaged works, which had been hurled high into the air completely over the premises, and which descended like an arrow from its bow to impale itself in an adjoining field.[16]

Following Bolton Road West for about 700 yards, Frankenburg dropped an incendiary in a field at Lumb Carr Farm as L 21 approached the village at Holcombe Brook. There another incendiary smashed through the roof of a house at Pot Green on Summerseat Lane, sparking sudden terror inside. The father told a newspaper: '...there were flames bursting from the room in which our two little girls were sleeping... It was just a mad dash into the room... confused perception that the children were unhurt... then I was outside, feeling scorched and stifled, with one child in each arm.'[17]

From his command gondola Kurt Frankenburg could now see what appeared to be a most tempting target. Just five miles away the town of Bolton, with its numerous mills and industrial complexes, was in full production. Frankenburg believed mistakenly that it was Derby, actually some 60 miles away.[18] No Zeppelin had previously threatened this area, so air raid defences were not a priority. The area had received a warning but closing down steel production, munitions manufacture and mill output was not a quick process. Leaving Holcombe Brook behind, Frankenburg passed over Old Bates' Farm near Tottington. There a 70-year-old woman, Elizabeth Cranshaw, died of shock when she saw the Zeppelin.

## 26 September 1916, 12.20am: Bolton, Lancashire

At 12.19am an observer reported L 21 approaching the north of Bolton.[19] Frankenburg commenced his attack a minute or two later, just west of

Astley Bridge. Quickly realising he faced no opposition, he flew two loops over the town, dropping 22 bombs.[20]

The first, an incendiary, crashed into a field at Sharples Park close to Eden's Orphanage where all the children were evacuated to a safe distance and the fire extinguished. It was only with the detonation of the first HE bomb that the residents of Bolton realised they were under attack. That exploded in Hobart Street smashing numerous windows while an incendiary in Darley Street just missed the Brownlow Fold cotton mill. Mortfield Lane snaked around a series of reservoirs supplying the Mortfield Bleach Works, while amongst the reservoirs stood Lodge Vale, a row of workmen's cottages. The next bomb exploded on the end cottage. Much to their amazement rescuers found all three occupants alive. Two incendiary bombs that dropped in Waldeck Street and another in Chorley Old Road, just yards from the Halliwell Cotton Works, caused no harm and a worker from the mill dashed out with a bucket of water to extinguish the flames. Passing over Queen's Park, L 21 began the first of its loops. Frankenburg released two more incendiary bombs as he approached the Bullfield district. If his target was the gas works and the concentration of railway tracks at Bullfield Sidings he was to be disappointed. Both overshot, one landing in Bolton Corporation's Wellington Yard, between the railway and Wellington Street, where a fire started at a stable, and the second set fire to a house on Wellington Street where a woman and her two children were asleep. Firemen were quickly on the scene and all three escaped without injury.

Frankenburg then released a group of five bombs. They missed the railway complex around Crook Street Goods Station by about a hundred yards. Instead they caused devastation amongst the terraced houses on Kirk Street, with an incendiary bomb also killing a horse in stables in neighbouring Back John Street.

> Four bombs, all explosive… had confined their actual violence to six or eight homes, the terrific impact and vibration had a remarkable impact on two streets, probably some two hundred cottages in all.[21]

Six of the modest homes in Kirk Street ceased to exist, while all around others suffered greatly as did those in John Street and James Street. In Kirk Street the bombs claimed 13 lives. The Irwin family resided at No.58. Joseph Irwin and his wife Bridget had moved to Bolton from Ireland to seek a better life. Four children shared a bed while the youngest, two-year-old Margaret Ellen, slept with her parents. When the house collapsed, the older children managed to escape and Joseph pulled himself free too, but Bridget, clutching their youngest daughter, remained pinned under the bed as more rubble crashed down. When a rescue attempt finally reached them, Bridget was dead and Margaret Ellen died shortly afterwards.

Next door at No.60, ironworker Michael O'Hara and his wife, Martha, died in the wreckage of their home, as did their neighbours at No.62, William and Ann McDermott, along with their five-year-old daughter, Mary Ellen. Their two other children survived after a rescue that took six hours. Four people died at No.64: James and Ellen Allison and their lodgers, David Davies, a 39-year-old coal heaver, and Frederick Guildford, a packing case maker. The final two victims in Kirk Street lived at No.66. Ellen Gregory, a 17-year-old weaver died in the ruins while her mother, Elizabeth, was pulled out alive only to die in a neighbour's house soon after. Elizabeth's husband, Robert, and their 10-month-old son were trapped for hours under the rubble but both survived. A newspaper reporter who visited Kirk Street in the hours after the raid summed up the devastation.

> What was yesterday the centre of a worker's colony, rows and rows of cottages is today a scene of woebegone desolation. One walks the whole length of the street without seeing an unbroken window and at the southern end is a vista of wanton havoc.[22]

Leaving this havoc behind, L 21 began circling anti-clockwise to complete its first loop, dropping an incendiary that struck a fruit warehouse at the corner of Ashburner Street and Old Hall Street.[23] From there L 21 returned to Queen's Park, where a HE bomb buried itself in a flowerbed after failing to detonate.

The second loop over Bolton was on a wider radius than the first. From Queen's Park L 21 passed over more mills before releasing two bombs as it approached Deane Road. An incendiary fell on a rope works off Washington Street just seconds before a bomb exploded at the Co-operative Laundry located between Washington Street and Deane Road, damaging the water storage cistern and boiler house as well as smashing windows and the roof. Turning now, L 21 released two more bombs as it approached the large Moor Cotton Mills on Parrot Street. One exploded with great force in Back Apple Street, just a hundred feet from the Mill, obliterating outside toilets, damaging the backs of a number of houses, smashing down walls and shattering windows, including those at the Mill. An incendiary bomb broke through the Mill's roof into a storeroom where a fire started amongst a stockpile of yarn and caused much damage, but the building's sprinkler system prevented the flames spreading further.

L 21's next bomb smashed through the roof of Holy Trinity Church, located between two important ironworks and Trinity Street Station. It broke apart on hitting the ground without exploding, the damage was restricted to the roof, an upper gallery and a number of pews reduced to splinters. L 21 now headed north, following a line about 150 yards east of the Town Hall, where an incendiary that hit Messrs Houghton solicitor's office in Mawdsley Street received quick attention as the final bomb fell in Mealhouse Lane where it caused no damage. Frankenburg left Bolton on a northerly course, observed about seven miles south-east of Blackburn, at 12.52am. From there L 21 passed Burnley and south of Skipton in Yorkshire at 1.30am. Five minutes later L 21 dropped a bomb in a field at the village of Bolton Abbey but it failed to explode and it was another four days before a farmer discovered it. Frankenburg exited the coast at Whitby at 3.05am.

Many of the children living in Kirk Street attended the Derby Street School. On the day after the raid 60 were absent, yet many others did appear as normal. The keeper of the school's logbook wrote admiringly: '... the calmness and absence of abnormality on the part of the poor children whose homes had been destroyed was a wonderful witness to their ability to undergo emergencies.'[24] Then, like in every other part of the country raided by Zeppelins, the visitors arrived, as the logbook continues.

> On the two following days the town was visited by thousands – yes, tens of thousands of people from places as far as Liverpool to view the damage and from early morning till late at night the streets near this school were crowded with curious sightseers.

There is also evidence in the logbook of the support given to those who suffered in the raid.

> The Mayor opened a fund on behalf of the poor stricken victims, numbers of families were housed and fed in the Flash St Special School and the benevolence of the town was showered upon the unfortunate sufferers in no stinted manner.

## 26 September 1916, 12.15am: Sheffield, Yorkshire

Zeppelin L 22 came inland at about 10.30pm, 45 minutes behind L 21 on the same stretch of coast. Her commander, Martin Dietrich, had a clear objective in mind – Sheffield. He dropped incendiary bombs at Maltby-le-Marsh and south of Market Rasen, both probably to get an estimate of ground speed because Dietrich was confused by the effects of a south-east tail wind. When he reached Yorkshire he believed he was still over Lincolnshire. Attracted by lights, which he thought indicated Lincoln, and with heavy cloud cover building, Dietrich decided to attack the city, abandoning hopes of reaching Sheffield. But the tail wind had actually carried him to the eastern edge of Sheffield and at 12.15am the seven incendiary bombs he dropped fell at the Tinsley Park Colliery although without causing any damage of note.[25]

While Dietrich flew around the outskirts of the city in a clockwise direction, many of the population were still awake after the earlier scare when L 21 passed by. From Hillsborough, north of the centre of the city, Dietrich was drawn towards the north-eastern districts, the seat of Sheffield's steel and iron industries. This area also contained a great concentration of railways, goods yards and sidings from where, like at Nottingham two days earlier, the lights were shining brightly. The first two bombs, both incendiaries, landed near the entrance to Burngreave Cemetery where they scorched a patch of grass and a notice board.[26] More bombs quickly followed. One that exploded in a recreation ground off Danville Street, shattered windows nearby and a bomb fragment flying through one killed 49-year-old Frederick Stratford in his bed. A woman and child also received injuries. In Earldom Road[27] another exploded in a yard, 'driving holes through walls of buildings', and injuring a man. The next shattered Nos.110 and 112 Grimesthorpe Road. Screams emanating from the shattered ruins of No.112 pierced the air, but before any rescue attempt was possible the remainder of the building collapsed and the screaming stopped. Search parties later recovered the bodies of Ann Coogan, aged 76, and her daughter, Margaret Taylor (59).

Having been flying east over the city, Dietrich now turned south, commencing a series of zig-zags as L 22 reached All Saints Church, dropping another bomb as he did so. It detonated behind houses at the corner of Lyons Street and Petre Street. Woken by the sound of exploding bombs Thomas Wilson, who lived at 73 Petre Street, had gone to the window. As he looked out the bomb exploded, sending razor sharp fragments flying in all directions. One struck him on the chin, killing

274

the 59-year-old engineer's fitter instantly. About 200 yards away another bomb exploded close to the corner of Writtle Street and Sutherland Road.

A woman who was lodging in Writtle Street woke to the sound of the first HE bomb and, throwing on some clothes, hurried down to the cellar where she found her landlady moments before a bomb exploded outside. As the Zeppelin moved away the terrified pair went upstairs to find that 'the furniture was all topsy-turvy, whilst large portions of shrapnel were embedded in the doors, the walls, and the furniture'. Then they heard screams for help.[28] At 45 Writtle Street, George Ineson and his wife both suffered serious injury. Fragments of the bomb struck George's head, fracturing his skull and lacerating his brain. He clung to life for five days before dying on 1 October.[29] Next door, at 43 Writtle Street, William and Elizabeth Bellamy had woken with a start. They shared their house with their daughter, her husband and the couple's 11-month-old child. Elizabeth rushed to get her granddaughter but as she passed a window the bomb exploded and 'shattered the end of the house'. Fragments of the bomb slashed into the room where Elizabeth was and ripped open her back. Her injuries were horrific and she died in hospital three hours later.

Dietrich and L 22 were now just 300 yards from the heart of Sheffield's industrial centre, where great steel and iron works produced the material of war on a mammoth scale. Before he reached them, however, Dietrich dropped two bombs with disastrous results for those living in Cossey Road. The Harrison family lived at No.26: George and Eliza, their 12-year-old daughter Vera, along with a married daughter, Nellie Rhodes, and her children Phyllis (six) and Elsie (four). On hearing the warning 'buzzers' earlier, their neighbours at No.24, William and Sarah Southerington, came to join them and while the women and children took shelter in the cellar, George Harrison and William Southerington remained upstairs talking and smoking. At No.28, the Harrison's other neighbours, Albert and Alice Newton, were asleep in bed. The bomb hit the roof of No.26, crashed down through the house and exploded within the confines of the cellar where it 'blew everything to smithereens'. All eight people died. When they found George Harrison he still clutched his pipe and matches.[30] The explosion also ripped through the Newton's home. Searchers found Albert's body in the back yard while that of Alice, blasted out of the front of the house, lay on the opposite side of the road. That night their six-year-old son, Albert Edward, was staying with his grandparents.

The second bomb exploded 'like a crack of doom' on 10 Cossey Road, home to the Hames family. Levi, his wife Beatrice and their 14-month-old son, Horace, all died in the same bed. Extensive damage to property extended into Babur Road and in Forncett Street an incendiary bomb set fire to a house. L 22 now missed a great opportunity as Dietrich released just a single incendiary bomb as he passed over the vast Atlas Steel & Iron Works. It smashed through the roof of a machine shop but only started a small fire. His next bomb overshot the Norfolk Steel & Iron Works by a hundred yards.[31]

Dietrich now made another turn on his zig-zag course and 450 yards on released two more bombs. One fell directly on the Princess Street Primitive Methodist Chapel, completely shattering the building and leaving just fragments of the outer walls standing. On one of those walls, a line from the New Testament remained legible for those who came to see the wreckage: 'A new commandment I give unto you, that ye love one another.' The second bomb of this pair obliterated a house at 136 Corby Street, home to seven members of the Tyler family. Joseph and Selina Tyler, along with their children, Ernest (11), Albert (eight), Amelia (five) and John (two) all died in the shattered ruins of their home. Their eldest child, 14-year-old Joseph, was extricated from the wreckage after many hours of painstaking and careful work but, suffering extensive injuries, he died later in hospital. Next door, at 134 Corby Street, 11-year-old Richard Brewington had exclaimed 'The Zepps are here!' moments before the bomb fell. The house collapsed and although his mother and a lodger escaped, Richard died under the rubble.

On the opposite side of the road, at No.143, there was further tragedy. As the sound of exploding bombs drew closer, William Shakespeare gathered his children from the attic and shouted to his wife Martha to follow them down to the cellar. Just as William reached the refuge the bomb exploded in Corby Street and he heard his wife cry out in shock: 'Oh Bill, my leg's off.' Martha Shakespeare died in hospital three hours later.[32] The explosion demolished four houses and damaged 40 more, many of which were considered no longer fit for habitation.

A viaduct carried the Midland Railway alongside Corby Street and L 22 moved parallel to it until the tracks crossed over Sutherland Street where Dietrich engaged in another turn, dropping a bomb as he did so. It destroyed two houses abutting the viaduct but had no impact on the structure itself. Now following Attercliffe Road, L 22 crossed the River Don near the Washford Bridge and dropped two bombs, a HE and an incendiary. Both fell in a yard surrounded by closely packed workmen's homes and, although there was much damage there and in Trent Street, only three children sustained any injuries when fallen rafters and plaster trapped them in their bed.[33]

Dietrich now executed his next turn and, crossing back over Attercliffe Road, dropped a bomb that damaged a public house, The Baltic Arms, at 420 Effingham Road. L 22 passed over the Baltic Steel Works, but an incendiary overshot by a hundred yards, causing only minor damage at the Park House Works on Bacon Lane. At the same time a four-man team from Sheffield Corporation was working in Woodbourn Hill. They heard bombs exploding and one of them, William Guest, realised a light was showing in the street. As he approached the building to tell the occupiers to extinguish it a bomb exploded. The explosion damaged 12 buildings and killed Guest, his body found just three yards from the bomb crater. Those in the house where the light was showing had left it on by mistake when they took shelter in their basement. An incendiary bomb then fell on the sidings of the Great Central Railway close to Woodbourn Bridge, setting fire to a storage facility and burning a number of railway sleepers.

Although Sheffield had at least three anti-aircraft guns none of them had opened fire because the atmospheric conditions prevented them locating the target.[34] A gun at Shiregreen, north of the city, however, did fire two rounds at the sound of the Zeppelin's engines and this may have been the reason why L 22 stopped zig-zagging and headed south. Appearing to follow the line of Manor Lane, Dietrich dropped at least seven bombs, some near the settlements at Manor Oaks and The Manor, but the countryside here was open and no damage occurred. At The Manor, Dietrich changed direction to the north-east and commenced his journey back to the coast, dropping an incendiary bomb at Darnell and setting fire to the home of a retired policeman in Britannia Road.[35] He was away at the time but neighbours responded quickly to extinguish the flames. The raid on Sheffield was over.

On his flight back to the coast, Martin Dietrich finally recognised the strength of the south-easterly wind and realised he had probably travelled further west than he had first supposed. He came to the correct conclusion that he had bombed Sheffield and not Lincoln. L 22 briefly came under fire from guns of the Humber garrison before passing out to sea east of Hull at about 2.05am. Back in Sheffield, Dietrich's raid had claimed the lives of 29 and injured another 10, five of them seriously.

After the raid the civic authorities in Sheffield raised their concerns about lighting on the railways, as had happened in Nottingham, and a deputation from 25 towns and cities from the Midlands and Eastern counties went to London to discuss this with the War Office. It, however, refused to sanction the stopping of railway traffic prior to raids. The transportation of munitions and the commerce of the country, the War Office insisted, would face tremendous dislocation, causing the cessation of railway traffic over great swathes of Britain and result in the paralysis of the business of the country. The War Office further pointed out that this was exactly what Germany wanted.[36]

There were no more attacks in the North and Midlands that night, but in the far south, Heinrich Mathy had opened up a new area to bombing – Portsmouth, with its important harbour and naval dockyard. But his raid did not go well.

Chapter 19

# 'I have a really bad feeling about this'

While the older Zeppelins, L 21 and L 22, had carried out attacks on Sheffield and Bolton, far to the south the new Zeppelins, L 30 and L 31, had orders to attack London, but to show caution. Having travelled over Belgium, clear starry skies over the English Channel caused them to abandon the capital. Heinrich Mathy, however, had a novel Plan B, he set out along the south coast to strike at the Portsmouth naval base, an ambitious and dangerous idea, something no Zeppelin commander had attempted before.

### 25 September 1916, 11.50pm: Portsmouth Harbour, Hampshire

Observers at Dungeness picked up engine sounds out to sea at 9.35pm, as L 31 passed down the English Channel. At 11.30pm Mathy reached Sandown on the Isle of Wight, remaining there for 15 minutes before crossing the Solent to the mouth of Portsmouth Harbour at 11.50pm. Two RNAS aircraft took off from Calshot in response, a White and Thompson No.3 flying boat and a Short 827 floatplane, but neither was up to the task. Although searchlights picked up L 31 immediately, estimates of her height varied from 12,000 to 15,000 feet. Consequently, when the eleven guns defending the harbour exploded into action, firing 138 shells, observers felt they were all bursting short of the target. L 31 made a sudden climb at full power. As the nose of the airship reared up, Pitt Klein thought she 'creaked and groaned all over like some living being'.[1]

Those reporting on the raid all seemed to agree that L 31 dropped no bombs.

The guns continued firing for some ten or fifteen minutes. Flashes were seen in the sky, and the first shell from the anti-aircraft guns appeared to explode in close proximity to the airship, which immediately altered its course and got out of range… It is not known whether any bombs were dropped, but so far as is known no damage was done.[2]

This is an interesting aspect of the raid. The official report states: 'Strange to relate, not a single bomb was thrown on or in the vicinity of Portsmouth by this airship as far as can be traced.'[3] This differs significantly from the account of Pitt Klein who reported bombs dropping 'in rapid succession'.[4]

There is, however, evidence that L 31 did release bombs. On 28 September, Major R.N. Andrews, produced a report collating signals sent during the raid to C-in-C Portsmouth, Admiral the Honourable Stanley C.J. Colville. The conflicting reports from the torpedo school ship HMS *Vernon* and the destroyers, HMS *Angler*, HMS *Conflict* and HMS *Hind*, Fort Blockhouse, the Royal Naval Barracks and shore establishments on Whale Island, resulted in Major Andrews concluding 'approximately 10 bombs dropped'. There were also descriptions by three witnesses. Petty Officer William Shales, Coxswain of No.2 Medical Guard Boat, was one who gave a statement.

> Came out of Pier Head Mess and saw two bombs in quick succession drop in water and throw up large columns of dirty water about 100 yards high with big flash in the explosions. The second was nearest and was not more than 150 yards from the Magazine at Pier Head off the West Shore.

For some unknown reason Andrews' report was shelved for two months, by which time the official report stating that no bombs had been dropped was already in circulation.[5]

Having crossed the harbour, Mathy reached land at Portchester. In his engine gondola Pitt Klein breathed a sigh of relief to be clear of the guns, considering the experience 'worse than London'.[6] From Portchester L 31 passed over Sussex, crossing the coast at Bexhill at 1.45am. Now over the sea, Mathy was off Dover at 2.25am where he dropped three bombs at shipping before heading back towards Belgium, losing a propeller on the way.

While Mathy and L 31 had been over Portsmouth, the movements of Horst von Buttlar and L 30 are again uncertain. Von Buttlar filed another imaginative report, claiming attacks on the Kent coastal towns of Margate and Ramsgate, yet neither was bombed. British reports placed him off the coast of Norfolk but there are other reports suggesting he may have trailed Mathy down the English Channel before turning back.

The raid of 25/26 September was over. It had demonstrated that the naval Zeppelins were not cowed by their recent losses, but it had failed to achieve anything of note, despite bombing two towns producing material for Britain's war effort, other than killing 43 people, injuring perhaps 31 more and destroying the homes of a few working families.

Later on 26 September, the day the raiders returned to northern Germany, Heinrich Mathy wrote to his wife Hertha and their baby daughter, Gisela. The losses of L 32 and L 33 had taken their toll on him and the impact of the gunfire over Portsmouth was fresh in his mind.

> Peterson is dead, Böcker captured. Hertha, the war is a serious business, we two have always kept this in mind and in our happiness we have praised the good fortune of Gisela's father. It is also my fervent wish that you both may be spared this most difficult sacrifice for the Fatherland and that I may stay with you and surround you with love. And when you put our little daughter to sleep in these days, a good angel will see it and read it in your heart, and he will hurry and guide my ship past the dangers that are in the air.[7]

This solemn mood extended to the crews too, as Pitt Klein remembered.

> Even in the Mess our old banter had gone. All talk was of heavy losses, especially the latest ones. Everyone's nerves were on edge, and even the most keen and impassioned crew members could not shake off the dark and sombre mood. It was only a matter of time before our turn would come... Our nerves were wasted. If anyone claimed that they weren't haunted by the spectre of an airship falling in flames, they were a downright liar.[8]

On 27 September the Naval Airship Division received a boost when the latest 'r-class' Zeppelin joined the fleet. Command of L 34 went to Kapitänleutnant der Reserve Max Dietrich, former commander of L 7, L 18 and L 21. Just four days later L 34 rose from Nordholz joining the rest of the Zeppelin fleet on the next raid, scheduled just before the cycle of the moon made raiding inadvisable again.

The raid that set out on 1 October coincided with a change in L 31's crew. They had first come together in January 1915 but now the executive officer Oberleutnant-zur-See Kurt Friemel was about to get his own command – L 24 – so a new officer joined on the day of the raid, Leutnant-zur-See Jochen Werner. Friemel remained behind at Ahlhorn as did Pitt Klein – he was due leave.

> This was the first time I had been left off a mission; I wasn't sure whether to be pleased or angry about it. The feeling of not taking part in a mission in my own airship, which was such an important part of my life, was so unusual, so strange, and so depressing that it preyed on my mind.[9]

As Klein said his farewells there was a fatalistic mood amongst the crew. Karl Dornbusch, Klein's replacement grabbed his hand: 'Pitt, I have a really bad feeling about this; I'm not sure what it is; I'm really anxious.' Others had similar worries. The last man Klein shook hands with was Siegfried Körber. 'Goodbye Pitt,' he whispered, 'Something's going to happen today – just wait and see; we're not going to come back from this one. I can feel it.'[10]

Strasser ordered 11 Zeppelins out: L 31 had orders for London if cloud cover permitted while the older ships and L 34 headed for the industrial Midlands. Four did not reach England – L 13, L 22, L 23 and, inevitably, von Buttlar's L 30. He reached the Yorkshire coast before turning around and heading slowly back to Germany where he reported bombing 'extensive installations on the south side of the Humber', an area that was untouched during the raid.[11]

## 1 October 1916, 11.55pm: Potter's Bar, Hertfordshire

Despite his personal concerns, Heinrich Mathy did not hesitate to follow orders and, with cloud cover evident, he set out to attack London. L 31 crossed the Suffolk coast near Lowestoft at 8pm and heading south-west steered towards Essex. At Kelvedon Hatch, at 9.45pm, a searchlight found L 31 and Mathy changed direction, first north and then north-west, working around to the north of London.

That night it appears No.39 Squadron were not anticipating a raid because Second Lieutenant Wulstan J. Tempest of 'B' flight received permission to fly over from Sutton's Farm to North Weald from where he went to meet friends at Epping.[12] The squadron received the patrol order when Mathy reached Kelvedon Hatch. First off at 9.50pm was James Mackay from North Weald, followed six minutes later by Lieutenant Lionel Payne from Hainault Farm. Meanwhile a phone message reached Tempest whereupon he leapt upon a motorcycle 'and drove like a lunatic to his aerodrome'.[13] A breathless Tempest took off from North Weald at 10pm. By the time all three pilots had made the slow climb up to patrol height there was no sign of L 31.

From Kelvedon Hatch, Mathy reached Buntingford in Hertfordshire at 10.30pm, Stevenage 25 minutes later then Hertford at 11.10pm. There observers reported that L 31 shut down her engines, drifting with the wind towards Ware, before resuming under power again at 11.30pm, and heading south towards Waltham Abbey with London beyond. Reports of L 31's progress resulted in No.39 Squadron sending up a fourth aircraft at 11.25pm, Second Lieutenant Philip McGuiness taking off from North Weald. None of the pilots saw anything until the searchlights of the Waltham Abbey Sub-Command came into play. At 11.37pm the light at Newmans, a farm about two and a half miles north-east of Waltham Abbey, located L 31, after which the lights never lost their grip on her. A minute later the two 3-inch, 20 cwt guns at Newmans opened fire, soon joined by the gun at Temple House. All four pilots now saw anti-aircraft shells exploding in the sky and then the unmistakeable sign, searchlight beams drawing together on a single spot, and pinned at their apex the elusive Zeppelin.

With shells now exploding close to L 31, Mathy dropped his entire load of 57 bombs (30 HE and 27 incendiary) in three salvoes as he zig-zagged over the Hertfordshire town of Cheshunt. The first 11 fell behind houses on Turner's Hill causing serious damage to four properties as well as other damage to 58 more. The shock wave rolled over fields inflicting additional damage in Blindman's Lane, Prospect Road, High Street, Church Lane and Windmill Lane. After a sharp turn to starboard L 31 dropped 27 bombs around College Road, near to the junction with Aldbury Walk, smashing windows, doors and ceilings in Lordship Lane and College Road. A sharp turn to port brought L 31 over the vast Walnut Tree Nursery, one of many horticultural establishments in the area. The sound of shattering glass filled the air as six bombs destroyed 40 greenhouses extending for six acres. More windows were shattered in Aldbury Ride and Crossbrook Street. The last 11 bombs fell in a line across Cheshunt recreation ground destroying the sports pavilion and inflicting injuries on a pony from which it did not survive. The local police reported that a 16-year-old girl, Catherine Bouette, received cuts to her hand, the only casualty of the attack. Lightened by the release of the bombs, L 31 gained height but continued to weave as Mathy now headed west, hoping to escape the guns and the lights. But any respite would be brief – the pilots of No.39 Squadron were closing in. Leading the chase was Wulstan Tempest.

Wulstan Joseph Tempest was working in Canada when war broke out. He returned home and in November 1914 received a commission as a second lieutenant in the 6th (Service) Battalion, King's Own Yorkshire Light Infantry. Following a wound in May 1915 at the Second Battle of Ypres he recuperated in England before a posting to garrison duty in Newcastle. But Tempest had seen and admired the men of the Royal Flying Corps while serving on the Western Front and applied for a transfer. After gaining his pilot's licence and further training he transferred to the RFC General List on 17 June 1916 before joining No.39 Squadron. This was his first encounter with a Zeppelin.

Homing in on the illuminated airship, Tempest pushed his engine to the maximum. By the time he had closed to five miles, he became aware of the anti-aircraft guns: 'Above the roar of my own plane I could hear their boom, see the gleam of bursting shells.'[14] L 31 was over Cheshunt when Tempest closed in.

> I must have been seen, for she suddenly turned about and began to climb. On I flew in pursuit and, finding she could not shake me off, she suddenly shed all her bombs, which helped her to climb even quicker.

At that moment Tempest's petrol pressure pump failed: 'If I was to maintain height, I would have to keep the supply going. There was nothing for it but to use the hand pump.' At that moment he was flying slightly higher than L 31, estimating her at 12,700 feet and, reluctant to let her climb out of reach, furiously hand-pumping fuel he made his move.

> I made a dive straight at her and, passing under her enormous envelope, which seemed to overshadow me, I put in a burst of fire from my Lewis gun… Turning about, I flew under her in the same direction she was going and let her have a further burst.

Tempest thought his bullets might have pierced a fuel tank during the attack and he may be right.[15] Major Charles Lloyd, R.G.A., commanding the Waltham Abbey guns, saw 'Two thin pencils of white flame' falling from the forward part of the Zeppelin. 'They had the appearance,' he concluded, 'of two streams of petrol flowing from the ship and blazing up as they fell.'[16]

Those manning the machine guns on L 31 were also in action 'blazing at him hammer and tongs', but Tempest appeared out of the darkness too quickly for them to hope for accuracy.[17] Coming around behind her, Tempest sat under her tail, beyond the reach of the machine guns and fired again.

> I had almost begun to despair of bringing her down, when suddenly, after letting her have another burst, I saw her begin to go red inside like an immense Chinese lantern. And then I knew it was all up!... Flames burst from her glowing envelope and licked her bows. Brighter they grew, ruby, orange, yellow, paler. And then she seemed to be coming straight for me. I did a frantic nosedive with the wreckage tearing down on me. Only by putting my machine into a spin did I manage to corkscrew out of the way as the blazing mass roared past me... There was a smell of burning everywhere in the sky.[18]

For those watching from below the destruction of Zeppelin L 31 was a 'magnificent yet awful spectacle' that would last in their memories forever, but 'an eternity of torture' for the crew.

> There, in the western sky, an oval of bright flame, hung the doomed airship casting forth a flush of pure light which illuminated fields and hedgerows and houses for many miles around... And as she dipped so her back broke, with the result that she fell in two pieces, side by side, slowly, and burning with immense fierceness, for all the world like a fiery comet falling to earth, with threads of fire trailing behind and around her.[19]

Immediately after the flames engulfed L 31, Tempest confessed to his father that 'he went mad', shouting, yelling and swooping down. Having regained his composure he watched the fall of L 31: 'Far below that white-bright mass was receding, till a cloud of sparks told me it had hit the ground.'

For the crew of L 31, Tempest's attack meant their journey had run its course. When the time came to make that final, fateful decision – to jump or burn – Heinrich Mathy threw himself from the doorway of the command gondola and fell to his death. His body, and the wreckage of his airship, smashed into the earth at Oakmere Park, Potter's Bar, just two and a half miles from Cuffley, where SL 11 had crashed a month earlier.

While L 31 met its date with destiny, six other Zeppelins were already over Britain or on their way. Their impact was minimal, with heavy clouds and mist hampering navigation. Two of the older Zeppelins came inland over the Lincolnshire coast, L 16 just after midnight and L 14 about 40 minutes later. Erich Sommerfeldt in L 16 circled over south-east Lincolnshire dropping 16 bombs over ten villages. They killed a cow and injured two horses on Mr Clarey's farm at Hameringham. L 16 crossed back over the coast near Wainfleet at 2am.[20] The raid achieved nothing of value to Germany, yet it was matched in futility by the progress of L 14.

Kuno Manger brought L 14 inland over south-east Lincolnshire and remained near Boston for almost an hour, before penetrating about 25 miles inland. The first of his 38 bombs dropped at 2.40am. They killed a horse and two sheep at Blankney, smashed a window at Woodhall Spa, killed another horse and three sheep at Stixwould, finally breaking a window and killing a rabbit at Hemingby, yet most had no effect at all. At 3.10am a final bomb fell in Burwell Wood, about four miles south-east of Louth, before L 14 crossed over the coast at Mablethorpe and returned to Germany.[21]

While L 16 and L 14 had been wandering over Lincolnshire, Hermann Kraushaar brought L 17 inland over Weybourne on the north Norfolk coast. At 1.35am he dropped a parachute flare, which illuminated the coast from Sheringham to Cromer, then meandered around north-eastern Norfolk for almost an hour and a half before dropping two bombs at Marlingford, six miles west of Norwich, followed by one at Easton, but they caused no damage. At 3.35am L 17 went back out to sea at Caister.[22]

The experience that night, however, was a little different for the remaining three Zeppelins who, between 9.20 and 10.15pm, all came inland over an eight-mile stretch of the north Norfolk coast. The first of these, Kurt Frankenburg's L 21, crossed at Weybourne from where he headed west until reaching The Wash at Heacham where he dropped two incendiary bombs. Following the shore of The Wash, L 21 reached

Kirton, south of Boston from where he commenced an erratic path to the south-west as though London was his target. He dropped an incendiary over Kirkby Underwood at 11.20pm but 35 minutes later, when L 21 had reached the Rutland village of Manton, the crew saw a distant fireball illuminate the sky. Although it was 68 miles away, Frankenburg, who had witnessed the destruction of SL 11, knew it was a burning Zeppelin. He abandoned his plans and turned back, eventually flying the length of Lincolnshire but dropping only one more bomb, at South Kyme at 12.30am where it killed a sheep. L 21 passed over the coast at Donna Nook at 1.10am and a few minutes later the lighthouse crew at Spurn Head heard the sound of bombs exploding at sea.[23]

## 1 October 1916, 23.55pm: Corby, Northamptonshire

The second of this group of three Zeppelins, the new L 34 on her first mission, crossed the coast at Overstrand at 9.42pm. Her commander, Max Dietrich, set a course to the south-west but a parachute flare and three requests for wireless bearings, at 10.40pm, 11.20pm and 11.32pm, suggest he was unsure where he was. At 11.45pm, L 34 was heading towards Corby when a searchlight uncovered, trying to locate the Zeppelin through the mist and clouds. It was operating with two mobile 6-pdr Nordenfelt guns positioned at Shire Lodge Farm on the road between Corby and Rockingham. Presuming he had found a worthy target, Dietrich began dropping the first of 17 HE bombs as he passed over Kirby Hall. The line of bombs ran for about two miles through fields and woods, ending near the southern end of the Corby railway tunnel. To the gun crews, who had fired eight rounds at fleeting glimpses of the Zeppelin, it seemed as though it was heading directly towards them but it suddenly veered away to starboard. The time was approaching midnight – it was also the time L 31 took fire 60 miles to the south. Turning onto a north-east course, L 34 dropped 13 incendiary bombs in fields alongside the Rockingham to Gretton road. The only damage caused by all 30 bombs was a broken telegraph wire. Max Dietrich gradually turned on to an easterly course and reached the coast again just south of Sea Palling in Norfolk at 1.40am.[24]

## 2 October 1916, 1.05am: Willian, Hertfordshire

The last of this trio of Zeppelins came inland at Weybourne at 10.15pm. Her commander, Robert Koch, set off across Norfolk taking a south-west direction into Cambridgeshire and heading for London. But just before midnight, when passing over Wicken Fen, Koch saw an unmistakeable flare of light in the sky about 45 miles to the south that could only be a burning Zeppelin. Over Waterbeach, Koch changed course to the north-west but, after progressing 12 miles to St Ives, he had a change of heart and resumed his course for London. At 1.05am L 24 reached Shefford in Bedfordshire from where he observed an urban area with a concentration of lights east of it. Koch believed he had reached north London where, he reported, 'the whole bomb load was dropped with good effect on the districts of Stoke Newington and Hackney'.[25] But he never reached London; the urban area he saw was the Hertfordshire town of Hitchin and the lights were landing flares burning at an RFC emergency landing ground south of the village of Willian.

Private William Hawkes of No.56 Protection Company, Royal Defence Corps, was on the landing field when L 24 approached at 1.14am. Nine bombs exploded in quick succession. Private Hawkes had nowhere to hide when one burst just five yards from where he stood, a wound near the heart proving fatal.[26] In all, L 24 dropped 54 bombs (28 HE and 26 incendiary) along a straight line from the landing ground to Tilekiln Farm, south of the village of Weston, a distance of two and a half miles. The bombs all fell on open ground. With his attack on 'London' over, Koch turned L 24 back towards the coast, exiting at Kessingland in Suffolk at 2.35am.

\* \* \*

Back in the sky above Potter's Bar, Wulstan Tempest had lost all sense of time and direction after his attack on L 31, but felt a curious calm: 'It was a sensation I shall always remember... it was almost as though I came from another world.'[27]

Eventually he sighted the landing flares at North Weald airfield and began his descent but as he came in to land he fainted for a moment and his BE2c struck the ground with a crash, wrecking the landing gear, smashing the propeller into the ground and cracking his head against his Lewis gun. Those on the airfield rushed to his aircraft to congratulate him then, carrying him in triumph on their shoulders, they took him to the flight office where he made out his report. With just four sentences it was understated, but actions speak louder than words. Tempest received the Distinguished Service Order for shooting down L 31.

In Potter's Bar the townsfolk watched nervously as the falling Zeppelin, with flames streaming in her wake, roared down towards them but to their great relief it crashed on farmland on the Oakmere Estate. Rushing to the spot, the farmer, M.W. Bird, found much of the burning wreckage stacked around or hanging from a stout British oak tree. He also found Police Constable Herbie Pyne who had just had quite an experience. He was about 50 yards from where the wreckage smashed into the field when a burning propeller broke free and began to cartwheel towards him. Pyne lay down and with great relief saw the propeller bog down in the mud.

Fire now ignited machine gun bullets, which whizzed and zipped in all directions while the two men ran around desperately trying to round up Bird's cattle, which appeared drawn towards the flames.[28] As more people arrived, including the fire brigade and doctors, some order was restored before the army appeared and secured the area. The bodies of those who had jumped from the doomed airship were lying in the field away from the wreckage, the impact of their bodies making indentations in the soft earth, while others were terribly burned and disfigured. Stretcher-bearers carried them all to Farmer Bird's barn. A linen tag on his clothing identified the body of Heinrich Mathy. Although rumours that he was alive for a short period soon made their way as fact into the newspapers, a doctor who saw Mathy's body vehemently denied this at the inquest, as did a police inspector.

The following morning the London journalist Michael MacDonagh travelled out to Potter's Bar and trekked 'over the miry roads and sodden fields' to Oakmere Park. His newspaper office had received confirmation that the commander of the downed Zeppelin was Heinrich Mathy. MacDonagh gained permission to enter the makeshift mortuary specifically to see Mathy's body.

> The sergeant removed the covering from one of the bodies which lay apart from the others. The only disfigurement was a slight distortion of the face. It was that of a young man, clean-shaven. He was heavily clad in a dark uniform and overcoat, with a thick muffler round his neck.[29]

MacDonagh pondered Mathy's role in the death of many British civilians, Mathy 'the destroyer of humble homes, this slayer of women and children!' But then his own feelings towards Mathy mellowed.

Mathy is a soldier of Germany. He had but obeyed orders. In his own land he is esteemed, no doubt, for his daring, resolution, fortitude. He is our enemy, and we are glad he is no more. But apart from that, it is hardly for us to judge him for his particular military service to his country… War, even at its best, is barbarous. This war is wholesale murder of the most hideous kind. Mathy is dead, and for us, as a doer of terrible things, he is not dead for nothing. So may he rest in peace.[30]

It was less than a week since Mathy had written the heartfelt letter to his wife, Hertha, in which he conveyed an unmistakeable sense of foreboding. A feeling shared by many amongst the crew prior to the raid.

\* \* \*

On this, Mathy's final raid, for the loss of L 31 and her highly experienced crew, the 200 bombs dropped by seven Zeppelins killed just one man, a cow, four horses, six sheep, a rabbit and shattered a lot of glass. It was a high price to pay for such a paltry return.

Back in Germany, the news of the loss of L 31 with all hands had a devastating effect on Pitt Klein, the mechanic left behind. Those men were his comrades, his friends, with whom he had shared countless dangers. Now they were all gone but he was alive. Provisionally posted to the crew of L 14, who were due to transfer to one of the latest Zeppelins in January 1917, he never joined them. A medical report declared him unfit to fly, with Klein admitting that his 'nerves were so shot'. Instead he worked in the engine workshop at Ahlhorn until an accident left him unfit for military service. For the rest of the war he taught engine maintenance on a training ship. When he wrote his book in 1935 he dedicated it to the memory of Heinrich Mathy and the crew of L 31, whose loss, he confided, 'tormented and ate away at me'.

Chapter 20

# 'They've got her! She's hit!'

There can be little doubt that the death of Heinrich Mathy deeply affected Peter Strasser, while the loss of three of the long awaited 'r-class' airships – the 'Super Zeppelins' – in the space of just a week was a shocking blow. Since his appointment as commander of the Naval Airship Division in September 1913, it was Strasser's most significant test of character, but outwardly he remained positive and confident. His subordinates' reports of successful, damaging raids helped him to rationalise these losses. He was unaware that many of those reports contained unrealistic appraisals of their effectiveness and they helped convince him to keep the pressure on Britain as more airships became available to replace the losses.

The latest 'r-class', L 34, had joined Strasser's fleet on 27 September, followed by L 35 in October and three more in November – L 36, L 37 and L 38. Experienced crews and their commanders, however, could not be replaced so easily. The only long term naval Zeppelin commander still operational was Horst von Buttlar, who made his first raid on England back in April 1915. He, however, owed his survival to avoiding risks and rarely penetrating far inland, if crossing the coast at all – yet he invariably made extravagant but fictitious claims of success. The British authorities, who tracked the Zeppelins' movements, had long noted the behaviour of von Buttlar's airships: 'L 30 exhibited her now familiar tendency of just crossing the coast and then returning home.'[1] The strategy, however, served von Buttlar well – he survived the war.

## 22 October 1916, 1.37pm: Sheerness, Kent

When the next moon cycle arrived the naval Zeppelins were supporting fleet operations in the North Sea and so there were no airship raids towards the latter part of October. Aeroplanes, however, made what was becoming a monthly visit to the Kent coast. On Sunday 22 October an aeroplane of Marine Landflieger Abteilung I, now relocated from Mariakerke to Gistel, south of Ostend, set out for England, the two-seater commanded by Leutnant Walter Ilges who had raided on at least two previous occasions.

Ilges' aeroplane, believed to be a LVG, appeared over Sheerness on the Isle of Sheppey at 1.37pm. Flying at a great height, few people saw it and with haze adding to the difficulty in locating the raider, the local anti-aircraft guns remained silent. Ilges dropped four bombs over the north-western part of Sheerness with three falling in the harbour and one at the Dockyard Station. The bombs in the harbour caused no damage although one exploded between the pier head and a battleship. The bomb at the station sidings made a small crater 18 inches in diameter, smashed windows in four railway carriages and a horsebox, broke two more in a signal box and cut telegraph wires. No one was hurt. Just two or three minutes after it appeared, the aeroplane departed before any defending aircraft could intervene.

## 23 October 1916, 10am: Margate, Kent

The following day, 23 October, another short, sharp attack took place, this time on Margate. The unidentified aeroplane made its approach just after 10am. No one noticed it until bombs began to drop in the Cliftonville district. According to a newspaper: 'Nothing could be heard of aircraft engines, but high in the sky a small speck was eventually discerned.' The first bomb dropped in the sea, followed by one on the shore near Walpole Rocks. Another exploded on the grass at the north end of Fifth Avenue, smashing the glass in a shelter and leaving a lady sitting there shocked but unhurt. Fragments of the bomb, however, injured a man as he walked along the promenade. The final bomb demolished a chimneystack as it smashed down through the St George's Hotel on Eastern Esplanade, damaging the staircase and walls as it passed through the building. A chambermaid working on the top floor needed hospital treatment for injuries to her feet.

As the raider made off across land towards Ramsgate, a gun at Sackett's Hill opened fire. Although the crew found it hard to spot the aircraft in the bright sunlight, they fired off 16 rounds in its general direction before it went back out to sea near Ramsgate. An aircraft from RNAS Manston took off in pursuit but was unable to close the gap.

## 23 November 1916: Berlin

In Germany at this time a slight reorganisation took place within the Naval Aviation Divisions. From the beginning of the war there had been two divisions – airships and aeroplanes – commanded by Konteradmiral Otto Philipp. In May 1916, however, Admiral Eduard von Capelle, the new State Secretary for the Navy, redefined regulations governing the Airship Division and, although still technically subordinate to Philipp, Strasser gained some independence inasmuch that von Capelle now provided the link between his division and the High Seas Fleet. On 23 November 1916 this separation became official. Peter Strasser was given a new title, *Führer der Luftschiffe* (Leader of Airships), and was now responsible directly to Admiral Reinhard Scheer, commander of the High Seas Fleet, regarding the deployment and development of airships, and to von Capelle in matters relating to experimental work and training. Under Strasser, Victor Schütze was promoted to command all airship troops two weeks later, his new command, L 36, transferring to Franz Eichler, but overall Strasser's day-to-day involvement changed very little, he remained very much a 'hands-on' leader.[2]

Bad weather over the North Sea through November prevented a resumption of Zeppelin raids. With the new moon rising on 25 November, the ideal time for raiding, the weather continued to disappoint in Germany. On the evening of 26 November, however, weather charts showed a possible window of opportunity for the following day. A hectic flurry of activity broke out in the Zeppelin sheds at Nordholz, Hage, Ahlhorn and Tondern on the morning of 27 November but still no confirmation came that the raid was on. Heinrich Hollender, commander of L 22 at Nordholz, relates a story that he and the commanders of L 21 and L 34, Kurt Frankenburg and Max Dietrich, were in the officers' mess at noon, having all but given up hope of the raid taking place, and were about to celebrate Dietrich's 46th birthday. At that moment an adjutant burst in: 'Gentlemen, orders to attack the industrial district of the English Midlands; splendid prospects; the first ship must be in the air by one o'clock at the latest!' As the three officers dashed from the mess, Kurt Frankenburg said: 'Leave the birthday things as they are; we'll have our celebrations tomorrow.'[3]

In L 22's shed Richard Frey, the executive officer, waited impatiently with the crew for the return of Hollender with news. When he burst in to announce the raid was on, Frey noted, 'Now the eyes of the crew were seen to sparkle for the longed-for raid on England was to take place at last.[4] It was their first raid on Britain; whether the more experienced crews shared their enthusiasm is debatable.

Strasser's plan split his 10 Zeppelins into two groups, one targeting the north and the other the midlands. The raiders made their way out over the North Sea but the failure of two engines caused von Buttlar's L 30 to turn back when midway across. Meanwhile, Leutnant-zur-See Frey was thrilled to be taking part in his first raid.

> After a short time, we caught sight of L 13, L 14 and L 16, which had started from Hage, in East Friesland, and later of L 24 from Tondern. Forming a bold front of seven airships, we proceeded on our westward course. It was an impressive sight, which always remained with me during my later flights. No one at home had any idea of the forthcoming raid, and in England too, no one had yet thought of it.[5]

In England, however, the Zeppelins' progress was being closely monitored as always from their radio reports and at 8.45pm, all along the east and north-eastern coast the Field Marshal's Warning Only order put the defences on the alert and at 10.13pm the TARA order instigated the blackout. After a previous aborted flight, at 10.22pm a pilot from No.36 (Home Defence) Squadron at Seaton Carew, Second Lieutenant Ian Vernon Pyott, received orders to patrol. At least one other of the squadron's pilots ascended too: Second Lieutenant Francis Turner. Both pilots were flying the BE2c.

The northern group, having lost L 30 on the way, comprised L 34, L 35, L 36 and L 24. The first two were heading for the Newcastle area; L 36 had orders for Edinburgh while L 24 had Stockton as its target. No.36 Squadron patrolled much of this area and although they had so far had no success against Zeppelin raiders, there was a new confidence amongst the pilots of the RFC, and the RNAS too. They now had the weapons that gave them the edge over their adversaries – as long as they could be found in the night skies.

## 27 November 1916, 11.45pm: West Hartlepool, County Durham

The first of the northern group to come inland was Max Dietrich's L 34; it was just her second time over England. Dietrich crossed the coast at Blackhall Rocks, about four miles north of Hartlepool, at 11.30pm and headed inland. The commander of the local special constables,

W. Nimmo, was at Castle Eden, about three miles from the coast, where he heard the sound of engines.

> I was trying to see it against the stars when the Hutton Henry searchlight flashed right across the sky and passed over the Zeppelin. It immediately swung back and settled on it and never left it again for a moment.[6]

As Dietrich turned south, towards the searchlight, others at Elwick and Greatham found L 34, as did 21-year-old Second Lieutenant Pyott.

Although of Scottish background, Ian Pyott was in South Africa where his family ran a business when war broke out. In January 1916 he left for England to join the army, destined for a future in tanks with a commission in the Heavy Section Machine Gun Corps. Soon realising it was not for him he successfully applied for a transfer to the Royal Flying Corps. After completing his training, Pyott joined No.36 (Home Defence) Squadron in late August 1916. As L 34 headed towards him, Pyott made his move.

> At this moment I was at 9,800 and the Zepp seemed a few hundred feet below me. I flew towards the Zepp and flew at right angles to and underneath him amidships, firing as I went under.

As L 34 approached Elwick, Dietrich released a string of 12 bombs aimed at the searchlight. The third of these brought down telegraph wires at a crossroads just south west of Elwick, while the sixth, seventh and eighth bombs all detonated in the searchlight field but it was unaffected. The ninth bomb caused some damage at Dovecote Farm but the other seven all exploded harmlessly in surrounding fields.

After Pyott's first pass, L 34 turned to the east, flying a zig-zag course towards Hartlepool and the sea. Flying parallel, Pyott fired short bursts from his Lewis gun. The anti-aircraft guns at Hartlepool and Seaton Carew joined in the action too. As he reached West Hartlepool, Dietrich commenced dropping 16 bombs. The first four fell in fields at West Park, on the edge of the town, followed immediately by two that exploded in Ward Jackson Park before five more fell amongst the tightly packed rows of terraced houses between Grosvenor Street and Hart Road.

At No.2 Bentick Street, George Linton, a 40-year-old provision's dealer, was at home with his family. The children were in bed but when

Mrs Linton heard an unusual noise, she asked her husband to bring the children downstairs. George decided to look outside first: 'He saw a flash, heard an explosion, and knew no more.' Fragments from a bomb in a neighbouring street had struck him. His wife found him in the doorway lying in a pool of blood that flowed from his legs. George Linton died in hospital two days later.[7] A bomb that exploded outside 15 Hartley Street fatally injured Mary Ann Pritchard who lived at No.13 and Elizabeth Rumble's death at 4 Back Eden Street was attributed to shock caused by the exploding bombs. A newspaper report listed most of the damage as occurring in Hartley Street, Lowthian Road, Poplar Grove and Rugby Terrace. The next three bombs exploded on allotments between Hart Road and the Victoria Football Ground, home to Hartlepools United football club,[8] then two destroyed the football ground's main stand on Clarence Road.[9] L 34 was now over the docks. Behind her were 15 wrecked houses with 20 or 30 suffering significant damage, while the police reported that nearly 600 other homes and shops lost windows and roof tiles. And amongst the destruction four people were dead or dying and 11 more lay injured.

Pyott had continued to fly parallel with L 34 as the anti-aircraft guns ceased firing. Reports indicate at least one of their shells may have damaged L 34 but there was little time to note any effect as Pyott attacked again.

> I was aiming at his port quarter, and I noticed first a small patch become incandescent where I had seen tracers entering his envelope. I first took it for a machine gun firing at me from the Zeppelin, but this patch rapidly spread and the next thing was that the whole Zeppelin was in flames.[10]

Lieutenant C.B. Williamson, the officer commanding the searchlights that had so effectively held on to L 34, was able to confirm Pyott's observation.

> ... a number of small bright lights [incendiary bullets] could be seen darting from close range, slightly below on the left-hand side in quick succession and apparently entering the envelope. After a short space of time a small red glow arising from a point (port quarter) where the light struck.[11]

Like a huge flaming torch, the doomed airship began to fall.

It fell endways on, and when still at a tremendous height seemed gradually to separate into two sections. The larger part fell with increased velocity and amid a sheet of intenser flame. The other, and apparently lighter, section of the structure fell more slowly, and glowed a dull red colour... Finally the whole structure plunged into the sea.[12]

Already awoken by the guns and bombs, the residents of Hartlepool waited nervously for the raid to end. In later years Emma Cussons (née Harrison) recalled her experience of the raid; she was eight-years-old at the time.

Dad got us all out of bed and said. 'If we have got to be killed, we'll all go together.'... we heard terrible screams and we assumed the Zeppelin had dropped a bomb nearby, but then Dad said to my mother, 'My God, I think they've hit something.' Mum said, 'Don't go out' but he opened the back kitchen door and it was absolutely red, like a ball of fire, and he said, 'They've got it, they've hit it. Come on, kids, come out and have a look at this, you'll never see anything like this again.'[13]

Badly injured in December 1914 during the naval bombardment on the town, Emma's mother was horrified when her husband later brought home a piece of the Zeppelin wreckage as a souvenir. 'I don't want that in my house,' she told him, 'it smells of death.'

For others, however, it was a moment for celebration, as Cora Tucker remembered when her father appeared.

'Come on quick, the Zeppelin's coming down, when you're a big girl you can say you saw it.' By this time everyone had rushed out to see it. One poor man was in his nightshirt and when the Zeppelin was coming down he threw up his arms and said, 'Let them burn in hell.' Well, of course, as his arms went up his nightshirt went up, much to the delight of the women and they kept saying to him, 'Say it again, Mr so and so,' and so he'd throw his arms up and say, 'Let them burn in hell,' and they howled with laughter. I had no thought of the men in the Zeppelin, serve them right, they shouldn't be over bombing us, should they?'[14]

The wreckage of L 34 came down about a mile out to sea, east of the Heugh Battery, shortly before midnight and remained burning for about 30 minutes. Major S. Horsley of the Durham Royal Garrison Artillery gathered some armed men, boarded a boat and headed out.

> We arrived at the scene of the wreck shortly after 1.0 [1am], but the remains had entirely disappeared, and there was nothing to be seen except a considerable amount of oil on the water. We cruised about in the vicinity for a couple of hours but nothing further was seen.[15]

Max Dietrich and the nineteen men of his crew were dead. It was still Dietrich's birthday. Not until 9 January 1917 were the first bodies found, when two washed ashore at Seaton Carew, about two miles from where they had crashed. Six days later another appeared at Redcar, about six miles away. Then between 18 and 24 January three more washed ashore. Dietrich was not among them.

Max Dietrich's family did not hear what happened to him until some years later. His niece, the actress Marlene Dietrich, spoke to a British reporter in 1935.

> My uncle never came back. My aunt was broken-hearted, but she would not believe her husband had really gone. She insisted he would come back but the years passed, and there was no news. At last she lost hope and bowed to the hand of fate. It is very sad but of course in Germany my Uncle Max was mourned as a hero. He gave his life for his country.[16]

Approaching the coast of County Durham, six minutes behind L 34, Herbert Ehrlich brought L 35 inland about three miles further north near the village of Hawthorn. Heading north, no sooner had he come inland than a searchlight at New Seaham fixed L 35 in its beam and a mobile 13-pdr, 6cwt gun at Seaham opened fire, blasting 34 shells skywards in nine minutes. Already losing hydrogen due to ice forming on gas escape valves and aware of the barrage aimed at L 34 behind him, Ehrlich went back out to sea where the crew were to witness the inferno that engulfed L 34 just eight miles away.

With an engine out of action, L 24 trailed behind both L 34 and L 35. She was still about 15 miles from the coast when Pyott destroyed L 34. Her commander, Kurt Friemel, L 31's former executive officer now commanding his own airship for the first time, gave up his plan to attack Stockton and returned to Germany.

The last of the northern group, Korvettenkapitän Viktor Schütze, commanding L 36 before taking on his new role under Strasser, was heading up the coast to attack Edinburgh when he too saw the end of L 34. Running into difficult atmospheric conditions he abandoned Scotland and hoped to attack Newcastle or Sunderland but then an engine broke down and L 36 became stern heavy. Schütze released bombs and fuel to trim the ship then limped back to Germany. But unlike Max Dietrich, Schütze, Ehrlich and Friemel all made it home safely.

There were more troubles ahead for those Zeppelins in the second raiding group heading for the Midlands. All five crossed the Yorkshire coast on a 30-mile stretch between Filey and Tunstall. The first of these, Kuno Manger's L 14 came inland at 9.10pm east of Hull. Ten minutes later two mobile 13-pdr guns at Cowden fired 26 rounds at L 14, with the crews believing they may have hit her. In response Manger released 44 bombs (18 HE and 26 incendiary), which fell in fields between Mappleton and Rowlston Hall where they caused no damage. Manger then headed north up the coast but on coming under fire from two mobile 13-pdr guns at Barmston he turned back. Heading south, at 10.15pm L 14 was attacked by a 12-pdr, 12cwt gun at Sutton, north-east of Hull. Unable to free himself from the guns, Manger went back out to sea north of Spurn at 10.25pm.

The industrial heartland of Yorkshire was L 16's destination, commanded for the first time by Kapitänleutnant Hans-Karl Gayer. Having crossed the coast near Filey at 9.20pm, Gayer followed a south-west course but, between Selby and Howden at 10.15pm, three 3-inch, 20 cwt guns at Hemingborough Grange, Cliffe and Wood House Farm, forced Gayer to take evasive action. At 10.30pm, having passed south of Pontefract and Featherstone, it appeared that Gayer was about to attack Wakefield but lights at the New Sharlston Colliery caught his attention and he dropped nine bombs (three HE and six incendiary) there instead. They only caused minor damage at Sharlston and the settlement at Streethouse. From there L 16 steered towards Barnsley, but the town, like others in the area, was effectively blacked out. An incendiary dropped at Cudworth landed in a field alongside the Snydale Road, and two HE bombs also fell in fields by the Barnsley Road in Monk Bretton at 10.42pm, a couple of miles from the centre of Barnsley. L 16 now turned and headed back towards Pontefract, dropping four bombs at South Hiendley that broke a few windows.

In Pontefract many people had left their homes, making for the perceived safety of Pontefract Park, which also served as an emergency landing ground for the RFC. Many occupied the elevated northern end of the park overlooking the landing ground, now illuminated by flares, in the hope of seeing a Zeppelin. Concerned by their proximity to the landing ground, special constables ushered them away from their vantage point.[17] It was a fortunate move because, attracted by the flares, L 16 dropped four bombs on the recently vacated area of the park just before 11pm. Four incendiaries also fell between the park and the Prince of Wales Colliery, but all failed to ignite. Circling back to Featherstone, L 16 dropped six HE bombs but again to no effect.

At Knottingley, L 16 headed north towards Tadcaster dropping two incendiary bombs at the villages of Lumby and Monk Fryston at 11.15pm. It then appeared that L 16 was about to attack York but at 11.35pm the 3-inch, 20cwt gun at Acomb came into action firing 12 rounds and forcing Gayer west of the city before he eventually turned east towards the coast. He dropped seven more bombs. The first two fell on West Farm at Helperthorpe and on Jepson's Farm at Boythorpe; neither bomb had a fuze fitted. The final salvo of five bombs dropped at about 12.25am on a farm at Foxholes where they caused some damage to the farmhouse. About ten minutes later, L 16 crossed the coast south of Scarborough from where two 13-pdr, 6cwt guns fired 20 rounds at the departing airship.

## 27 November 1916, 11.15pm: York, Yorkshire

Two of the raiders, L 13 and L 22 crossed the coast at Flamborough Head at 10.05pm. Five minutes later they separated at Burton Agnes with L13, commanded by Franz Eichler, heading for York. About 11pm Eichler spotted some lights. After dropping a single incendiary at Yapham, about 12 miles east of the city centre, he headed straight for the lights and bombarded them with 21 HE and three incendiary bombs. His bombs landed near the village of Barmby Moor where flares were burning on a RFC landing ground. Continuing on to Stamford Bridge, L 13 then appeared over the northern part of York and dropped a number of incendiary bombs, observed by the officers on board L 22, which was also approaching the city. After parting company with L 13 at Burton Agnes, Heinrich Hollender in L 22 headed south-west as far as the village of Holme-on-Spalding-Moor. Moments later, the searchlight and gun at Willitoft found her and opened fire, forcing Hollender away to the north-west. York lay 12 miles ahead. As L 22 steered for the fires started by L 13's bombs, she came under fire from the anti-aircraft gun at Acomb, which blasted five rounds in 30 seconds.[18]

The city escaped relatively lightly. It would appear that the Rowntree's Cocoa Works on Haxby Road was the main target, which no doubt looked like any other industrial plant from high above. All the bombs fell just to the south of Works. Richard Frey, on board L 22, recalled dropping two large 300kg bombs that exploded with such force that at least one member of the crew thought a shell had hit them.[19] Those two bombs landed within 70 yards of each other, just 300 yards from Rowntree's. One 'completely smashed' a house at the end of Faversham Crescent, with only the dining room left standing, and the other exploded at the junction of Fountayne Street and Wigginton Road: 'The noise of the explosion was terrific and every house in Feversham Terrace [Crescent], a row of residential houses, sustained greater or less damage.'[20]

Before the bomb exploded at the end of Feversham Crescent, Mr and Mrs Hall were bringing their children downstairs, Mr Hall carrying their little girl, Sheila. The window over the stairs shattered inwards.

> Pieces of tar macadam and shrapnel were hurled into the house, and one piece of the latter, nearly three inches square, struck the little girl, penetrating the scalp, but fortunately not touching the skull. It was deeply embedded in the flesh, and it was removed under an anaesthetic, the child making a good recovery.[21]

Elsewhere in York there were injuries to a man and a woman. Of the incendiary bombs, two also fell in Fountayne Street, with others on the corner of Haxby Road and Stanley Street.

It appears that L 13 headed away to the east, passing Pocklington at 11.35pm and Driffield. At 12.25am she dropped five incendiaries in fields at Wold Newton before reaching the coast just north of Scarborough at 12.50am from where the two guns that had engaged L 16 about 15 minutes earlier were in action again, firing 24 rounds to send L 13 on her way.

Meanwhile L 22 returned towards the Humber, passing to the north of Hull and back out to sea at Hornsea at 12.20am, under fire from the guns at Cowden that had previously engaged L 14. They fired 26 rounds at L 22 and had some success. Shrapnel ripped 150 holes in two gas cells, which quickly began to lose hydrogen. Hollender jettisoned excess weight and L 22 limped home, although she was unable to reach Nordholz and took shelter at Hage where the landing caused further damage that took six days to repair. It was a sobering first raid for the crew.

About five minutes after L 13 passed out over the coast at Scarborough, a BE2c took off from RNAS Scarborough, piloted by Flight sub-Lieutenant J.F. Roche. He crash-landed 50 minutes later. But other pilots also patrolled the skies searching for the Zeppelins. While No.36 Squadron searched for those in the north-east, three other Home Defence squadrons were on the alert further south. No.33 Squadron was patrolling over Lincolnshire, No.38 Squadron over Leicestershire and southern Lincolnshire and No.51 Squadron in Norfolk was standing by. This was to prove problematical for the final raider, Kurt Frankenburg's L 21 (see Map 7).

Frankenburg came under fire from the guns at Barmston as soon as he crossed the coast. Going back out to sea, he came inland again a little further north. Having got his bearings, Frankenburg then snaked south-west across country until at 11.25pm he reached the village of Sherburn in Elmet, about 8 miles north-east of Pontefract. He seemed intent on attacking Leeds but gunfire from Brierlands at 11.34pm and Rothwell Heigh drove him away from the town. Now heading south, L 21 reached Sharlston at 11.48pm, where L 16 had dropped bombs over an hour earlier and from where light still shone from the colliery because, according to a police report, 'The nightwatchman appears to have been so much unnerved that he failed to take the necessary action.'[22]

Frankenburg released three bombs over the colliery but there was no damage of consequence. From Sharlston L 21 headed towards a darkened Barnsley, concealed by the blackout, appearing over the town at about 12.05am.

> The Zeppelin appeared to be lost, and it descended a considerable distance, but perfect darkness prevailed... and to this fact its escape is attributed, for without dropping any bomb the airship suddenly rose and sped away on a westerly course. Almost immediately a loud report was heard, and [three] bombs were dropped... close to the spoil-bank of the old Silkstone Colliery, Dodworth.[23]

## 28 November 1916, 1.10am: Stoke-on-Trent, Staffordshire

From there L 21 passed over the Peak District between Manchester and Sheffield; at 12.50am Frankenburg dropped a single incendiary bomb over Hammond's Brickworks at the village of Pott Shrigley, probably offloaded to check ground speed and drift. Twenty minutes later a single HE bomb landed at Birchenwood near Kidsgrove. To the south lay Stoke-on-Trent and surrounding districts where many ironstone mine hearths, burning colliery waste heaps and furnaces were glowing in the otherwise darkened landscape. Frankenburg prepared to attack.

The first three bombs fell at Goldenhill, close to the Goldenhill Colliery, but they exploded harmlessly, before three fell at Tunstall. The first of these exploded in the narrow streets, landing in the backyard of 6 Sun Street (now St Aidan's Street), ripping away the sculleries and outhouses of Nos.2 to 8, wrecking the interiors of two homes and damaging many others there and in neighbouring Bond Street. At No.8 Sun Street, Mr Cantliffe had just returned from a shift at a nearby pit and was having supper with his wife when the bomb exploded. Flying fragments struck him in the chest but he made a good recovery in hospital. The other two detonated alongside burning slag heaps, one between the Goldendale Ironworks and Ravensdale Ironworks, and the other close to the Ravensdale New Forge. Frankenburg now crossed over Bradwell Woods, lured by the glow from ironstone-burning hearths two miles away at Chesterton. At 1.20am, he released 23 bombs (16 HE and seven incendiary) but although they fell close to various collieries and brick and tile works, the net result was just broken windows and a demolished shed. Continuing its sinuous course, Frankenburg's L 21 passed over Newcastle-under-Lyme and Hanley before dropping an incendiary at Trentham and three more at Fenton, where all but one failed to ignite. From a wireless bearing he received, Frankenburg believed he had attacked Manchester. At 1.30am he commenced his return flight across England; it would be a long night.

From the area around Stoke-on-Trent, Frankenburg headed east but engine breakdowns plagued the return to the coast. He first shut down the engines to allow mechanics to work on them as he approached Nottingham, drifting with the wind. But when a searchlight at Ruddington found L 21, Frankenburg restarted the engines. At 2.35am, as he entered the area patrolled by No.38 Squadron, he requested wireless bearings when near Melton Mowbray in Leicestershire. At 2.50am a searchlight at the squadron's Buckminster airfield found L 21 and two pilots, Captain George Birley and Second Lieutenant David Allan gave chase. Birley reported L 21 flying at about 7,000 feet when the airship began to climb and fly first north-west and then south-east in a series of long evasive loops. During these manoeuvres L 21 climbed to 13,000 feet leaving Birley unable to close the gap. He fired two drums of ammunition from 2,000 feet below, but lost sight of her when loading a third. Allan never managed to position himself for an attack. When Frankenburg reached Essendine at 3.25am he had shaken off his pursuers and resumed an eastwards course, but extensive manoeuvring north and south for 40 minutes had restricted progress towards the coast to just 10 miles, and there were more problems ahead.

## 28 November 1916, 3.50 - 6.00am: Norfolk

At 3.50am L 21 was over Norfolk but Frankenburg was troubled. He requested wireless bearings near King's Lynn and again from Hillington, about seven miles away, as engine problems recurred. Reports state that L 21 drifted with the wind towards East Dereham, reaching the town at 4.55am. Six pilots of No.51 Squadron now searched for the intruder. At East Dereham one of them, Lieutenant Walter Gayner flying a FE2b, found L 21 at 7,500 feet and noticed a light shining from one of the gondolas where it appears repairs were underway. Gayner closed in but just before coming into range his own engine began to malfunction then failed. With great skill he managed to glide down and crash-landed on Tibenham emergency landing ground. Frankenburg restarted L 21's engines at East Dereham but about ten minutes later, near Reepham, he drifted with them off again. Around that time, 5.05am, Frankenburg radioed a message to Germany that one of his four engines was out of action. It took the beleaguered Zeppelin about an hour to cover the 30 miles to the coast, reaching Great Yarmouth at 6am. L 21 had now been over British soil for almost nine hours and although she had reached the coast, there was fresh danger ahead. Pilots of the RNAS were out over the sea while anti-aircraft guns lay in wait on land – and the sun would rise within the hour.

L 21 was still drifting with the wind when she passed over Great Yarmouth and at 6.05am two 13-pdr, 9cwt guns at Bradwell, south-west of the town, opened fire. The sky was brightening and the guns did not need searchlights to help them find the target. Observers believed at least two shells exploded very close to L 21. From Great Yarmouth L 21 drifted south about a mile off the coast until she reached Lowestoft.

There her remaining three engines spluttered back to life and L 21 headed out to sea.

## 28 November 1916, 6.45am: North Sea, off Lowestoft

Alerted to the approach of L 21 over Norfolk, four RNAS pilots were patrolling the coastline: Egbert Cadbury from Yarmouth, Edward Pulling from Bacton, Flight sub-Lieutenant Gerard Fane from Burgh Castle and Flight sub-Lieutenant A.V. Robinson from Holt. All were flying the BE2c.

Cadbury had landed at Burgh Castle after problems with his spark plugs forced him down. Problem rectified he was airborne again at 6.18am and a few minutes later he saw L 21 and set off in pursuit. The gunfire from Bradwell attracted the attention of Fane and Pulling and they also set a course towards the raider, now silhouetted against the lightening pre-dawn sky. When she left the coast, L 21 was flying at 8,200 feet and had now pushed her speed up to 55mph. Cadbury closed in and from a position about 700 feet below fired the first of four drums of mixed ammunition into her rear as he gradually closed the distance. While he did so, Fane came up very close on her starboard side but it did not go well.

> I only got off one round, however, when the gun jambed [sic] and so I soon cleared out of the position I was in owing... to the slipstream of her... engines which made the machine very difficult to control, and also there was another machine some way below me firing like mad and evidently could not see me.[24]

Fane was witnessing Cadbury's determined attack as the crew of L 21 manned the machine guns and made a spirited defence. With his gun out of action, 18-year-old Fane tried to climb above the Zeppelin and bomb it. As he did so, Pulling closed in to make his attack, approaching at right angles to L 21's port quarter and passing underneath, but it did not go according to plan either: 'The Lewis gun fired two shots, both hitting and stopped.' Pulling turned sharply to get away from L 21's machine guns while he cleared his own. But he never got the chance to fire again: 'A few seconds later, on looking over my shoulder, I saw the Zeppelin was on fire by the stern.'[25]

Fane was higher than L 21 and under fire from the machine gunner on the upper platform on top of the envelope as the fire took hold. 'At

305

the same moment,' he explained, 'the gunner… saw the flames, stopped firing at me, whether or not he had a parachute I don't know, but he ran straight over the nose of the ship just before she exploded and disappeared.' Pulling, having passed under L 21, flew parallel to her, and as L 21 began to fall stern first, one machine gunner stuck to his post until engulfed in flames. L 21 hit the water about nine miles south-east of Lowestoft and sank almost immediately – the time was 6.45am.

Alerted by the firing of the guns, great crowds had gathered on the Great Yarmouth sea front, watching in silence as the Zeppelin slowly receded against the dawn sky. Then the mood changed.

> A vivid flash burst from the Zeppelin, and hundreds of voices shouted, 'They've got her! She's hit!' In a second or two the flash had spread until the whole airship was in flames and then the whole crowd cheered with might and main, while the syrens (sic) of steamers hooted out in triumph.[26]

Some steamers were sent out to find the wreckage, 'but nothing was found but black scum and floating oil'. The Zeppelin crew that the British press had 'buried' back in September at Cuffley had died a second time – but this time it was final.

Although Cadbury made the main attack, his fire all against the stern from where the flames originated, the naval authorities gave the main credit to Pulling, who only fired two rounds, neither of them at the stern. Pulling received the Distinguished Service Order, Cadbury and Fane the Distinguished Service Cross. There is a suggestion that Pulling received the higher award as recognition of the fact that he had made thirteen anti-Zeppelin sorties, the most by any pilot to that date.[27] Another DSO went to Ian Pyott for his destruction of L 34 over Hartlepool.

At Nordholz, Dietrich's birthday decorations remained in place but neither he nor Frankenburg, who had shouted, 'We'll have our celebrations tomorrow', came back. In Germany there was no way of avoiding the truth. The loss of five naval Zeppelins in less than ten weeks was a major blow to the ambitions of the new *Führer der Luftschiffe*. And for the first time Peter Strasser recognised that his airships were the victims of aeroplane attacks. These losses appeared to signify that the Zeppelins' days were numbered, and a foretaste of the future appeared over London later on the same day that the surviving Zeppelins returned home from this latest disastrous raid on England.

# Chapter 21

# A Portent for the Future

On the morning of 28 November, while Peter Strasser was still coming to terms with the loss of two more Zeppelins, an audacious plan was underway to bomb the Admiralty building in central London. A plan not carried out by Zeppelins after dark but by a single two-seater aeroplane – in broad daylight.

The enterprising Leutnant Walter Ilges, who had made the raid on Sheerness a month earlier, with his pilot, Deckoffizier Paul Brandt, had plans to engage in a photo-reconnaissance mission in their aeroplane, a LVG C IV, before making an attack on the Admiralty. Flying at around 13,000 feet, no one saw the aircraft pass over the Thames Estuary, giving Margate, Westgate and the Isle of Sheppey a wide berth. Once past the familiar town of Sheerness, Brandt turned inland, keeping west of the River Medway as Ilges began taking photographs. Near Maidstone at 11.15am, the aircraft turned west and, shortly after passing Reigate, it turned north near Dorking and followed the railway line towards London's Victoria Station. Ilges had taken about 20 photos, amongst which he believed there were images of a new aerodrome, army camps and munition works.

Just before midday, the LVG appeared over the fashionable Knightsbridge area of London, still unnoticed in a hazy sky by those on the ground two and a half miles below, and began the bomb run that Ilges and Brandt aimed at the Admiralty. They carried six 10kg HE bombs and the first of these stuck the premises of Spiking & Co, bakers and confectioners, at 108 Brompton Road, a mile and a half short of the target. Inside, Henrietta Simmonds and two other girls were working in an upstairs room.

> By a lucky chance, the bomb, instead of striking the roof direct, spent its force against a chimney stack 14ft high, and,

also by good fortune the stack fell outwards into an empty yard. The three girls were thrown off their feet. They behaved very pluckily, said a foreman. They calmly made their way downstairs unaided, and then the injured hand [of Henrietta] was quietly attended to, afterwards receiving six stitches in hospital.[1]

As the aircraft passed over Brompton Road, the next bomb struck a building at 15 Pavilion Road, running parallel with Sloane Street, premises occupied by the London Pure Milk Association.

> A bomb came hurtling through the roof of an office in which a young woman [Joan Farnborough] was employed. She was slightly injured, her hand being cut, besides which she was thrown against the wall and suffered some shock. She escaped from the noxious fumes with which the apartment became charged, and emerged covered with a fine dust – 'white as a miller,' a colleague expressed it.[2]

Minor damage extended to the building next door and to 12 Sloane Street, while smashed windows were evident in Basil Street. Crossing over Sloane Street into Belgravia, the LVG dropped a third bomb on 13 Lowndes Square where it wrecked half the roof and damaged the contents of the rooms at the back of the house. Now passing over Belgrave Square, the next bomb detonated in the roadway at Belgrave Mews East (now Montrose Place), punching a hole in the cobblestones and breaking windows at Nos.6 to 8 on one side of the road and at Nos.43 to 46 on the other. One woman was slightly hurt and four coachmen and stable staff sustained minor injuries from bomb fragments and flying stones: Albert Emery, John Tate, Albert Taylor and Frederick Morley.

The fifth bomb, which struck the rear part of 112 Eaton Square, also impacted on neighbouring houses and in Eccleston Mews and Eaton Place. Most bomb damage in Britain had generally affected the homes of the working class, but this bomb struck at the homes of a lieutenant general, a lieutenant colonel and a colonel, all of them knighted, and one a baronet, as well as one owned by a lord and another by a lady. Although 13 properties suffered damage, in most cases it was restricted to broken windows. There were only two injuries, both in Eccleston Mews. At No.16 a coachman's wife, Sarah Bidwell, suffered cuts to her face and an arm, while at No.14, Yvonne Boucquey from Brussels received a cut to her neck. The final bomb fell on the Victoria Palace Music Hall near Victoria Station. Here the bomb smashed through a roof over dressing rooms and injured a cleaner, Louisa Cameron. The police summed up her injuries: '2 wounds on upper part of chest & back; larger lacerated wound at bottom of ribs and numerous bruises on right leg, side & arm; considerable shock but injuries are not considered serious.'[3]

Their last bombs dropped, Ilges and Brandt made off towards the south-east. On the streets in this part of London, the sound of the sharp reports led to some confusion as to their cause, but little appeared to suggest they were the sound of exploding bombs. A man working in the street near where one of them fell thought it sounded like 'the bursting of motor tyre'. A woman who was just 50 yards from another was surprised when she learnt later that it was a bomb: 'She thought it was a 'bus back-firing, so did not trouble to turn around.' And at the Victoria Palace, those present initially thought the blast was a gas explosion. In fact, it was not until an hour after the attack that official advice went out that it had been a raid, and it was 1pm when the RFC and RNAS ordered pilots to take off and search for the lone raider. By then it was too late.

Having reached the Maidstone area, Ilges and Brandt changed course first to the south-west then south, crossing the coast just west of Hastings and avoiding any aircraft that might intercept their path. They planned to cross to Abbeville, then pass over the front line at height, but things did not go according to plan. While over the English Channel, their engine's oil feed pipe became blocked and the crew began to throw excess weight overboard – including Ilges' precious camera and photographic plates. By the time they reached Abbeville they were down to 2,000 metres, too low to cross the front line safely. Instead, they decided to follow the French coast northwards, keeping out to sea, and hoping to reach Belgium that way, but their engine failed and they were forced to come inland, touching down about three and a half miles north-east of Boulogne. The two men managed to set fire to their aircraft and documents, except a map of London, before French soldiers appeared and took them captive.

In the subsequent interrogation, Ilges explained he was aiming his bombs at the Admiralty building but had found it difficult through the haze, although he believed his last bomb had exploded about 300 yards from the target. The report of the interrogation states that Ilges 'expressed some disappointment on being told that this was not the case'. That final bomb fell about a mile short of the Admiralty building, but it raises an interesting possibility – had Ilges mistaken it for another building? The Admiralty was a large square building on the edge of a park. About 400 yards from where that last bomb fell there was a large square building on the edge of a park – Buckingham Palace.

\* \* \*

Back in Germany there was much to consider. 1916 had started on a high, with the great raid over the Midlands continuing the largely unopposed procession over the British countryside that had begun in the previous year. With the long-awaited arrival of the 'r-class' Zeppelins, known to their crews as the 'Big 30s' and in Britain as the 'Super Zeppelins', with their greater carrying capacity and ability to fly higher, Peter Strasser expected even greater results from the naval airship fleet. The greater the height, however, the more difficult navigation became, and Britain was not standing idly by. Finally, some level of co-ordination in the nation's air defences saw anti-aircraft guns and searchlights working effectively together, and her aeroplanes armed with the new bullets, both explosive and incendiary, provided a lethal antidote to the Zeppelin menace. Their introduction at the same time as the appearance of the new 'r-class' Zeppelins had an immediate impact. In 1915, the loss of only one Zeppelin had resulted from the actions of Britain's air defences.[4] In 1916, however, those defences brought down six naval Zeppelins and an army Schütte-Lanz, all but one of these lost after the introduction of the new bullets (see Map 8). And other Zeppelins failed to reach home from raids due to engine problems or lack of fuel. This became more of a problem as Zeppelins ventured further inland than they had done in 1915.

In 1915 German airships made 20 raids on Britain, involving 35 vessels. In 1916 there were a similar number of raids, 21, but the number of appearances by individual airships rose significantly to 121.[5] Those 35 airships in 1915 dropped an estimated 34.9 tons (35,467 kg) of bombs on land, causing material damage valued at £815,406 as they roamed freely over Britain, while inflicting 740 casualties (208 killed, 532 injured). In 1916, as the defences tightened, the far greater number of raiders dropped 119.5 tons (121,442 kg) of bombs over land but inflicted less damage, estimated at £594,543, but with casualties rising to 988 (300 killed, 688 injured).[6] Britain's blackout in towns proved effective, but far out in the countryside, beyond the areas covered by lighting regulations, many isolated farms and country houses attracted Zeppelin bombs as they often provided the only source of visible light in an otherwise darkened landscape. Zeppelin commanders wasted a huge weight of bombs on agricultural land.

In addition, the stinging seaplane and aeroplane raids in 1916, which culminated with the attack on London at the end of November, had little overall impact other than to serve as an irritant. At least 26 aeroplanes and seaplanes dropped bombs over England in 14 raids, causing damage estimated at £10,937 and inflicting 79 casualties (18 killed, 61 injured), but this was a marked increase over 1914-1915 when five raids inflicted eight casualties (two killed, six injured) with damage estimated at just £570.

While in the autumn the German Army had concluded that raiding Britain in airships now carried too much risk, the Navy, however, remained committed to Strasser's strategy. On 18 December he took delivery of their latest Zeppelin, L 39. Strasser now had 14 Zeppelins and four Schütte-Lanz airships available, although five of the Zeppelins were of the old 'p-type' introduced in May 1915. Of these 18 airships, 12 Zeppelins and a Schütte-Lanz operated over the North Sea and two Zeppelins and three Schütte-Lanz in the Baltic region. At the end of the year the personnel of the Naval Airship Division numbered over 5,000 men.

While Strasser pondered the changes needed to give his Zeppelins the advantage again over the British defences, he sent out a raid on 28 December against southern England to attack, if possible, London. But there was caution evident in his orders: 'Attack only with cloud cover, otherwise turn back.'[7] Six airships set out for England: L 13, L 14, L 22, L 30, L 39 and SL 12. In addition, Strasser sent out L 35 and L 38 to attack Russian positions in the Baltic region, while two Zeppelins, L 16 from Hage and L 24 from Tondern, undertook scouting duties with the fleet's minesweepers. Having sent ten airships out, Strasser anticipated some success but he was to suffer yet more disappointment as his losses continued to mount. Once out over the North Sea, the main force encountered a strong rising wind, prompting their recall. As SL 12 came in to land at Ahlhorn, a strong gust of wind pulled the landing ropes away from the ground crew and carried SL 12 towards a hydrogen gasometer. Her commander, Waldemar Kölle, managed to lift the nose clear of impending doom but the trailing ropes caught, tipping the airship forward and smashing in the nose. The ship had escaped one disaster but now, having broken free, was taken by the wind until her crew managed to unceremoniously force it down a couple of kilometres further on. An approaching storm broke up the airship where she lay and battered SL 12 to a wreck.

And there was more. Over the Baltic, L 38 encountered horrific winter weather, with snow and ice forming on the envelope and control surfaces. Her commander, Martin Dietrich, abandoned the mission and turned back but, flying nose up and with failing engines, he deliberately landed in a wood at Seemuppen (now Ziemupe, Latvia) so the trees would prevent the heavy ship smashing into the ground. Having saved what they could, the crew had no choice but to abandon the wreck. And yet there was still more heartbreak for Strasser. L 24, one of those scouting for the minesweepers, returned to her shed at Tondern, which she shared with L 17. As the ground crew pulled L 24 into the shed, she broke free, smashing against the entrance and into lighting equipment. The impact ripped open a gas cell and a spark did the rest. The flames that erupted from L 24 quickly spread to L 17. There was nothing anyone could do as fire engulfed both airships in another great inferno, their girders twisting and screeching in the airships' final agonising moments. Strasser had lost four airships in a day – the only redeeming feature being that all four crews survived. But it was a not an end to the year that he could ever have imagined after the success at the beginning of 1916.

In those 12 months, Strasser had lost 16 airships (14 Zeppelins and two Schütte-Lanz). He had also lost nine commanders and their crews: Karl Hempel (L 7 - killed), Joachim Breithaupt (L 15 - captured), Odo Loewe (L 19 - killed), Franz Stabbert (L 20 - interned), Kurt Frankenburg (L 21 - killed), Heinrich Mathy (L 31 - killed), Werner Peterson (L 32 - killed), Alois Böcker (L 33 - captured), Max Dietrich (L 34 - killed). After absconding from internment in Norway, however, Stabbert returned to take command of L 23 on 20 December 1916.

Despite the high cost in men and airships, Strasser remained fully committed to the cause but needed to fight his corner as questions raised at a high level probed the value of continuing the raids in the face of mounting losses. He put his case to Reinhard Scheer, commander of Germany's High Seas Fleet. Scheer recognised the important role Zeppelins played in long-range reconnaissance for the fleet[8] and Strasser managed to convince him of the value continued raiding would bring, but his bullish mood of August, when he claimed that 'airships offer a certain means of victoriously ending the war', had taken on a more pragmatic tone.

> It was not on the direct material damage that the value of the airship attacks depended, but rather on the general result of the German onslaught upon England's insularity, otherwise

undisturbed by war. The disturbance of transportation, the dread of airships prevailing in wide strata of society, and above all the occupation of very considerable material and military personnel were considered outstanding reasons for continuing the attacks.[9]

Scheer and Strasser shared a mutual respect and the commander of the High Seas Fleet later wrote:

> It was our business to make as much use as possible of our superiority in airships, and to increase their efficiency so fear of them might be a contributory cause in inducing England to make peace possible.

> Such an ideal of perfection can only be attained if it is perseveringly sought in spite of the set-backs we endured, and although the opposition we had to overcome was increasingly great.

> That is the right warlike spirit – not to give in, but to redouble one's efforts as our airship men did in an exemplary way.[10]

To Strasser, however, it was starkly clear that if Zeppelins were to continue raiding Britain, a new improved type was needed, one that could reach heights far above those attainable by British aircraft and beyond the range of her guns. Strasser would get his new Zeppelins in 1917 – the 's-class' – as he led them to new heights. By the end of the war, Zeppelin development had progressed through the alphabet to the 'x-class'.

Strasser's claims that the Zeppelin raids had affected vast numbers of the population is undeniable, and there was an impact on industrial output, but the morale of the British nation was never broken nor its production dangerously curtailed by German bombing raids. Throughout the war London remained a prime target, yet reaching that target became increasingly difficult as defences improved. When bombs did drop on London's streets the results could be shocking and costly, even so, critical damage was limited. Yet, even as the bombs fell, the government resisted calls for a public air raid warning system for the capital. There were concerns that great numbers would congregate in the streets to watch if they knew a raid was likely, and that would put those people at greater risk than if they had stayed at home, while their presence would also hinder the efforts of the emergency services. There was also a fear that munitions workers, amongst others, would not return to work once the raid was over. After the raid on London by L 31 and L 33 on 23/24 September, sections of the population had taken matters into their own hands by finding shelter in the Underground stations.

> Many thousands of people flocked to the tube railways without waiting for any warning. Many of them began to take up their places about 5.30pm prepared to camp out until the danger, real or imaginary, was over. They went in family parties and carried with them pillows, bedding, provisions, and household treasures.[11]

When no more raids on the capital materialised in the following days, those people gradually forsook the Underground and resumed their normal night time routines. Away from London, where many towns did have their own warning systems, often alerted by hooters at industrial sites known locally as 'buzzers', many would leave their homes and trek out to seek safety in the surrounding countryside.

The perceived vulnerability of the working population in industrial areas, where production of vital war materials continued throughout the day and night, had an impact on production, in some cases for days after raids had taken place – even in places where no bombs dropped. Areas of iron production that received warning of a potential raid were required to douse blast furnaces. This was costly as it could take eight or nine hours for the furnaces to return to full output. In just one district in the north-east, the Cleveland area, there were 13 weeks in 1916 when Zeppelin warnings sounded. This resulted in a fall in production of pig-iron on average of 30,000 tons per week, or 390,000 tons in total, about 17 per cent of the region's annual production.[12]

At Palmer's Shipbuilding and Iron Company in Jarrow, itself subject to a Zeppelin attack in June 1915, there were three Zeppelin warnings in early April 1916, causing great concern amongst the management.

> In this department, on the alarm signal being received, practically everybody leaves the place. Metal is left in the large furnaces and also in ladles, or in whatever manner the circumstances find it. The whole aspect of these air raids on

a steel works is one of extreme gravity... and it is our opinion
that in the event of a sustained number of such raids, sooner
or later much material harm will be done to the plant.[13]

The raids induced absenteeism amongst the workforce too. On the day
after a raid, it was not unusual for only 10 per cent of the workers to
arrive at the beginning of the morning shift, and although more would
arrive later, about 20 per cent would stay away completely. There was
also a reluctance to work overtime after a raid.[14]

Strasser's claim that his raids caused 'the occupation of very
considerable material and military personnel' is also true. By the end
of 1916 there were 11 Home Defence squadrons, as well as the RNAS
flights, distributed the length of Britain, from the south coast all the way
up to Scotland, as well as a Depot Squadron in Essex. The 11 regular
squadrons should have mustered 222 aircraft, but they were just under
half strength when the year ended. The total strength of those committed
to defence against aerial attack amounted to 17,341 officers and men,
of which 2,200 manned the Home Defence squadrons, 12,000 the anti-
aircraft guns and searchlights, with the remaining 3,100 allocated to
the Observer Companies who reported the raider's progress overland.
While this number is swamped by the vast numbers who served in the
war, these were all specialists and would certainly have proved valuable
assets if deployed at the Front. The numbers, however, were probably far
less than that estimated in Germany.

The outcome of the Zeppelin and aeroplane raids over the night of
27 November and the daylight hours of 28 November, gave a huge boost
to those involved in Home Defence, as well as to the public. The fact that
the defences beyond London were equally as capable of inflicting a killer
blow as those around the capital was something *The Times* newspaper
thought should be applauded.

> The public may legitimately feel satisfaction at the results of the
> Zeppelin raid on England on Monday night. The destruction
> of two German airships – a destruction of the completest
> possible kind for both fell into the sea in flames – at points far
> removed from the London area shows that our anti-aircraft
> measures have not only maintained the effectiveness revealed
> by the bringing down of the previous four since September 3,
> but have largely increased their scope...

Equally satisfactory is the news which reaches us at an early hour this morning. We are familiar with German claims to have dropped bombs on London itself when they have as a matter of fact fallen well outside that extensive target. Yesterday, however, a raid shortly before noon by a single aeroplane did succeed in landing half a dozen bombs in London proper. In this case again the damage was insignificant... Moreover there seems no reasonable ground for doubt that the raider has also paid the penalty...That makes an excellent finish to a thoroughly successful day.[15]

Those concerned with Home Defence approached the final days of 1916 in buoyant mood. Back in February, when the War Office had assumed responsibility for the air defence of Britain, there was much work required to develop an efficient and co-ordinated defence system, but German raiders now appeared over Britain at their peril. There was an undeniable sense of confidence in the air. *The Times* sagely raised a note of caution amidst the wave of enthusiasm that followed these successes at the end of November, particularly in reference to the lone aeroplane that bombed London.

We and our Allies have every reason for congratulations, and we would only add a warning to our own public that, like all fresh portents of the kind, this isolated visit is by no means to be ignored. It may have been largely an act of bravado, or it may have had some definite object of reconnoitring or destruction. In any case it is wise to regard it as the prelude to further visits of the kind on an extensive scale, and to lay our plans accordingly. We have always believed that the method of raiding by aeroplanes, which are relatively cheap and elusive, has far more dangerous possibilities than the large and costly Zeppelin.[16]

The writer had hit the nail on the head, but it appears that those commanding Britain's air defences were not quite so perceptive and did not anticipate Germany's evolving strategy in 1917.

By the end of 1916, despite Strasser's endless optimism, the Zeppelin campaign was all but over. Airships had menaced Britain on 41 nights in 1915 and 1916 but their heyday had passed; they would make only nine more raids in the final two years of the war. In their place Germany was planning to unleash a new terror in the skies over Britain, the *Grosskampfflugzeug*, better known as the Gotha bomber. Instead of raiding furtively under the cover of darkness, it would arrive in swarms in the daylight hours with devastating effect. In time it would spawn a new aerial defence system and even force the Royal Family to change its name. It was a technological and strategic shift that Strasser and his Zeppelins were unable to compete with.

# German Airship Numbering

The identification numbers of German Zeppelins can appear confusing as each airship had two numbers: a manufacturer's number (the sequential number given it by the Zeppelin Company who built them) and a service number, designated by the Navy or the Army. In most cases these two numbers differed, but for a while the Army service number was the same as the manufacturer's number, one of three different systems used by the Army.

## Navy Zeppelins

The Navy system was the simpler of the two services. The Navy named their first Zeppelin L 1 (L = Luftschiff = Airship). As L 1 was the fourteenth airship made by the Zeppelin Company it also had a manufacturer's number: LZ 14 (Luftschiff Zeppelin 14). Throughout this book I have only used service numbers. The Navy continued with this system throughout the war. So the Navy's fifteenth Zeppelin, for example, was L 15, but as it was the forty-eighth airship built by Zeppelin it also had a manufacturer's number of LZ 48. Zeppelin crews only referred to the service number.

## Army Zeppelins

Army numbering was more complex. The Army first used Roman numerals to denote service numbers. The Army designated its first Zeppelin as Z I (Zeppelin I). It was the third Zeppelin built by the Zeppelin Company so had manufacturer's number LZ 3. The Army continued in this way sequentially until Z XII (twelve), then it appears there was an uneasiness about giving the next Zeppelin the number Z XIII (thirteen). Instead, the Army chose to adopt the manufacturer's number as the service number. This meant their next Zeppelins were numbered LZ 34, LZ 35, LZ 37, LZ 38 and LZ 39. The Army did not have LZ 36 as the Zeppelin with this manufacturer's number went to the Navy, becoming L 9.

After taking delivery of LZ 39, the Army changed to a third system. Although still based on the manufacturer's number, the new system added 30 to it. When the Zeppelin Company handed over LZ 42, the Army gave it the service number LZ 72. It seems the idea was an attempt to confuse the Allies as to just how many Zeppelins there were.

## Schütte-Lanz airships

The wooden-framed Schütte-Lanz airships had a sequential numbering system, which served as both a manufacturer's number and service number for both services, with one small change. The first two airships built were numbered using Roman numerals – SL I and SL II. From the third airship, numbering changed to SL 3, SL 4, etc.

## Appendix II

# Airship Raids 1916

| Date | Airships over England | Material Damage (£) | Casualties | |
|---|---|---|---|---|
| | | | Killed | Injured |
| 31 Jan./1 Feb. | L 11, L 13, L 14, L 15, L 16, L 17, L 19, L 20, L 21 | 53,832 | 72 | 113 |
| 5/6 Mar. | L 11, L 13, L 14 | 25,005 | 19 | 52 |
| 31 Mar./1 Apr. | L 13, L 14, L 15, L 16, L 22 | 19,431 | 51 | 64 |
| 1/2 Apr. | L 11, L 17 | 25,568 | 22 | 130 |
| 2/3 Apr. | L 14, L 16, L 22, LZ 88, LZ 90 | 73,113 | 13 | 24 |
| 3/4 Apr. | L 11 | 0 | 0 | 0 |
| 5/6 Apr. | L 11, L 16 | 7,983 | 1 | 9 |
| 24/25 Apr. | L 11, L 13, L 16, L 17, L 21, L 23 | 6,412 | 1 | 1 |
| 25/26 Apr. | LZ 87, LZ 88, LZ 93, LZ 97 | 568 | 0 | 1 |
| 26 Apr. | LZ 93 | 0 | 0 | 0 |
| 2/3 May | L 11, L 13, L 14, L 16, L 17, L 20, L 21, L 23 | 12,030 | 9 | 30 |

| Date | Airships over England | Material Damage (£) | Casualties | |
|---|---|---|---|---|
| | | | Killed | Injured |
| 29 Jul. | L 11, L 13, L 16, L 17, L 24, L 31 | 257 | 0 | 0 |
| 31 Jul./1 Aug. | L 11, L 13, L 14, L 16, L 17, L 22, L 23, L 31 | 139 | 0 | 0 |
| 2/3 Aug. | L 11, L 13, L 16, L 17, L 21, L 31 | 796 | 0 | 1 |
| 9 Aug. | L 11, L 13, L 14, L 16, L 21, L 22, L 24, L 30, L 31 | 13,196 | 11 | 16 |
| 23/24 Aug. | LZ 97 | 3 | 0 | 0 |
| 24/25 Aug. | L 16, L 21, L 31, L 32 | 130,203 | 9 | 40 |
| 2/3 Sep. | L 11, L 13, L 14, L 16, L21, L 22, L 23, L 24, L 30, L 32, SL 8, LZ 90, LZ 98, SL 11 | 21,072 | 4 | 12 |
| 23/24 Sep. | L 13, L 14, L 17, L 21, L 22, L 23, L 31, L 32, L 33 | 135,068 | 40 | 130 |
| 25/26 Sep. | L 14, L 16, L 21, L 22, L 31 | 39,698 | 43 | 31 |
| 1/2 Oct. | L 14, L 16, L17, L 21, L 24, L 31, L 34 | 17,687 | 1 | 1 |
| 27/28 Nov. | L 13, L 14, L 16, L 21, L 22, L 34, L 35 | 12,482 | 4 | 37 |
| | **TOTALS** | 594,543 | 300 | 688 |

## Aeroplane Raids 1916

| Date | Material Damage (£) | Casualties | |
| --- | --- | --- | --- |
| | | Killed | Injured |
| 22/23 January | 1,591 | 1 | 6 |
| 23 January | 0 | 0 | 0 |
| 9 February | 305 | 0 | 3 |
| 20 February | 1,168 | 1 | 1 |
| 1 March | 497 | 1 | 0 |
| 19 March | 3,809 | 14 | 26 |
| 3 May | 720 | 0 | 4 |
| 20 May | 960 | 1 | 2 |
| 9/10 July | 48 | 0 | 0 |
| 12 August | 0 | 0 | 7 |
| 22 September | 5 | 0 | 0 |
| 22 October | 20 | 0 | 0 |
| 23 October | 229 | 0 | 2 |
| 28 November | 1,585 | 0 | 10 |
| **TOTALS** | **10,937** | **18** | **61** |

Appendix III

# Individuals Killed in Air Raids — 1916

O ne of the questions I am most often asked is 'Where can I find a list of those killed in air raids on the Home Front in the First World War?' And there is a simple answer – there isn't one. The government at the time made no attempt to compile a central register and as such those lists that do exist are the fruits of the labours of local historians working on their own town's history, leaving many places with no casualty lists at all. When I started the 'Forgotten Blitz' project I set out to try to correct this, creating for the first time a national list of those who were killed, victims of this first sustained aerial campaign. It has been challenging at times, has involved much detective work and the following up of hunches but, following my list for 1915 published in 'Zeppelin Onslaught', I can now add that covering 1916. Interestingly, although the official totals show 293 killed in Zeppelin raids, I have evidence of 300 deaths. In some cases this is due to people dying of their injuries after the numbers were collated (at least four), while in other cases it demonstrates a lack of consistency in including those whose deaths are attributed to 'shock' suffered during an air raid. Of the 300 deaths I have traced, I have been able to put names to the victims in all but six cases: a child in Wednesbury, two women in Sunderland, two men in NE London and a woman in West Hartlepool. If anyone can help fill in the blanks I would love to hear. www.IanCastleZeppelin.co.uk

## Deaths during Zeppelin Raids

| Date | Name | Age | Place |
| --- | --- | --- | --- |
| 31 January/<br>1 February | Maud Fellows | 24 | Bradley |
| | William Fellows | 23 | Bradley |
| | Margaret Anderson | 60 | Burton |
| | Ada Brittain | 15 | Burton |
| | John Lees Finney | 53 | Burton |
| | Bertie Geary | 13 | Burton |
| | Charles Gilson | 52 | Burton |
| | Edith Measham | 10 | Burton |
| | Mary Rose Morris | 55 | Burton |
| | Lucy Simnett | 15 | Burton |
| | Elizabeth Smith | 45 | Burton |
| | George Stephens | 16 | Burton |
| | Rachel Wait | 78 | Burton |
| | Flora L. Warden | 16 | Burton |
| | George Warrington | 6 | Burton |
| | Mary Warrington | 11 | Burton |
| | Florence Jane Wilson | 23 | Burton |
| | Sidney Baines | 21 | Derby |
| | William Bancroft | 32 | Derby |
| | Sarah Constantine | 71 | Derby |
| | James Gibbs Hardy | 55 | Derby |
| | Harry Hithersay | 23 | Derby |
| | James Hall | 56 | Ilkeston |
| | Walter Wilson | 41 | Ilkeston |
| | Annie Adcock | 42 | Loughborough |
| | Annie Elizabeth Adkin | 29 | Loughborough |
| | Joseph Williamson Adkin | 27 | Loughborough |
| | Ethel Alice Higgs | 25 | Loughborough |
| | Josiah Gilbert | 49 | Loughborough |

| Date | Name | Age | Place |
|------|------|-----|-------|
| | Elsie Page | 16 | Loughborough |
| | Joseph Page | 18 | Loughborough |
| | Mary Anne Page | 44 | Loughborough |
| | Martha Shipman | 49 | Loughborough |
| | Arthur Christian Turnill | 50 | Loughborough |
| | Ernest Wilkinson Benson | 31 | Scunthorpe |
| | Thomas William Danson | 29 | Scunthorpe |
| | Cyril Jack Wright | 24 | Scunthorpe |
| | Elizabeth Cartwright | 35 | Tipton |
| | Thomas Henry Church | 57 | Tipton |
| | Arthur Edwards | 26 | Tipton |
| | Mary Greensill | 67 | Tipton |
| | William Greensill | 64 | Tipton |
| | Benjamin Goldie | 43 | Tipton |
| | Martin Morris | 11 | Tipton |
| | Nellie Morris | 8 | Tipton |
| | Sarah Jane Morris | 44 | Tipton |
| | George Henry Onions | 12 | Tipton |
| | Daniel Whitehouse | 34 | Tipton |
| | Anne Wilkinson | 44 | Tipton |
| | Frederick N. Yates | 9 | Tipton |
| | Louisa Yorke | 30 | Tipton |
| | Charles Cope | 34 | Walsall |
| | William Henry Haycock | 50 | Walsall |
| | Frank Thompson Linney | 36 | Walsall |
| | Thomas Merrylees | 28 | Walsall |
| | John Thomas Powell | 59 | Walsall |
| | Mary Julia Slater | 55 | Walsall |
| | Matilda May Birt | 10 | Wednesbury |
| | Mary Emma Evans | 57 | Wednesbury |
| | Rachel Higgs | 36 | Wednesbury |

| Date | Name | Age | Place |
|------|------|-----|-------|
| | Susan Howells | 50 | Wednesbury |
| | Mary Ann Lee | 59 | Wednesbury |
| | Albert Gordon Madeley | 21 | Wednesbury |
| | Betsy Shilton | 39 | Wednesbury |
| | Edward Shilton | 33 | Wednesbury |
| | Ina Smith | 7 | Wednesbury |
| | Joseph Horton Smith | 37 | Wednesbury |
| | Nellie Smith | 13 | Wednesbury |
| | Thomas Horton Smith | 11 | Wednesbury |
| | Rebecca Sutton | 51 | Wednesbury |
| | Samuel Arthur Whitehouse | 16 | Wednesbury |
| | Unknown child | ? | Wednesbury |
| 5/6 March | Frank Cattle | 8 | Hull |
| | James William Collinson | 63 | Hull |
| | Edward Cook | 38 | Hull |
| | Ethel M. Ingamells | 33 | Hull |
| | Martha R. Ingamells | 35 | Hull |
| | Mira Lottie Ingamells | 28 | Hull |
| | Edward Ledner | 89 | Hull |
| | John Longstaff | 71 | Hull |
| | William Jones | 80 | Hull |
| | Annie Naylor | 6 | Hull |
| | Charlotte Naylor | 36 | Hull |
| | Edward Naylor | 4 | Hull |
| | Jeffrey Naylor | 2 | Hull |
| | Ruby Naylor | 8 | Hull |
| | James Pattison | 68 | Hull |
| | Edward Slip | 45 | Hull |
| | John Smith | 30 | Hull |
| | George Henry Youell | 40 | Hull |
| | James Beswick | 39 | Killingholme |

| Date | Name | Age | Place |
|---|---|---|---|
| 31 March/ 1 April | Alfred Dennington | 31 | Braintree |
| | Annie Dennington | 32 | Braintree |
| | Ella M. Hammond | 3 | Braintree |
| | Ann Herbert | 70 | Braintree |
| | George K. Adams | 15 | Bury St Edmonds |
| | Henry Adams | 60 | Bury St Edmonds |
| | Annie E. Dureall | 29 | Bury St Edmonds |
| | James I. Dureall | 5 | Bury St Edmonds |
| | Kathleen Dureall | 3 | Bury St Edmonds |
| | Harry Frost | 44 | Bury St Edmonds |
| | *4/1st Battalion, Cambridgeshire Regiment* | | |
| | Pte. Hubert Hardiment | 19 | Bury St Edmonds |
| | *3rd (Reserve) Battalion, Manchester Regiment* | | |
| | Pte. Wilfred Ernest Ball | 30 | Cleethorpes |
| | Pte. Joseph Beardsley | 30 | Cleethorpes |
| | Pte. Louis A Beaumont | 34 | Cleethorpes |
| | Pte. Samuel Bell | 28 | Cleethorpes |
| | Pte. William Bodsworth | 23 | Cleethorpes |
| | Pte. Thomas Brierley | 24 | Cleethorpes |
| | Pte. W H Brown | 19 | Cleethorpes |
| | Pte. Ernest Budding | 19 | Cleethorpes |
| | Pte. F Chandler | 19 | Cleethorpes |
| | Pte. Joseph Chandler | 19 | Cleethorpes |
| | Pte. Job Clowes | 19 | Cleethorpes |
| | Pte. John H. Corfield | 19 | Cleethorpes |
| | Pte. Harry Cuthbert | 34 | Cleethorpes |
| | Pte. Frederick Dimelow | 20 | Cleethorpes |
| | Pte. Thomas Diviney | 37 | Cleethorpes |
| | Pte. Albert E. Downs | 20 | Cleethorpes |

| Date | Name | Age | Place |
|------|------|-----|-------|
| | Pte. Robert Fox | 18 | Cleethorpes |
| | Pte. William Francis | 19 | Cleethorpes |
| | Pte. Thomas Hannon | 30 | Cleethorpes |
| | Pte. Percy Harrison | 21 | Cleethorpes |
| | L/cpl Alfred Haynes | 20 | Cleethorpes |
| | Pte. W. Hetherington | 20 | Cleethorpes |
| | Pte. Tom Pierce | 35 | Cleethorpes |
| | Pte. J Radford | 19 | Cleethorpes |
| | Pte. Henry Ramsden | 23 | Cleethorpes |
| | Pte. James Russell | 21 | Cleethorpes |
| | Pte. Thomas Stott | 18 | Cleethorpes |
| | L/cpl Jack Swift | 23 | Cleethorpes |
| | Pte. Thomas Tomkinson | 18 | Cleethorpes |
| | Pte. John Wheeler | 19 | Cleethorpes |
| | Pte. William Wild | 34 | Cleethorpes |
| | Pte. Robert Wood | 32 | Cleethorpes |
| | David Bishop Cattermole | 57 | Ipswich |
| | Jane Hopestill Hoff | 75 | Ipswich |
| | Ester Louisa Olding | 64 | Ipswich |
| | Ellen Ambrose | 37 | Sudbury |
| | Thomas Ambrose | 50 | Sudbury |
| | John Edward Smith | 50 | Sudbury |
| | Ellen Wheeler | 64 | Sudbury |
| | *2/6th (City of London) Battalion (Rifles)* | | |
| | Rfn. Frederick Robert Wilson | 42 | Sudbury |
| 1/2 April | Herbert Archibald Chater | 47 | Sunderland |
| | Thomas Shepherd Dale | 55 | Sunderland |
| | Henry Dean | 28 | Sunderland |

| Date | Name | Age | Place |
|------|------|-----|-------|
| | Alfred Wood Dunlop | 17 | Sunderland |
| | Alfred Finkle | 39 | Sunderland |
| | Robert Garbutt Fletcher | 68 | Sunderland |
| | John Glasgow | 17 | Sunderland |
| | Florence May Johnson | 17 | Sunderland |
| | Ernest Liddle Johnstone | 31 | Sunderland |
| | Hannah Lydon | 33 | Sunderland |
| | John Thomas Lydon | 14 | Sunderland |
| | Gertrude Patrick | 19 | Sunderland |
| | Henry Patrick | 16 | Sunderland |
| | Elizabeth Ann Ranson | 5 | Sunderland |
| | George Holmes Rogerson | 53 | Sunderland |
| | Thomas Rogerson | 55 | Sunderland |
| | Elizabeth Jane Thirkell | 16 | Sunderland |
| | Joseph Thompson | 46 | Sunderland |
| | Elizabeth Weldon | 67 | Sunderland |
| | John Joseph Woodward | 35 | Sunderland |
| | Unknown woman | ? | Sunderland |
| | Unknown woman | ? | Sunderland |
| 2/3 April | Cora Edmond Bell | 4 | Edinburgh |
| | William Breakey | 45 | Edinburgh |
| | William Ewing | 23 | Edinburgh |
| | James Farquhar | 74 | Edinburgh |
| | David Thomas Graham | 5 | Edinburgh |
| | Victor McFarlane | ? | Edinburgh |
| | Henry George Ramble | 17 | Edinburgh |
| | David Robertson | 27 | Edinburgh |
| | John Smith | 41 | Edinburgh |
| | William Smith | 15 | Edinburgh |

| Date | Name | Age | Place |
|------|------|-----|-------|
| | *3/4ᵗʰ Battalion, Royal Scots* | | |
| | Pte Thomas Donoghue | ? | Edinburgh |
| | Robert Love | 66 | Leith |
| | David Robb | 1 | Leith |
| 5/6 April | Robert Moyle | 9 | Close House, Co. Durham |
| 24/25 April | Fanny Gaze | 79 | Dilham, Norfolk |
| 2/3 May | George Avison | 70 | York |
| | Sarah Avison | 69 | York |
| | Emily Chapman | 28 | York |
| | William Chappelow | 49 | York |
| | Ernest Coultish | 27 | York |
| | Benjamin Sharpe | 20 | York |
| | Susan Waudby | 65 | York |
| | *3/1ˢᵗ East Riding Yeomanry* | | |
| | Pte. Leslie Hinson | 18 | York |
| | *1ˢᵗ Div. Ammunition Column, Royal Field Artillery* | | |
| | Sgt. Edward Gordon Beckett | 29 | York |
| 8/9 August | Emmie Bearpark | 14 | Hull |
| | Mary Louisa Bearpark | 44 | Hull |
| | Elisabeth Jane Bond | 76 | Hull |
| | John Charles Broadley | 3 | Hull |
| | Emma Louise Evers | 46 | Hull |
| | Elizabeth Hall | 9 | Hull |
| | Mary Hall | 7 | Hull |
| | Rose Alma Hall | 31 | Hull |

| Date | Name | Age | Place |
| --- | --- | --- | --- |
| | Charles Lingard | 64 | Hull |
| | Esther Stobbart | 21 | Hull |
| | Revd. Arthur Wilcockson | 86 | Hull |
| 24/25 August | Annie Allen | 38 | SE London |
| | Frederick Thomas Allen | 40 | SE London |
| | Gladys Allen | 10 | SE London |
| | Ellen Rosina Pearce | 34 | SE London |
| | Elsie Pearce | 2 | SE London |
| | Walter George Turnball Pearce | 40 | SE London |
| | Annie Funnell | 29 | SE London |
| | Richard Turner | 31 | SE London |
| | Elizabeth Emma Vane | 70 | SE London |
| 2/3 September | Violet Ellen Dungar | 36 | Dersingham, Norfolk |
| | Eleanor Bamford | 12 | Essendon, Herts. |
| | Frances Bamford | 26 | Essendon, Herts. |
| | Horace Oughton | 17 | Boston, Lincs. |
| 23/24 September | Sylvia Adams | 20 | E London |
| | Sylvia Adams | 1 | E London |
| | Blanche Bradford | 22 | E London |
| | Henry Brown | 53 | E London |
| | Harriett Drewett | 57 | E London |
| | Michael Harris | 20 | E London |
| | George Jones | 41 | E London |
| | Mary Lunnis | 71 | E London |
| | Mary Ann Potter | 63 | E London |

| Date | Name | Age | Place |
|------|------|-----|-------|
| | Queenie Grace Reynolds | 19 | E London |
| | Henry Taylor | 4 | E London |
| | Charles Rogers | 50 | NE London |
| | George Sexton | 52 | NE London |
| | Virginia Sexton | 50 | NE London |
| | Henry Stoneham | 47 | NE London |
| | Henry Stoneham | 13 | NE London |
| | William Webb | 25 | NE London |
| | Unknown man | ? | NE London |
| | Unknown man | ? | NE London |
| | Walter Archer | 67 | S London |
| | Henry Edward Bloomfield | 55 | S London |
| | Charles Boys | 38 | S London |
| | Mary Chadwick | 74 | S London |
| | John Gayner | 45 | S London |
| | Betty Hobbs | ? | S London |
| | Florence Annie Hogg | 38 | S London |
| | Gaston Leonard | 32 | S London |
| | William Lorimer | 5 | S London |
| | Roger William Curtis Shaw | 23 | S London |
| | Elijah Wade | 53 | S London |
| | Alfred Ward | 50 | S London |
| | Grace Ward | 21 | S London |
| | William Wood | 48 | S London |
| | Alfred Fletcher (AA shell) | 58 | N London |
| | Frederick William Monk (AA shell) | 22 | E London |
| | Edward Patrick O'Brien (AA shell) | 43 | E London |

| Date | Name | Age | Place |
|------|------|-----|-------|
| | *10th Anti-Aircraft Coy.,*<br>*Royal Garrison Artillery* | | |
| |    Gnr John McDougall | 35 | SE London |
| | Harold Renshaw | 21 | Nottingham |
| | Alfred Rogers | 44 | Nottingham |
| | Rosanna Rogers | 43 | Nottingham |
| 25/26 September | Ellen Allison | 32 | Bolton |
| | James Allison | 34 | Bolton |
| | David Davies | 39 | Bolton |
| | Elizabeth Gregory | 42 | Bolton |
| | Ellen Gregory | 17 | Bolton |
| | Frederick James Guildford | 62 | Bolton |
| | Bridget Ellen Irwin | 44 | Bolton |
| | Margaret Ellen Irwin | 2 | Bolton |
| | Ann McDermott | 36 | Bolton |
| | Mary Ellen McDermott | 5 | Bolton |
| | William McDermott | 42 | Bolton |
| | Martha O'Hara | 41 | Bolton |
| | Michael O'Hara | 42 | Bolton |
| | Elizabeth Bellamy | 57 | Sheffield |
| | Richard Brewington | 11 | Sheffield |
| | Ann Coogan | 76 | Sheffield |
| | William Guest | 32 | Sheffield |
| | Beatrice Hames | 22 | Sheffield |
| | Horace William Hames | 1 | Sheffield |
| | Levi Hames | 23 | Sheffield |
| | Eliza Harrison | 48 | Sheffield |
| | George Harrison | 59 | Sheffield |

| Date | Name | Age | Place |
|------|------|-----|-------|
| | Vera Harrison | 12 | Sheffield |
| | George Ineson | 28 | Sheffield |
| | Albert Newton | 28 | Sheffield |
| | Alice Newton | 27 | Sheffield |
| | Elsie Rhodes | 4 | Sheffield |
| | Nellie Rhodes | 28 | Sheffield |
| | Phyllis Rhodes | 6 | Sheffield |
| | Martha Shakespeare | 36 | Sheffield |
| | Sarah Southerington | 47 | Sheffield |
| | William Southerington | 37 | Sheffield |
| | Frederick Stratford | 49 | Sheffield |
| | Margaret Taylor | 59 | Sheffield |
| | Albert Tyler | 8 | Sheffield |
| | Amelia Tyler | 5 | Sheffield |
| | Ernest Tyler | 11 | Sheffield |
| | John Tyler | 2 | Sheffield |
| | Joseph Henry Tyler | 45 | Sheffield |
| | Joseph Henry Tyler | 14 | Sheffield |
| | Selina Tyler | 41 | Sheffield |
| | Thomas Wilson | 59 | Sheffield |
| | Elizabeth Cranshaw | 70 | Tottington, Lancs. |
| 1/2 October | *No. 56 Protection Coy., Royal Defence Corps* | | |
| | Pte. William Hawkes | 49 | Willian, Herts. |
| 27/28 November | George Linton | 40 | W. Hartlepool |
| | Mary Ann Pritchard | 33 | W. Hartlepool |
| | Elizabeth Rumble | 54 | W. Hartlepool |
| | Unknown woman | ? | W. Hartlepool |

## Deaths during Aeroplane Raids

| Date | Name | Age | Place |
|------|------|-----|-------|
| 22/23 January | Harry Sladden | 43 | Dover |
| 20 February | George Castle | 16 | Walmer |
| 1 March | Jack Dodman | 9 months | Margate |
| 19 March | Francis A. Hall | 7 | Dover |
| | Jane James | 47 | Dover |
| | Edith M. Stoker | 23 | Dover |
| | *5th (Reserve) Battalion, Royal Fusiliers* | | |
| | Corp. Daniel H. Dolphin | 41 | Dover |
| | Pte. Alfred Greig | 30 | Dover |
| | Pte. Frank M. Roseberry | 18 | Dover |
| | Pte. Walter Venables | ? | Dover |
| | Gertrude M. Bishop | 23 | Ramsgate |
| | Harry H. Divers | 49 | Ramsgate |
| | Herbert Gibbons | 9 | Ramsgate |
| | Frank Hardwick | 7 | Ramsgate |
| | Ernest Robert Philpott | 12 | Ramsgate |
| | Gladys Saxby | 6 | Ramsgate |
| | James Saxby | 4 | Ramsgate |
| 19/20 May | *3rd (Reserve) Battalion, East Surrey Regiment* | | |
| | Pte. Henry Frederick Sole | 34 | Dover |

# Bibliography

Ashmore, Maj Gen E.B.: *Air Defence*, (London 1929)

Austen, Chas, A.F.: *Ramsgate Raid Records 1915-1918*, (originally published around 1919, reprint Ramsgate 2006)

Beesly, Patrick, *Room 40 - British Naval Intelligence 1914-18*, (London 1982)

Bennett, J.E.: *The Potters Bar Zeppelin*, (Potters Bar 1989)

Bostle, Eileen: *Enfield's Night to Remember - The Airship Raid of 2nd/3rd September 1916*, (Enfield 2014)

Bott, Ian M., *The Midlands Zeppelin Outrage,* (Privately published 2015)

Brown, John W., *Zeppelins Over Streatham,* (Streatham 1996)

Buttlar-Brandenfels, Freiherr Treusch von: *Zeppelins Over England,* (London 1931)

Carter-Clavell, Scott, *The First Air Raid on Lancashire - The Zeppelin Menace,* (Stroud 2016)

Castle, H.G.: *Fire Over England – The German Air Raids in World War 1,* (London 1982)

Castle, Ian: *The First Blitz – Bombing London in the First World War,* (Oxford 2015)

Castle, Ian: *The First Blitz in 100 Objects,* (Barnsley 2019)

Castle, Ian: *Zeppelin Onslaught - The Forgotten Blitz 1914-1915,* (Barnsley 2018)

Charlton, L.E.O.: *War Over England,* (London 1936)

Cole, Christopher, & Cheesman, E.F.: *The Air Defence of Britain 1914-1918,* (London 1984)

Coxon, Stanley W., *Dover During the Dark Days,* (London 1919)

Credland, Arthur G.: *The Hull Zeppelin Raids 1915-1918,* (Stroud 2014)

Dover Express: *Dover and the European War 1914-18,* (Dover 1919)

Easdown, Martin, with Genth, Thomas: *A Glint in the Sky,* (Barnsley 2004)

Fegan, Thomas: *The 'Baby Killers' – German Air Raids on Britain in the First World War*, (Barnsley 2002)

Gerhardt, Frederik C., *London 1916*, (Paderborn 2019)

Grayzel, Susan R.: *At Home and Under Fire – Air Raids and Culture in Britain from the Great War to the Blitz*, (Cambridge 2012)

Green, Bernard A.N., *Zeppelin L15 & The Wakefield Medal*, (Privately published, 2018)

Griel, Manfred, & Dressel, Joachim: *Zeppelin! The German Airship Story*, (London 1990)

Hackwood, Frederick, *The History of Wednesbury* (Wednesbury 1920)

Hall, Ian: *Zeppelins Over the North East*, (Alnwick 2014)

Hoeppner, General Ernest von, *Germany's War in the Air*, (English translation, Nashvlle 1994)

Hook, John, *Warriors for the Working Week*, (Privately published, London, 1994)

Jenkins, Gareth: *Zeppelins Over Bury*, (Revised edition, Needham Market 2016)

Jones, H.A.: *The War in the Air – Being the Story of the part played in the Great War by the Royal Air Force*, Vol. III, (Oxford 1931)

Kirk, P., Felix. P., and Bartnik, G.: *The Bombing of Rolls-Royce at Derby*, (Derby 2002)

Klein, Pitt (trans. Reid, Alastair): *Bombs Away! Zeppelins at War*, (Privately Printed 2016). Originally published as *Achtung! Bomben fallen!*, (Leipzig 1934)

Kollman, Franz: *Das Zeppelinluftschiff – seine Entwicklung, Tätigkeit und Leistungen*, (Berlin 1924)

Lehmann, Ernst: *Zeppelin - The story of lighter-than-air craft*, (1937 - reprinted 2015)

Lehmann, Capt. E.A., & Mingos, H.: *The Zeppelins*, (London 1927)

Long, David, *Night of the Zeppelin - The German airship raid on Loughborough*, (Privately published)

MacDonagh, Michael: *In London During the Great War – The Diary of a Journalist*, (London 1935)

Marben, Rolf: *Zeppelin Adventures*, (London 1931)

Marks, David: *Let The Zeppelins Come*, (Stroud 2017)

Marks, David: *The Zeppelin Offensive — A German perspective in Pictures & Postcards*, (Barnsley 2019)

Miles, Hallie Eustace, *Untold Tales of War-time London*, (London 1930)

Morison, Frank: *War on Great Cities – A Study of the Facts*, (London 1937)

Morris, Joseph: *German Air Raids on Britain 1914-1918*, (orig, 1925. Reprinted Dallington 1993)

Munsun, J. (ed.), *Echoes of the Great War - The Diary of the Reverend Andrew Clark, 1914-1919*, (Oxford 1985)

Neumann, Major Georg Paul (trans. Gurdon, J.E.): *The German Air Force in the Great War*, (originally published 1921, reprinted Bath 1969)

Oak-Rhind, Edwin Scoby: *The North Foreland Lookout Post in the Great War 1915-1917*, (Ramsgate 2005)

Poolman, Kenneth: *Zeppelins Over England*, (London 1960)

Powis, Mick: *Zeppelins Over the Midlands*, (Barnsley 2016)

Rawlinson, A.: *The Defence of London 1915-1918*, (London 1923)

Reay, Colonel W.T.: *The Specials - How They Served London*, (London 1920)

Rimell, Raymond L.: *Zeppelin! A Battle for Air Supremacy in World War I*, (London 1984)

Rimell, Raymond L.: *The Airship VC*, (Bourne End 1989)

Rimell, R.L.: *The Last Flight of the L31*, (Berkhamsted 2016)

Rimell, R.L.: *The Last Flight of the L32*, (Berkhamsted 2016)

Rimell, R.L.: *Zeppelins at War 1914-1915*, (Berkhamsted 2014)

Rimell, R.L.: *Zeppelin*, Vol. 1, (Berkhamsted 2006)

Robinson, Douglas H.: *The Zeppelin In Combat – A History of the German Naval Airship Division, 1912-1918*, (Atglen, PA 1994)

Scheer, Admiral Reinhardt: *Germany's High Sea Fleet in the World War*, (English translation, London 1920)

Scott, Admiral Sir Percy: *Fifty Years in the Royal Navy*, (London 1919)

Simpson, Alan: *Air Raids on South-West Essex in the Great War*, (Barnsley 2015)

Smith, Peter J.C.: *Zeppelins Over Lancashire*, (Radcliffe 1991)

Smith, Richard C., *Hornchurch's Air Heroes of the First World War*, (Rainham 2014)

Snowden Gamble, C.F.: *The Story of a North Sea Air Station*, (Original 1928, Reprint, London 1967)

Strahlmann, Dr. Fritz (Ed.): *Zwei deutsche Luftschiffhäfen des Weltkrieges, Ahlhorn und Wildeshausen*, 1926 (English translation by Alex Reid retitled, *Memories of Ahlhorn*, (privately published 2016)

Stuart, Denis: *History of Burton upon Trent, Part II, 1914-74*, (Hanley 1977)

Sutton, Sqn Ldr H.T.: *Raiders Approach*, (Aldershot 1956)

Thanet Advertiser: *Thanet's Raid History*, (Ramsgate 1919, reprinted Ramsgate 2006)

Van Emden, Richard, and Humphries, Steve: *All Quiet on the Home Front - An Oral History of Life in Britain during the First World War*, (London 2003)

## Magazines and Journals

Author unknown: *The Hornets of Zeebrugge,* In *Cross & Cockade Journal,* Vol. 11, No. 1, Spring 1970

Breithaupt, Kapitänleutnant: *How We Bombed London.* In *The Living Age,* Vol. 334, No. 4322, 15 Jan. 1928

Fergus, David: *The Zepps are Coming,* in *The Scots Magazine,* Vol.132, No.5, Feb 1990

Ferris, John: *Airbandit: C3I and Strategic Air Defence During the First Battle of Britain 1915-1918.* In Dockrill M. and French D, (Ed.), Strategy and Intelligence; British Policy During the First World War, London 1996

Logan, David Dale, *Detonation of High Explosive in Shell and Bomb and its Effects.* In Horner, N.G. (Ed.), articles from British Medical Journal republished as: *War Wounds and Air Raid Casualties,* (London 1939)

Ovenall, J.C.: Letter. In *Essex Countryside,* Volume 18, Number 165, October 1970

Suddaby, Steven C.: *Buzzer Nights: Zeppelin Raids on Hull.* In *Over the Front - Journal of the League of WW1 Aviation Historians,* Vol. 12, No. 2, Summer 1997

Tempest, Major W.J.: *How I Shot Down L.31.* In Hammerton, Sir John (ed.): *The Great War... I Was There! – Undying memories of 1914-1918,* Part 22, (London 1939)

Weddell, Col. J.M.: *The Treatment of Wounds in War.* In Horner, N.G. (ed.), *op. cit.*

## Archival Sources

### The National Archives (TNA), Kew, London

AIR 1     Air Ministry: Air Historical Branch: Papers (Series 1)

WO 158     War Office: Military Headquarters: Correspondence and Papers, First World War

MEPO 2     Metropolitan Police: Office of the Commissioner: Correspondence and Papers

### Essex Archives, Chelmsford, Essex

J/P 12/7     Telegrams, Reports, Statements, and Correspondence Concerned with Zeppelin Raids on Essex.

### The Times Digital Archive (TDA) - Online
### The British Newspaper Archive (BNA) - Online

# Notes

## Chapter 1: Frightfulness

1. Miles, Hallie Eustace, *Untold Tales of War-Time London*, pp.58-59
2. *Ibid*, pp.64-65
3. *Ibid*, pp.76-77
4. Weddell, Col. J.M., *The Treatment of Wounds in War*, p.2
5. Logan, David Dale, *Detonation of High Explosive in Shell and Bomb and its Effects*, pp.230-231
6. The words 'Frightfulness' and *'Schrecklichkeit'* were both used in Britain in reference to the perceived German tendency towards brutal acts of war.
7. Times Digital Archive (TNA): *The Times*, 18 January 1916, p.9
8. TNA: *Ibid*, 19 January 1916, p.9
9. TNA: *Ibid*
10. Account of the Dover raid based on those given in TNA: WO 158/975 and AIR 1/573/16/15/154, and *Dover and the European War 1914-18*
11. Coxon, Stanley W.: *Dover During the Dark Days*, p.125
12. *Ibid*, pp.122-123
13. Miles: *op. cit.*, pp.88-89
14. *Ibid*, pp.90-91

## Chapter 2: 'Attack England Middle or South, if at all possible Liverpool'

1. Robinson, *The Zeppelin in Combat*, p. 141
2. 'H.V.B.' was a radio signal (abbreviation of *Handelsschiffsverkehrsbuch* - a codebook officially used for communications between German Navy ships and merchant vessels). It denoted that the Zeppelin was carrying only this already compromised codebook, and none that were unknown to the Allies. For more see Castle, Ian: *Zeppelin Onslaught - The Forgotten Blitz 1914-1915*, pp.89-90

3. Robinson, *op. cit.*, p.143

4. Jones, H.A.: *The War in the Air*, Vol. III, p.136

5. Robinson, *op. cit.*, p.144

6. British Newspaper Archive (BNA): *Evening Despatch*, 3 February, p.4

7. TNA: AIR1/573/16/15/156.

8. *Ibid*

9. The original report on the raid (TNA:WO158/938) admits to struggling to reconcile the movements of individual Zeppelins, while a later historian, H.A.Jones, noted that there was a possibility they could have been dropped by L 16 (Jones: *op. cit.*, p.143). Later Robinson (*op. cit.*, p.144) refers to Peterson's report in which he claimed he dropped all L 16's bombs on Great Yarmouth. It seems likely therefore that the concentration of bombs dropped in the Fens were those released by Peterson from L 16.

10. Robinson, *op. cit.*, p.139

11. *Ibid*, p.142

12. BNA: *Staffordshire Advertiser*, 5 February 1916, p.10

13. BNA: *Midland Daily Telegraph*, 3 February 1916, p.3

14. BNA: *Birmingham Gazette*, 4 February 1916, p.1

15. Information from Ian Holmes, from letter written by his grandmother on 1 Feb 1916.

16. Hackwood, Frederick, *The History of Wednesbury*, pp.119-120

17. *Ibid*, p.119

18. TNA: AIR1/573/16/15/156

19. BNA: *Birmingham Gazette*, 4 February 1916, p.3. Samuel Whitehouse is one of the forgotten victims of the raid on Wednesbury. After some detective work I found him while researching this chapter. His death certificate confirms he suffered fatal burns during the raid at the Crown Tube Works.

20. BNA: *Ibid*

21. Albert Madeley is often listed as one of those killed in King Street but his Death Certificate states he sustained his fatal injuries in Oldbury Street.

22. BNA: *Walsall Observer and South Staffordshire Chronicle*, 28 December 1918, p.2

23. https://www.expressandstar.com/news/great-war/2014/07/31/horror-of-zeppelin-bombings/ accessed 20 Feb. 2019

24. http://www.historywebsite.co.uk/articles/Walsall1/memories.htm accessed 20 Feb. 2019

25. BNA: *Walsall Observer and South Staffordshire Chronicle*, 28 December 1918, p.2

26. https://www.expressandstar.com/news/great-war/2014/07/31/horror-of-zeppelin-bombings/ accessed 20 Feb. 2019

27. BNA: *Birmingham Gazette*, 5 February 1916, p.3

28. http://www.historywebsite.co.uk/articles/Zeppelins/zeppelins.htm accessed 20 February 2019

29. BNA: *Walsall Observer and South Staffordshire Chronicle*, 26 February 1916 and *Wolverhampton Chronicle*, 23 February 1916

30. BNA: *Northampton Mercury*, 13 February 1920, p.8
31. Robinson: *op. cit.*, p.143
32. *Derby Daily Telegraph*, 3 Feb. 1916
33. BNA: *Lincolnshire Echo*, 3 Feb. 1916, p.2
34. *Derby Daily Telegraph*, 3 Feb. 1916
35. Powis, Mick, *Zeppelins Over the Midlands*, pp.70-71
36. Scunthorpe and Lindsey United were the forerunners of Scunthorpe United Football Club
37. BNA: *Lincolnshire Echo*, 3 Feb. 1916, p.2
38. *Ibid*
39. Information supplied by Nigel Wood who interviewed Thomas Charity in the late 1990s
40. *Derby Daily Telegraph*, 20 December 1918
41. Kirk, P., Felix. P., and Bartnik, G., *The Bombing of Rolls-Royce at Derby*, p.36
42. TNA: AIR2/18/MA/Misc/351 - Report on Zeppelin Raid on Midlands (Derby & Burton-on-Trent)
43. *Ibid*
44. Litchurch Villa is now the Rolls-Royce Foremans' Club and the garden where the bomb exploded is the Club's bowling green.
45. *Derby Daily Telegraph*, 20 December 1918
46. TNA: AIR2/18/MA/Misc/351 - Report on Zeppelin Raid on Midlands (Derby & Burton-on-Trent)
47. *Derby Daily Telegraph*, 5 February 1916 and 20 December 1918
48. TNA: AIR2/18/MA/Misc/351
49. *Derby Daily Telegraph*, 20 December 1918
50. Recent writers name this fourth victim as Charles Henry Chapman. This is incorrect. Chapman's death, at home, was unconnected to the air raid. A report in the *Derby Daily Telegraph*, 20 December 1918, and Baines' Death Certificate confirm he was the fourth victim.
51. TNA: AIR2/18/MA/Misc/351

## Chapter 3: Gott strafe England

1. 'May God Punish England'
2. It was the second Crown and Cushion public house damaged by bombs that night, the other being in Wednesbury.
3. *Loughborough & North Leicestershire Gazette*, 30 January 1919 - quoted in: Long, David, *Night of the Zeppelin*, p.28
4. *Ibid*, p.34
5. *Ibid.*, pp.39-40
6. *Ibid*, p.44
7. *Ibid*, p.69

8. The bombs in The Rushes and Empress Road are commemorated by small granite squares set into the roadway where they exploded. They are still there. See, Castle, *The First Blitz in 100 Objects*, pp.99-101
9. BNA: *The Loughborough Echo*, 11 February 1916, p.5
10. BNA: *Nottingham Daily Express*, 7 February 1916, p.6
11. TNA: *Derby Daily Telegraph*, 4 February 1916, p.4
12. TNA: *Ibid*, 5 February 1916, p.2
13. Stuart, Denis: *History of Burton Upon Trent*, p.20
14. As shown in Chapter 2, the bombs in the fens are now attributed to L 16.
15. Robinson, *op. cit.*, p.145
16. Stuart: *op. cit.*, p.21
17. TNA: AIR2/18/MA/Misc/351
18. BNA: *Staffordshire Advertiser*, 26 February 1916, p.10 and *Lichfield Mercury*, 4 February 1916, p.5
19. BNA: *Lichfield Mercury*, 4 February 1916, p.5
20. BNA: *Staffordshire Advertiser*, 26 February 1916, p.10
21. Stuart: *op. cit.*, p.19
22. BNA: *Staffordshire Advertiser*, 26 February 1916, p.10, and Stuart: op. cit., p.18
23. BNA: *Ibid*, and *Lichfield Mercury*, 4 February 1916, p.5
24. Stuart: *op. cit.*, pp.20-21
25. Robinson: *op.cit.*, p.145
26. Bott, Ian M.: *The Midlands Zeppelin Outrage*, p.56
27. TNA: AIR1/573/16/15/156
28. Information from Ian Holmes, from a letter written by his grandmother on 1 Feb. 1916.
29. BNA: *Lichfield Mercury*, 4 February 1916, p.5 and Bott: *Ibid*, p.66
30. BNA: *Walsall Observer and South Staffordshire Chronicle*, 28 December 1918, Bott: *op.cit.*, p.68, Powis, Mick: *Zeppelins Over the Midlands*, p.28
31. BNA: *Birmingham Gazette*, 3 February 1916, p.5
32. BNA: as reported in *Walsall Observer and South Staffordshire Chronicle*, 12 February 1916, p.3
33. Cole, C. & Cheesman, E.F., *The Air Defence of Britain 1914-1918*, p.85
34. Snowden Gamble, C.F., *The Story of a North Sea Air Station*, p.165
35. Robinson: *op.cit,.* p.146
36. BNA: *Lancashire Daily Post*, 5 February 1916, p.2. The accounts by William Martin and George Denny.
37. BNA: *Liverpool Daily Post*, 4 February 1916, p.5
38. BNA: *Daily Mirror*, 4 February 1916, p.3
39. TDA: *The Times*, 4 February 1916, p.7
40. Jones, *op. cit.*, p.142 (note 1). Other translations have appeared which differ slightly.
41. TDA: *The Times*, 4 June 1916, p.8

## Chapter 4: A New Beginning

1. BNA: *The Scotsman*, 7 February 1916, p.9
2. *Ibid*
3. Chamberlain, Geoffrey, *Airships: Cardington*, (Lavenham 1984), pp.48-49
4. BNA: *Sheffield Daily Telegraph*, 26 February 1917, p.6
5. BNA: *Newcastle Daily Journal*, 17 December 1918, p.8
6. Chamberlain later served as British Prime Minister, 1937-1940.
7. Jones, *op. cit.*, p.146
8. *Ibid*, pp.156-157
9. See *Zeppelin Onslaught*, pp.234-237
10. Jones, *op. cit.*, pp.162-163
11. BNA: *Thanet Advertiser*, 12 February 1916, p.5
12. *Ibid*
13. *Ibid*
14. TNA: AIR1/574/16/15/157
15. Thanet Advertiser, *Thanet's Raid History*, p.6
16. BNA: *Thanet Advertiser*, 12 February 1916, p.5
17. Thanet Advertiser, *Thanet's Raid History*, p.6
18. Cole & Cheesman, *op. cit.*, pp.89-90
19. TDA: *The Times*, 12 February 1916, p.7
20. Account of the Lowestoft raid is compiled from TNA: AIR1/574/16/15/158, and BNA: *Framlingham Weekly News*, 26 February 1916, p.2
21. I have been unable to establish which side of the harbour the restaurant stood.
22. BNA: *Framlingham Weekly News*, 26 February 1916, p.2
23. Snowden Gamble, *op. cit.*, p.171
24. TDA: *The Times*, 22 February 1916, p.5
25. TDA: *The Times*, 21 February 1916, p.9
26. BNA: *Dover Express and East Kent News*, 25 February 1916, p.5
27. TNA: AIR1/574/16/15/158
28. BNA: *Dover Express and East Kent News*, 25 February 1916, p.5
29. Grayzel, Susan, *At Home and Under Fire*, p.58
30. BNA: *Thanet Advertiser*, 4 March 1916, p.5
31. TNA: AIR1/574/16/15/159
32. BNA: *Thanet Advertiser*, 4 March 1916, p.5
33. TNA: AIR1/574/16/15/159
34. Lehmann & Mingos, *The Zeppelins*, pp.152-153
35. Lehmann was a reserve naval officer before the war, but when war broke out he was commanding the civilian airship, *Sachsen*, which was taken over by the army and he continued to serve.
36. Ibid
37. Robinson, *op. cit.*, p.147

38. Lehmann, *op. cit.*, pp.153-154
39. *Flight Magazine*, 2 March 1916, p.186
40. Lehmann, *op. cit.*, p.152

# Chapter 5: 'This is not war — but ghastly work of Hell'

1. TNA: AIR1/574/16/17/160
2. Klein, Pitt: *Bombs Away! Zeppelins at War*, p.73
3. TNA: WO158/939, p.4
4. TNA: AIR1/574/16/17/160, uncensored *Daily Mail* report
5. Klein: *op. cit.*, p.73
6. TNA: AIR1/574/16/17/160
7. Sources for account of the Hull raid are taken from TNA: AIR1/574/16/17/160, BNA: *Sheffield Daily Telegraph*, 8 March 1916, p.4, *Hull Daily Mail*, 7 March 1916, p.4, *Lincolnshire Echo*, 7 March 1916, p.3
8. Suddaby, Steven C.: *Buzzer Nights: Zeppelin Raids on Hull*, pp.101 & 108
9. Robinson: *op. cit.*, p.149
10. I have only found one reference to the Walker Street bomb, a letter written by T.C. Turner included in TNA: AIR1/574/16/17/160
11. Suddaby: *op. cit.*, p.106
12. TNA: AIR1/574/16/17/160
13. Jones: *op.cit.*, p.185
14. BNA: *Hull Daily Mail*, 7 March 1916, p.4
15. BNA: *Sheffield Daily Telegraph*, 8 March 1916, p.4
16. *Ibid*
17. Jones: *op. cit.*, pp.185-186
18. BNA: *Hull Daily Mail*, 7 March 1916, p.4
19. Confirmed by William Jones' death certificate.
20. The exact sequence of bombs is unclear but having read all the information available this appears to me to be the most likely course. With incendiary bombs weighing less than HE bombs there is a case for a slight southward drift of the bombs in the high winds.
21. BNA: *Sheffield Daily Telegraph*, 8 March 1916, p.4
22. TNA: AIR1/574/16/17/160
23. Credland: *op. cit.*, p.58
24. Jones: *op. cit.*, p.188 (note)
25. *Ibid*, pp.188-189
26. TNA: AIR1/574/16/17/160
27. BNA: *The Dover Express*, 24 March 1916, p.5
28. *Ibid*
29. *Ibid*
30. Dover Express, *Dover and the European War 1914-18*, p.20
31. TNA: AIR1/574/16/15/161

32. *Ibid*, and BNA: *The Dover Express*, 24 March 1916, p.5
33. Account of raid on Ramsgate complied from TNA: AIR1/574/16/15/161 and BNA: *Thanet Advertiser*, 25 March 1916, p.5
34. TNA: AIR1/574/16/15/161
35. *Ibid*
36. Cole & Cheesman, *op. cit.*, p.116
37. BNA: *Thanet Advertiser*, 25 March 1916, p.5
38. TNA: AIR1/574/16/15/161

## Chapter 6: 'Dante's Inferno'

1. Jones: *op. cit.*, pp.157-158
2. *Ibid*, pp.175-176
3. *Ibid*, 173-174
4. Robinson: *op. cit.*, p.150
5. The two Zeppelin commanders Martin Dietrich and Max Dietrich were unrelated.
6. BNA, *Lincolnshire Echo*, 3 April 1916, p.4
7. TNA, AIR1/575/16/15/162
8. From *Heritage to Legacy* reproduced at http://www.greatermanchester blitzvictims.co.uk/index.php?memorials=TRUE&memorial_id=68 (accessed 24/6/2019)
9. Article by Dr Alan Dowling, *Cleethorpes and the Zeppelin Raid*, Friends of Cleethorpes Heritage http://friendsofcleethorpesheritage.co.uk/home/ alan-dowling-articles (accessed 24/6/2019)
10. From *Heritage to Legacy*, see note 8 above.
11. Private Stott is the forgotten victim. Most sources give 31 killed and fail to include Stott who died of his injuries two months later. The official figures only list 29 killed — those who had died by 3 April, the day before the first funerals took place.
12. Klein: *op. cit.*, p.71
13. *Ibid*, p.72
14. BNA, *Lincolnshire Echo*, 3 April 1916, p.3
15. Robinson: *op. cit.*, p.150
16. *Ibid.*, p.152
17. TNA: AIR1/575/16/15/162
18. I have taken the sequence of bombs from that given on a map produced to accompany his report by the Chief Constable, Major E.P. Prest, now in the National Archives. The report was compiled on 4 May 1916 and included a number of bombs that had not been located when the first reports were compiled the day after the raid.
19. Jenkins, Gareth: *Zeppelins Over Bury*, pp.49-50

20. The GHQ, Home Forces official report states there were eight HE and 19 incendiaries dropped on Sudbury. However, police reports filed up to 3 April state only 'about 8' HE bombs and record no incendiaries. There is little information as to where bombs dropped in Sudbury, other than those that claimed lives. There is certainly one known incendiary, perhaps the others fell in fields outside the town only to be discovered some days later.
21. Although not listed amongst the casualties, a local newspaper reports two men (possibly soldiers of 2/6th) injured when an incendiary bomb smashed through the roof of their lodging house, 'scattering burning fluid over the face of one'. The other man heaved the fiery bomb out of a window, badly burning his hands, before rescuing his friend. (*Ipswich Evening Star*, 4 April 1916)
22. 'Memories of the late Doris Bardell, née Carter', provided by her son, Michael Bardell
23. BNA: *Essex County Chronicle*, 7 April 1916, p.5
24. Munsun, J. (ed.), *Echoes of the Great War*, p.120
25. The house was 'Lulworth' at 5 London Road, occupied by Charles Joscelyne, a prominent stationer in the town.
26. BNA: *Essex County Chronicle*, 7 April 1916, p.5
27. Munsun: *op. cit.*, p.120
28. Essex Society for Archaeology and History: *Zeppelins Over Essex 31 March 1916*, http://esah160.blogspot.com/2016/03/high-country-history-group-zeppelins.html (accessed 4/7/2019)
29. Munsun: *op. cit.*, pp.120-121

## Chapter 7: 'Why, haven't you heard — our boys brought the Zeppelin down!'

1. Castle: *Zeppelin Onslaught*, pp.270-276
2. TNA, AIR1/2397/267/1
3. BNA, *Bury Free Press*, 8 April 1916, p.6
4. TNA, AIR1/575/16/15/162
5. TNA: AIR1/575/16/15/162, proofs of a *Daily Sketch* article dated 2 April 1916
6. TNA: AIR1/575/16/15/162
7. TNA: *Ibid*
8. TNA: AIR1/2397/267/1
9. Marben, Rolf: *Zeppelin Adventures*, p.38
10. TNA: AIR1/575/16/15/162
11. The 3.45-inch incendiary bomb was released through a tube in the cockpit floor where it was ignited by electrical contact strips and had two three-pointed hooks that would, hopefully, catch the airship's envelope.
12. Robinson: *op. cit.*, p.152
13. Marben: *op. cit.*, pp.40-41
14. TNA: AIR1/2397/267/1

15. *Ibid*
16. *Ibid*
17. *Ibid*
18. Essex Readers' Forum.: *Essex Countryside*, Volume 18, Number 165, October 1970, p.61
19. TNA: AIR1/2579
20. http://sussexhistoryforum.co.uk/index.php?topic=1825.0;wap2, (accessed 12/9/19)
21. There was no reason for the authorities to make this information public and for many months all illustrations of Zeppelins produced for public consumption continued to be based on pre-war types.
22. TDA: *The Times*, 3 April 1916, p.9
23. *Ibid*
24. Otto Kühne was repatriated via Switzerland in December 1916. Joachim Breithaupt transferred to Holland in April 1918 before repatriation in September.
25. BNA: *Lincolnshire Echo*, 8 April 1916, p.2
26. Many of the men later moved to other camps, the majority ending up at Brocton, Staffordshire, which opened in 1917. One man, *Obersignalmaat* Erich Grund, was repatriated via Switzerland in December 1916.
27. From the diary of Private Alexander F. Morley, 3rd (Reserve) Battalion, Northamptonshire Regiment, courtesy of Northamptonshire Records Office
28. Worth in the region of £50,000 in current terms.
29. TNA: AIR1/575/16/15/162
30. Essex Readers' Forum, *op. cit.*, p.61
31. AIR1/575/16/15/162. Proofs of a *Daily Sketch* article dated 2 April 1916
32. Unfortunately no official list of recipients appears to have survived. However, Bernard Green in his book, *Zeppelin L15 & The Wakefield Gold Medal*, has made an excellent start in creating one.

## Chapter 8: A Zeppelin Moon

1. *Sunderland Echo*, 10 March 2016, (accessed online 20/9/2019). Tributes to Sunderland victims of wartime Zeppelin attack to be unveiled. Quote from Harriet O'Leary.
2. BNA: *Sunderland Daily Echo*, 3 April 1916, p.3
3. BNA: *Sunderland Daily Echo*, 4 April 1916, p.6
4. Her name is often given as Sally Ann Holmes but this appears to be incorrect.
5. *Sunderland Echo*, 10 March 2016, Quote from Malcolm Holmes.
6. BNA: *Sunderland Daily Echo*, 4 April 1916, p.6 & 23 December 1918, p.3
7. BNA: *Sunderland Daily Echo*, 23 December 1918, p.3

8. Scheer: Admiral Reinhardt, *Germany's High Sea Fleet in the World War*, pp.120-121
9. *Ibid*, p.121
10. TNA: WO 158/940
11. TNA: AIR1/576/16/15/163
12. *Ibid*
13. *Ibid*
14. *Ibid*
15. Cole & Cheesman, *op. cit.*, pp.121-122
16. Jones, op. cit., pp.196 & 199
17. Castle, *Zeppelin Onslaught*, pp.27-30
18. *Ibid*, pp.168-171
19. BNA: *Sunderland Daily Echo*, 4 April 1916, p.3
20. https://www.coquetandcoast.co.uk/amble-northumberland/showthread. php?t=168, (accessed 24/9/2019)
21. BNA: *The Scotsman*, 5 April 1916, p.7
22. *Ibid*
23. *Ibid*
24. TNA: AIR1/576/16/15/164
25. Jones: *op. cit.*, p.197
26. The timing is disputed. Other sources say 11.40pm or 11.50pm
27. Location of bombs from report by Leith Police in TNA:, AIR1/576/16/15/164
28. BNA: *Sunday Post*, 9 Feb. 1919, p.16
29. BNA: *The Scotsman*, 4 April 1916, p.5
30. Almost £4m today
31. BNA: *The Scotsman*, 4 April 1916, p.5
32. *The Watsonian*, 1987-88 (magazine of George Watson's College), Alastair C. McLaren, *Edinburgh's First Air Raid* pp.27-28,
33. University of Edinburgh: http://libraryblogs.is.ed.ac.uk/untoldstories/ 2016/03/30/i-100th-anniversary-of-zeppelin-air-attack-on-edinburgh-a-school-student-walks-among-the-wreckage/ (accessed 11/10/2019)
34. University of Edinburgh: http://libraryblogs.is.ed.ac.uk/untoldstories/ 2016/04/01/ii-100th-anniversary-of-zeppelin-air-attack-on-edinburgh-incendiary-bombs-and-the-infirmary/ (accessed 11/10/2019)
35. It is unclear whether this bomb exploded or not. The police report says it did while a newspaper (*The Scotsman*, 4 April 1916) says: 'A considerable hole, about eight feet by nine, was made in the roof where the shell seems to have burst, or partially so, on contact.' The holes made in the floors and ceilings as it plunged down through the house measured only about 'a square foot or so'.
36. King's Park is more commonly known today as Holyrood Park.
37. A report in *The Scotsman*, 4 April 1916, indicated that Donoghue died instantly but he survived for eight days, dying from his injuries on 11 April. This brought the total deaths from the Marshall Street bomb to seven.

38. BNA: *The Scotsman*, 4 April 1916, p.5
39. The official statistics show eleven people killed in Edinburgh and two in Leith. However the police records list only nine killed in Edinburgh, the missing being Thomas Donoghue and James Farquhar. Both fatally injured, they were still alive when the police report was made.
40. BNA: *The Scotsman*, 4 April 1916, p.5

## Chapter 9: 'Such a rain of destruction... so little harm'

1. British records are confused as to which Zeppelins were involved, but settled on LZ 88, LZ 90 and LZ 93. LZ 93, however, only made her first raid on 2 April 1916 according to German flight records. Those same records show that LZ 81 set out on the raid.
2. Lehmann & Mingos: op. cit., pp.169-170
3. TNA: AIR1/575/16/15/162
4. Lehmann & Mingos: *op. cit.*, p.147. See also page 57 above.
5. *Ibid*, pp.171-172
6. BNA: *Suffolk and Essex Free Press*, 5 April 1916, p. 6
7. Jones: *op. cit.*, p.199 (note)
8. This bomb was not discovered until 8 April.
9. TNA: AIR1/577/16/15/165
10. It seems L 17 needed repairs because she undertook a test flight three days later then transferred to Hanover on 9 April, returning to Nordholz on 15 April.
11. Klein: *op. cit.*, p.71
12. TNA: AIR1/577/16/15/166
13. *Ibid*
14. TNA: AIR/577/16/15/166
15. BNA: *Sunderland Daily Echo*, 7 April 1916, p.3
16. https://thefallenservicemenofsouthwestcountydurham.com/the-zeppelin-raid-on-evenwood-5-april-1916/ (accessed 8 Nov 2019)
17. Information from local historian Colin Turner.
18. BNA: *Sunderland Daily Echo*, 8 April 1916, p.3
19. BNA: *Sunderland Daily Echo*, 7 April 1916, p.3
20. Beith, Margaret: *The story of the WW1 Zeppelin Raid on Eldon*, p.1
21. TNA: AIR1/577/16/15/166
22. BNA: *Sunderland Daily Echo*, 8 April 1916, p.3
23. It is worth noting that £44,000 of this was attributable to damage at the Leith whisky warehouse on 2 April.
24. Strahlmann, Dr. Fritz (Ed.). *Zwei deutsche Luftschiffhäfen des Weltkrieges, Ahlhorn und Wildeshausen* (English translation - *Memories of Ahlhorn*, Alex Reid), p.72
25. TNA: WO 158/940
26. BNA: *Cambridge Independent Press*, 28 April 1916, p.5

27. *Ibid*
28. BNA: *Cambridge Independent Press*, 28 April 1916, p.5
29. BNA: *Lancashire Daily Post*, 26 April 1916, p.2
30. TNA: WO 158/941. Information from rescued crew of Zeppelin L 7, shot down at sea on 4 May 1916.
31. It was the same target attacked by Mathy and L 13 on the night of 31 March 1916.

## Chapter 10: Germany's Old Problems — Britain's New Weapons

1. Jones: *op. cit.*, p.164
2. British authorities mistook LZ 81 for the old Z XII, however she was on the Eastern Front at the time.
3. TNA: WO 158/941
4. BNA: *Dover Express and East Kent News*, 28 April 1916, p.5
5. TNA: Details of the raid extracted from WO 158/941 and AIR1/578/16/15/168
6. Information from Phil Redman, Albert Redman's grandson.
7. BNA: *Essex Newsman*, 29 April 1916, p.5
8. Neumann, Major Georg Paul: *The German Air Force in the Great War*, p.118. This account by Lt Rohde was collected by Leutnant Peter Martin Lampel, one of a number of officers who assisted Neumann.
9. Neumann: *op. cit.*, p.118-119
10. TNA: AIR1/578/16/15/168
11. *Ibid*
12. Linnarz's flight report
13. Neumann: op. cit., p.122
14. TNA: AIR1/578/16/15/168
15. *Ibid*
16. *Ibid*
17. Arthur Travers Harris is better known for his role as Commander-in-Chief of Bomber Command in the Second World War
18. TNA: AIR1/578/16/15/168
19. Cole & Cheesman: op. cit., p.32
20. Although a bullet with both explosive and incendiary properties, it was originally classed as an incendiary. Officially 'Cartridge S.A. Incendiary BIK .303 inch (VIIK) Mark I'
21. TNA: MUN 7/429.
22. Officially the 'Cartridge S.A. Ball .303 inch PSA (VII.A) Mark 1'
23. Jones: *op. cit.*, pp.384-385
24. TNA: AIR1/719/35/8
25. Officially the 'Cartridge S.A. Incendiary Buckingham .303 inch (VII.B) Mark II'

26. Jones: *op. cit.*, p.384
27. Officially the 'Cartridge S.A. Tracer SPK .303 inch Mark VII.T'
28. The first raid had been against Dunkirk.
29. TNA: AIR1/578/16/15/170. It is not clear if the report was published
30. BNA: *Yorkshire Post*, 4 May 1916, p.5
31. Letter written by Annie Ryder, a friend and work colleague of Norah Chapman. Kindly provided by Haydn Gate, Annie Ryder's great great nephew.
32. http://www.clementshallhistorygroup.org.uk/projects/world-war-1/exploring-the-impact-of-the-may-1916-zeppelin-attack/ (accessed 16 Jan 2020)
33. BNA: *Yorkshire Post*, 4 May 1916, p.5
34. TNA: AIR1/578/16/15/170
35. BNA: *Sheffield Daily Telegraph*, 4 May 1916, p.5
36. *Ibid* and BNA: *Yorkshire Post*, 28 December 1918, p.7
37. TNA: AIR1/578/16/15/170
38. Cole & Cheesman, *op. cit.*, pp.133-134

## Chapter 11: The Coming of the Super Zeppelins

1. Robinson: *op. cit.*, p.158
2. TNA: AIR1/578/16/15/170
3. Fergus, David: *The Zepps are Coming*, The Scots Magazine, Vol.132, No.5, Feb 1990, p.506
4. TNA: AIR1/578/16/15/170
5. Fergus: *op. cit.*, p.507
6. TNA: AIR1/578/16/15/170. The police report states 40 feet, a military report says 40 yards.
7. Fergus: *op .cit.*, p.507
8. Robinson: *op. cit.*, p.159
9. Exact details are vague but it appears that seven bombs fell at Deal, with another three near a gun battery at Sandwich.
10. Easdown, M., *A Glint in the Sky*, p.38
11. AIR1/579/16/15/171
12. Easdown: *op. cit.*, p.38
13. Name changed to The Farrier in 2016.
14. Thanet Advertiser, *Thanet's Raid History*, p.8
15. TNA: WO158/ 975, p.15
16. TNA: AIR1/579/16/15/171 and BNA: *Western Times*, 22 May 1916, p.4
17. Dover Express: *Dover and the European War 1914-18*, pp.20-21
18. *Ibid*, p.21 and AIR1/579/16/15/171
19. BNA: *Dover Express and East Kent News*, 26 May 1916, p.5
20. Dover Express: *Dover and the European War 1914-18*, p.21
21. Jones: *op. cit.*, p.165
22. Jones: *op. cit.*, pp.165-166

23. *Ibid*, p.166
24. The Navy took delivery of 10 'p-class' Zeppelins and five 'q-class'. The German Army received 12 'p-class' and seven 'q-class'.
25. Robinson: *op. cit.*, p.385 & p.389
26. Robinson: *op. cit.*, p.171
27. Author unknown: *The Hornets of Zeebrugge*, In *Cross & Cockade Journal*, Vol. 11, No.1, Spring 1970
28. TNA: AIR1/579/16/15/173
29. TNA: WO 158/942: L 14, L 21, L 22 and L 23
30. TNA: AIR 1/579/16/15/174 and WO158/942
31. Klein: *op. cit.*, p.80
32. TNA: AIR 1/579/16/15/174 and WO158/942
33. *Ibid*
34. TDA: *The Times*, 31 July 1916, p.3
35. TNA: AIR 1/579/16/15/174

## Chapter 12: A Fruitless Summer

1. TNA: AIR 1/579/16/15/175. The bombs at Stanford are not included in WO 158/942. In WW2 the village was taken over by the army for training purposes.
2. Klein: *op. cit.*, p.81
3. BNA: *Hull Daily Mail*, 14 August 1916, p.3. Report of article in German newspaper.
4. Snowden Gamble: *op. cit.*, pp.180-181
5. Cole & Cheesman: *op. cit.*, pp.143-144
6. BNA: *Birmingham Gazette*, 4 Aug. 1916, p.1
7. TNA: AIR 1/580/16/15/176
8. Hewetson: First World War letters and Family Papers, MC 643, Norfolk Record Office
9. BNA: *Birmingham Gazette*, 4 Aug. 1916, p.1
10. Klein: *op. cit.*, p.83
11. TNA: AIR1/580/16/15/177. This flare was only discovered ten months later, in June 1917
12. TNA: AIR1/580/16/15/177. Undated article from *The Daily Chronicle*
13. *Ibid*
14. BNA: *Hull Daily Mail*, 10 August 1916, p.4
15. TNA: AIR1/580/16/15/177. Undated article from *The Daily Chronicle*
16. Credland: *op. cit.*, p.70
17. Although official figures give 10 killed, there are 11 names.
18. One elderly man sheltering in a mine died of shock. There is inconsistency in regards to recording victims who died of shock. In this instance the unnamed victim was not included as an air raid casualty.

19. Later in the war de Roeper was credited with five victories on the Western Front.
20. Robinson: *op.cit.*, p.188
21. http://www.marsdenbannergroup.btck.co.uk/SalmonsHall (accessed 7 April 2020)
22. TNA: AIR1/580/16/15/177. Undated article from *The Daily Chronicle*

## Chapter 13: The Return to London

1. Eleven different Zeppelins took part in these four raids. L 11, L 13, L 16 and L 31 took part in all four, L 17 was involved in three, L 14, L 21, L 22 and L 24 in two and both L 23 and L 30 appeared once.
2. The bombs killed 10 and injured perhaps only 16 people.
3. Robinson: *op. cit.*, pp.187-188
4. *Ibid*, p.188
5. The six men were: 2nd Lt. S.J. Parker and Privates R.J. Eagle, J. Robinson, J. McCarthy, E. Green and J.W. Harper.
6. http://www.ww1worcestershire.co.uk/key-dates/1916/08/worcester-boy-narrowly-escapes-german-seaplane-bombing-raid-at-dover/ (accessed 11 April 2020)
7. Von Buttlar: *op. cit.*, p.111
8. TDA: *The Times*, 25 August 1916, p.6
9. TNA: WO 158/943 & AIR1/581/16/15/180
10. This figure is from the police report and is used in the Home Forces, Intelligence Branch report (WO 158/943). It differs from that given by the searchlight commander who reported 11 HE and six incendiaries (AIR 1/581/16/15/180)
11. TDA: *The Times*, 26 August 1916, p.7
12. Robinson: *op. cit.*, p.190
13. TNA: AIR 1/581/16/15/180 Part 1, Cutting from *Daily News*, unknown date
14. BNA: *The Globe*, 28 August 1916, p.2
15. Mrs Turner received £300 as compensation for her loss - currently worth about £26,000.
16. Now Belushi's
17. TNA: AIR 1/581/16/15/180 Part 1, Cutting from *Daily Mail*, unknown date
18. *Ibid*
19. The van was owned by J. Bartholomew & Sons of Southfleet, Kent.
20. TDA: *The Times*, 26 August 1916, p.7
21. Now renamed West Grove
22. BNA: *The People*, 27 August 1916, p.3
23. BNA: *Pall Mall Gazette*, 25 August 1916, p.2
24. BNA: *Western Daily Press*, 31 August 1916, p.5

25. The seven were: Robert Barrell, age 23, Robert Pulling (24), John Holmes (8), Mary Hurry (22), Annie Hurry (20), Winnie Hurry (17) and Rebecca Hurry (53).
26. At a later date the house numbers were changed; the house is now No. 290.
27. TNA: AIR 1/581/16/15/180 Part 2
28. BNA: *The Globe* , 28 August 1916, p.2
29. TNA: AIR 1/581/16/15/180 Part 1. Cutting from *Daily Chronicle*, unknown date
30. Reay, Colonel W.T., The Specials - How They Served London, (London 1920), pp.175-176
31. TNA: AIR 1/581/16/15/180 Part 1. Cutting from *Daily Mail*, unknown date.
32. TNA: AIR1/2417/303/42, *London Evening News*, 31 January 1935
33. BNA: *The Globe*, 28 August 1916, p.1
34. *Ibid*
35. TNA: AIR 1/581/16/15/180 Part 1. Cutting from *Daily Mail*, unknown date.
36. *Ibid*, Cutting from *Daily Chronicle*, unknown date
37. Now Myrtledene Road
38. On 8/9 September 1915, Mathy's raid on London in L 13 caused damage estimated at £530,787.

## Chapter 14: A Bright Flare of Light

1. See Beesly, *Room 40*.
2. See Ferris, *Airbandit* and TNA: WO 32/10776
3. Gerhardt, Frederik C.: *London 1916*, pp.85-86, 103-105
4. BNA: *Boston Guardian*, 11 January 1919, p.9
5. BNA: *Lincolnshire Echo*, 6 September 1916, p.3
6. BNA: *Boston Guardian*, 11 January 1919, p.9
7. *Ibid*
8. Gerhardt: *op. cit.*, p.98
9. TNA: WO158/944
10. TNA: WO15/944
11. BNA: *Sheffield Daily Telegraph*, 4 December 1918, p.7
12. *Ibid*
13. *Ibid*: *Nottingham Daily Express*, 8 September 1916, p.3
14. Castle: *Zeppelin Onslaught*, p.251. During the raid of 13/14 October 1915 he reported bombing West Ham, the London Docks and Woolwich but had actually attacked various Norfolk villages.
15. In, *London 1916,* Gerhardt considers whether these bends, viewed through clouds from altitude, convinced von Buttlar that he had found the horseshoe bend of the Thames around the docks on the Isle of Dogs.
16. TNA: AIR1/582/16/15/181 Part I. All details about bomb locations from this file.
17. Cole & Cheseman: *op. cit.*, p.162

18. AIR1/582/16/15/181 Part II. Correction issued by Rawlinson 20 Dec 1916.
19. TNA: AIR1/582/16/15/181 Part II
20. *Ibid.*
21. BNA: *The Yarmouth Independent,* 9 Sep. 1916. p.5
22. Gerhardt: *op. cit.,* p.107
23. TNA: AIR1/582/16/15/181 Part I
24. The Spähkorb is now in the collection of the Imperial War Museum, London.
25. Lehmann & Mingos: *op. cit.,* p.92
26. Although the teeth of the winch's gear wheels showed damage possibly caused by jamming a metal bar into them to stop them running free, La Quiante states he deliberately dropped *the Spähkorb* and winch to reduce weight as he battled against the wind. See Gerhardt: *op. cit.,* p.92.
27. Gerhardt: *op. cit.,* p.92
28. Gerhardt: *op, cit.,* p.96
29. Lehmann, Ernst, *Zeppelin - The story of lighter-than-air craft,* p.153

# Chapter 15: 'One Glowing Blazing Mass'

1. For more information on Robinson's background see Rimell's *The Airship VC.*
2. TNA: AIR1/582/16/15/181 Part II
3. Lehmann & Mingos: *op. cit.,* p.196
4. TNA: AIR1/582/16/15/181 Part II
5. *Ibid,* Part III
6. II meaning 2 in Roman numerals, not to be confused with SL 11
7. TNA: AIR1/582/16/15/181 Part II
8. *Ibid.* A clock found in the wreckage of SL 11 had stopped at 3.10am (German time), which corresponds with the time the Clapton gun was in action.
9. TNA: AIR1/582/16/15/181 Part III
10. Castle, *Zeppelin Onslaught,* pp.180-181
11. Lieutenant Brown had been admonished for opening fire when the target was out of range during a raid in April. His commanding officer thought he would 'do better in the future'. See page 137.
12. TNA: AIR1/582/16/15/181 Part III
13. *Ibid*
14. Robinson only mentions Brock and Pomeroy bullets. He fails to mention Buckingham incendiary bullets, which also acted as tracers. It is unlikely he would have none loaded for a night action. He may have failed to mention them as it was assumed a tracer would be employed.
15. Rimell, *Airship VC,* pp.112-114
16. TNA: AIR1/583/16/15/181 Part IV Report from *The Guardian,* 5 Sept 1916
17. BNS: *Lincolnshire Echo,* 4 Sept 1916, p.2
18. BNA: *Daily Mirror,* 4 Sept 1916, p.2
19. BNA: *Illustrated Police News,* 7 Sept 1916, p.2

20. Robinson: *op. cit.*, p.194
21. Rimell, *Airship VC*, p.62
22. AIR1/583/16/15/182, Report from *Daily News*, 23 Sep.1916
23. Strange, Mike: *In Memoriam*, in *Village Voice - The Dersingham Magazine*, Oct/ Nov 2017, pp.67-69 https://dersingham.org.uk/magazine.html (accessed 12/6/20)

# Chapter 16: 'Mother, they have got me this time'

1. Rimell: *Airship VC*, p. 112
2. TNA: WO 158/944
3. Lehmann & Mingos, *op. cit.*, pp.197-198
4. Von Hoeppner, *Germany's War In The Air*, p.90
5. TNA: AIR1/583/16/15/182. Report from *Daily Chronicle*, 23 Sept. 1916
6. TNA: AIR1/584/16/15/181, Part I. Report by commander, Harwich Garrison.
7. Ganzel in L 23 reported searchlight activity and gunfire at 10.45pm (UK time) from Lincoln where he dropped his bombs. British reports credit this to L 14 but her commander reports making an attack an hour later.
8. BNA: *Boston Guardian*, 18 January 1919, p.4
9. BNA: *Nottingham Evening Post*, 27 September 1916, p.3
10. *Nottingham Daily Express*, 26 September 1916
11. This would be classed as post-traumatic stress disorder (PTSD) today.
12. BNA: *Nottingham Evening Post*, 12 September 1919, p.3
13. BNA: *Nottingham Evening Post*, 27 September 1916, p.3
14. *Ibid*
15. TNA: AIR1/584/16/15, 183, Part II
16. Hook, John, *Warriors for the Working Week*, (Privately published, London, 1994), p.39
17. *Ibid*, p.42
18. *Ibid*, p.44
19. *Ibid*, p.41
20. *Ibid*, p.42
21. The timings given in Manger's report tie in with the raid near Sleaford, while L 13 was in action 45 minutes later.
22. British reports credited the movements of this Zeppelin to L 23 but comparing British timings with those from the reports by Eichler (L 13) and Ganzel (L 23) it appears that this attack should be credited to L 13.
23. BNA: *Boston Guardian*, 18 January 1919, p.4
24. Details from information supplied to author by local historian Ron Borsberry.
25. BNA: *Boston Guardian*, 18 January 1919, p.4
26. TNA: WO158/945. This report attributes these bombs to L 32, but Mathy's own report is clear that he dropped them.

27. Robinson never took to the air again as a Home Defence pilot but, frustrated, he successfully lobbied to be allowed to return to active service and arrived in France as a flight commander with No. 48 squadron in March 1917. He was shot down behind enemy lines the following month and remained a POW for the rest of the war. Suffering harsh treatment he was severely weakened when he returned home in December 1918 and died a victim of the 'Spanish flu' pandemic on 31 December 1918.
28. Klein: *op. cit.,* p.93
29. TNA: AIR 1/584/16/15/183 Part I
30. TNA: AIR1/2417/303/41, *London Evening News,* 23 February 1935
31. TNA: *Ibid,* 20 February 1935
32. TNA: *Ibid,* 7 February 1935
33. The area was redeveloped to create the 2012 Olympic Park and Stadium
34. TNA: WO158/945
35. Rimell, *Zeppelin!,* p.120.

## Chapter 17: 'They are all someone's sons'

1. TNA: AIR 1/584/16/15/183 Part I
2. Brown, John W: *Zeppelins Over Streatham,* pp.14-15
3. TNA: AIR1/2417/303/41,*London Evening News,* 9 March 1935
4. *Ibid,* 28 February 1935
5. BNA: *Liverpool Post and Mercury,* 25 September 1916, p.5
6. TNA: AIR1/2417/303/41,*London Evening News,* 8 February 1935
7. In his autobiography, Max Wall says Betty was the wife of Bill Hobbs, 'a performer of sorts'. Frustratingly I have been unable to find Betty in the GRO Death Index and the London Fire Brigade only lists her as 'female, name and age unknown'.
8. BNA: *Liverpool Post and Mercury,* 25 September 1916, p.5
9. BNA: *The Globe,*28 September 1916, p.5
10. *Ibid*
11. TNA: AIR1/584/16/15/183 Part II, *Daily Telegraph,* 26 September 1916, p.9
12. Part of Essex in 1916.
13. Mathy believed these 10 bombs fell on Islington after he dropped two on the City. His two bombs prior to Leyton were those at 269 Brixton Road and at Kennington Park when, inexplicably, Mathy thought he was over the City of London.
14. TNA: AIR1/584/16/15/183 Part II, *Daily Telegraph,* 26 September 1916, p.9
15. TNA: AIR1/584/16/15/183 Part II
16. See Castle, *Zeppelin Onslaught,* pp.181-182
17. TNA: AIR1/2417/303/41. *London Evening News,* 16 February 1935
18. TNA: *Ibid,* 18 February 1935
19. TNA: AIR1/584/16/15/183 Part II, *Daily Telegraph,* 26 September 1916, p.9

20. TNA: AIR1/2417/303/41 *London Evening News*, 18 February 1935
21. Renamed Whipps Cross Hospital in 1917.
22. TNA: AIR1/2417/303/41, *London Evening News*, 12 February 1935
23. TNA: *Ibid*, 4 March 1935
24. TNA: *Ibid*, 18 February 1935
25. Bundesarchiv, Militärarchiv Freiburg, RM 116/28-353-354
26. TNA: AIR1/584/16/15/183 Part I
27. Rimell, *Zeppelin!*, p.130
28. TNA: AIR 1/584/16/15/183 Part I
29. Tracer refers to either Buckingham or 'Sparklet' incendiary bullets.
30. TNA: AIR 1/584/16/15/183 Part II, *Morning Post*, 25 September 1916, p.7
31. Rimell, *Zeppelin!*, p.128
32. TNA: AIR 1/608/16/15/264
33. TNA: AIR 1/584/16/15/183 Part II, *Morning Post*, 25 September 1916, p.8
34. *Ibid*
35. BNA: *Daily Mirror*, 25 September 1916, p.2
36. *Ibid*
37. TDA: *The Times*, 25 September 1916, p.10
38. Essex Archives, J/P 12/7. *Telegrams, Reports, Statements, and Correspondence Concerned with Zeppelin Raids on Essex*. Report by Capt. Ffinch.
39. *Ibid*
40. He had served as Chaplain in the Suffolk Regiment at Gallipoli where he was awarded the Military Cross, earning the nickname 'The Fighting Parson'.
41. TNA: AIR1/584/16/15/183 Part II, *Daily Telegraph*, 26 September 1916, p.9
42. *Ibid*
43. Zeppelina Clark married Jack Williams in 1939. She died in 2004. But she was not the first to bear the name. On 28 May 1915, Edward and Alice Risley's daughter was born in Stoke Newington, London, three days prior to London's first Zeppelin raid, which started in that area. They registered their daughter as May Zeppilina Risley. I am grateful to Mark Barnes for this information about the earlier birth.

## Chapter 18: 'A scene of woebegone desolation'

1. MacDonagh: *In London During the Great War*, pp.131-132
2. *Ibid*, pp.132-133
3. *Ibid*, p.133
4. TNA: AIR2/123/B10869
5. Beesly, *Room 40*, pp.3-7 & 145
6. Klein: *op. cit.*, p.96
7. Rimell, R.L., *The Last Flight of the L32*, p.14
8. BNA: *Yorkshire Post*, 2 January 1919, p.8

9. A police report shows this as the first bomb dropped in the York raid, while a newspaper reports it as the last.

10. BNA: *Yorkshire Post*, 2 January 1919, p.8 and AIR1/584/16/15/184, *Daily Telegraph*, 27 September 1916. Account of the raid on the outskirts of York is based on these sources.

11. TNA: AIR1/584/16/15/184

12. BNA: *Yorkshire Post*, 2 January 1919, p.8

13. Sheffield Archives: MD7126/1

14. This incendiary bomb is now in the collection of 'The Whitaker' museum in Rawtenstall, Lancashire.

15. TNA: AIR1/584.16/15/186 Part II. *Daily Telegraph*, 27 September 1916

16. BNA: *Liverpool Echo*, 26 September 1916. p.6

17. Carter-Clavell, Scott, *The First Air Raid on Lancashire*, p.67

18. Robinson: *op. cit.*, p.212

19. The official report in WO/158/945 states L 21 south-west of Bolton at 12.40am and commencing the attack at 12.45am. This appears to be an error and differs from local reports given by police and other eyewitnesses.

20. This account of the raid on Bolton relies heavily on local newspaper coverage, as well as Smith: *Zeppelins Over Lancashire*, and Carter-Clavell: op. cit., and documents in TNA: AIR1/584/16/15/184

21. Carter-Clavell, Scott: *op. cit.*, p.76. Quote from *Bolton Evening News*

22. *Ibid*, p.77

23. This bomb is usually included in the second loop flown over Bolton by L 21, but I believe it may have dropped during the first.

24. https://gm1914.wordpress.com/2015/01/15/zeppelin-over-bolton/ (accessed 2/10/20)

25. Robinson: *op. cit.*, p. 211

26. This account of the Sheffield raid relies heavily on an article in the *Sheffield Independent*, 3 December 1918, pp. 1 & 3, documents in TNA: AIR1/584/16/15/184, and other references *passim*.

27. Police reports state the bomb fell in Earldom Street, but Earldom Road appears more likely.

28. BNA: *Sheffield Daily Telegraph*, 27 September 1916, p.9

29. At the time of the raid the figure of 28 deaths in Sheffield was generally given and continues to be so. However, George Ineson died after the main inquest and was forgotten. His name did appear in the *Sheffield Independent* on 5 December 1918, confirming 29 deaths in the city.

30. BNA: *Sheffield Daily Independent*, 29 September 1916, p.5

31. This bomb was discovered 11 years later at Mill Race Dam (alongside Sanderson's Weir) on the River Don. *Sheffield Daily Telegraph*, 16 August 1927.

32. BNA: *Sheffield Independent*, 29 September 1916, p.5

33. BNA: *Sheffield Independent*, 3 December 1918, p.3

34. There is a myth still quoted that the guns did not fire because the officers were at a function at the Grand Hotel in the city centre. Even if they had been away from their gun stations earlier, the TARA order given at about 10.30pm would have resulted in their return, about 95 minutes before L 22 appeared.
35. In 1919 a newspaper stated the Darnell bomb landed in Nightingale Street but the police report compiled at the time shows it as Britannia Road.
36. Jones: *op. cit.*, p.231

## Chapter 19: 'I have a really bad feeling about this'

1. Klein: *op. cit.*, p.98
2. BNA: *Pall Mall Gazette*, 26 September 1916, p.1
3. TNA: WO158/945, p.20
4. Klein: *op. cit.*, p.98
5. To add further confusion there are also reports in newspapers (eg: *Pall Mall Gazette*, 26 September 1916, p.1) of two policemen diving for cover during a raid on a 'south coast town' and subsequently rescuing children from a burning house. Portsmouth was the only place on the south coast bombed that night.
6. Klein: *op. cit.*, p.99
7. Gerhardt: *op. cit.*, p.155. (My translation).
8. Klein: *op. cit.*, p.101. Slight variations of this quote have appeared in numerous publications over the years, but invariably incorrectly attributed to Heinrich Mathy.
9. *Ibid*, p.102
10. *Ibid*, p.103
11. Robinson: *op. cit.*, p.214
12. Smith, Richard C., *Hornchurch's Air Heroes of the First World War*, p.34
13. Rimell, *Zeppelin!*, p.145. Letter written by Tempest's father
14. Tempest, Major W.J.: *How I Shot Down L.31*, in *The Great War...I Was There!*, p.871
15. Rimell: *Zeppelin!*, p.145
16. TNA: AIR1/585/16/15/185
17. Rimell: *Zeppelin!*, p.145
18. Tempest: *op. cit.*, p.871
19. BNA: *Hertfordshire Mercury*, 7 October 1916, p.6
20. TNA: WO158/945 and AIR1/585/16/15/185
21. *Ibid*
22. *Ibid*
23. *Ibid*
24. *Ibid*

25. Robinson: *op. cit.*, p.214
26. BNA: *Hertfordshire Mercury,* 7 October 1916, p.6
27. Tempest: *op. cit.*, pp.871-872
28. Bennett, J.E.: *The Potters Bar Zeppelin*, pp.6-7
29. MacDonagh: *op. cit.*, p.138
30. *Ibid*, p.139

## Chapter 20: 'They've got her! She's hit!'

1. TNA: WO 158/944. Report of 2/3 September raid.
2. Information supplied by Alexander Cordes, archivist at the Aeronauticum Museum, Nordholz.
3. Neumann: *op. cit.*, pp.126-127
4. TNA:AIR 1/2397/267/9
5. *Ibid*
6. TNA: AIR1/586/16/15/188 Part I
7. BNA: *Northern Daily Mail*, 1 December 1916, p.6
8. Hartlepools United became Hartlepool in 1968, then Hartlepool United in 1977.
9. After the war the football club tried to get compensation from the German government but failed. The 'temporary' stand built to replace the one destroyed remained in use until the 1980s.
10. TNA: AIR1/586/16/15/188 Part I
11. *Ibid*
12. BNA: *Northern Daily Mail*, 29 November 1916, p.3
13. Van Emden, Richard, and Humphries, Steve: *All Quiet on the Home Front*, pp.169-170
14. *Ibid*, p.170
15. TNA: AIR1/586/16/15/188 Part I
16. Undated *Daily Sketch* newspaper cutting in Pyott family scrapbook.
17. BNA: *Yorkshire Post*, 4 January 1919, p.9
18. TNA: WO 158/946. The official report states that only L 13 bombed York but there is some confusion evident in reports submitted that night.
19. TNA: AIR 1/2397/267/9
20. BNA: *Yorkshire Post*, 4 January 1919, p.9
21. *Ibid*
22. TNA: AIR1/586/16/15/188 Part I
23. BNA: *Yorkshire Post*, 4 January 1919, p.9
24. Snowden Gamble: *op. cit.*, pp.198-199
25. *Ibid*, p.199
26. BNA:*Northern Daily Mail*, 29 November 1916, p.3
27. Cole & Cheesman: *op. cit.*, p.183

## Chapter 21: A Portent for the Future

1. BNA: *Northern Daily Mail*, 29 November 1916, p.3
2. *Ibid*
3. TNA: AIR1/587/16/15/189
4. Zeppelin L 12 damaged by the Dover AA guns, 10 August 1915, See Castle, *Zeppelin Onslaught*, p.169
5. See Appendix II
6. This figure is slightly different from that given at the time in official reports. Some listed as injured died after figures were first collated, some were just missed out completely. See Appendix II and Appendix III.
7. Robinson: *op. cit.*, p.222
8. Robinson: *op. cit.*, p.398. In 1916 there were 253 individual reconnaissance flights over the North Sea carried out over 89 days.
9. *Ibid*, p.225
10. Scheer: *op. cit.*, p.212
11. Jones: *op. cit.*, p.247
12. *Ibid*
13. *Ibid*, p.245
14. *Ibid*, p.246
15. TDA: *The Times*, 29 November 1916, p.9
16. *Ibid*

# General Index

# Index of Places Bombed

Due to the great number of locations where bombs fell, I have generally excluded places where only one or two bombs dropped and failed to inflict any damage, although these are mentioned in the text. The County locations are as they were at the time.

# Index of Airfields (RFC) & Air Stations (RNAS)

## RFC Airfields

Co. Durham
  Seaton Carew 294

Derbyshire
  Coal Aston 268

Essex
  Chingford 7
  Hainault Farm 7, 41-42, 88, 91, 120, 133, 136, 138, 210-211, 214, 239, 241, 283
  North Weald Bassett 195, 210-211, 214, 215, 239, 283, 288
  Sutton's Farm 7, 41, 88, 120, 133, 138, 195, 210-211, 213, 214, 226, 239, 241, 256, 283

Hertfordshire
  Willian (Emergency Landing Ground – ELG) 288

Kent
  Dover (Swingate) 10, 49, 54, 186, 229
  Farningham 7, 41, 213
  Joyce Green 7, 41, 88, 210, 211, 213, 214, 256

Leicestershire
  Buckminster 303

Middlesex
  Hendon 7, 41
  Hounslow 7, 120, 133, 138, 195
  Northolt 7, 41

Norfolk
  Mattishall 165, 167
  Sedgeford (ELG) 173
  Snarehill 164, 169
  Tibenham (ELG) 304

Northumberland
  Cramlington 49, 106, 107, 126, 148, 156
  High West Houses (ELG) 107

Surrey
  Croydon 7, 41, 120
  Wimbledon Common 7, 41

Warwickshire
  Castle Bromwich 157-158, 211

Yorkshire
  Barmby Moor (ELG) 300
  Beverley 106, 126
  Bramham Moor 148, 156, 268
  Doncaster 49, 121, 148
  Dunkeswick (ELG) 267
  Pontefract Park (ELG) 300

## RNAS Air Stations

# Index of AA gun and Searchlight positions

## Anti-Aircraft Guns

Co. Durham
Fulwell Quarry 104
Hartlepool 295
Seaham 104, 298
Seaton Carew 295

Essex
Belhus Park 254–255
Chigwell Row 136
Farm Hill 119
Grange Hill 119
Harwich 135, 171, 185, 205
Hayes Hill Farm 119
Kelvedon Hatch 85, 119, 243
Kynochtown 86
Monkhams Hill 119
Newmans 283
Pitsea 86
Purfleet 89–90, 97–98
Shenfield Common 255
Shoeburyness 59
Shonks 255
Thames Haven 86
Tilbury 213, 254
Tunnel Farm 254–255
Warlies Park 218

Hampshire
Portsmouth 279–280

Hertfordshire
Cheshunt 119
Temple House 137, 216, 218, 219–220, 283

Kent
Capel-le-Ferne 185
Dartford 89, 97–98, 212
Deal 185, 229
Dover 9–10, 67–69, 106, 172, 185, 229
Faversham 60
Harty Ferry 60
Manston 166
Ramsgate 167, 185
Sackett's Hill 292
Sheerness 60, 292
Southfleet 212
Southern Outfall 255
Walmer 133
Westgate 142

Lincolnshire
Canwick 230
Cleefields 237
Immingham Halt 160
Killingholme 62, 65
Rauceby 236–237
Scartho Top 237
Waltham 24, 76

## Searchlights